Reading Pop Culture

A Portable Anthology

Reading
Pop Culture

A Portable Anthology

Second Edition

JEFF OUSBORNE
Suffolk University

Bedford/St.Martin's
A Macmillan Education Imprint

Boston • New York

For Bedford/St. Martin's
Vice President, Editorial, Macmillan Higher Education Humanities:
    Edwin Hill
Editorial Director for English and Music: Karen S. Henry
Publisher for Composition, Business and Technical Writing, and
    Developmental Writing: Leasa Burton
Executive Editor: John Sullivan
Developmental Editor: Leah Rang
Production Editor: Lidia MacDonald-Carr
Production Supervisor: Lisa McDowell
Executive Marketing Manager: Joy Fisher Williams
Project Management: Jouve
Director of Rights and Permissions: Hilary Newman
Senior Art Director: Anna Palchik
Cover Design: John Callahan
Cover Image: © Paul Bradbury/Getty Images
Composition: Jouve
Printing and Binding: RR Donnelley and Sons

Manufactured in the United States of America.

0   9   8   7   6   5
f   e   d   c   b   a

For information, write: Bedford/St. Martin's, 75 Arlington Street, Boston, MA 02116   (617-399-4000)

ISBN 978-1-319-00662-4 (Student Edition)
ISBN 978-1-319-02569-4 (Instructor's Edition)

Acknowledgments

Text acknowledgments and copyrights appear at the back of the book on pages 461–63, which constitute an extension of the copyright page. Art acknowledgments and copyrights appear on the same page as the art selections they cover. It is a violation of the law to reproduce these selections by any means whatsoever without the written permission of the copyright holder.

Contents

For political theorist Barber, the economic problems of the last several years illustrate the downside of consumerism: "The 'Protestant ethos' of hard work and deferred gratification has been replaced by an infantilist ethos of easy credit and impulsive consumption that puts democracy and the market system at risk."

Lutz, former editor of the *Quarterly Review of Doublespeak*, focuses on "weasel words" in dubious advertising: This language allows advertisers to appear to be making a claim for a product when "in fact they are making no claim at all."

Preeminent semiotician Barthes shows how toys condition children to accept a ready-made and constructed world as natural and given. Toys "reveal the list of all the things the adult does not find unusual: war, bureaucracy, ugliness . . ." and encourage children to identify as owners, not creators or inventors.

CHAPTER 3   Technology:
How do new devices and apps
transform experience?   137

CHAPTER 4   Music: How does popular music reflect and express our identities?

CHAPTER 7   Immersive Media: Can we get lost—and can we be found—in media?   393

Rhetorical Contents

NARRATION

DESCRIPTION

EXEMPLIFICATION

PROCESS

CAUSE AND EFFECT

COMPARISON AND CONTRAST

Introduction:
Analyzing Popular Culture

*"This is our collective fear projection: that we will be con-
sumed. Zombies are like the Internet and the media and every
conversation we don't want to have. All of it comes at us
endlessly (and thoughtlessly), and—if we surrender—we will
be overtaken and absorbed."*
　　　　　　—Chuck Klosterman, "My Zombie, Myself" (p. 425)

WHAT IS POPULAR CULTURE?

When we consider specific examples, we see popular culture everywhere. The *Hunger Games* books and movies. Beyoncé. Instagram.
Bob's Burgers. Chicken McNuggets. *Frozen.* Abercrombie & Fitch
advertisements. Cats playing the piano on YouTube. Reality television shows. When we generalize about pop culture's relationship to "culture," however, we run into complications—especially
in an academic context. In part, they result from the connotations
of the word *culture,* which long ago calcified around Victorian
critic Matthew Arnold's phrase "the best that has been thought
and said." That means high culture with a capital "C": a legacy of
art, music, and literature, with names like Michelangelo, Bach,
and Shakespeare. Dressing up to hear the symphony (*Be quiet!*)
or visit an art museum (*Don't touch!*)? Culture. Dressing up as an
obscure superhero for Comic-Con? Pop culture.

　　We can also make a distinction within pop culture: the difference
between *folk* culture and *mass* culture. Folk culture emerges from
a particular place, community, or group: Appalachian folk music,
Amish quilts, Southern cooking, the sea chanteys of working sail-
ors, even the graffiti of street artists. Folk culture embodies the
particular. In contrast, mass culture products such as commercial

1

television, retail chain stores, and fast-food restaurants are usually fashioned and distributed by corporations. Mass culture embodies the *standardized*: A McDonald's french fry is the same in Portland, Oregon, as it is in Portland, Maine. And that's the point of McDonald's food. The essays in this book address the mass culture that buzzes, pulses, and sizzles around us constantly; all the writers included here assume that it is worthy of consideration and study. You probably do, too, whether you know it or not. When you write an online review, when you engage in a Twitter argument about your favorite band, when you read a blog post about television shows—or write one about your favorite professional sports team—you are responding, evaluating, analyzing, and participating in popular culture. Some of this activity is escapist fun, of course. But it also reflects the knowledge and authority you bring to these topics. You can use that literacy for rigorous analysis of mass-culture phenomena that deserve more serious scrutiny.

Despite how much we naturally engage with mass culture, the idea that we should take it seriously as an academic subject is a relatively recent one. For much of the last century or so, critics and scholars put a higher value on both high culture and folk culture than on mass culture. Timeless, universal, leather-bound, museum-curated capital "C" culture ennobled and enriched us. To these critics and scholars, great books, art, and music were intrinsically valuable—the flowers of civilization. Likewise, genuine folk culture expressed worthy values like authenticity, spontaneity, and democracy. American critic Dwight MacDonald—an unrepentant highbrow snob—identified these virtues in his influential 1953 essay "A Theory of Mass Culture." Folk culture "grew up from below" as a "spontaneous expression of the people, shaped by themselves . . . to suit their needs." He sharpened his point by contrasting endearing, democratic folk culture with its ugly, authoritarian twin, mass culture. The latter was "imposed from above . . . fabricated by technicians hired by businessmen." For MacDonald and many others, mass culture—say a film like *The Sound of Music*—was a con job imposed on passive consumers, a deceptive shell game that reduced all participation to the "choice between buying and not buying." According to this view, culture invariably becomes shoddy, formulaic, and manipulative when it is subjected to the economic marketplace. We can still find critics denouncing popular culture in similar terms today: when

© Vince Bucci/Invision/AP

Even celebrities have a fear of missing out.

they claim it is shallow, coarse, cheap, materialistic, and mindless, or when they argue that it brainwashes children with advertising or traffics in sensationalism and stereotypes to draw viewers.

Yet stable categories like "high" and "low" culture tend to dissolve under historical scrutiny. For example, eighteenth-century English novels were popular entertainments, cultural products disparaged for their corrupting influence, much like video games are today. Popular culture has a way of transcending its low origins. After all, Shakespeare did not write his plays for the pleasure of English teachers or graduate students. He was a businessman as well as a dramatist and poet, a savvy entrepreneur whose plays pleased a popular audience with their trashy puns and sensational violence. The nineteenth-century English novelist Charles Dickens dominated the Victorian literary marketplace with mass-produced and serialized fictions; his novels were the equivalent of our cable television series or blockbuster movies. Now we study them as leather-bound "classics," culture with a capital "C." To take more recent American examples: In the early and mid-twentieth century, many culture critics disparaged popular jazz or ignored it altogether. But from our vantage point, jazz long ago put on a good suit and ascended to the plush concert hall, becoming high culture. That process seems endless, as rap lyrics now appear regularly in academically sanctioned literary anthologies and hip-hop increasingly becomes a field for academic study.

If the border between "high" and "low" culture is often porous, so is the boundary separating mass culture and folk culture. That is especially true for cultural artifacts not created by large corporations or sold in the traditional sense. If one anonymous individual posts silly amateur videos of his dog online, and millions of people view them, are the videos folk culture or mass culture? What if an advertising agency seizes on the videos' popularity and the dog becomes a mascot for a fast-food restaurant or an energy drink company? Where do we draw the line? Is local or regional folk culture inherently superior to standardized mass culture? At what point in its creation or distribution does folk culture become mass culture? Does it lose its value in the process? How does the creation of a popular YouTube video or the posting of an image that goes viral on the Internet become a media event? Several of the selections in this book explore these questions, dichotomies, tensions, and paradoxes.

THE IMPORTANCE OF STUDYING POP CULTURE

When we reflect on the value of analyzing—and writing about—popular culture, we might heed words of poet and critic T. S. Eliot, the personification of elite cultural values and infamously "difficult" poetry: "It is just the literature that we read for amusement, or purely for pleasure, that may have the greatest and least suspected influence on us. . . . Hence, it is that the influence of popular novelists, and of popular playwrights of contemporary life, requires to be scrutinized most closely."[1] His basic point is more relevant than ever: Mass-produced amusements and products suffuse our lives. Consequently, we should give them as much attention as we devote to the lofty artifacts of "high" culture. Literary history includes a long tradition of engagement with popular entertainment and consumer culture. In *The Tatler* and *Spectator*, eighteenth-century magazines long considered models of English criticism, Joseph Addison and Richard Steele wrote about commerce, fashion, and entertainment, as well as poetry and philosophy. Even Samuel Johnson, a writer central to the canon of English literature, turned his keen gaze to the proliferation of print advertising in his time (the 1700s), as well as to the tendency of readers to filter out these ads—over two centu-

---

[1]Indeed, Eliot's notoriously dense and allusive poem "The Waste Land" incorporates popular culture references into its matrix of allusions. It's also revealing that many years after Eliot's death, his book of verse *The Old Possum's Book of Practical Cats* became the basis for the musical *Cats*.

ries prior to DVRs: "Advertisements are now so numerous that they are very negligently perused, and it is therefore become necessary to gain attention by magnificent promises, and by eloquence sometimes sublime and sometimes pathetic."

But the academic study of popular culture grew from many disparate developments in twentieth-century scholarship and criticism—literary, sociological, linguistic, anthropological, political, and economic. In the 1920s and 1930s, American figures such as Vernon Parrington and F. O. Matthiesson developed the academic discipline now known as "American Studies," a field with a more holistic and inclusive notion of culture than the traditional study of literature. Influential German critics from the Frankfurt School argued that consumption deserved close scrutiny. Walter Benjamin's *Arcades Project*, for example, used shopping as the focus for a study of Paris. Many of these critics also thought mass culture deserved derision as an oppressive instrument of state and corporate capitalism. In their seminal essay, "The Culture Industry: Enlightenment as Mass Deception" (1944), Frankfurt School figures Theodor Adorno and Max Horkheimer dissected their subject with instruments from the Marxist tool kit: "The deception is not that the culture industry supplies amusement, but that it ruins the fun by allowing business considerations to involve it in the ideological clichés of a culture in the process of self-liquidation." When Adorno and Horkheimer looked behind pop culture phenomena like jazz, shiny cars, and the smiling face of Mickey Rooney on a movie screen, they saw the grim specter of fascism.

In the 1950s and 1960s, British cultural studies pioneers like Raymond Williams and Richard Hoggart expanded the scope of literary study from its focus on a select canon of masterpieces. For these critics, "culture" encompassed commerce, labor, technology, sports, leisure activities, and the practices of everyday life. So Hoggart's *The Uses of Literacy: Aspects of Working-Class Life* (1957), for example, investigated how emerging mass culture—movies, popular literature, magazines—destroyed and replaced traditional, local, and communal forms of popular culture. In their roles as professors, these critics moved away from training students to be comfortable connoisseurs and custodians of great art and literature. Instead, their pedagogy focused on culture as a fluid process and worked toward an explicit political goal: radical social change.

The middle of the twentieth century saw many "serious" scholars and writers turning their attention to popular culture. Canadian literary critic and media theorist Marshall McLuhan analyzed advertisements in *The Mechanical Bride: Folklore of Industrial Man* (1951), teasing out their symbolism and revealing their cultural implications. For McLuhan, advertising was the "greatest art form of the twentieth century." French semiologist Roland Barthes deployed techniques from anthropology and linguistics to unravel the significance of popular amusements such as Marlon Brando movies, professional wrestling, and striptease shows in his *Mythologies* (1957). As McLuhan did, Barthes brought a sense of pleasure to his encounters with the "culture industry," even as he exposed the dishonesty of its claims. On the pages of American literary journals and general interest magazines of the 1960s, figures such as Susan Sontag and Tom Wolfe brought startling insight and sharp writing to subjects like "camp" culture, custom cars, and the city of Las Vegas.

Still, while fields like cultural studies became legitimate academic disciplines, many scholars remained skeptical of *popular* culture studies. When Ray Browne, an English professor at Bowling Green State University, founded the Center for Popular Culture Studies over forty years ago, many of his colleagues thought he was wasting time and (as he recalled) "disgracing the university in the eyes of the public and academics." Browne did not approach mass culture with the reflexive contempt displayed by so many earlier academic critics. He was intellectually engaged, but he also brought a sense of openness and idealism to the project: "Popular culture democratizes society and makes democracy truly democratic. It is the everyday world around us: the mass media, entertainments, and diversions. It is our heroes, icons, rituals, everyday actions, psychology, and religion—our total life picture. It is the way of living we inherit, practice, and modify as we please, and how we do it. It is the dreams we dream while asleep." These essays, and the spirit behind this book, share that expansive view, which is broad enough to include meditations on Vietnamese food, hip-hop, Snapchat, television zombies, country music, video games, and disaster movies.

But that broad perspective affects the style as well as the substance of many selections chosen here. Some earlier critics of mass culture wrote about it as condescending outsiders worried about getting their hands dirty. Adorno and Horkheimer had little interest in—or feel for—the formal qualities and pleasures of popular entertainment, for example, even as their ideas remain prescient (see Nikil Saval's "Wall of Sound" [p. 139] which is grounded in the work of Adorno). Several essays in this book, like William Lutz's classic "With These Words I Can Sell You Anything" (p. 26) are essentially how-to pieces for resisting the manipulations of mass culture. Even when encouraging resistance, however, almost all these authors bring a fluency and familiarity with their subjects: They write as insiders. For all its intellectual dexterity and critical detachment, Susan Sontag's "The Imagination of Disaster" (p. 324) suggests a genuine intimacy with popular science fiction films. Bill Bryson's "The Hard Sell: Advertising in America" (p. 53) encourages critical thinking about the advertising industry; yet, the essay is also a supple and closely argued formal analysis of advertisements by someone deeply familiar with Madison Avenue craft.

The study of popular culture should be compatible with the study of "serious" academic subjects like literature or philosophy, not antagonistic or competitive. That is especially true in the context of composition classes. Students can apply the same skills that deconstruct children's playthings or identify clichéd tropes in contemporary films to poetry, history, sociology, political economy, social psychology, or any other discipline that requires critical thinking and writing. The habits and procedures are transferrable: reading closely, recognizing patterns, questioning assumptions, apprehending analogies, citing examples, making logical inferences and establishing connections. The selections here are excellent prompts for such intellectual investigation. Moreover, this book begins with the premise that in many ways, popular culture has become much smarter—more dense, more sophisticated, and more cognitively demanding—over the last fifty years, not less so. In its own way, each essay functions as an important reminder: *Keep your brain turned on when you leave class and put your earbuds in.*

CRITICAL THINKING

Much of our media and entertainment encourages passive consumption. But clear thinking—and good writing—about movies, music, television shows, and other mass-culture products require active, critical engagement. Perhaps the epigraph at the start of this introduction provides the best reason to study popular culture: to avoid being overtaken, absorbed, and assimilated by "zombies." Yet our zombification has less to do with the quality of popular culture and more to do with our reaction to it. We may even find any particular example of popular culture unappealing or uninteresting by itself, say, a specific reality television show. Yet in a wider context—a discussion of increasing cultural narcissism, changing notions of privacy, or shifting attitudes toward voyeurism—we might discover a revealing and sophisticated intellectual conversation. In other words, we may like or dislike specific elements of popular culture—*this* movie, *that* video game, *this* hip-hop star, *that* phone app—but the larger goal is to get involved in the conversation and become a critical reader of the world around us rather than a passive consumer. Ultimately, pop culture is mindless only if we approach it mindlessly.

When you are mindful of pop culture, you remain attentive, self-aware, and engaged. You ask questions and practice **critical thinking** to understand the world around you. Critical thinking takes many forms and draws on different strategies. It might include *analyzing* a text, image, or cultural phenomenon by breaking it into its component parts, looking for cause-and-effect relationships, defining it, or classifying it; *evaluating* claims, argu-

Times Square in New York City, where exposure to popular entertainment and consumer culture is unavoidable.

© Eye Ubiquitous/Alamy

ments, assertions, and supporting examples and discriminating between them; *reasoning* through the use of sound logic and persuasive evidence; and *synthesizing,* or making connections, between texts, events, products, films, trends, and other aspects of popular culture. Critical thinking is skeptical but not merely "critical" in the sense of leveling negative judgments or adopting a position of knee-jerk cynicism. Most of all, critical thinking means persistent *questioning*—of claims, texts, arguments, assumptions, images, implications, and (perhaps most importantly) your own biases and blind spots.

Questions critics (and critical thinkers) ask about pop culture in general might resemble the following:

Analyzing

- What does a trend reveal about the current cultural climate?
- What factors have caused a particular pop-cultural media event or sensation?
- How have pop-cultural representations of a particular group changed over time?

Evaluating

- What formal qualities—textual, visual, aural, stylistic—account for the appeal of this pop culture artifact?
- What effects is this pop culture artifact or phenomenon designed to achieve—and how do its creators want their audiences to react?
- Given the aesthetic standards of the cultural form or genre, how "good" or "bad" is the film (song, movie, television show, video game)?
- Is this pop culture artifact or phenomenon sincere, ironic, honest, deceptive, manipulative, beneficial, harmful, meaningful, empty, overhyped, or underrated?

Reasoning

- Does it seem logical that a pop culture form has emerged—or become wildly popular or declined in popularity—at this particular time?
- Is there enough evidence to make any broad arguments about the topic or its significance?

Synthesizing

- In what ways is a pop culture product or event similar to—and different from—comparable ones in the past?

- Can the topic be compared to other cultural forms (video games to novels, hip-hop lyrics to poetry) regarding either its innate qualities or the critical conversation around it?
- How has my perspective on this topic changed over time, with new information about or exposure to a topic, etc.?
- What have critics been saying about the topic? Are their arguments valid and their perspectives useful in judging the topic?

Similar questions can be narrowed to focus on a particular topic. For example, a student thinking critically about a popular viral marketing and advertising campaign might ask questions such as the following:

- What formal qualities—visual, aural, stylistic—account for the appeal of this campaign?
- How is it like or unlike similar products and campaigns aimed at the same demographic?
- Who is the target audience for this campaign, and what assumptions do its creators make about that audience?
- In what ways is the advertising effective, subtle, indirect, manipulative, or dishonest about achieving its purpose?
- What trends, technologies, cultural tendencies or other factors account for its popularity?
- What does the popularity of this product—and the prevalence of the ad campaign—suggest about our current cultural values?

CRITICAL READING: FROM COMPREHENSION TO ANALYSIS

You should apply critical-thinking skills—including questioning and careful analysis—to the essays in this book as you would apply them to any other cultural artifact. Essentially, **critical reading** is critical thinking applied to the reading process. When you read critically, you respond to writing on every level—from the sound of the prose to the soundness of the logic. You consider everything from the writer's underlying assumptions and the kinds of evidence she uses to support her claims to the argument's place in a wider cultural context. Then you turn those responses into analysis and ideas of your own.

But basic comprehension is essential: We need to know the basic meaning of the words on the page, the thesis of the essay, the plot of the story, the difference between *mitosis* and *meiosis* in a biology text, and the dates of the Civil War in the history book. But reading for analysis suggests a deeper—and more lasting—transaction between writer and reader. When readers approach a text analytically, they recognize and grasp the significance, arguments, and context as well as the basic information provided in the text. They may look for (and challenge) underlying premises; they may consider the relationship between specific pieces of evidence and the writer's general argument; they may discover thematic patterns or find links to larger issues. On the surface, for example, the subject of Lessley Anderson's "Seduced by 'Perfect' Pitch" (p. 220) is the musical technology Auto-Tune: its history, along with various attitudes toward the pitch-correction device. But the essay is about more than its subject: The writer meditates on music, identity, authenticity, and the meaning of Auto-Tune. Like a good critical reader, she makes connections, proposes arguments, and questions assumptions.

Readers sometimes confuse a story or essay's **subject**—"what happens" in a piece of writing, or its general topic—with its **themes**: what it is really *about,* as well as its connections to larger ideas, broader conversations, or even events in the reader's life. That crucial distinction reveals the difference between comprehension (understanding the content) and analysis (understanding how and to what effect the content is conveyed by using theme, form, and style and by considering audience and purpose). We might think about this distinction in the different ways we ask questions of a text. When we read for comprehension, we might ask questions like *What is the writer's thesis? What year did Auto-Tune debut as a plug-in for Pro Tools? Why did the band Death Cab for Cutie wear blue ribbons to the 2009 Grammy Awards?* While analysis requires an accurate understanding of these basic textual details, the critical, analytical reader also asks different questions—ones designed to illuminate what a text is really "about": *In what way is Auto-Tune different from—or worse than—other devices that electronically alter "natural" sounds, as electric guitars do? Why do debates about Auto-Tune often turn into moralistic arguments about integrity? How does the writer's tone reinforce her main points? What are the implications of her thesis?*

Notice that, unlike simple matters of recall and comprehension, these questions can lead to differing answers from well-informed readers. As you read and comprehend the details of a piece of writing, try to formulate questions that reveal more than its topic, subject, or plot: Look for ways to understand and express what a text is really "about." Keep in mind that the same principles of comprehension and analysis apply beyond written texts as well, whether you are thinking about an advertisement, an online video, or an iconic celebrity. You may be scrutinizing the visual composition of a widely disseminated image from the Web or listening carefully to decode the relationship between a pop song's message and its studio production methods, but you are still using the analytical tools of critical thinking and active reading. The essays in the book provide many examples of analysis across different pop culture and media forms, from Roland Barthes's deft interpretations of toys to Paul Cantor's provocative analysis of television's *The Walking Dead*.

Not surprisingly, all good pop culture writers are perceptive, analytical readers—of songs, technologies, television shows, movies, advertisements, video games, and other media forms. The writers included here are great noticers, too; they pay attention, make connections, and perceive thematic patterns in their chosen subjects.

The Practice of Critical Reading

You can become a better "noticer" by slowing down when you read. That is not always easy, especially in a culture that values speed and immediacy. But to improve as a writer, you must give yourself time and space for active, deliberate, even playful reading, as you grasp and reflect on key elements of a text.

Thesis and main points. This may seem obvious, but we sometimes approach texts hampered by our preconceptions and clichéd ideas. Then we read selectively and use this cognitive shorthand to plaster over gaps in our comprehension. If the following essays were mere vessels for conventional wisdom or platitudes, they would be worthless in a composition class—or any other class. Likewise, when we impose bland clichés on writers or filter their arguments through our own unexamined assumptions about what we think teachers want to hear, we block the grace of good writing. For example, if we have some vague sense that racial diversity is "good," then read Hua Hsu's "The End of White America?" (p. 96) and assume he agrees and wants to provide us with evidence for what we already know, we miss most of what makes his essay provocative and powerful. If we approach Clay Shirky's "Gin, Television, and Social Surplus" (p. 167) assuming everyone already agrees that messing around on the Internet is a waste of time and that no professor would assign an essay that argued otherwise, we will probably miss Shirky's main point. So make sure to read the words that the author wrote and not what you *think* he or she wrote, or what you think your instructor wants you to say. Similarly, some writers may imply thesis statements and main points without expressing them directly, which means you may need to reread passages or reflect on them after you have finished reading. Doing so is an essential component of critical reading—and worth the effort. You may find some familiar subjects and arguments in these essays, but you will also find provocations, challenges, and surprises. To that end, note what's confusing or unclear. It may turn out to be the most important part of the reading.

Purpose, audience, and writing situation. Some of the writers here aim to inform; others are trying to persuade; still others are reflecting, investigating, interpreting, expressing, proposing, evaluating, and writing for various, often overlapping, purposes. Try to analyze the writer's **purpose** and respond accordingly. If you are reading an argument, you may want to be especially mindful of the quality of the text's logic and the effectiveness of the evidence, as well as the way the writer addresses or anticipates counterarguments; if the goal of the writer is to express or entertain, pay special attention to style, tone, diction, and figurative language. Similarly, try to discover the intended **audience** of a text. For example, does the writer assume the reader has specialized knowledge of a particular film genre or specific era of American alternative music? If the text is argumentative, is the writer's approach likely to persuade those who disagree—or will it alienate them? Note the way the **writing situation**—which encompasses purpose, audience, subject, medium, and publication, as well as the relevant **context** (cultural, historical, political, etc.)—may influence the writer's style or use of sources. A column from a general interest online magazine may require only personal observations, anecdotal evidence, and casual references to other texts; in contrast, a scholarly article will likely require scholarly sources (like academic journals) and formal citations. But questions of purpose, audience, and situation are applicable beyond traditional texts: a pop-up video advertisement on a sports Web site has a purpose, audience, and writing situation, as does the Twitter feed of a celebrity or a television show like *Girls*.

Form and structure. Try to figure out *how* a piece of writing means as well as *what* a piece of writing means. Pay attention to **introductions**. How do the essays begin? With a case study, like Ellen Huet's "Snaps to Riches: The Rise of Snapchat Celebrities" (p. 70)? With a brief narrative that establishes the author's personality and connection to the topic, like Will Wilkinson's "Country Music, Openness to Experience, and the Psychology of Culture War" (p. 214)? How do different essays unfold and develop in different patterns? Some of these writers make their arguments in a linear way, moving directly from point to point; others set up oppositions and contrasts; still others use analogies. Many deploy all these techniques, and more. Look for the connective tissue between general assertions and specific examples. In the novel *A Prayer for Owen Meany*, author John Irving writes, "Any good book is always in motion—from the general to the specific, from the particular to the whole, and back again. Good reading—and good writing about reading—moves in the same way." Notice how writers manage that motion and achieve that balance throughout their work. Consider the **conclusions** of these essays. For example, how do these writers avoid stock endings that begin, "All in all . . ." or "In sum . . ."? How do they avoid just reiterating their arguments and, instead, leave readers with an evocative thought or a clever turn—like a toy surprise in a cereal box?

Evidence, research, and sources. Arguments, assertions, and generalizations require **evidence**. Pay attention to the ways in which writers support their claims. Does the writer use statistical data or empirical research? Does the writer cite expert testimony? Does the writer rely on observation and personal experience? If the writer cites sources, can the reader follow up on them to see that they are credible—and that the writer has used them accurately? Analyzing the research you find in a reading to determine how

and why a writer is using his or her sources helps you draw conclusions about the writer's own ideas and decide whether the
writer is a reliable or useful source. Keep in mind: Different **writing situations** require different kinds of evidence. A personal
essay about an individual's evolving musical tastes or social media
habits will likely depend on different kinds of evidence than a
more empirical study of the nature of television addiction. Likewise, a music review from an online newspaper will usually be
less rigorous in its citations than an article on a similar subject
from a scholarly journal.

Style. You are probably perceptive about questions of style as
they apply to fashion, sports, music, or other pop culture topics
that interest you. Try to apply that fluency and insight to the prose
you read. Which voices hover off the page and stay with you—
and why? All the authors here are competent, correct, and clear,
but some of them are distinctive stylists whose prose is as identifiable as their thumbprints. They compose with their ears tuned
to sound, rhythm, and tone; such writers go beyond choosing language adequate for communication and instead choose the *best*
words and phrases, which not only make their point but shimmer
on the page. Allow yourself to be influenced by your preferences.
Which essayists here would you want to sound like, and why?
T. S. Eliot once claimed that "immature poets imitate; mature
poets steal; bad poets deface what they take, and good poets make
it into something better, or at least something different." This is
not an endorsement of theft or plagiarism, of course. Rather,
Eliot's overstatement reminds us that good writing comes from
absorbing *other good writing*, and from our attempts to take what
we learn from the writers we admire and make it our own. So find
writers that you like and then figure out what you like about
them—the ways they open their essays, incorporate evidence,
choose examples, shape paragraphs, sustain a tone, achieve sentence variety, push readers beyond the obvious. Notice how they
solve these and other writing problems because their problems
are the same as yours, ultimately.

Tools and Strategies for Active Reading

To read actively, you need to do more than look at the words on
the page or wait for something to happen as you run your eyes

over paragraphs. Here are some practical tips for getting the most out of a text.

Know your purpose. Are you reading to learn more about a pop culture event or artifact that interests you? Will you be tested on the content of the material? Are you reading for class discussion? Will you be writing a response to the reading, or a journal entry? Are you reading to get background or context on a related research project? All of these purposes can shape your approach. For example, if you are trying to find sources for your own essay, you may focus your attention and analysis on a specific section of an article that is relevant to your preliminary thesis.

Preview the reading. Look over the entire text to get a general sense of the writer's purpose, thesis, and supporting arguments. Along with reading the title and introduction, do not hesitate to read the last paragraph of the essay, which may contain a concise summary or restatement of the writer's main point. If you are reading to find or retrieve a specific piece of information, you might skim the text to discover the passage you need. Do not worry about "spoilers," particularly when reading for information and comprehension: You are not looking for a plot or a surprising, whodunit ending. Rather, you are reading to get as much out of a text as possible to suit your purposes.

Often, the title, format, and even typography encourage comprehension and interpretation: numbered sections, topic headings, bullet points, and titles can indicate or suggest a thesis. For some of the essays in this book, the structure and organization will be subtle. But in others, previewing will give you a sense of the text's overall shape and design: titles that suggest subjects and themes; introductions that establish topic, context, purpose, and point of view; sections that address counterarguments or provide qualifications.

Talk back to the text. Annotate, underline, write comments, ask questions in the margins, and look up unfamiliar words. In his book *Here at the New Yorker*, writer Brendan Gill recalls lending a copy of the novel *Moby Dick* to his cranky Uncle Arthur, who asked permission to annotate the book: "His weapon was a little stub of yellow pencil, with which he would indicate his disapproval of the contents of a book, writing in the margins, 'Bah!,' 'Nonsense!,' and the like. He never got through *Moby Dick*, but how savagely he fought with Melville throughout the first fifty or a hundred pages." Uncle Arthur was an active reader. So were Mark Twain, Susan Sontag, and David Foster Wallace — fine writers, all known for their sparkling marginal comments. Your responses should go beyond "Bah!" and "Nonsense!" of course, but gut reactions can provide openings for criticism, analysis, and counterarguments. Start with what you *notice*: what you like, what you do not like, where you agree with the writer, and where you disagree — or even where the writer confuses you. Then figure out *why*. This habit will help you immeasurably with writing assignments. Your annotations, quibbles, and comments can form the basis for your own thesis questions, arguments, ideas, examples, counterexamples, and pathways for further research.

Make Connections. Look for links and tensions *between* these essays and other pop culture you've seen or read about as well. Apply the theoretical approach, intellectual framework, or method of analysis from one essay to another reading or topic. Can Susan Sontag's analytical strategy in "The Imagination of Disaster" (p. 324) be adapted and applied to contemporary horror movies? How does Neil Postman's "The Judgment of Thamus" (p. 151) illuminate discussions of immersive media or debates about "IRL"? As you join a conversation with a text, get texts talking to each other as well.

Read to Write. Record your responses and questions, and you will already have taken the key step in creating and shaping material for your own writing. Think quality, not quantity: Highlighting every topic sentence in an essay is less useful than finding — and annotating — the passages that capture the essence of the writer's thesis, suggest the argument's widest implications, or even show the essay's *least convincing* logical leaps and blind spots. Mark passages that open spaces for your point of view and provide opportunities for you to enter the conversation as a writer.

To show what active reading looks like, let's take a look at one student's annotation of paragraphs 19–20 from Hua Hsu's "The End of White America?" (The full essay is on page 96.)

In this regard, Combs is both a product and a hero of the new cultural mainstream, which prizes diversity above all else, and whose ultimate goal is some vague notion of racial transcendence, rather than subversion or assimilation. Although Combs's vision is far from representative — not many hip-hop stars vacation in St. Tropez with a parasol-toting manservant shading their every step — his industry lies at the heart of this new mainstream. Over the past 30 years, few changes in American culture have been as significant as the rise of hip-hop. The genre has radically reshaped the way we listen to and consume music, first by opposing the pop mainstream and then by becoming it. From its constant sampling of past styles and eras — old records, fashions, slang, anything — to its mythologization of the self-made black antihero, hip-hop is more than a musical genre: it's a philosophy, a political statement, a way of approaching and remaking culture. It's a lingua franca not just among kids in America, but also among young people worldwide. And its economic impact extends beyond the music industry, to fashion, advertising, and film.

But hip-hop's deepest impact is symbolic. During popular music's rise in the 20th century, white artists and producers consistently "mainstreamed" African American innovations. Hip-hop's ascension has been different. Eminem notwithstanding, hip-hop never suffered through anything like an Elvis Presley moment, in which a white artist made a musical form safe for white America. This is no dig at Elvis — the constrictive racial logic of the 1950s demanded the erasure of rock and roll's black roots, and if it hadn't been him, it would have been someone else. But hip-hop — the sound of the post-civil-rights, post-soul generation — found a global audience on its own terms.

Marginal annotations (left):

What does "mainstream" mean, exactly?

Fame and money undercuts "street" authenticity?

Why "antihero" and not just "hero"?

Symbolic of what?

"Suffered through" — negative.

Compare with Hollander essay: Is hip-hop still on its "own terms"?

Marginal annotations (right):

Is this a negative statement — "vague" notion?

True? What about the Internet?

Lingua franca?

With jazz, too.

"Constrictive racial logic" of an era. This essay is about today's "racial logic."

Notice how the student has underlined and highlighted important terms (such as "antihero") or ones he doesn't understand (such as "lingua franca"). These markings, particularly the marginal annotations, are an excellent way of understanding and engaging with the ideas in the text, as well as a useful tool for preparing for class discussion. They are also extremely useful for beginning the process of responding to a piece of writing with an essay of your own.

CHAPTER 1

Consumption and Advertising
How can we become more critical consumers?

"Capitalism's core virtue is that it marries altruism and self-interest," writes Benjamin Barber in an essay from this section. "In producing goods and services that answer real consumer needs, it secures a profit for producers." But what, exactly, are "real consumer needs"? From the stalls of the *agora*, which served as a marketplace in ancient Greece, to the endless aisles of a contemporary Wal-Mart, shopping has often meant more than just a simple financial transaction to satisfy bare human necessities. That is especially true in the United States. If we associate American consumerism with debt, excess, and self-indulgence, we also associate it with prosperity, liberty, and the egalitarian democracy of the market. After 9/11, shopping became patriotic, too, as public officials like former New York mayor Rudolph Giuliani urged Americans—the "best shoppers in the world"—to help New York recover by spending money. This notion of excessive American consumption is hardly new. The French political philosopher Alexis de Tocqueville long ago noted the American propensity for consumer desire. Observing this country in the 1830s, he wrote that Americans "never stop thinking of the good things they have not got," even as they "hurry after some new delight."

Of course, if we ever stopped hurrying "after some new delight," the advertising industry would be quick to remind us of the "good things" that we "have not got." Indeed, consumption and advertising are largely inseparable. While basic forms of advertising go back at least as far as ancient Egyptian papyrus posters, our familiar, modern form developed alongside print media over

19

three centuries ago. At the beginning of the twentieth century, copywriter John E. Kennedy famously defined advertising as "salesmanship in print." But as the century progressed, commercial radio and television superseded print media in the proliferation of advertising. Consumers became more sophisticated, of course, but so did marketers and advertisers. Edward Bernays, political consultant and author of books such as *This Business of Propaganda* (1928), applied the psychological theories of his uncle, Sigmund Freud, to marketing, branding, and public relations. As the ad industry grew in size and influence, its legion of skeptics and detractors grew as well. For example, in 1957, journalist and social critic Vance Packard published *The Hidden Persuaders*, which exposed the manipulative tactics and psychological techniques used to influence consumers.

The essays in this section look at consumption and consumer habits, as well as our relationship to products, retail stores, and new technologies. They also address the advertising and mass persuasion that suffuse our economy and our society. In "Overselling Capitalism with Consumerism," Barber argues that consumerism ultimately perverts capitalism, as producers in search of buyers must "dumb down consumers" and "invent new needs." In "With These Words I Can Sell You Anything," William Lutz focuses on the specific language of marketers and advertisers; he also encourages consumers to view the claims of advertisers skeptically. Roland Barthes's "Toys" shows how seemingly innocent consumer products—children's playthings—burst with significance, ideological and otherwise, when they are given a close reading. Soleil Ho examines consumption in a more literal sense in "Craving the Other": Exploring the facile appropriation of ethnic cuisines among American "foodies," she argues that this trend has only led to inaccurate generalizations and stereotypes of Asian culture. Virginia Postrel's "In Praise of Chain Stores" provides a bracing defense of retail chain stores, as the writer responds to snobby "cosmopolites" whose misguided "contempt for chains represents a brand-obsessed view of place." Bill Bryson's witty "The Hard Sell: Advertising in America" gives historical perspective on the theory and practice of modern American advertising, especially the way advertisements identify and exploit the American consumer's anxiety.

The chapter's paired readings investigate how new technologies and social media are shaping consumption, branding, and buying habits. In "Snaps to Riches: The Rise of Snapchat Celebrities," Ellen Huet looks at Snapchat, a social media platform that has quickly evolved from an app that allows users to share images, texts, and videos into a potential marketing tool for brands seeking access to a "hard-to-reach youth audience." In "Public Displays of Transaction," Chiara Atik discusses the online payment app Venmo, which brings our intimate consumer habits and financial transactions into the exhibitionistic—and voyeuristic—arena of Internet social media.

As you read, consider these essays in the context of your own experience as both a consumer and a target for advertising:

- How do the arguments here align with—or challenge—your own views?
- Can you detect or identify any ideas or themes that seem to unify these disparate essays? What are they?
- What underlying assumptions about consumption or advertising can you discover?

BENJAMIN BARBER

Overselling Capitalism with Consumerism

Benjamin R. Barber is founder and president of the international project CivWorld and of the Interdependence Movement, Walt Whitman Professor Emeritus at Rutgers University, and author of nineteen books, including the classic Strong Democracy, *the international best seller* Jihad vs. McWorld *(1995), and, published from Yale University Press,* If Mayors Ruled the World *(2013).*

In this Los Angeles Times *opinion column (2007), Barber considers the economic problems of the last several years in the context of consumerism and the decline of an "ethos of hard work and deferred gratification."*

As you read, *reflect on your own views of capitalism and your role in a consumer economy. Why does consumerism threaten democracy and the economy, according to Barber? Do you think Barber's proposed solutions to the problem of consumerism are specific and realistic enough to be effective?*

The crisis in subprime mortgages betrays a deeper predicament facing consumer capitalism triumphant: The "Protestant ethos" of hard work and deferred gratification has been replaced by an infantilist ethos of easy credit and impulsive consumption that puts democracy and the market system at risk.

Capitalism's core virtue is that it marries altruism and self-interest. In producing goods and services that answer real consumer needs, it secures a profit for producers. Doing good for others turns out to entail doing well for yourself.

Capitalism's success, however, has meant that core wants in the developed world are now mostly met and that too many goods are chasing too few needs. Yet capitalism requires us to "need" all that it produces in order to survive. So it busies itself manufacturing needs for the wealthy while ignoring the wants of the truly needy. Global inequality means that while the wealthy have too few needs, the needy have too little wealth.

Capitalism is stymied, courting long-term disaster. We still work hard, but only so that we can pay and play. In order to turn reluctant consumers with few unsatisfied core needs into permanent shoppers, producers must dumb down consumers, shape their wants, take over their life worlds, encourage impulse buying, cultivate shopoholism, and invent new needs.

At the same time, they empower kids as shoppers by legitimizing their unformed tastes and mercurial wants and detaching them from their gatekeeper mothers and fathers and teachers and pastors. The kids include toddlers who recognize brand logos before they can talk and commodity-minded baby Einsteins who learn to shop before they can walk. 5

Consumerism needs this infantilist ethos because it favors laxity and leisure over discipline and denial, values childish impetuosity and juvenile narcissism over adult order and enlightened self-interest, and prefers consumption-directed play to spontaneous

© Vincent Yu/AP Images

Customers in line for the iPhone 6. "In order to turn reluctant consumers with few unsatisfied core needs into permanent shoppers," writes Barber, "producers must dumb down consumers, shape their wants . . . and invent new needs."

recreation. The ethos feeds a private-market logic ("What I want is what society needs!") and combats the public logic fashioned by democracy ("What society needs is what I want to want!").

This is capitalism's all-too-logical way of solving the problem of too many goods chasing too few needs. It makes consuming ubiquitous and omnipresent, turning shopping into an addiction facilitated by easy credit.

Compare any traditional town square with a modern suburban mall. In the square, you'll find a school, town hall, library, general store, park, movie house, church, art gallery, and homes — a true neighborhood exhibiting our human diversity as beings who do more than simply consume. But our new town malls are all shopping, all the time.

When we see politics permeate every sector of life, we call it totalitarianism. When religion rules all, we call it theocracy. But when commerce dominates everything, we call it liberty. Can we redirect capitalism to its proper end: the satisfaction of real human needs? Well, why not?

The world teems with elemental wants and is peopled by billions who are needy. They do not need iPods, but they do need potable water, not colas but inexpensive medicines, not MTV but their ABCs. They need mortgages they can afford, not funny-money easy credit.

To serve such needs, however, capitalism must once again learn to defer profits and empower the needy as customers. Entrepreneurs wanted! With micro-credit, villagers can construct hand pumps and water filters from the clay under their feet.

Pharmaceutical companies ought to be thinking about how to sell inexpensive retrovirals to Africans with HIV instead of pushing Botox to the "forever young" customers they are trying to manufacture here.

And parents can refuse to relinquish their gatekeeping roles and let marketers know they won't allow their kids to be targeted anymore.

To do this, we will require the assistance of democratic institutions and an adult ethos. Public citizens must be restored to their proper place as masters of their private choices. To sustain itself, capitalism once again will have to respond to real needs instead of trying to fabricate synthetic ones — or risk consuming itself.

For Discussion and Writing

1. **Comprehension** According to Barber, what is the deep predicament that faces consumer capitalism?

2. **Critical Reading** Barber wrote this essay in 2007. What aspects of the author's **writing situation** can you identify from your reading? For example, what is the social and economic **context** for "Overselling Capitalism with Consumerism"? Has the context changed since it was written, and does that affect its relevance? Explain your answer.

3. **Analysis** The author refers to capitalism's "core virtue" (par. 2), and proposes that capitalism be redirected to its "proper end" (par. 9). How do you respond to these—and other—characterizations of our economic system in the essay? Do you agree with Barber's assumptions about the nature and function of capitalism?

4. **Connections** Barber writes about an "infantilist ethos" as it applies to consumerism (par. 6). Do you think the advertising industry encourages that "ethos," or do marketers and advertisers cultivate another kind of ethos among consumers? Consider using Bill Bryson's historical analysis of the Kodak camera advertising campaigns in "The Hard Sell: Advertising in America" (p. 53) to address these questions.

5. **Writing** Barber proposes an opposition between an "infantilist ethos" and an "adult ethos." How would you compare and contrast them? In a compare and contrast essay, use specific examples from your own life, society, and culture to illustrate the difference between the two.

WILLIAM LUTZ

With These Words
I Can Sell You Anything

William Lutz (b. 1940) taught English at Rutgers University from 1991 to 2006. He also edited the Quarterly Review of Doublespeak, *a publication that collected misleading language and euphemisms by politicians, advertisers, educators, and others. Lutz has worked with dozens of corporations and government agencies, consulting and conducting workshops on clear language. His books include* Doublespeak: From Revenue Enhancement to Terminal Living *(1989),* The New Doublespeak: No One Knows What Anyone's Saying Anymore *(1996), and* Doublespeak Defined *(1999). In this selection from* Doublespeak, *Lutz approaches the language of advertising in much the way a literary critic approaches a poem. He encourages his readers to use the same rigor: "Your job is to figure out exactly what each word is doing in the ad — what each word really means, not what the advertiser wants you to think it means." We often presume that the goal of language is clear and accurate communication, but Lutz shows us that this assumption is often false.*

As you read, *notice how words can mask reality or mislead us. What common qualities define "weasel words"? Do you think most consumers understand that advertising is often misleading? Is it possible that, on some level, we like to be misled by advertisers and invite the deception?*

One problem advertisers have when they try to convince you that the product they are pushing is really different from other, similar products is that their claims are subject to some laws. Not a lot of laws, but there are some designed to prevent fraudulent or untruthful claims in advertising. Generally speaking, advertisers have to be careful in what they say in their ads, in the claims they make for the products they advertise. Parity claims are safe

26

because they are legal and supported by a number of court decisions. But beyond parity claims there are weasel words.

Advertisers use weasel words to appear to be making a claim for a product when in fact they are making no claim at all. Weasel words get their name from the way weasels eat the eggs they find in the nests of other animals. A weasel will make a small hole in the egg, suck out the insides, then place the egg back in the nest. Only when the egg is examined closely is it found to be hollow. That's the way it is with weasel words in advertising.

"HELP"—THE NUMBER ONE WEASEL WORD

The biggest weasel word used in advertising doublespeak is "help." Now "help" only means to aid or assist, nothing more. It does not mean to conquer, stop, eliminate, end, solve, heal, cure, or anything else. But once the ad says "help," it can say just about anything after that because "help" qualifies everything coming after it. The trick is that the claim that comes after the weasel word is usually so strong and so dramatic that you forget the word "help" and concentrate only on the dramatic claim. You read into the ad a message that the ad does not contain. More importantly, the advertiser is not responsible for the claim that you read into the ad, even though the advertiser wrote the ad so you would read that claim into it.

The next time you see an ad for a cold medicine that promises that it "helps relieve cold symptoms fast," don't rush out to buy it. Ask yourself what this claim is really saying. Remember, "helps" means only that the medicine will aid or assist. What will it aid or assist in doing? Why, "relieve" your cold "symptoms." "Relieve" only means to ease, alleviate, or mitigate, not to stop, end, or cure. Nor does the claim say how much relieving this medicine will do. Nowhere does this ad claim it will cure anything. In fact, the ad doesn't even claim it will do anything at all. The ad only claims that it will aid in relieving (not curing) your cold symptoms, which are probably a runny nose, watery eyes, and a headache. In other words, this medicine probably contains a standard decongestant and some aspirin. By the way, what does "fast" mean? Ten minutes, one hour, one day? What is fast to one person can be very slow to another. "Fast" is another weasel word.

Look at ads in magazines and newspapers, listen to ads on   5
radio and television, and you'll find the word "help" in ads for all
kinds of products. How often do you read or hear such phrases as
"helps stop . . . ," "helps overcome . . . ," "helps eliminate . . . ,"
"helps you feel . . . ," or "helps you look . . ."? If you start looking
for this weasel word in advertising, you'll be amazed at how often
it occurs. Analyze the claims in the ads using "help," and you will
discover that these ads are really saying nothing.

VIRTUALLY SPOTLESS

One of the most powerful weasel words is "virtually," a word so
innocent that most people don't pay any attention to it when it is
used in an advertising claim. But watch out. "Virtually" is used in
advertising claims that appear to make specific, definite promises
when there is no promise. After all, what does "virtually" mean?
It means "in essence of effect, although not in fact." Look at that
definition again. "Virtually" means not in fact. It does not mean
"almost" or "just about the same as," or anything else.

The next time you see the ad that says that this dishwasher
detergent "leaves dishes virtually spotless," just remember how
advertisers twist the meaning of the weasel word "virtually." You
can have lots of spots on your dishes after using this detergent
and the ad claim will still be true, because what this claim really
means is that this detergent does not in fact leave your dishes
spotless. Whenever you see or hear an ad claim that uses the word
"virtually," just translate that claim into its real meaning. So the
television set that is "virtually trouble free" becomes the television set that is not in fact trouble free, the "virtually foolproof
operation" of any appliance becomes an operation that is in fact
not foolproof, and the product that "virtually never needs service"
becomes the product that is not in fact service free.

NEW AND IMPROVED

If "new" is the most frequently used word on a product package,
"improved" is the second most frequent. In fact, the two words
are almost always used together. It seems just about everything
sold these days is "new and improved." The next time you're in

the supermarket, try counting the number of times you see these words on products.

Just what do these words mean? The use of the word "new" is restricted by regulations, so an advertiser can't just use the word on a product or in an ad without meeting certain requirements. For example, a product is considered new for about six months during a national advertising campaign. If the product is being advertised only in a limited test market area, the word can be used longer, and in some instances has been used for as long as two years.

What makes a product "new"? Some products have been 10 around for a long time, yet every once in a while you discover that they are being advertised as "new." Well, an advertiser can call a product new if there has been "a material functional change" in the product. What is "a material functional change," you ask? Good question. In fact it's such a good question it's being asked all the time. It's up to the manufacturer to prove that the product has undergone such a change. And if the manufacturer isn't challenged on the claim, then there's no one to stop it. Moreover, the change does not have to be an improvement in the product. One manufacturer added an artificial lemon scent to a cleaning product and called it "new and improved," even though the product did not clean any better than without the lemon scent. The manufacturer defended the use of the word "new" on the grounds that the artificial scent changed the chemical formula of the product and therefore constituted "a material functional change."

Which brings up the word "improved." When used in advertising, "improved" does not mean "made better." It only means "changed" or "different from before." So, if the detergent maker puts a plastic pour spout on the box of detergent, the product has been "improved," and away we go with a whole new advertising campaign. Or, if the cereal maker adds more fruit or a different kind of fruit to the cereal, there's an improved product. Now you know why manufacturers are constantly making little changes in their products. Whole new advertising campaigns, designed to convince you that the product has been changed for the better, are based on small changes in superficial aspects of a product. The next time you see an ad for an "improved" product, ask yourself what was wrong with the old one. Ask yourself just how "improved" the product is. Finally, you might check to see whether the "improved" version costs more than the unimproved one.

ADVERTISING DOUBLESPEAK: QUICK QUIZ

Test your awareness of advertising doublespeak. The following is a list of statements from some recent ads. Your job is to figure out what each of these ads really says.

DOMINO'S PIZZA: "Because nobody delivers better."
SINUTAB: "It can stop the pain."
TUMS: "The stronger acid neutralizer."
LISTERMINT: "Making your mouth a cleaner place."
CASCADE: "For virtually spotless dishes."
NUPRIN: "Little. Yellow. Different. Better."
ANACIN: "Better relief."
ADVIL: "Advanced medicine for pain."
ALEVE COLD AND SINUS: "12 hours of relief."
PONDS COLD CREAM: "Ponds cleans like no soap can."
MILLER LITE BEER: "Tastes great. Less filling."
PHILLIPS MILK OF MAGNESIA: "Nobody treats you better than MOM."
BAYER: "The wonder drug that works wonders."
KNORR: "Where taste is everything."
ANUSOL: "Anusol is the word to remember for relief."
DIMETAPP: "It relieves kids as well as colds."
LIQUID DRANO: "The liquid strong enough to be called Drano."
JOHNSON & JOHNSON BABY POWDER: "Like magic for your skin."
PURITAN: "Make it your oil for life."
PAM: "Pam, because how you cook is as important as what you cook."
TYLENOL GEL-CAPS: "It's not a capsule. It's better."
ALKA-SELTZER PLUS: "Breaks up your worst cold symptoms."

"New" is just too useful and powerful a word in advertising for advertisers to pass it up easily. So they use weasel words that say "new" without really saying it. One of their favorites is "introducing," as in, "Introducing improved Tide," or "Introducing the stain remover." The first is simply saying, here's our improved soap; the second, here's our new advertising campaign for our detergent. Another favorite is "now," as in, "Now there's Sinex," which simply means that Sinex is available. Then there are phrases like "Today's Chevrolet," "Presenting Dristan," and "A fresh way to start the day." The list is really endless because advertisers are always finding new ways to say "new" without really saying it.

ACTS FAST

"Acts" and "works" are two popular weasel words in advertising because they bring action to the product and to the advertising claim. When you see the ad for the cough syrup that "Acts on the cough control center," ask yourself what this cough syrup is claiming to do. Well, it's just claiming to "act," to do something, to perform an action. What is it that the cough syrup does? The ad doesn't say. It only claims to perform an action or do something on your "cough control center." By the way, what and where is your "cough control center"? I don't remember learning about that part of the body in human biology class.

Ads that use such phrases as "acts fast," "acts against," "acts to prevent," and the like are saying essentially nothing, because "act" is a word empty of any specific meaning. The ads are always careful not to specify exactly what "act" the product performs. Just because a brand of aspirin claims to "act fast" for headache relief doesn't mean this aspirin is any better than any other aspirin. What is the "act" that this aspirin performs? You're never told. Maybe it just dissolves quickly. Since aspirin is a parity product, all aspirin is the same and therefore functions the same.

WORKS LIKE ANYTHING ELSE

If you don't find the word "acts" in an ad, you will probably find   15
the weasel word "works." In fact, the two words are almost interchangeable in advertising. Watch out for ads that say a product "works against," "works like," "works for," or "works longer." As with "acts," "works" is the same meaningless verb used to make you think that this product really does something, and maybe even something special or unique. But "works," like "acts," is basically a word empty of any specific meaning.

"Advertisers use weasel words to appear to be making a claim for a product when in fact they are making no claim at all." This ad for Method Soap uses two: the advertiser's misdirection "like" and the meaningless verb "works." "Like" is used to identify the soap's literal scent (cucumber) and then deployed in a vague simile that is unsubstantial: "Works like gangbusters." Yet the ad attempts a more sophisticated sleight-of-hand: it not only promotes Method Soap, but also responds to the rhetoric of other soap advertisements: "So why do so many brag about their 99.99% death rate?" By doing so, the ad attempts to co-opt suspicion of advertising to service its own claims. How does the visual composition of the ad reflect the claims made by the text?

LIKE MAGIC

Whenever advertisers want you to stop thinking about the product and to start thinking about something bigger, better, or more attractive than the product, they use that very popular weasel word, "like." The word "like" is the advertiser's equivalent of a magician's use of misdirection. "Like" gets you to ignore the product and concentrate on the claim the advertiser is making about it. "For skin like peaches and cream" claims the ad for a skin cream. What is that ad really claiming? It doesn't say this cream will give you peaches-and-cream skin. There is no verb in this claim, so it doesn't even mention using the product. How is skin

"Your job is to figure out exactly what each word is doing in an ad—what each word really means, not what the advertiser wants you to think it means." But what if an advertisement contains no words? This ad implies the effectiveness of Glassex without making any explicit claim about the product. Consider the paradoxes: a glass cleaner connotes clarity and transparency, but an illusionist's floating-woman trick implies deception, mystery, and incredulity. We might say that "Glassex works like magic." As it conjures a world of illusion and misdirection while saying nothing about the product, this Glassex ad may be an ideal metaphor for advertising itself. Would the addition of text be beneficial or detrimental to the ad? Why?

ever like "peaches and cream"? The ad is making absolutely no promise or claim whatsoever for this skin cream. If you think this cream will give you soft, smooth, youthful-looking skin, you are the one who has read that meaning into the ad.

The wine that claims "It's like taking a trip to France" wants you to think about a romantic evening in Paris as you walk along the boulevard after a wonderful meal in an intimate little bistro. Of course, you don't really believe that a wine can take you to France, but the goal of the ad is to get you to think pleasant, romantic thoughts about France and not about how the wine tastes or how expensive it may be. That little word "like" has taken you away from crushed grapes into a world of your own imaginative making. Who knows, maybe the next time you buy wine, you'll think those pleasant thoughts when you see this brand of wine, and you'll buy it. Or, maybe you weren't even thinking about buying wine at all, but now you just might pick up a bottle the next time you're shopping. Ah, the power of "like" in advertising.

THE WORLD OF ADVERTISING

A study some years ago found the following words to be among the most popular used in U.S. television advertisements: "new," "improved," "better," "extra," "fresh," "clean," "beautiful," "free," "good," "great," and "light." At the same time, the following words were found to be among the most frequent on British television: "new," "good-better-best," "free," "fresh," "delicious," "full," "sure," "clean," "wonderful," and "special." While these words may occur most frequently in ads, and while ads may be filled with weasel words, you have to watch out for all the words used in advertising, not just the words mentioned here.

Every word in an ad is there for a reason; no word is wasted. Your job is to figure out exactly what each word is doing in an ad—what each word really means, not what the advertiser wants you to think it means. Remember: the ad is trying to get you to buy a product, so it will put the product in the best possible light, using any device, trick, or means legally allowed. Your only defense against advertising (besides taking up permanent residence on the moon) is to develop and use a strong critical reading, listening, and looking ability. Always ask yourself what the ad is really saying. When you see ads on television, don't be misled by the pictures, the visual images. What does the ad say about the product? What does the ad not say? What information is missing from the ad? Only by becoming an active, critical consumer of the doublespeak of advertising will you ever be able to cut through the doublespeak and discover what the ad is really saying.

For Discussion and Writing

1. **Comprehension**   According to Lutz, "If 'new' is the most frequently used word on a product package, 'improved' is the second most frequent" (par. 8). What do these words mean in the context of

packaging and advertising? What words do advertisers sometimes use in place of "new"?

2. ***Critical Reading*** Lutz addresses the readers in his **audience** as "you" throughout the essay. Why do you think he writes in the second person? How does this choice suggest his **purpose** and affect the essay's overall effectiveness?

3. ***Analysis*** Lutz writes, "Every word in an ad is there for a reason; no word is wasted. Your job is to figure out exactly what each word is doing in an ad—what each word really means, not what the advertiser wants you to think it means" (par. 19). How is this kind of analytical reading similar to the way one might interpret a poem, a novel, a short story, or any other artistic form? How is it different?

4. ***Connections*** According to Bill Bryson in "The Hard Sell: Advertising in America" (p. 53), advertisers made a great breakthrough in their art with the "identification and exploitation of the American consumer's Achilles' heel: anxiety" (par. 14). How do Lutz's weasel words illustrate Bryson's claim, if at all? What other emotions, aspirations, or tendencies do weasel words exploit?

5. ***Writing*** Lutz gives a quiz within his essay to test our awareness of taglines, slogans, and doublespeak in advertising. Choose an advertisement—online, in a magazine, on television—and examine its language in a brief interpretive essay. Does it contain "weasel words"? What do they mean? Is the ad misleading or deliberately ambiguous? If the advertisement contains images, do they trick us, or redirect our attention from the product?

ROLAND BARTHES

Toys

Roland Barthes (1915–1980) was a literary theorist and semiotician born in the Normandy region of France. As a critic and essayist, his interests ranged from anthropology, existentialism, and Marxism to fashion and mass culture. While he deployed a variety of critical approaches, Barthes is probably best known for his interest in semiotics, a branch of linguistics that analyzes signs and symbols as elements of communication. Barthes used semiotics to analyze popular culture—perhaps most famously in Mythologies *(1957), a book that includes "Toys." By scrutinizing phenomena like toys, cars, and professional wrestling, Barthes revealed their hidden meanings. He also uncovered the unexamined assumptions, values, and myths of the society that consumes such products. The essays in* Mythologies *originally appeared in the literary magazine* Les Lettres Nouvelles *between 1954 and 1956. Barthes's other works include* Writing Degree Zero *(1953),* S/Z: An Essay *(1970), and* The Pleasure of the Text *(1973). While Barthes's style is witty and playful, he has a serious purpose in* Mythologies: *"I resented seeing Nature and History confused at every turn, and I wanted to track down, in the decorative display of what-goes-without-saying, the ideological abuse which, in my view, is hidden there."*

As you read, notice how Barthes uncovers this meaningful "what-goes-without-saying" through keen observation and vivid description. What toys does Barthes focus on? What are the "myths" and "techniques" of modern adult life? Why does Barthes seem to dislike plastic toys?

French toys: one could not find a better illustration of the fact that the adult Frenchman sees the child as another self. All the toys one commonly sees are essentially a microcosm of the adult world; they are all reduced copies of human objects, as if in the

Barthes writes that toys "are usually based on imitation, they are meant to produce children who are users, not creators." Do the toys in this image support his claim?

eyes of the public the child was, all told, nothing but a smaller man, a homunculus to whom must be supplied objects of his own size.

Invented forms are very rare: a few sets of blocks, which appeal to the spirit of do-it-yourself, are the only ones which offer dynamic forms. As for the others, French toys *always mean something*, and this something is always entirely socialized, constituted by the myths or the techniques of modern adult life: the Army, Broadcasting, the Post Office, Medicine (miniature instrument-cases, operating theatres for dolls), School, Hair-Styling (driers for permanent-waving), the Air Force (Parachutists), Transport (trains, Citroëns, Vedettes, Vespas, petrol-stations), Science (Martian toys).

The fact that French toys *literally* prefigure the world of adult functions obviously cannot but prepare the child to accept them all, by constituting for him, even before he can think about it, the alibi of a Nature which has at all times created soldiers, postmen, and Vespas. Toys here reveal the list of all the things the adult does not find unusual: war, bureaucracy, ugliness, Martians, etc. It is not so much, in fact, the imitation which is the sign of an abdication, as its literalness: French toys are like a Jivaro head, in which one recognizes, shrunken to the size of an apple, the wrinkles and hair of an adult. There exist, for instance, dolls which urinate; they have an esophagus, one gives them a bottle, they wet their nappies; soon, no doubt, milk will turn to water in their stomachs. This is meant to prepare the little girl for the causality of house-keeping, to "condition" her to her future role as mother. However, faced with this world of faithful and complicated objects, the child can only identify himself as owner, as user, never as creator; he does not invent the world, he uses it: there are, prepared for him, actions without adventure, without wonder, without joy. He is turned into a little stay-at-home house-holder who does not even have to invent the mainsprings of adult causality; they are supplied to him ready-made: he has only to help himself, he is never allowed to discover anything from start to finish. The merest set of blocks, provided it is not too refined, implies a very different learning of the world: then, the child does not in any way create meaningful objects, it matters little to him whether they have an adult name; the actions he performs are not those of a user but those of a demiurge. He creates forms which walk, which roll, he creates life, not property: objects now act by themselves, they are no longer an inert and complicated material in the palm of his hand. But such toys are rather rare: French toys are usually based on imitation, they are meant to produce children who are users, not creators.

The bourgeois status of toys can be recognized not only in their forms, which are all functional, but also in their substances. Current toys are made of a graceless material, the product of chemistry, not of nature. Many are now molded from complicated mixtures; the plastic material of which they are made has an appearance at once gross and hygienic, it destroys all the pleasure, the sweetness, the humanity of touch. A sign which fills one with consternation is the gradual disappearance of wood, in spite of its being an ideal material because of its firmness and its softness, and the natural warmth of its touch. Wood removes, from all the forms which it supports, the wounding quality of angles which are too sharp, the chemical coldness of metal. When the child handles it and knocks it, it neither vibrates nor grates, it has a sound at once muffled and sharp. It is a familiar and poetic substance, which does not sever the child from close contact with the tree, the table, the floor. Wood does not wound or break down; it does not shatter, it wears out, it can last a long time, live with the child, alter little by little the relations between the object and the hand. If it dies, it is in dwindling, not in swelling out like those mechanical toys which disappear behind the hernia of a broken spring. Wood makes essential objects, objects for all time. Yet there hardly remain any of these wooden toys from the Vosges, these fretwork farms with their animals, which were only possible, it is true, in the days of the craftsman. Henceforth, toys are chemical in substance and color; their very material introduces one to a coenaesthesis[1] of use, not pleasure. These toys die in fact very quickly, and once dead, they have no posthumous life for the child.

---

[1]*coenaesthesis:* the condition of experiencing sensations (such as sight, hearing, taste, touch, smell) that make one aware of one's own body. [Editor's note.]

For Discussion and Writing

1. **Comprehension**   Why does Barthes prefer wooden toys to toys made from plastic or metal?

2. **Critical Reading**   What is Barthes's **thesis**? How would you state it in your own words?

3. **Analysis**   According to Barthes, toys "*literally* prefigure the world of adult functions" and therefore "cannot but prepare the child to accept them all, by constituting for him, even before he can think about it, the alibi of a Nature . . ." (par. 3). What does he mean by the "alibi of a Nature"? Does he prove his claim persuasively throughout the essay? Why or why not?

4. **Connections**   In "Why Videogames Should Be Played with Friends, Not Online with Strangers" (p. 436), Bo Moore discusses the social aspects of "play" in the context of video games. How might you view video games using Barthes's framework? Do video games "socialize" or "condition" players to accept certain "myths" or a certain view of the world? Are video game players like "owners" and "users," or are they more like "creators"?

5. **Writing**   Barthes writes that "French toys *always mean something*" (par. 2). Choose a toy, product, or common object, and in a brief descriptive analysis essay, interpret its meaning as Barthes interprets toys in his essay. Focus on its function, material, and formal details: What do they suggest about its user's relationship to the world? How does the object reflect social values? What does the object "mean"?

SOLEIL HO

Craving the Other

Soleil Ho is a freelance writer who lives and works in New Orleans. Her essays have appeared in bitch, *the* Heavy Table, Interrupt Mag, Impreachable, Art Review & Preview, *and other publications. She is also the nonfiction editor at* Quaint *magazine. In this essay from* Bitch *magazine, Ho ties her experiences as the Americanized child of Vietnamese immigrants who longs to be an assimilated "white American" to the glib, pretentious connoisseurship of Western sophisticates who believe that liking authentic ethnic food gives them authority and cachet. "Their commonality is their insistence on appreciating a culture that exists mostly in their heads," she writes. "They share a nostalgia for someone else's life."*

As you read, pay close attention to Ho's style and tone. How would you describe it? In what ways does it reinforce her argument? How would you characterize her attitude toward the authenticity-seeking consumers of "ethnic" food?

For a long time, Vietnamese food made me uncomfortable. It was brothy, weirdly fishy, and full of the gross animal parts that other people didn't seem to want. It was too complicated.

I wanted the straightforward, prefabricated snacks that I saw on television: Bagel Bites, Pop-Tarts, chicken nuggets. When my grandmother babysat me, she would make tiny concessions, preparing rice bowls with chopped turkey cold cuts for me while everyone else got caramelized pork. I would make my own Bagel Bites by toasting a normal-size bagel and topping it with Chinese sausage and a dash of Sriracha. My favorite snack was a weird kind of fusion: a slice of nutrient-void Wonder Bread sprinkled with a few dashes of Maggi sauce, an ultraplain proto-*banh mi* that I came up with while rummaging through my grandmother's pantry. In our food-centric family, I was the barbarian who demanded twisted simulacra of my grandmother's masterpieces, perverted so far beyond the pungent, saucy originals that they looked like the national cuisine of a country that didn't exist. When I entered my first year of college in Iowa, a strange pattern began to emerge as I got to know my classmates. "Oh, you're Vietnamese?" they'd ask. "I love *pho*!" And then the whispered question—"Am I saying that right?" The same people who would have made fun of me for bringing a stinky rice-noodle salad to school 10 years ago talked to me as if I were the gatekeeper to some hidden temple that they had discovered on their own. Pho seemed like a shortcut for them, a way that they could tell me that they knew about my culture and our soupy ways without me having to tell them. I would hear this again and again from that point on. I'm Vietnamese? They love pho! I told people to pronounce it a different way each time they asked, knowing that they would immediately march over to their racially homogenous group of friends to correct them with the "authentic" way to pronounce their favorite dish. I'm sure that they were happy to learn a little bit about my family's culture, but I found their motivations for doing so suspect.

What can one say in response? "Oh, you're white? I love tuna salad!" It sounds ridiculous, mostly because no one cares if a second-generation immigrant likes American food. Rather, the burden of fluency with American culture puts a unique pressure on the immigrant kid. I paid attention during playdates with my childhood friends, when parents would serve pulled-pork sandwiches and coleslaw for lunch. (It took me a long time to understand the appeal of mayonnaise, which, as a non-cream, non-cheese, non-sauce, perplexed the hell out of me.) From watching my friends, I learned to put the coleslaw in the sandwich and sop the bread in the stray puddles of sauce in between bites. There's a similar kind of self-checking that occurs when I take people out to Vietnamese restaurants: Through unsubtle side glances, they watch me for behavioral cues, noting how and if I use various condiments and garnishes so they can report back to their friends and family that they learned how to eat this food the "real way" from their real, live Vietnamese friend. Their desire to be true global citizens, eaters without borders, lies behind their studious gazes.

When I go to contemporary Asian restaurants, like Wolfgang Puck's now-shuttered 20.21 in Minneapolis and Jean-Georges Vongerichten's Spice Market in New York City, it seems the entrées are always in the $16–$35 range and the only identifiable person of color in the kitchen is the dishwasher. The menus usually include little blurbs about how the chefs used to backpack in the steaming jungles of the Far East (undoubtedly stuffing all the herbs and spices they could fit into said backpacks along the way, for research purposes), and were so inspired by the smiling faces of the very generous natives—of which there are plenty of tasteful black-and-white photos on the walls, by the way—and the hospitality, *oh, the hospitality*, that they decided the best way to really crystallize that life-changing experience was to go back home and sterilize the cuisine they experienced by putting some microcilantro on that $20 curry to really make it worthy of the everyday American sophisticate. American chefs like to talk fancy talk about "elevating" or "refining" third-world cuisines, a rhetoric that brings to mind the *mission civilisatrice* that Europe took on to justify violent takeovers of those same cuisines' countries of origin. In their publicity materials, Spice Market uses explicitly objectifying language to describe the culture they're appropriating: "A timeless paean to Southeast Asian sensuality, Spice Market titillates Manhattan's Meatpacking District with Jean-Georges Vongerichten's piquant elevations of the region's street cuisine." The positioning of Western aesthetics as superior, or higher, than all the rest is, at its bottom line, an expression of the idea that no culture has value unless it has been "improved" by the Western Midas touch. If a dish hasn't been eaten or reimagined by a white person, does it really exist?

Andrew Zimmern, host of *Bizarre Foods*, often claims that to know a culture, you must eat their food. I've eaten Vietnamese food my whole life, but there's still so much that I don't understand about my family and the place we came from. I don't know why we can be so reticent, yet so emotional; why Catholicism, the invaders' religion, still has such a hold on them; why we laugh so hard even at times when there's not much to laugh about. After endless plates of *com bi, banh xeo*, and *cha gio*, I still don't know what my grandmother thinks about when she prays. 5

Others appear to be on a similar quest for knowledge, though they seem to have fewer questions than answers. Like a plague of culture locusts, foodies, Chowhounders, and food writers flit from *bibimbap* to *roti canai*, fetishizing each dish as some adventure-in-a-bowl and using it as a springboard to make gross generalizations about a given culture's "sense of family and community," "lack of pretense," "passion," and "spirituality." Eventually, a hole-in-the-wall reaches critical white-Instagrammer mass, and the swarm moves on to its next discovery, decrying the former fixation's loss of authenticity. The foodies' cultural cachet depends on being the only white American person in the room, braving inhumane spice levels and possible food poisoning in order to share with you the proper way to handle Ethiopian *injera* bread. But they can't cash in on it unless they share their discoveries with someone else, thereby jeopardizing that sense of exclusivity. Thus, happiness tends to elude the cultural foodie.

Why am I being such a sourpuss about people who just want to show appreciation for another culture? Isn't the embrace of multiculturalism through food a beautiful expression of a postracial milieu? Aren't *I* being the *true* racist here?

Item: "Asian Girlz" by Day Above Ground, a wannabe–Red Hot Chili Peppers bro-band, is full of references to East Asian food juxtaposed with violently misogynistic lines about their yellow fever: "I love your sticky rice / Butt fucking all night / Korean barbecue / Bitch, I love you." (Yum!) When criticism surfaced in summer 2013, the band insisted that the charges of racism were ridiculous because none of them were racists, that their many Asian friends thought it was hilarious, and that, at its heart, the song was about sharing their love for the culture. You know what they say: If you really love something, treat it with flippant disrespect.

Item: Alton Brown's "Asian Noodles" episode of *Good Eats* takes us on an educational trip to the typical Asian American grocery store—by having its host travel through a lengthy underground tunnel that is a visual echo of the idea of "digging a hole to China." He emerges onto a set decorated with noodles, a red-and-gold Chinese scroll, and that typically "chinky" erhu music that plagues any mention of Asia in any media, ever. Also on the set is a bearded white man wearing a kimono and a sumo top-knot wig who acts out the stereotype of the severe Asian American grocery store clerk. As Brown shares his vast pool of knowledge with the viewer, the clerk harasses him in fake Japanese

("Waduk! Chiyabemada!"). Clearly, knowing a lot about Asian food does not preclude one's ability to be an asshole about it anyway.

These items speak to the Westerner as cultural connoisseur 10 and authority, a theme that has shone like a brilliant Angolan diamond in the imperialist imagination ever since Marco Polo first rushed back to Europe to show off the crazy Chinese "ice cream" that he discovered on his travels. I don't doubt that these guys love *bulgogi* and soba and want more people to enjoy them, but that kind of appreciation certainly doesn't seem to have advanced their understanding of the Asian American experience beyond damaging and objectifying generalities.

Their commonality is their insistence on appreciating a culture that exists mostly in their heads; they share a nostalgia for someone else's life. Nostalgia traps the things you love in glass jars, letting you appreciate their arrested beauty until they finally die of boredom or starvation. The sought-after object cannot move on from you or depart from the fixed impression that you have imposed upon it. After all, a thing can't be "authentic" if it's allowed the power to change. Robbed of its ability to evolve on its own, the only way such a thing can venture into the future is as an accessory worn by someone who can. The pho you had at a dirty little street stall in Saigon or the fresh goat's milk you tasted in Crete as a child may both be beautiful in and of themselves, but their value diminishes if they are allowed an ounce of banality. In order for them to make you look like a more exciting, more interesting person, they must remain firmly outside the realm of the mundane.

All of this makes the experiences of the immigrant's Americanized children particularly head scratching. We're appreciated for our usefulness in giving our foodie friends a window into the off-menu life of our cuisines, but the interest usually stops there. When I tell white Americans about the Maggi-and-margarine sandwiches and cold-cut rice bowls that I used to eat, they tend to wrinkle their noses and wonder aloud why I would reject my grandmother's incredible, authentic Vietnamese food for such bastardizations. What I don't tell them is, "It's because I wanted to be like you."

We live in a time where the discriminating American foodie has an ever-evolving list of essentials in their pantry: *ras el hanout*, shrimp paste, lemongrass, fresh turmeric. With a hugely expanded palate of flavors, you can experiment with these ingredients in ways that used to be possible only for medieval kings and nobles who spent fortunes on chests of spices from the Orient. By putting leaves of cabbage kimchi on a slice of pizza, you're destroying the notion of the nation–state and unknowingly mimicking the ways in which many Korean American children took their first awkward steps into assimilation, one bite at a time, until they stopped using kimchi altogether. Over time, you grow to associate nationalities with the quaint little restaurants that you used to frequent, before they were demolished and replaced with soulless, Americanized joints. You look at a map of the world and point a finger to Mongolia. "Really good barbecue." El Salvador. "Mmm, pupusas." Vietnam. "I love pho!" When you divorce a food from its place and time, you can ignore global civil unrest and natural disasters (see: Zagat declaring Pinoy cuisine the "next great Asian food trend" this past fall as deadly floods swept through the Philippines), knowing as you do that the world's cultural products will always find safe harbor in your precious, precious mouth.

For Discussion and Writing

1. **Comprehension**   What is the specific kind of food "rhetoric" (par. 4) that Ho often sees? Who uses it? Why does it bother Ho?

2. **Critical Reading**   What does Ho assume about her **audience**—and where does she anticipate their objections or counterarguments? Does she address those hypothetical objections effectively?

3. **Analysis**   Ho asserts that "happiness tends to elude the cultural foodie" (par. 6), despite the connoisseur's authority and taste. Why? What, exactly, does the "foodie" want, and how is its pursuit paradoxical or ironic? How do these ironies tie into Ho's larger themes?

4. **Connections**   How is Ho's figure of the "American sophisticate" similar to the "bored cosmopolite" described by Virginia Postrel in "In Praise of Chain Stores" (p. 47)? Do the writers share the same view of "soulless, Americanized joints" (par. 13)? How do you think Postrel would respond to Ho's argument? Explain.

5. **Writing**   Ho's essay is polemical and invites discussion and disagreement. Find a point of disagreement with "Craving the Other": a claim, a line of argument, an example, an assumption, etc. Then write a response that complicates or refutes her argument, shows a flaw in her reasoning, or corrects some other aspect of her essay that you see as problematic.

VIRGINIA POSTREL

In Praise of Chain Stores

*Critic Virginia Postrel (b. 1960) covers a broad swath of American pol-
itics, commerce, and culture—from fashion and design to health care
and technology. The editor of* Reason *magazine from 1989 to 2000, her
columns and articles have appeared in the* New York Times, *the* Atlantic, *the* Wall Street Journal, Forbes, Bloomberg View, *and other publications. Postrel's books include* The Future and Its Enemies: The
Growing Conflict Over Creativity, Enterprise, and Progress *(1998),*
The Substance of Style: How the Rise of Aesthetic Value Is Remaking
Commerce, Culture, and Consciousness *(2003), and* The Power of
Glamour: Longing and the Art of Visual Persuasion *(2013). "In Praise
of Chain Stores," like much of Postrel's work, challenges conventional
wisdom—in this case, received opinions about geography and commerce in America.*

As you read, *note how the writer tries to overturn common perceptions of suburbs and chain stores. What are these common perceptions? What rhetorical strategies does she use to address those she disagrees with (that is, how does she incorporate their views into her
essay)? How effective is her approach?*

"Every well-traveled cosmopolite knows that the United States is
mind-numbingly monotonous—the most boring country to tour,
because everywhere looks like everywhere else," as the *New York
Times* columnist Thomas Friedman once told Charlie Rose. Boston has the same stores as Denver, which has the same stores as
Charlotte or Seattle or Chicago. We live in a "Stepford world,"
says Rachel Dresbeck, the author of *Insiders' Guide to Portland,
Oregon.* Even Boston's historic Faneuil Hall, she complains, is
"dominated by the Gap, Anthropologie, Starbucks, and all the
other usual suspects. Why go anywhere? Every place looks the
same."

This complaint is more than the old worry, dating back to the 1920s, that the big guys are putting Mom and Pop out of business. Today's critics focus less on what isn't there—Mom and Pop—than on what is. Faneuil Hall actually has plenty of locally owned businesses, from the Geoclassics store selling minerals and jewelry, to Pizzeria Regina ("since 1926"). But you do find the same chains everywhere.

The suburbs are the worst. Take Chandler, Ariz., just south of Phoenix. At Chandler Fashion Center, the area's big shopping mall, you'll find P. F. Chang's, California Pizza Kitchen, Chipotle Mexican Grill, and the Cheesecake Factory. Drive along Chandler's straight, flat boulevards, and you'll see PetSmart and Petco; Lowe's and Home Depot; CVS and Walgreens. Chandler has the Apple Store and Pottery Barn, the Gap and Ann Taylor, Banana Republic and DSW, and, of course, Target and Wal-Mart, Starbucks and McDonald's. For people allergic to brands, Chandler must be hell—even without the 110-degree days.

One of the fastest-growing cities in the country, Chandler is definitely the kind of place urbanists have in mind as they intone, "When every place looks the same, there is no such thing as place anymore." Like so many towns in the U.S., it has lost much of its historic character as a farming community. The annual Ostrich Festival still honors one traditional product, but these days Chandler raises more subdivisions and strip malls than ostrich plumes or cotton, another former staple. Yet it still refutes the common assertion that national chains are a blight on the landscape, that they've turned American towns into an indistinguishable "geography of nowhere."

The first thing you notice in Chandler is that, as a broad empirical claim, the cliché that "everywhere looks like everywhere else" is obvious nonsense. Chandler's land and air and foliage are peculiar to the desert Southwest. The people dress differently. Even the cookie-cutter housing developments, with their xeriscaping and washed-out desert palette, remind you where you are. Forget New England clapboard, Carolina columns, or yellow Texas brick. In the intense sun of Chandler, the red-tile roofs common in California turn a pale, pale pink.

Stores don't give places their character. Terrain and weather and culture do. Familiar retailers may take some of the discovery out of travel—to the consternation of journalists looking for

Postrel writes "Stores don't give places their character. Terrain and weather and culture do." How would you describe the "character" of this place?

obvious local color—but by holding some of the commercial background constant, chains make it easier to discern the real differences that define a place: the way, for instance, that people in Chandler come out to enjoy the summer twilight, when the sky glows purple and the dry air cools.

Besides, the idea that the U.S. was once filled with wildly varied business establishments is largely a myth. Big cities could, and still can, support more retail niches than small towns. And in a less competitive national market, there was certainly more variation in business efficiency—in prices, service, and merchandise quality. But the range of retailing *ideas* in any given town was rarely that great. One deli or diner or lunch counter or cafeteria was pretty much like every other one. A hardware store was a hardware store, a pharmacy a pharmacy. Before it became a ubiquitous part of urban life, Starbucks was, in most American cities, a radically new idea.

Chains do more than bargain down prices from suppliers or divide fixed costs across a lot of units. They rapidly spread economic discovery—the scarce and costly knowledge of what retail concepts and operational innovations actually work. That knowledge can be gained only through the expensive and time-consuming process of trial and error. Expecting each town to independently invent every new business is a prescription for real monotony, at least for the locals. Chains make a large range of choices available in more places. They increase local variety, even as they reduce the differences from place to place. People who mostly stay put get to have experiences once available only to frequent travelers, and this loss of exclusivity is one reason why frequent travelers are the ones who complain. When Borders was a unique Ann Arbor, Mich., institution, people in places like Chandler—or, for that matter, Philadelphia and Los Angeles—didn't have much in the way of bookstores. Back in 1986, when California Pizza Kitchen was an innovative local restaurant about to open its second location, food writers at the L.A. *Daily News* declared it "the kind of place every neighborhood should have." So what's wrong if the country has 158 neighborhood CPKs instead of one or two?

The process of multiplication is particularly important for fast-growing towns like Chandler, where rollouts of established stores allow retail variety to expand as fast as the growing population can support new businesses. I heard the same refrain in Chandler that I've heard in similar boomburgs elsewhere, and for similar reasons. "It's got all the advantages of a small town, in terms of being friendly, but it's got all the things of a big town," says Scott Stephens, who moved from Manhattan Beach, Calif., in 1998 to work for Motorola. Chains let people in a city of 250,000 enjoy retail amenities once available only in a huge metropolitan center. At the same time, familiar establishments make it easier for people to make a home in a new place. When Nissan recently moved its headquarters from Southern California to Tennessee, an unusually high percentage of its Los Angeles–area employees accepted the transfer. "The fact that Starbucks are everywhere helps make moving a lot easier these days," a rueful Greg Whitney, vice president of business development for the Los Angeles County Economic Development Corporation, told the *Los Angeles Times* reporter John O'Dell. Orth Hedrick, a Nissan product manager, decided he could stay with the job he loved when he turned off the interstate near Nashville and realized, "You could really be

Anywhere, U.S.A. There's a great big regional shopping mall, and most of the stores and restaurants are the same ones we see in California. Yet a few miles away you're in downtown, and there's lots of local color, too."

Contrary to the rhetoric of bored cosmopolites, most cities 10 don't exist primarily to please tourists. The children toddling through the Chandler mall hugging their soft Build-A-Bear animals are no less delighted because kids can also build a bear in Memphis or St. Louis. For them, this isn't tourism; it's life—the experiences that create the memories from which the meaning of a place arises over time. Among Chandler's most charming sights are the business-casual dads joining their wives and kids for lunch in the mall food court. The food isn't the point, let alone whether it's from Subway or Dairy Queen. The restaurants merely provide the props and setting for the family time. When those kids grow up, they'll remember the food court as happily as an older generation recalls the diners and motels of Route 66—not because of the businesses' innate appeal but because of the memories they evoke.

The contempt for chains represents a brand-obsessed view of place, as if store names were all that mattered to a city's character. For many critics, the name on the store really *is* all that matters. The planning consultant Robert Gibbs works with cities that want to revive their downtowns, and he also helps developers find space for retailers. To his frustration, he finds that many cities actually turn away national chains, preferring a moribund downtown that seems authentically local. But, he says, the same local activists who oppose chains "want specialty retail that sells exactly what the chains sell—the same price, the same fit, the same qualities, the same sizes, the same brands, even." You can show people pictures of a Pottery Barn with nothing but the name changed, he says, and they'll love the store. So downtown stores stay empty, or sell low-value tourist items like candles and kites, while the chains open on the edge of town. In the name of urbanism, officials and activists in cities like Ann Arbor and Fort Collins, Colo., are driving business to the suburbs. "If people like shopping at the Banana Republic or the Gap, if that's your market—or Payless Shoes—why not?" says an exasperated Gibbs. "Why not sell the goods and services people want?"

For Discussion and Writing

1. **Comprehension**   According to Postrel, the "idea that America was once filled with wildly varied business establishments is largely a myth" (par. 7). What other myths and misperceptions does she try to correct in this essay?

2. **Critical Reading**   Postrel refers to "bored cosmopolites" (par. 10) and "urbanists" (par. 4). How does she characterize them? Why are they important to her overall **purpose**? Do you think they are her primary **audience**? Why or why not?

3. **Analysis**   In paragraph 3, Postrel provides a long list of brand names and chain stores. What is the rhetorical purpose of this paragraph? How does it support her argument?

4. **Connections**   How is Postrel's argument similar to Nathan Jurgenson's in "The IRL Fetish" (p. 191)? What purposes, themes, and rhetorical strategies do the two writers share, despite their divergent subjects?

5. **Writing**   What are some of the benefits of chain stores, according to Postrel? List them in your own words. Do you agree? Why or why not? Use these responses to write an essay exploring your own view of retail and restaurant chains.

BILL BRYSON

The Hard Sell:
Advertising in America

A versatile American author of several books on travel, science, and literature, Bill Bryson (b. 1951) has spent much of his career working and living in Britain. From 2005 to 2011, he served as chancellor of Durham University in England; in 2006, he was awarded the Order of the British Empire, an honorary order of chivalry granted by Queen Elizabeth II. His books include A Short History of Nearly Everything *(2003),* Shakespeare: The World as Stage *(2007),* At Home: A Short History of Private Life *(2010), and* One Summer: America 1927 *(2013). "The Hard Sell" is excerpted from Bryson's 1994 book* Made in America: An Informal History of the English Language in the United States.

As you read, *notice how Bryson highlights the comical aspects of branding and advertisements. How would you describe Bryson's style as a writer? How does he achieve comic effects in his writing? How would you characterize his attitude toward advertising? Reverent? Playful? Skeptical? Ironic?*

In 1885, a young man named George Eastman formed the Eastman Dry Plate and Film Company in Rochester, New York. It was rather a bold thing to do. Aged just 31, Eastman was a junior clerk in a bank on a comfortable but modest salary of $15 a week. He had no background in business. But he was passionately devoted to photography and had become increasingly gripped with the conviction that anyone who could develop a simple, untechnical camera, as opposed to the cumbersome, outsized, fussily complex contrivances then on the market, stood to make a fortune.

Eastman worked tirelessly for three years to perfect his invention, supporting himself in the meantime by making dry plates

53

for commercial photographers, and in June 1888 produced a camera that was positively dazzling in its simplicity: a plain black box just six and a half inches long by three and a quarter inches wide, with a button on the side and a key for advancing the film. Eastman called his device the *Detective Camera*. Detectives were all the thing—Sherlock Holmes was just taking off with American readers—and the name implied that it was so small and simple that it could be used unnoticed, as a detective might.

The camera had no viewfinder and no way of focusing. The *photographer* or *photographist* (it took a while for the first word to become the established one) simply held the camera in front of him, pressed a button on the side, and hoped for the best. Each roll held a hundred pictures. When a roll was fully exposed, the anxious owner sent the entire camera to Rochester for developing. Eventually he received the camera back, freshly loaded with film, and—assuming all had gone well—one hundred small circular pictures, two and a half inches in diameter. . . .

In September 1888, Eastman changed the name of the camera to *Kodak*—an odd choice, since it was meaningless, and in 1888 no one gave meaningless names to products, especially successful products. Since British patent applications at the time demanded full explanation of trade and brand names, we know how Eastman arrived at his inspired name. He crisply summarized his reasoning in his patent application: "First. It is short. Second. It is not capable of mispronunciation. Third. It does not resemble anything in the art and cannot be associated with anything in the art except the Kodak." Four years later the whole enterprise was renamed the Eastman Kodak Company.

Despite the considerable expense involved—a Kodak camera   5 sold for $25, and each roll of film cost $10, including developing—by 1895, over 100,000 Kodaks had been sold and Eastman was a seriously wealthy man. A lifelong bachelor, he lived with his mother in a thirty-seven-room mansion with twelve bathrooms. Soon people everywhere were talking about snapshots, originally a British shooting term for a hastily executed shot. Its photographic sense was coined by the English astronomer Sir John Herschel, who also gave the world the terms *positive* and *negative* in their photographic senses.

From the outset, Eastman developed three crucial strategies that have been the hallmarks of virtually every successful consumer goods company since. First, he went for the mass market, reasoning that it was better to make a little money each from a lot of people rather than a lot of money from a few. He also showed a tireless, obsessive dedication to making his products better and cheaper. In the 1890s, such an approach was widely perceived as insane. If you had a successful product you milked it for all it was worth. If competitors came along with something better, you bought them out or tried to squash them with lengthy patent fights or other bullying tactics. What you certainly did not do was create new products that made your existing lines obsolescent. Eastman did. Throughout the late 1890s, Kodak introduced a series of increasingly cheaper, niftier cameras — the Bull's Eye model of 1896, which cost just $12, and the famous slimline Folding Pocket Kodak of 1898, before finally in 1900 producing his eureka model: the little box Brownie, priced at just $1 and with film at 15 cents a reel (though with only six exposures per reel).

Above all, what set Eastman apart was the breathtaking lavishness of his advertising. In 1899 alone, he spent $750,000, an unheard-of sum, on advertising. Moreover, it was *good* advertising: crisp, catchy, reassuringly trustworthy. "You press a button — we do the rest" ran the company's first slogan, thus making a virtue of its shortcomings. Never mind that you couldn't load or unload the film yourself. Kodak would do it for you. In 1905, it followed with another classic slogan: "If It Isn't an Eastman, It Isn't a Kodak."

Kodak's success did not escape other businessmen, who also began to see virtue in the idea of steady product refinement and improvement. AT&T and Westinghouse, among others, set up research laboratories with the idea of creating a stream of new products, even at the risk of displacing old ones. Above all, everyone everywhere began to advertise.

Advertising was already a well-established phenomenon by the turn of the twentieth century. Newspapers had begun carrying ads as far back as the early 1700s, and magazines soon followed. (Benjamin Franklin has the distinction of having run the first magazine ad seeking the whereabouts of a runaway slave, in 1741.) By 1850, the country had its first *advertising agency*, the American Newspaper Advertising Agency, though its function was to buy advertising space rather than come up with creative campaigns. The first advertising agency in the modern sense was

N. W. Ayer & Sons of Philadelphia, established in 1869. To *adver-tise* originally carried the sense of to broadcast or disseminate news. Thus a nineteenth-century newspaper that called itself the *Advertiser* meant that it had lots of news, not lots of ads. By the early 1800s the term had been stretched to accommodate the idea of spreading the news of the availability of certain goods or services. A newspaper notice that read "Jos. Parker, Hatter" was essentially announcing that if anyone was in the market for hats, Jos. Parker had them. In the sense of persuading members of the public to acquire items they might not otherwise think of buying—items they didn't know they needed—advertising is a phenomenon of the modern age.

By the 1890s, advertising was appearing everywhere—in news- 10 papers and magazines, on *billboards* (an Americanism dating from 1850), on the sides of buildings, on passing streetcars, on paper bags, even on matchbooks, which were invented in 1892 and were being extensively used as an advertising medium within three years.

Very early on, advertisers discovered the importance of a good slogan. Many of our more venerable slogans are older than you might think. Ivory Soap's "99 44/100 percent pure" dates from 1879. Schlitz has been calling itself "the beer that made Milwaukee famous" since 1895, and Heinz's "57 varieties" followed a year later. Morton Salt's "When it rains, it pours" dates from 1911, the American Florist Association's "Say it with flowers" was first used in 1912, and the "good to the last drop" of Maxwell House coffee, named for the Maxwell House Hotel in Nashville, where it was first served, has been with us since 1907. (The slogan is said to have originated with Teddy Roosevelt, who pronounced the coffee "good to the last drop," prompting one wit to ask, "So what's wrong with the last drop?")

Sometimes slogans took a little working on. Coca-Cola described itself as "the drink that makes a pause refreshing" before realizing, in 1929, that "the pause that refreshes" was rather more succinct and memorable. A slogan could make all the difference to a product's success. After advertising its soap as an efficacious way of dealing with "conspicuous nose pores," Woodbury's Facial Soap came up with the slogan "The skin you love to touch" and won the hearts of millions. The great thing about a slogan was that it didn't have to be accurate to be effective. Heinz never actually

A 1904 Kodak camera ad. What strategies does Kodak use to persuade prospective consumers? How do you interpret the company's slogan?

had exactly "57 varieties" of anything. The catchphrase arose simply because H. J. Heinz, the company's founder, decided he liked the sound of the number. Undeterred by considerations of verity, he had the slogan slapped on every one of the products he produced, already in 1896 far more than fifty-seven. For a time the company tried to arrange its products into fifty-seven arbitrary clusters, but in 1969 it gave up the ruse altogether and abandoned the slogan.

Early in the 1900s, advertisers discovered another perennial feature of marketing—the *giveaway*, as it was called almost from the start. Consumers soon became acquainted with the irresistibly tempting notion that if they bought a particular product they could expect a reward—the chance to receive a prize, a free book (almost always ostensibly dedicated to the general improvement of one's well-being but invariably a thinly disguised plug for the manufacturer's range of products), a free sample, or a rebate in the form of a shiny dime, or be otherwise endowed with some gratifying bagatelle. Typical of the genre was a turn-of-the-century tome called *The Vital Question Cook Book*, which was promoted as an aid to livelier meals, but which proved upon receipt to contain 112 pages of recipes all involving the use of Shredded Wheat. Many of these had a certain air of desperation about them, notably the "Shredded Wheat Biscuit Jellied Apple Sandwich" and the "Creamed Spinach on Shredded Wheat Biscuit Toast." Almost all involved nothing more than spooning some everyday food on a piece of shredded wheat and giving it an inflated name. Nonetheless the company distributed no fewer than four million copies of *The Vital Question Cook Book* to eager consumers.

The great breakthrough in twentieth-century advertising, however, came with the identification and exploitation of the American consumer's Achilles' heel: anxiety. One of the first to master the form was King Gillette, inventor of the first safety razor and one of the most relentless advertisers of the early 1900s. Most of the early ads featured Gillette himself, who with his fussy toothbrush mustache and well-oiled hair looked more like a caricature of a Parisian waiter than a captain of industry. After starting with a few jaunty words about the ease and convenience of the safety razor—"Compact? Rather!"—he plunged the reader into the heart of the matter: "When you use my razor you are exempt from the dangers that men often encounter who allow their faces to come in contact with brush, soap, and barbershop accessories used on other people."

Here was an entirely new approach to selling goods. Gillette's 15 ads were in effect telling you that not only did there exist a product that you never previously suspected you needed, but if you *didn't* use it you would very possibly attract a crop of facial diseases you never knew existed. The combination proved irresistible. Though the Gillette razor retailed for a hefty $5—half the average workingman's weekly pay—it sold by the millions, and King Gillette became a very wealthy man. (Though only for a time, alas. Like many others of his era, he grew obsessed with the idea of the perfectibility of mankind and expended so much of his energies writing books of convoluted philosophy with titles like *The Human Drift* that he eventually lost control of his company and most of his fortune.)

By the 1920s, advertisers had so refined the art that a consumer could scarcely pick up a magazine without being bombarded with unsettling questions: "Do You Make These Mistakes in English?"; "Will Your Hair Stand Close Inspection?"; "When Your Guests Are Gone—Are You Sorry You Ever Invited Them?" (because, that is, you lack social polish); "Did Nature fail to put roses in your cheeks?"; "Will There be a Victrola in Your Home This Christmas?"[1] The 1920s truly were the Age of Anxiety. One ad pictured a former golf champion, "now only a wistful onlooker," whose career had gone sour because he had neglected his teeth. Scott Tissues mounted a campaign showing a forlorn-looking businessman sitting on a park bench beneath the bold caption "A Serious Business Handicap—These Troubles That Come from Harsh Toilet Tissue." Below the picture the text explained: "65% of all men and women over 40 are suffering from some form of rectal trouble, estimates a prominent specialist connected with one of New York's largest hospitals. 'And one of the contributing causes,' he states, 'is inferior toilet tissue.'" There was almost nothing that one couldn't become uneasy about. One ad even asked: "Can You Buy a Radio Safely?" Distressed bowels were the

---

[1]The most famous 1920s ad of them all didn't pose a question, but it did play on the reader's anxiety: "They Laughed When I Sat Down, but When I Started to Play. . . ." It was originated by the U.S. School of Music in 1925.

most frequent target. The makers of Sal Hepatica warned: "We rush to meetings, we dash to parties. We are on the go all day long. We exercise too little, and we eat too much. And, in consequence, we impair our bodily functions—often we retain food within us too long. And when that occurs, poisons are set up—*Auto-Intoxication begins.*"

In addition to the dread of auto-intoxication, the American consumer faced a gauntlet of other newly minted maladies—*pyorrhea, halitosis* (coined as a medical term in 1874, but popularized by Listerine beginning in 1922 with the slogan "Even your best friend won't tell you"), *athlete's foot* (a term invented by the makers of Absorbine Jr. in 1928), *dead cuticles, scabby toes, iron-poor blood, vitamin deficiency* (*vitamins* had been coined in 1912, but the word didn't enter the general vocabulary until the 1920s, when advertisers realized it sounded worryingly scientific), *fallen stomach, tobacco breath,* and *psoriasis,* though Americans would have to wait until the next decade for the scientific identification of the gravest of personal disorders—*body odor,* a term invented in 1933 by the makers of Lifebuoy soap and so terrifying in its social consequences that it was soon abbreviated to a whispered *B.O.*

The white-coated technicians of American laboratories had not only identified these new conditions, but—miraculously, it seemed—simultaneously come up with cures for them. Among the products that were invented or rose to greatness in this busy, neurotic decade were *Cutex* (for those deceased cuticles), *Vick's VapoRub, Geritol, Serutan* ("Natures spelled backwards," as the voiceover always said with somewhat bewildering reassurance, as if spelling a product's name backward conferred some medicinal benefit), *Noxzema* (for which read: "knocks eczema"), *Preparation H, Murine* eyedrops, and *Dr. Scholl's Foot Aids.*[2] It truly was an age of miracles—one in which you could even cure a smoker's cough by smoking, so long as it was Old Golds you smoked, because as the slogan proudly if somewhat untruthfully boasted, they contained "Not a cough in a carload." (As late as 1943, L&M cigarettes were advertised as "just what the doctor ordered!")

---

[2]And yes, there really was a Dr. Scholl. His name was William Scholl, he was a real doctor, genuinely dedicated to the well-being of feet, and they are still very proud of him in his hometown of LaPorte, Indiana.

By 1927, advertising was a $1.5-billion-a-year industry in the United States and advertising people were held in such awe that they were asked not only to mastermind campaigns but even to name products. An ad man named Henry N. McKinney, for instance, named *Keds* shoes, *Karo* syrup, *Meadow Gold* butter, and *Uneeda Biscuits*.

Product names tend to cluster around certain sounds. Break- 20 fast cereals often ended in *-ies* (*Wheaties*, *Rice Krispies*, *Frosties*); washing powders and detergents tended to be gravely monosyllabic (*Lux*, *Fab*, *Tide*, *Duz*). It is often possible to tell the era of a product's development by its termination. Thus products dating from the 1920s and early 1930s often ended in *-ex* (*Pyrex*, *Cutex*, *Kleenex*, *Windex*), while those ending in *-master* (*Mixmaster*, *Toastmaster*) generally betray a late-1930s or early-1940s genesis. The development of *Glo-Coat* floor wax in 1932 also heralded the beginning of American business's strange and long-standing infatuation with illiterate spellings, a trend that continued with *ReaLemon* juice in 1935, *Reddi-Wip* whipped cream in 1947, and many hundreds of others since, from *Tastee-Freez* drive-ins to *Toys 'R' Us*, along with countless others with a *Kwik*, *E-Z*, or *U* (as in *While-U-Wait*) embedded in their titles. The late 1940s saw the birth of a brief vogue for endings in *-matic*, so that car manufacturers offered vehicles with *Seat-O-Matic* levers and *Cruise-O-Matic* transmissions, and even fitted sheets came with *Ezy-Matic* corners. Some companies became associated with certain types of names. DuPont, for instance, had a special fondness for words ending in *-on*. The practice began with *nylon*—a name that was concocted out of thin air and owes nothing to its chemical properties—and was followed with *Rayon*, *Dacron*, *Orlon*, and *Teflon*, among many others. In recent years the company has moved on to what might be called its *Star Trek* phase with such compounds as *Tyvek*, *Kevlar*, *Sontara*, *Cordura*, *Nomex*, and *Zemorain*.

Such names have more than passing importance to their owners. If American business has given us a large dose of anxiety in its ceaseless quest for a healthier *bottom line* (a term dating from the 1930s, though not part of mainstream English until the 1970s), we may draw some comfort from the thought that business has suffered a great deal of collective anxiety over protecting the names of its products.

A certain cruel paradox prevails in the matter of preserving brand names. Every business naturally wants to create a product that will dominate its market. But if that product so dominates the market that the brand name becomes indistinguishable in the public mind from the product itself—when people begin to ask for a *thermos* rather than a "Thermos brand vacuum flask"— then the term has become generic and the owner faces loss of its trademark protection. That is why advertisements and labels so often carry faintly paranoid-sounding lines like "Tabasco is the registered trademark for the brand of pepper sauce made by McIlhenny Co." and why companies like Coca-Cola suffer palpitations when they see a passage like this (from John Steinbeck's *The Wayward Bus*):

> "Got any coke?" another character asked.
> "No," said the proprietor. "Few bottles of Pepsi-Cola. Haven't had any coke for a month. . . . It's the same stuff. You can't tell them apart."

An understandable measure of confusion exists concerning the distinction between patents and trademarks and between trademarks and trade names. A *patent* protects the name of the product and its method of manufacture for seventeen years. Thus from 1895 to 1912, no one but the Shredded Wheat Company could make shredded wheat. But because patents require manufacturers to divulge the secrets of their products—and thus make them available to rivals to copy when the patent runs out—companies sometimes choose not to seek their protection. *Coca-Cola*, for one, has never been patented. A *trademark* is effectively the name of a product, its *brand name*. A *trade name* is the name of the manufacturer. So *Ford* is a trade name, *Taurus* a trademark. Trademarks apply not just to names, but also to logos, drawings, and other symbols and depictions. The MGM lion, for instance, is a trademark. Unlike patents, trademark protection goes on forever, or at least as long as the manufacturer can protect it.

For a long time, it was felt that this permanence gave the holder an unfair advantage. In consequence, America did not enact its first trademark law until 1870, almost a century after Britain, and then it was declared unconstitutional by the Supreme Court. Lasting trademark protection did not begin for American companies until 1881. Today, more than a million trademarks have been issued in the United States and the number is rising by about thirty thousand a year.

A good trademark is almost incalculably valuable. Invincible-seeming brand names do occasionally falter and fade. *Pepsodent*, 25

Rinso, Chase & Sanborn, Sal Hepatica, Vitalis, Brylcreem, and
Burma-Shave all once stood on the commanding heights of consumer recognition but are now defunct or have sunk to the status
of what the trade calls "ghost brands"—products that are still
produced but little promoted and largely forgotten. For the most
part, however, once a product establishes a dominant position in
a market, it is exceedingly difficult to depose it. In nineteen of
twenty-two product categories, the company that owned the leading American brand in 1925 still has it today—*Nabisco* in cookies, *Kellogg's* in breakfast cereals, *Kodak* in film, *Sherwin-Williams*
in paint, *Del Monte* in canned fruit, *Wrigley's* in chewing gum,
Singer in sewing machines, *Ivory* in soap, *Campbell's* in soup,
Gillette in razors. Few really successful brand names of today
were not just as familiar to your grandparents or even great-
grandparents, and a well-established brand name has a sort of
self-perpetuating power. As the *Economist* has noted: "In the category of food blenders, consumers were still ranking General Electric second twenty years after the company had stopped making
them."

An established brand name is so valuable that only about 5
percent of the sixteen thousand or so new products introduced in
America each year bear all-new brand names. The others are variants on an existing product—*Tide with Bleach, Tropicana Twister
Light Fruit Juices,* and so on. Among some types of product a
certain glut is evident. At last count there were 220 types of
branded breakfast cereal in America. In 1993, according to an
international business survey, the world's most valuable brand
was *Marlboro,* with a value estimated at $40 billion, slightly ahead
of *Coca-Cola.* Among the other top ten brands were *Intel, Kellogg's,
Budweiser, Pepsi, Gillette,* and *Pampers; Nescafé* and *Bacardi* were
the only foreign brands to make the top ten, underlining American dominance.

Huge amounts of effort go into choosing brand names. General Foods reviewed 2,800 names before deciding on *Dreamwhip.*
(To put this in proportion, try to think of just ten names for an
artificial whipped cream.) Ford considered more than twenty thousand possible car names before finally settling on *Edsel* (which
proves that such care doesn't always pay), and Standard Oil a
similar number of names before it opted for *Exxon.* Sometimes,
however, the most successful names are the result of a moment's
whimsy. *Betty Crocker* came in a flash to an executive of the Wash-

burn Crosby Company (later absorbed by General Mills), who chose *Betty* because he thought it sounded wholesome and sincere and *Crocker* in memory of a beloved fellow executive who had recently died. At first the name was used only to sign letters responding to customers' requests for advice or information, but by the 1950s, Betty Crocker's smiling, confident face was appearing on more than fifty types of food product, and her loyal followers could buy her recipe books and even visit her "kitchen" at the General Foods headquarters.

Great efforts also go into finding out why people buy the brands they do. Advertisers and market researchers bandy about terms like *conjoint analysis technique, personal drive patterns, Gaussian distributions, fractals,* and other such arcana in their quest to winnow out every subliminal quirk in our buying habits. They know, for instance, that 40 percent of all people who move to a new address will also change their brand of toothpaste, that the average supermarket shopper makes fourteen impulse decisions in each visit, that 62 percent of shoppers will pay a premium for mayonnaise even when they think a cheaper brand is just as good, but that only 24 percent will show the same largely irrational loyalty to frozen vegetables.

To preserve a brand name involves a certain fussy attention to linguistic and orthographic details. To begin with, the name is normally expected to be treated not as a noun but as a proper adjective—that is, the names should be followed by an explanation of what it does: *Kleenex facial tissues, Q-Tip cotton swabs, Jell-O brand gelatin dessert, Sanka brand decaffeinated coffee.* Some types of products—notably cars—are granted an exemption, which explains why General Motors does not have to advertise *Cadillac self-propelled automobiles* or the like. In all cases, the name may not explicitly describe the product's function though it may hint at what it does. Thus *Coppertone* is acceptable; *Coppertan* would not be.

The situation is more than a little bizarre. Having done all they 30 can to make their products household words, manufacturers must then in their advertisements do all in their power to imply that they aren't. Before trademark law was clarified, advertisers positively encouraged the public to treat their products as generics. Kodak invited consumers to "Kodak as you go," turning the brand name into a dangerously ambiguous verb. It would never do that now. The American Thermos Product Company went so far as to boast, "Thermos is a household word," to its considerable cost. Donald F. Duncan, Inc., the original manufacturer of the *Yo-Yo*, lost its trademark protection partly because it was amazingly casual about capitalization in its own promotional literature. "In case you don't know what a yo-yo is . . ." one of its advertisements went, suggesting that in commercial terms Duncan didn't. Duncan also made the elemental error of declaring, "If It Isn't a Duncan, It Isn't a Yo-Yo," which on the face of it would seem a reasonable claim, but was in fact held by the courts to be inviting the reader to consider the product generic. Kodak had long since stopped saying "If it isn't an Eastman, it isn't a Kodak."

Because of the confusion, and occasional lack of fastidiousness on the part of their owners, many dozens of products have lost their trademark protection, among them *aspirin, linoleum, yo-yo, thermos, cellophane, milk of magnesia, mimeograph, lanolin, celluloid, dry ice, escalator, shredded wheat, kerosene,* and *zipper*. All were once proudly capitalized and worth a fortune.

On July 1, 1941, the New York television station WNBT-TV interrupted its normal viewing to show, without comment, a Bulova watch ticking. For sixty seconds the watch ticked away mysteriously, then the picture faded and the normal programming resumed. It wasn't much, but it was the first television *commercial*.

Both the word and the idea were already well established. The first commercial—the term was used from the very beginning—had been broadcast by radio station WEAF in New York on August 28, 1922. It lasted for either ten or fifteen minutes, depending on which source you credit. Commercial radio was not an immediate hit. In its first two months, WEAF sold only $550 worth of airtime. But by the mid-1920s, sponsors were not only flocking to buy airtime but naming their programs after their products—*The Lucky Strike Hour, The A&P Gypsies, The Lux Radio Theater*, and so on. Such was the obsequiousness of the radio networks that by the early 1930s, many were allowing the sponsors to take complete artistic and production control for the programs. Many of the most popular shows were actually written by the advertising agencies, and the agencies naturally seldom missed an opportunity to work a favorable mention of the sponsor's products into the scripts.

With the rise of television in the 1950s, the practices of the radio era were effortlessly transferred to the new medium. Advertisers inserted their names into the program title—*Texaco Star Theater, Gillette Cavalcade of Sports, Chesterfield Sound-Off Time, The U.S. Steel Hour, Kraft Television Theater, The Chevy Show, The Alcoa Hour, The Ford Star Revue, Dick Clark's Beechnut Show,* and the arresting hybrid *The Lux-Schlitz Playhouse,* which seemed to suggest a cozy symbiosis between soapflakes and beer. The commercial dominance of program titles reached a kind of hysterical peak with a program officially called *Your Kaiser Dealer Presents Kaiser-Frazer "Adventures in Mystery" Starring Betty Furness in "Byline."* Sponsors didn't write the programs any longer, but they did impose a firm control on the contents, most notoriously during a 1959 *Playhouse 90* broadcast of *Judgment at Nuremberg,* when the sponsor, the American Gas Association, managed to have all references to gas ovens and the gassing of Jews removed from the script.

Where commercial products of the late 1940s had scientific-sounding names, those of the 1950s relied increasingly on secret ingredients. Gleem toothpaste contained a mysterious piece of alchemy called *GL-70.*[3] There was never the slightest hint of what GL-70 was, but it would, according to the advertising, not only rout odor-causing bacteria but "wipe out their enzymes"! 35

A kind of creeping illiteracy invaded advertising, too, to the dismay of many. When Winston began advertising its cigarettes with the slogan "Winston tastes good like a cigarette should," nationally syndicated columnists like Sydney J. Harris wrote anguished essays on what the world was coming to—every educated person knew it should be "as a cigarette should"—but the die was cast. By 1958, Ford was advertising that you could "travel smooth" in a Thunderbird Sunliner and the maker of Ace Combs was urging buyers to "comb it handsome"—a trend that continues today with "pantihose that fits you real comfortable" and other grammatical manglings too numerous and dispiriting to dwell on.

We may smile at the advertising ruses of the 1920s—frightening people with the threat of "fallen stomach" and "scabby toes"—

---

[3]For purposes of research, I wrote to Procter & Gamble, Gleem's manufacturer, asking what GL-70 was, but the public relations department evidently thought it eccentric of me to wonder what I had been putting in my mouth all through childhood and declined to reply.

but in fact such creative manipulation still goes on, albeit at a slightly more sophisticated level. The *New York Times Magazine* reported in 1990 how an advertising copywriter had been told to come up with some impressive labels for a putative hand cream. She invented the arresting and healthful-sounding term *oxygenating moisturizers* and wrote accompanying copy with reference to "tiny bubbles of oxygen that release moisture into your skin." This done, the advertising was turned over to the company's research and development department, which was instructed to come up with a product that matched the copy.

If we fall for such commercial manipulation, we have no one to blame but ourselves. When Kentucky Fried Chicken introduced "Extra Crispy" chicken to sell alongside its "Original" chicken, and sold it at the same price, sales were disappointing. But when its advertising agency persuaded it to promote "Extra Crispy" as a premium brand and to put the price up, sales soared. Much of the same sort of verbal hypnosis was put to work for the benefit of the fur industry. Dyed muskrat makes a perfectly good fur, for those who enjoy cladding themselves in dead animals, but the name clearly lacks stylishness. The solution was to change the name to *Hudson seal*. Never mind that the material contained not a strand of seal fur. It sounded good, and sales skyrocketed.

Truth has seldom been a particularly visible feature of American advertising. In the early 1970s, Chevrolet ran a series of ads for the Chevelle boasting that the car had "109 advantages to keep it from becoming old before its time." When looked into, it turned out that these 109 vaunted features included such items as rearview mirrors, backup lights, balanced wheels, and many other components that were considered pretty well basic to any car. Never mind; sales soared. At about the same time, Ford, not to be outdone, introduced a "limited edition" Mercury Monarch at $250 below the normal list price. It achieved this, it turned out, by taking $250 worth of equipment off the standard Monarch.

And has all this deviousness led to a tightening of the rules 40 concerning what is allowable in advertising? Hardly. In 1986, as William Lutz relates in *Doublespeak*, the insurance company John Hancock launched an ad campaign in which "real people in real situations" discussed their financial predicaments with remarkable candor. When a journalist asked to speak to these real people, a company spokesman conceded that they were actors and "in that sense they are not real people."

During the 1984 presidential campaign, the Republican National Committee ran a television advertisement praising President Reagan for providing cost-of-living pay increases to federal workers "in spite of those sticks-in-the-mud who tried to keep him from doing what we elected him to do." When it was pointed out that the increases had in fact been mandated by law since 1975 and that Reagan had in any case three times tried to block them, a Republican official responded: "Since when is a commercial supposed to be accurate?" Quite.

In linguistic terms, perhaps the most interesting challenge facing advertisers today is that of selling products in an increasingly multicultural society. Spanish is a particular problem, not just because it is spoken over such a widely scattered area but also because it is spoken in so many different forms. Brown sugar is *azucar negra* in New York, *azucar prieta* in Miami, *azucar morena* in much of Texas, and *azucar pardo* pretty much everywhere else—and that's just one word. Much the same bewildering multiplicity applies to many others. In consequence, embarrassments are all but inevitable.

In mainstream Spanish, *bichos* means *insects*, but in Puerto Rico it means *testicles*, so when a pesticide maker promised to bring death to the *bichos*, Puerto Rican consumers were at least bemused, if not alarmed. Much the same happened when a maker of bread referred to its product as *un bollo de pan* and discovered that to Spanish-speaking Miamians of Cuban extraction that means a woman's private parts. And when Perdue Chickens translated its slogan "It takes a tough man to make a tender chicken" into Spanish, it came out as the slightly less macho "It takes a sexually excited man to make a chick sensual."

Never mind. Sales soared.

For Discussion and Writing

1. **Comprehension**   What is the "cruel paradox" (par. 22) of brand names, particularly for popular products that come to dominate a market?

2. **Critical Reading**   Bryson begins his essay with a narrative account of George Eastman and the development of the Kodak camera. Why do you think the writer chose to start with this story? What **purpose** does it serve? How is it tied to the main point? How else might he have begun his essay?

3. ***Analysis*** Bryson looks closely at language, including brand names, slogans, and rhetorical tricks he describes as "verbal hypnosis" (par. 38). What does this essay suggest about the power of words to shape people's perceptions and responses? Does the essay change your view of language and rhetoric? Explain your answer.

4. ***Connections*** According to Frank Rose in "The Art of Immersion" (p. 409), "Every new medium that has been invented, from print to film to television, has increased the transporting power of narrative" (par. 37). Do you think that the persuasive or "transporting" power of advertisements has increased with new media forms as well? In what way is advertising itself a type of "immersive media"?

5. ***Writing*** Bryson writes: "Great efforts also go into finding out why people buy the brands they do" (par. 28). Consider your own brand preferences and loyalties in a reflective personal essay. Why are you attached to a particular brand? Are brands connected with your sense of personal, social, or professional identity? Bryson spends much of his essay closely reading the language of branding and advertising. In your own reflection on these questions, pay similar attention to words, sounds, and images. How are they connected to the brand's meaning and associations?

ELLEN HUET

Snaps to Riches: The Rise of Snapchat Celebrities

A graduate of Stanford University, Ellen Huet (b. 1989) is a staff writer for Forbes *magazine. Previously, she covered technology for the* San Francisco Chronicle *and wrote for the* San Jose Mercury News *and* SF Weekly. *In this article from* Forbes, *Huet considers the photo messaging application Snapchat, which lets users take photos, videos, and texts, and share them with a selected group of recipients. But as the writer notes, Snapchat is more than another social media outlet: It is also a powerful platform for brands, marketers, and advertisers.*

As you read, *pay special attention to the reasons that brands are so interested in Snapchat. What app does Snapchat seem to be replacing in popularity, according to the article? What is the source of Snapchat's appeal? Likewise, notice the meaning of "celebrity": How does social media, like Snapchat, alter our understanding of the term?*

Shaun McBride takes no risks when drawing a Snapchat. He takes screenshots instead, to protect his works in progress in case of calamity.

"If 20 people decide to send me a snap at the same time, my app will crash and I'll lose my work," he explained as he took a quick mid-drawing screenshot. "But I can go back in and load this one up to keep going."

These safeguards may seem extreme, but they're vital when a Snapchat image is worth several thousand dollars—like it is for McBride.

McBride, better known as "Shonduras," is Snapchat's first home-grown celebrity and one of the first people to make money off of his intricate Snapchat art. Brands are shelling out up to $30,000 for advertising deals with McBride and other power users, hoping to reach Snapchat's demographic: the fickle and influential 13- to 25-year-old bracket.

Brands like Disney, Taco Bell, Major League Soccer, and tele- 5 vision networks see what McBride, a 27-year-old from Utah, can make for them: branded content with authentic Snapchat style that teens will actually pay attention to.

"I think brands are starting to notice now that they can put something on Instagram or Facebook, but the youth isn't on Facebook, and if they're on Instagram, they're going to just scroll past it," McBride said. "But with Snapchat you have their undivided attention, they're holding down the screen, and it's awesome. When else does that demographic spend seven seconds just soaking something in? They don't. They're too fast. So I think Snapchat really nails that."

> "Having a blast at the **#FrozenSummer** event on the 'WaltDisneyWorld' snapchat account!! Follow along! **#snapchat**
> —Shonduras (**@Shonduras**) July 5, 2014

SNAPCHAT GROWS UP

Snapchat's much more than a disappearing photo messaging app. It became a mobile video platform in October, when it introduced Snapchat Stories. With Stories, a user can string together photos and videos—sometimes up to two minutes or more—and the story is broadcast to all his or her followers, stays live on the app for 24 hours, and can be played over and over again.

Snapchat Stories changed everything. Creative types now see the app as a way to post videos to the public—with the added allure of a one-day-only urgency.

Internet celebrities who made it big on Vine are taking notice of the new kid in town. Vine, an app that lets users post looping six-second videos, debuted in early 2013 and quickly became known for rapid-fire comedy videos. It also launched the careers of dozens of stars, mostly young men who won hearts with physical comedy tricks or teen heartthrob looks.

Brands, eager to reach teens, flocked to Vine. Popular "Viners" 10 were offered lucrative advertising deals and began making thousands per sponsored Vine.

Shaun "Shonduras" McBride's Snapchat art. What factors make this image and platform appealing to its users—and to brands looking for marketing opportunities?

But after a year and a half, "it's clear that Vine is sort of plateauing," said Vine star Logan Paul. He and his fellow Viners are eager to hop onto the next trend so they can stay relevant. That's why they turn to Snapchatters like McBride.

"INCREDIBLY BULLISH ON SNAPCHAT"

GrapeStory, a talent agency that signs Vine and Instagram stars and helps them get branded gigs, recruited and signed McBride as its first Snapchatter in June. Niche, a company that helps brands connect with social media stars on platforms like Instagram and Vine, is working with Michael Platco, or "mplatco," a 25-year-old Snapchat artist who has done branded content for Disney and Grubhub.

"We're incredibly bullish on Snapchat as a new medium," said Darren Lachtman, the cofounder of Niche. "Tons of our brand clients are asking what we can do on the Snapchat stage. We haven't done standalone Snapchat campaigns, but if we talk again in a month I'm sure that's going to be different."

Jerome Jarre, a 24-year-old Vine star and a GrapeStory cofounder, believes Snapchat is the future. Jarre gained millions of followers on Vine with goofy videos starring unsuspecting strangers. But in the past month, he has set Vine aside and shifted his focus almost entirely to Snapchat.

He tweets constantly about his new Snapchat stories, consults 15 with McBride when brainstorming Snapchat ideas, and is convinced McBride is on the verge of making it big, just like he did last year on Vine.

"I remember the month I moved from 20,000 to 1 million followers," Jarre said. "That's happening to him right now. Two months from now Shaun's going to have a million followers. It's history repeating."

A SNAPCHAT STAR IS BORN

McBride, a fast-talking Mormon who often tucks his long, curly hair under a backward baseball cap, has his six younger sisters to thank for his Snapchat success. He travels frequently for his job as a sales rep for various skateboard and snowboard apparel companies, and he would often text back photos to his sisters, who range from 13 to 22 years old.

Get on Snapchat, they told him, so he did. He used the app to draw funny doodles on top of his photos and sent them to his sisters—who showed their friends, who added him in turn. As his following grew, he began taking it seriously, formed a business, and dedicated his time to sending out a high-quality Snapchat each day. Within a few months, his drawings had spread past local high schoolers to Reddit and a few online articles—and caught the attention of marketing departments.

One day when McBride was riding a ski lift in Colorado, Disney called. They asked him to come out to Disneyland and take over their official Snapchat account for 24 hours. Since then, he's gone back to Disney World to do a Snapchat story for a *Frozen* event—in which he tracks Olaf, the movie's obliviously cheerful snowman, through the park. He now has more than 60,000 followers and has done branded snaps for Major League Soccer and consulted with various companies about how best to build a presence on Snapchat.

Brands love Snapchat for several reasons: It's a gateway to the 20 hard-to-reach youth audience. It's still mostly a messaging app,

so it has a personal, friendly feel to it. Its disappearing aspect—
stories are only up for 24 hours—makes it feel exclusive and
urgent, and is great for timed events like film and television pre-
mieres. And it has yet to be flooded by brands, like Vine has—
though clearly that won't last forever.

> "EDIT: prior tweet had a typo: **@clint_dempsey** of **@SoundersFC**
> freezing people in their tracks and charging the goal!! **pic.twitter.com
> /G9mY52UkiG**
>
> —Shonduras (**@Shonduras**) June 11, 2014

IN A YEAR, "IT'LL COST EVEN MORE"

McBride can make "several thousand dollars" per image, he said.
Platco, who has fewer followers, can make up to $500 a snap or
$150 an hour, he said.

Those prices are likely to skyrocket over the next year, if Snapchat's trajectory mirrors Vine's. "A year ago, we were sending
them a Viner who did a Vine for $5,000 and now it's $25,000,"
Jarre said. "Now it's the same for Snapchat."

Jarre has more than two million followers on Snapchat—a
serious head start he gets from rallying his existing fans on Vine to
follow him on a new platform. Because of his following, he's about
to make $30,000 on a Snapchat story for a television premiere, he
said. "I think a year from now, it'll cost even more," he said.

Other Vine stars have already started exploring their Snapchat
options. Logan Paul, a Viner known for his gymnastic stunts, just
finished a five-day Snapchat campaign where he took to the streets
with someone in a Sour Patch Kids costume and posted videos to
the candy's official Snapchat account, though he declined to say
how much he was paid. Cody Johns, another Vine star, just signed
on to his first ad campaign, one for a TNT television show premiere, that includes a branded Snapchat.

Vine stars like Jarre, Paul, and Nicholas Megalis have also 25
started to collaborate with McBride on Snapchat. It's a win-win,
McBride said: They can learn his Snapchat insights, and he gets
a boost from their ample followings.

In one collaboration, Jarre posted a Snapchat story where
he took an ice cream bar on adventures through New York City.

When she began to melt, he put her in a "time machine"—and told his followers to add McBride to follow the rest of the story. McBride, many states away, pulled an identical ice cream out of the "time machine"—a fax machine—and took her on more adventures. The moral of the story? Everyone melts, so enjoy life while you can. (Both Jarre and McBride focus on lighthearted, positive content, keeping in mind that their fans can be as young as eight years old.)

McBride is full of innovative ways to use Snapchat, such as a "water balloon fight" he staged in June with Logan Paul. Both sides encouraged their followers to add the other and send images of them throwing water balloons—usually drawn in on the app—at the other.

> "TEAM I NEED YOUR HELP! I am in a snapchat battle with **@LoganPaul** so everyone . . . START THROWING WATER BALLOONS!!"
> —Shonduras (**@Shonduras**) June 29, 2014

> "Who saw the 'secret snapchat story' I did with **@nicholasmegalis** yesterday? It was only up for a couple hours ;)"
> —Shonduras (**@Shonduras**) July 16, 2014

ADAPT TO SURVIVE

Snapchat audiences respond to content that's uniquely fit to the app, McBride said. Vine stars need to adapt to a new medium to survive.

"Vine is slowly becoming less and less popular and relevant," McBride said. "I feel like there's a lot of branding on Vine now, so kids are hopping over to Snapchat because it's the cool new thing. So Viners need to hop over there and do more than just shout out their Vine. They need to create unique new Snapchats."

Snapchat's charm today is the same Vine had a year ago. The app is still raw—it crashes often, users can't easily check how many followers they have, and there's no way for an image to go viral. Before Snapchat offered a "story" option, McBride used to have to click every follower's name to send out a new Snapchat—a 45-minute process that took longer than creating the Snapchat itself.

McBride said that Vine veterans can't help but compare Snapchat now to the early days of Vine. "They're like, 'Dude, this is the exact same excitement we had about Vine a year and a half ago,'" McBride said. "It's new, it's raw, no one knows what's going on, the app sucks, you have to work around it. That's the fun. Those were the fun days of Vine, when people loved it. And now Vine is tons of advertisements, perfectly edited videos with background music and slo-mo. It's not organic like it used to be. Snapchat is like that now."

CAN IT LAST?

The great irony is that everything that's appealing to brands and creators about Snapchat today—its youth appeal, its novelty, its authenticity—will fade as more brands and creators flock to it. McBride tries to keep his Snapchat brand personal by responding to every fan who reaches out to him. But it takes hours, and it clearly can't continue if his following grows. And no one's counting on Snapchat lasting forever: Paul wants to be a movie director, and Platco hopes to turn his Snapchat prowess into a digital marketing career.

But Jarre thinks Snapchat can surpass Vine. Vine, he said, "never reached that tipping point where it gets mainstream," he said. It only became a place for comedy, whereas other platforms like YouTube offer everything: music, inspirational videos, tutorials, and more.

"We kind of know what Vine became—Vine is for comedy," Jarre said. "For Snapchat it's unknown. If Snapchat succeeds at not being only comedy, then it can win mobile—I think Snapchat has the power to be the YouTube on mobile."

For Discussion and Writing

1. **Comprehension**   What kind of content do brands like Disney and Taco Bell want from a Snapchat "celebrity" like Shaun McBride?
2. **Critical Reading**   What do you think is Huet's primary **purpose** in writing this article? Is she trying to persuade? Inform? Interpret? Explain your answer.
3. **Analysis**   The writer notices a "great irony" in the story of Snapchat (par. 32). What is the irony? Does it have any broader implications

for American consumerism and consumer culture more generally? What are they?

4. **Connections**   In both Huet's article and Chiara Atik's "Public Displays of Transaction" (p. 78), the writers refer to their respective topics getting "mainstream." What does that word mean? What connotations does it have? Do the writers use the word in the same way? For example, will becoming more mainstream have the same effect on Venmo that it will on Snapchat? Why or why not? Consider other trending applications and platforms that have recently gone "mainstream" to support your answer.

5. **Writing**   McBride makes a broad generalization about teenagers— and the benefits of Snapchat for reaching that audience: "But with Snapchat you have their undivided attention, they're holding down the screen, and it's awesome. When else does that demographic spend seven seconds just soaking something in? They don't" (par. 6). Do you agree with his assertion about this demographic? Does it seem fair and accurate? Write an argumentative essay that either refutes McBride's claim or supports and refines his claim. In either case, choose specific examples and evidence to support your thesis.

CHIARA ATIK

Public Displays of Transaction

A writer and playwright, Chiara Atik graduated from New York University in 2008. Her work has appeared in Glamour, Cosmopolitan, *the* Atlantic, *and other publications. She is also the author of* Modern Dating: A Field Guide *(2014) and* Paris is Lovely/Lovely When You're Alone *(2014). Her plays include* WOMEN *and* The Secret Catcher. *In this selection, which originally appeared on the blog platform* Medium, *Atik considers Venmo, a personal finance app and payment platform that applies the logic of online social networking to enable financial transactions between "friends." Venmo's visible feed allows other people in the network to see their friends' various transactions. For Atik, the app combines money, intimacy, and technology in surprising and revealing ways. She writes, "A lot of people seem unaware of the stories they're telling in their transactions."*

As you read, *consider the assumptions that Atik makes about money, sex, and intimacy: Do you agree with them? How does the writer use examples to support her generalizations? Would you be comfortable allowing others to see your financial transactions on an app like Venmo? Why or why not?*

There's this girl that I stalk on Venmo. Last fall, she showed up in my newsfeed, and though I don't know her very well, I was interested to note a series of payments she made to her live-in boyfriend:

"Half a couch."

"Bookshelves."

"Half a chandelier."

The notes were terse: no emojis, no jokes. Just economic transactions as she went through and calmly charged her boyfriend for his share of their life together. "Roku." "Half the security deposit." "U-Haul." 5

I later asked a mutual friend if she and her boyfriend had broken up. "Yeah, you see that on Facebook?" he asked me. Nope. The real social media platform for stalkers, gossips, and know-it-alls (in my case, all three) is Venmo.

Don't get me wrong. Facebook, Twitter, and Instagram are great for glimpses at how couples *want* to be perceived: that carefully cropped and filtered picture, the self-consciously flirtatious tweet. But money is intimate, far more intimate, in fact, than sex.

We're a generation that talks about sex comfortably and easily, but money is a different matter. (Would You Rather: A date see you naked or a date see your 2013 tax return?) Afraid of seeming cheap, or reckless, or broke, or unfashionably rich, we keep our credit cards close to the vest. But with Venmo — which automatically connects to your Facebook friends — we have a new way of seeing what each of us does with our money. And maybe because Venmo is a fairly new platform, a lot of people seem unaware of the stories they're telling in their transactions. This will likely change once it becomes more mainstream (in the same way Facebook use became more guarded once everyone's parents got an account), but for now, it's the Wild West of uninhibited, relatively public commerce. And if you want to get a snapshot of how people are dating in 2014, take a quick scroll through your Venmo newsfeed.

"Oooohh, I love you, oh, you pay my rent" writes one girl to her live-in fiancé, quoting The Pet Shop Boys and presumably paying her half of the rent. A guy friend paid his newfound summer fling for "Car rentalllll," another new couple transacted over "wine pairing!!!!" Men are paying women, women are paying men, couples are taking turns, alternating charging and receiving money for "dinner" "rock climbing" "Uber" "coachella!!" "utilities," "[plant emoji]" (which I presume is a euphemism for pot but for all I know could literally be a joint investment in houseplants).

But public displays of, if not affection, then at least economic 10 interaction, have their potential drawbacks. If you're wondering whether your ex has a new girlfriend, a Venmo transaction for concert tickets might be a better indicator than a Foursquare check-in. If you're paying attention, a mundane charge for "ConEd" may say more about couple's stability than a relfie (ugh) posted on Instagram and Facebook for public consumption and posterity.

Love affects how we spend money. And on Venmo, for better or for worse, these interactions are public, open to speculation and interpretation from your second cousin, your ex-boyfriend, your mom's work colleague, and, uhm, me.

Of course, when scrolling through a Venmo feed with the sole objective of measuring the relationship statuses of your friends and acquaintances, you're going to have to do a lot of filling in the blanks. But that's true of all social media, really: As telling as it is to see glimpses of how couples interact, or look together, or spend money with each other, all you're ever really getting is just glimpses. It's up to us (the voyeurs, the busybodies) to see what we want to see. It's just that Venmo makes this tantalizingly easy to do.

Take Melissa*, the girl who broke up with her boyfriend. Her appearances in my Venmo newsfeed over the course of last winter read like a truncated romantic comedy: Immediately following her breakup, most of her transactions seemed to be with her roommates, for things like [wine emoji] and [pizza emoji]. And then, sometime in February, I noticed a transaction for a "Taxi!" with a guy whose name I didn't recognize.

As winter turned to spring, this dude became a fixture in her life, and on my iPhone. Every time I opened the app, I would note, with a smile, their increasing (and increasingly cutesy) interactions. Movie tickets and drinks and payments for "lobstah dinner" were soon followed by airline tickets, hotels, and, perhaps most tellingly, "♥ ♥ ♥ ♥ ♥ ♥." I haven't seen Melissa in over a year, but this winter, dollar by dollar, I watched her fall in love.

*Not her real name. Obviously

For Discussion and Writing

1. **Comprehension**   Atik writes that "public displays of . . . economic interaction, have their potential drawbacks" (par. 10). According to her, what are the drawbacks?

2. **Critical Reading**   Is the **thesis** of this article implicit or explicit? How would you state Atik's thesis in your own words?

3. **Analysis**   What implicit contrast does Atik draw between social networking sites like Facebook and Twitter (on one hand) and Venmo (on the other) in paragraphs 7 and 8? What point does she make with this contrast? Do you agree? Why or why not?

4. ***Connections***   Both Huet's and Atik's articles identify the narrative possibilities of social media platforms. Atik writes that "people seem unaware of the stories they're telling" with their transactions on Venmo (par. 8). In "Snaps to Riches: The Rise of Snapchat Celebrities" (p. 70), Ellen Huet also refers to the storytelling aspects of Snapchat, as the app even has a "story" option. How are the stories on Venmo different from stories on Snapchat, in your view? According to Atik, how are the stories people tell on Venmo likely to change as the app becomes more popular? How does the storytelling of these apps differ from others you may use?

5. ***Writing***   Atik asserts that "money is intimate, far more intimate, in fact, than sex" (par. 7). Do you agree with this claim, in the context of online social media as well as in a broader context? Write an essay that takes a position on this question. Note that the writer places a generational qualification on her assertion, as she writes, "We're a generation that talks about sex comfortably and easily, but money is a different matter" (par. 8). You might address her generational observation in your essay, too.

CHAPTER 2

Identity

Where do we discover ourselves in pop culture?

When we consider the idea of identity, we might think of a divide between private and public. Our personality, our "individuality," our singular, autonomous "selves," with their conscious and unconscious thoughts and desires—these constitute our private identities. But our identities are also constructed and mediated socially and publicly. For example, when we are asked to identify our gender or race on a census form, or when we identify with an ethnic, religious, or national heritage—these acts suggest that identity is, in part, a function of a social and public context. No doubt, this private–public divide is permeable—and our public identities can be as complex as our distinctive privates "selves."

America has long tried to reconcile the paradoxes and tensions implicit in the notion of personal, social, and national identity—from its foundational myths of rugged individualism and its motto *E pluribus unum* ("Out of many, one"), to the metaphor of a melting pot, in which all identities would be dissolved, reconstituted, and unified in a transcendent "American" ideal. The country has always struggled with race and racial assimilation, from the colonial period and the Civil War up through the civil rights era and into the "postracial" presidency (as some had dreamed) of Barack Obama, who is biracial. Discussions of identity go well beyond race, ethnicity, and nationality. Identity encompasses the status of men and women, the meaning of feminism, and questions of sexuality—topics now discussed more openly, explicitly, and rigorously than at any time in American history.

Of course, our sense of identity is inextricably bound to our pop culture aesthetics and even our technologies. We construct our personas, in part, from our musical tastes, our consumer choices, our favorite brands, and even our tribal affiliations— from goths draped in black clothing to country music fans in cowboy hats. To add another layer of complexity, our lives are hyperconnected, mediated, and publicized by platforms like Internet social networks or animated by the virtual worlds of online gaming; we may even have multiple identities, depending on the social or technological context. Indeed, while we tend to view identity as part of a personal or private sphere, our identities—racial, ethnic, gender, sexual, online, off-line, and otherwise—are invariably social and have public implications.

The selections in this section look at those public and private implications through the lens of popular culture. In "An Argument for Being a Poser," Liz Armstrong recalls her adolescent experiences as a tentative "dabbler" among punks and ravers; she argues that committing to "One True Sub-genre" is less important than the process of exploring various communities, subcultures, and identities. Raquel Cepeda's "The N-Word Is Flourishing among Generation Hip-Hop Latinos: Why Should We Care Now?" explores the revival and meaning of a taboo racial term in a particular ethnic subculture. In "The End of White America?" Hua Hsu looks at the past, present, and future of "the real America" and "whiteness," moving fluidly from discussions of *The Great Gatsby* to reflections on hip-hop mogul Sean Combs. In "The Sports Taboo," Malcolm Gladwell focuses on the provocative intersections of genetics, race, and sports ability. Writer danah boyd ("Impression Management in a Networked Setting") considers the difficulties of identity construction and "impression management" among contemporary teens and young adults who must navigate these thorny issues while under the "constant surveillance" of newer technologies.

The paired readings consider gender roles and sexual identities as reflected in popular culture. In "Women and the Rise of Raunch Culture," Ariel Levy writes about social and cultural pressures that encourage supposedly "liberated" women to embrace a "tawdry, tarty, cartoonlike version of female sexuality." Sonali Kohl ("Pop Culture's Transgender Moment") finds the emergence of complex transgender characters and stories on Amazon's *Transparent* and Netflix's *Orange Is the New Black* a groundbreaking shift, even if it is still largely confined to "online spaces" rather than "traditional media."

As you read, pay attention to the different meanings—and contexts—that the word "identity" suggests:

- How do these writers define "identity"?
- Are the authors' definitions of identity compatible, or are they mutually exclusive?
- Does popular culture express and articulate our changing notions of identity, or does it merely reflect them?

LIZ ARMSTRONG

An Argument for Being a Poser

A graduate of the University of Missouri, Liz Armstrong is a writer and editor. She has held editorial positions at VICE, xoJane, Ready-Made, Hint, *the* Chicago Reader, *and* Las Vegas Weekly. *Her writing has appeared in* Flaunt, Rookie, Bullett, New York Magazine, *the* Pitchfork Review, *and other publications. In "An Argument for Being a Poser," from* Rookie, *Armstrong reflects on her adolescent exploration of subculture and personal identity. She ultimately draws a provocative and counterintuitive conclusion about what it means to "discover" yourself.*

As you read, *notice Armstrong's idea of adolescent identity. Is it static or fluid? Does it suggest that we all have one true "self" that we need to find? How is her topic both "totally ridiculous" and yet "important"?*

There comes a time in every young person's life when she is faced with a crucial dilemma: which alternative subgenre do I belong to? This question is both totally ridiculous on its face, and actually important: its answer forms the beginnings of how you figure out "who you are." Furthermore, when you're in high school, your chosen subculture is your escape—the place where people actually get you, where you don't have to pretend (as much) all the time. In this specific hidey-hole of rebellion, you will find freedom, and acceptance, and a kind of family—just as soon as you can figure out how to *look like that.* Because that's the first step to fitting in, right?

But aren't you not supposed to have to think about any of this? You're supposed to just KNOW WHO YOU ARE and BE YOUR-SELF, right? Your community will call to you from within your soul. Those of us who've really pondered this, and made premeditated, focused, and/or organized maneuvers on just how to start

John Hughes's *The Breakfast Club* (1985) explored—and complicated—
teenage stereotypes: "You see us as a brain, an athlete, a basket case, a princess
and a criminal." What are the visual clues that identify each in this image?

being this or that or that other thing, well, aren't we kind of *inauthentic*? You can't just decide one day that you feel seapunk and
then show up the next in an acid-washed frogskin bodysuit with
dyed green hair, can you? Doesn't that make you a *poser*?

Yes, you damn well sure can, and yes, it sure does. And both
those things are totally fine. I'll tell you why in a minute.

When you come across that thing that takes a seam-ripper to
the sewed-up reality you've been living in—the one that tells you
that you have to get perfect grades and stay out of trouble and
hang out with the "right" people so that you can get to the "right"
places later in life—suddenly there is a lot more possibility than

you ever realized. It could just be a photo you saw on someone's Instagram, or a quote on Tumblr. It could be a wild force of a human you met and desperately want to be friends with, because undoubtedly they will influence you to not only loosen up but possibly become consummately liberated. Whatever that thing is, it looks like freedom, and you want in. By all accounts (unless it looks like cocaine or something), please go chase it!

I had this feeling the first time I went to an underground show when I was 16 years old, a birthday party in a clubhouse that featured a couple of pop-punk bands and a legit raver DJ. This was in the mid-'90s, in the pre–Top 40 Green Day years, back when raves were huge, secret, and illegal. I had no idea beforehand what I was walking into. Here's my diary entry from that experience, slightly abridged to spare you the boring parts:

> Holy moly! This was probably the single most exciting event in my life. At first I felt really dumb because I was wearing a thermal top and farmer jeans. Everyone else's style was based on the same thing, but they all looked different. One guy thought he was Sherlock Holmes. Another guy carried a cellular phone and a bag of crap with him. I realized there were basically two groups: punks and ravers. The punks were the grungy, dressed-in-black ones who tended to be serious and aloof. The ravers wore big, bright, sporty clownish items and were more at ease with themselves. Most of them had shaved heads, ponytails, and a bad dye-job. I felt like a big nerd with my perfect, natural blond hair.
>
> My freaker friends who brought me were being totally cool to me. I was happy to be babied, because I had no clue what the hell was going on. I was introduced to some pretty girl who was embarrassed of her name (she was punk), then to a guy who kissed my hand (raver). Then I met two girls because I had the urge to pull one's rattail, so I did. They were ravers and didn't mind.
>
> At one point we were all told to go stand somewhere else, and I decided I didn't want to and refused, and I met this other girl because of that. "All right!" she said. "Start a trend!" I told her I felt dippy in my overalls and she told me I'm starting a new look. I thought she was gorgeous. She started raving her brains out and asked me to dance with her, but I was too shy. She said, "OK," and left.

That formative experience really yanked me out of the static boundaries of suburban life. These kids were simultaneously ridiculously role-playing from yore and pretending they were aliens from the future? And they were experimenting with their sexuality, which was pretty unheard of where I came from? Holy shit. From then on I decided, *Screw it, time to let go, I don't want to dress or be normal anymore,* so I didn't. One day I looked punk, in a kid's baseball shirt, a spiked collar, a crushed-velvet mini-skirt, and shredded fishnet stockings with visible garters; the next I was in enormous phat pants, a neon-yellow crop top printed with hot-pink flowers, and stickers all over my face. People did not know what to make of me, a straight-A former cheerleader who played soccer year-round, caused trouble incessantly, went to punk shows in skate parks, and snuck out on school nights to go to raves a state or two over. I didn't fit in with the art kids because I couldn't draw; I didn't fit in with the other honors students because I was way too weird. Therefore, on all accounts, I was a poser.

I really did try to commit to my One True Sub-genre, but I was too complicated (as are you), and it was all just way too perplexing of a puzzle to navigate. The ravers were so positive, fun, spiritual, and forward-thinking; the punks were raw, deep, and somewhat political, and they understood struggle. There was no way to choose between the two, and it hurt at the time to have my sincerity under inquisition from both camps and beyond just because I was curious.

But thank goodness for dabbling! It's how you develop dimension to your personality and interests. You get smart and possibly eccentric from experience; your fantasies become richer, your dreams engorged with possibility. Because that's what this is all about, right? The hope or belief that in a pocket of the big wide world, somewhere, there are things happening that are more interesting than your current surroundings might afford. And the more you dip in and out of escapist wormholes, the more you discover that your hunches are correct. So if you change your mind after a week on *S.S. Seapunk* and decide you're actually goth, great! Go bite that style as wholeheartedly as you can muster. Be a ho about culture. Be a poser—because everyone's posing, all the time, and the realest of us are at least honest about it.

For Discussion and Writing

1. **Comprehension**   How would you summarize Armstrong's advice to her readers in your own words?
2. **Critical Reading**   Who is Armstrong's intended **audience**? How do you know?

3. ***Analysis*** In the essay, Armstrong quotes a passage from her diary. Why does she do this? What does the excerpt illustrate? How is Armstrong's voice in the diary entry distinct from her voice in "An Argument for Being a Poser"?

4. ***Connections*** Armstrong writes about a "real-life" social situation and community at a rave; the experience gave her a chance to explore a subculture, as well as her own identity. In "Impression Management in a Networked Setting" (p. 122), danah boyd writes about a similar process, but one that takes place online. For example, boyd writes about a person who explored her sexual identity in a chat room for "queer girls" (par. 8). Do you think Armstrong's advice and argument are as applicable to online social settings as they are to "real-life" social settings? How does the term "poser" take on different meanings in the context of online social networks?

5. ***Writing*** In writing about a subculture, Armstrong means a "place where people actually get you, where you don't have to pretend . . . [where] you will find freedom, and acceptance, and a kind of family" (par. 1). Have you had an experience like this? Have you found a place like the one she describes? Was it mediated or created by your relationship with popular culture, such as shared tastes in music, preferences for certain kinds of books, or some other common interest? Narrate, describe, and interpret your experience—as Armstrong does—in a brief, personal essay.

RAQUEL CEPEDA

The N-Word Is Flourishing among Generation Hip-Hop Latinos: Why Should We Care Now?

Raquel Cepeda is a cultural activist, award-winning journalist, and documentary filmmaker whose interests include race in America, international hip-hop culture, and Latino American issues. Her work has appeared in the Village Voice, People, *and other publications. Cepeda edited* And It Don't Stop: The Best American Hip-Hop Journalism of the Last 25 Years *(2004). She directed and coproduced* Bling: A Planet Rock *(2010), a documentary film about the intersection of hip-hop and the diamond trade in Sierra Leone. Her memoir,* Bird of Paradise: How I Became Latina, *was published in 2013. In the following essay from the* Village Voice *(2008), she examines the use of the "n-word" among Afro-Latinos in New York City: "I'm interested in exploring, as a Dominican New Yorker, how we as a community have propagated it." But her essay raises more general issues as well.*

As you read, *consider the meaning of taboo words and the role that language plays in defining cultural and ethnic membership. How does Cepeda use the "n-word" to enter into a dialogue about broader issues of race in her community? What does it mean to look at national or ethnic identity "through a hip-hop lens"?*

"Yo, my nigga, *that* nigga's crazy," declares a young Dominican guy in his late teens, early twenties. "Yeah, my nigga, that nigga was buggin' last night, my nigga," responds another hermano. Chatter like this floated in the air like the whiff of days-old garbage smoldering in the heat while I took my frequent summer jaunts along Vermilyea Avenue way uptown in Inwood, with my 11-year-old daughter in tow.

Initially, you'd find mostly Caribbean Latinos dropping n-bombs into rap lyrics. "Pigs," off Cypress Hill's classic self-titled 1991 debut, is just one example—but nearly two decades later, the profusion of the word into the New York City Latino vocabulary is reaching an almost caricaturist quality. In Spanish Harlem, el Bronx, and the Lower East Side, it's enthusiastically deployed in an almost faddish manner, as if it's going out of style *literally* tomorrow. With Nas threatening to name his latest album *Nigga* (he relented, eventually, but most fans still call it that anyway) a few months ago, and iconic Latino artists from the authentic urban native Fat Joe[1] to one of my favorite internationalists, Immortal Technique,[2] still flinging it about freely, the word, its meaning, and our sense of who can and cannot use it still dominates public conversation. The palpable racial tension that's been rearing its head this historic presidential election, the subject of race and who is truly considered black or white in this black-and-white race, is something Latinos need to pay attention to. For many of us, especially those of Caribbean descent who make up a sizable chunk of New York Latinos, race should matter, and so should that one particular word.

Personal feelings, premonitions, and politics aside, I took the two young boys' exchange as an interesting opportunity, an exercise in thinking about Afro-Latino identity in an unlikely way: through a hip-hop lens. Aside from the fact that we're in the thick of a predominantly Dominican enclave (for now) in our beloved Uptown Manhattan, and the first guy I'd overheard wore an oversized white T-shirt emblazoned with our motherland's flag, homeboy could've passed for an African-American man on any other stretch of blocks stateside. By comparison, his comrade looked more like Fat Joe's skinnier brother, with light eyes and pale skin. Was it OK, or *more* OK, for the darker-skinned kid to use the term?

As many times as I've heard it yelled across the streets and in playgrounds lately, it doesn't take away the sting. But it's naive to think Puerto Rican, Dominican, and Cuban kids in New York City

---

[1]*Fat Joe:* stage name for Bronx-born rapper Joseph Antonio Cartagena. [Editor's note.]

[2]*Immortal Technique:* stage name for Peruvian-born rapper Felipe Andres Coronel. [Editor's note.]

aren't calling each other and themselves the n-word, especially in 2008. (It's a global phenomenon, too: In West African cities like Freetown and Accra, heads that find out you're from the States and part of the hip-hop community will find creative ways to work the word into a conversation.) For us, the word usually surfaces in the same context that arises among young African-Americans: as a term of inclusion and solidarity. "It's just a code of communication to us, a 'hood word people throw around frequently," says half-African-American, half-Dominican rapper AZ, who released his "rap thesis" on the subject, titled *N.4.L.* (Niggaz 4 Life) in August 2008. "I guess people want to use it now for press and all that; I don't understand what's all the big fuss about."

Somehow, the n-word has found its way back into hip-hop's 5 critical zeitgeist: I'm interested in exploring, as a Dominican New Yorker, how we as a community have propagated it. Recently, due to the mounting criticism of Boricua rapper Fat Joe's use of the term eight albums deep into his career (including his latest, *The Elephant in the Room*), Latinos are being challenged to introspect. But I can see why an impulse to laser-focus on the issue now would bewilder a veteran rapper like Joe; he's used the word consistently since emerging in 1993, as have the Beatnuts,[3] Hurricane G,[4] and his late Puerto Rican cohort Big Pun, to name a few. In an interview with Chicago-based WGCI radio personality Leon Rogers, Joe said that while he didn't know exactly when Latinos started using the n-word, he felt that "somehow it became a way to embrace each other." He added: "Crazy shit is, my man Reverend Al Sharpton,[5] whenever I see him, he'll be like, 'Wassup Joe, my nigga,' and he's the dude that protests 'my nigga.' He's my friend, so he says it to me as a term of endearment."

"It draws the racial differentiations into the Latino community, which I agree with," says New York University Professor of Social and Cultural Analysis, Juan Flores, who regularly teaches courses on Afro-Latino identity here and abroad. "It's just an opportunity

---

[3]*The Beatnuts:* hip-hop group and production company based in Queens, New York. [Editor's note.]

[4]*Hurricane G:* stage name for Brooklyn-born rapper Gloria Rodríguez. [Editor's note.]

[5]*Al Sharpton:* American minister, civil rights activist, and talk show host. [Editor's note.]

to check the power that Black Latinos reflect off each other and the Latino population." In other words, Latino artists use the n-word as a reminder that they too have been oppressed and are products of the transatlantic slave trade.

There may be a reason for the lack of attention: Many Caribbean Latinos are, to Americans at least, ethnically ambiguous products of miscegenation. Regardless of what we've learned in grade school, our history extends past Columbus and our Spanish conquistadores. "The European Spaniards have left a legacy of self-hatred and racism among the Latino population; without acknowledging that, we will not evolve past our own inequity," says Immortal Technique, an Afro-Peruvian hip-hop artist who also uses the n-word. "Racism in America, as horrible and ugly as it may be, still isn't as bad as what it is in Latin America, and the sad part is that we are being racist against ourselves."

Maybe, in a way, that's the statement Dania Ramirez intended to make when, as part of Nas's Grammy-night entourage earlier this year, the dark-brown Dominican actress sported a black T-shirt emblazoned with the n-word. Many folks in our parents' generation have rejected their blackness—I have older Latino neighbors who won't vote for Barack Obama simply because he's black—but those generations more informed by hip-hop are embracing their Afro-Latino identity and evolving past our own self-hatred. Perhaps. "One fallacy is that [the n-word is] blasé, like, 'Ah well, everyone can use it now that it has a different meaning,' because it's not completely meaningless," says Professor Flores. "The other extreme, though, is the absolutist who thinks no one can use it because it's taboo, under any circumstances. That's a problem, too, because every expression has the potential for ulterior meanings, depending on the *circumstances* of the person."

Crystal, a 13-year-old fair-skinned Dominican girl attending eighth grade in an Inwood public school, remembers first hearing the n-word in a song while hanging out with her aunt. "So then, we got on the computer and we looked it up, and it had the meaning and everything," she recalls. "I was like, 'Why would you *say* it in a song?' From there, you started hearing everybody on the street saying it, and then everybody started getting used to it." To be fair, parents aren't always able to interfere because they speak little to no English; those reared by hip-hop culture in the last two decades often use it themselves.

The similar term *cocolo*—most popularly used as an insult 10 against Haitians by Dominicans, and by Puerto Ricans against Dominican immigrants who look Haitian—is another word gradually being assigned a new meaning here among Latinos. Other words that translate to mean "black" among Caribbean Latinos are *moreno/a* and *negrito/a*, almost always used as terms of endearment. However, because none of these words have had the fraternal stamp of hip-hop approval, they have yet to receive their proverbial ghetto passes; speaking of which, Jennifer Lopez might've surrendered hers when she left the Bronx eons ago. While it's a fact that men in the hip-hop industry can get away with murder, women are held to impossibly high standards, and the question of authenticity played a role in how negatively the public reacted to J. Lo's use of the n-word on the remix for her 2001 single "I'm Real."

"I think that with that, it was really based more upon class than anything else," Immortal Technique says. "Many people saw Fat Joe as technically black even though he was a light-skinned Puerto Rican, and he had affiliations with the streets that Jennifer Lopez probably lost on the way to Hollywood."

With few exceptions within our community—Raquel Rivera's 2003 book *New York Ricans From the Hip Hop Zone* devoted prime real estate to the discussion of Latino identity in hip-hop—this is a conversation we've failed to have, whatever our personal feelings. "It really don't matter if you're white, you're black, you're brown, or from the Boogie Down—it irks me to death," says Alain "KET" Maridueña, 37, an entrepreneur and artist. "Latinos in our neighborhood use it a lot—like every other word—and I'm trying to check people because I find that we're suffering, we're going through our thing, times are hard, there aren't enough opportunities out there, and I want us to rise up." But we won't rise up if we can't talk about the reasons why we haven't quite gotten there yet, and the words that've risen in prominence as a result.

For Discussion and Writing

1. **Comprehension**   According to the article, why did some people react so negatively to Jennifer Lopez's use of the "n-word" in her 2001 song "I'm Real," even if the same people do not mind when rappers such as Fat Joe or Immortal Technique use the term?

2. *Critical Reading*   Reread Cepeda's **introduction**. What tension or problem does her first paragraph raise? How does this strategy lead the reader into her wider discussion? How else might she have opened the essay? Give an example.

3. *Analysis*   What do the words "authentic" (par. 2) and "authenticity" (par. 10) mean in the context of this essay? Why are they important? How do notions of authenticity shape perceptions of racial, ethnic, and cultural identity?

4. *Connections*   Both Raquel Cepeda and Tina Vasquez ("Riffs of Passage," p. 232) view bicultural Latino identity through the lenses of a particular musical culture: hip-hop and punk, respectively. Do their essays share a similar purpose? Are their approaches and claims compatible? Does one writer's lens seem more revealing than the other's? Explain your answers.

5. *Writing*   In Cepeda's article, Professor Juan Flores claims: "One fallacy is that [the n-word is] blasé, like, 'Ah well, everyone can use it now that it has a different meaning,' because it's not completely meaningless. . . . The other extreme, though, is the absolutist who thinks no one can use it because it's taboo, under any circumstances. That's a problem, too, because every expression has the potential for ulterior meanings, depending on the *circumstances* of the person" (par. 8). How do you understand the significance of this "taboo" word? Is its use ever acceptable? Does its meaning change, depending on the identity of the person using it? If so, why? Do certain people have a right to use this word, while others do not? Write a brief essay that addresses and answers these questions or responds to Cepeda's analysis.

HUA HSU

The End of White America?

Hua Hsu (b. 1977) earned a Ph.D. from the History of American Civilization program at Harvard University and now teaches English at Vassar College. His scholarly interests include cultural studies, arts criticism, and American intellectual history. Hsu also writes for publications such as the Atlantic, Slate, *and the* New York Times. *In "The End of White America?" which originally appeared in the* Atlantic, *Hsu investigates the decline of "whiteness"—demographically and culturally—as a fundamental aspect of American identity.*

As you read, *consider how our notions of race and ethnicity are changing as the United States population changes. Hsu refers to the "triumph of multiculturalism" and "postracialism." Do you see our society in those terms? Why or why not? Do you think that "to be white is to be culturally broke?"*

"Civilization's going to pieces," he remarks. He is in polite company, gathered with friends around a bottle of wine in the late-afternoon sun, chatting and gossiping. "I've gotten to be a terrible pessimist about things. Have you read *The Rise of the Colored Empires* by this man Goddard?" They hadn't. "Well, it's a fine book, and everybody ought to read it. The idea is if we don't look out the white race will be—will be utterly submerged. It's all scientific stuff; it's been proved."

He is Tom Buchanan, a character in F. Scott Fitzgerald's *The Great Gatsby*, a book that nearly everyone who passes through the American education system is compelled to read at least once. Although *Gatsby* doesn't gloss as a book on racial anxiety—it's too busy exploring a different set of anxieties entirely—Buchanan was hardly alone in feeling besieged. The book by "this man Goddard" had a real-world analogue: Lothrop Stoddard's *The Rising Tide of Color Against White World-Supremacy*, published in

96

1920, five years before *Gatsby*. Nine decades later, Stoddard's polemic remains oddly engrossing. He refers to World War I as the "White Civil War" and laments the "cycle of ruin" that may result if the "white world" continues its infighting. The book features a series of foldout maps depicting the distribution of "color" throughout the world and warns, "Colored migration is a universal peril, menacing every part of the white world."

As briefs for racial supremacy go, *The Rising Tide of Color* is eerily serene. Its tone is scholarly and gentlemanly, its hatred rationalized and, in Buchanan's term, "scientific." And the book was hardly a fringe phenomenon. It was published by Scribner, also Fitzgerald's publisher, and Stoddard, who received a doctorate in history from Harvard, was a member of many professional academic associations. It was precisely the kind of book that a 1920s man of Buchanan's profile—wealthy, Ivy League–educated, at once pretentious and intellectually insecure—might have been expected to bring up in casual conversation.

As white men of comfort and privilege living in an age of limited social mobility, of course, Stoddard and the Buchanans in his audience had nothing literal to fear. Their sense of dread hovered somewhere above the concerns of everyday life. It was linked less to any immediate danger to their class's political and cultural power than to the perceived fraying of the fixed, monolithic identity of whiteness that sewed together the fortunes of the fair-skinned.

From the hysteria over Eastern European immigration to the vibrant cultural miscegenation of the Harlem Renaissance,[1] it is easy to see how this imagined worldwide white kinship might have seemed imperiled in the 1920s. There's no better example of the era's insecurities than the 1923 Supreme Court case *United States v. Bhagat Singh Thind*, in which an Indian-American veteran of World War I sought to become a naturalized citizen by proving that he was Caucasian. The Court considered new anthropological studies that expanded the definition of the Caucasian race to include Indians, and the justices even agreed that traces of "Aryan blood" coursed through Thind's body. But these technicalities availed him little. The Court determined that Thind was

5

---

[1]*Harlem Renaissance:* a Harlem-based cultural movement of African American literature, music, and art during the 1920s and 1930s. [Editor's note.]

not white "in accordance with the understanding of the common man" and therefore could be excluded from the "statutory category" of whiteness. Put another way: Thind was white, in that he was Caucasian and even Aryan. But he was not *white* in the way Stoddard or Buchanan were white.

The '20s debate over the definition of whiteness—a legal category? a commonsense understanding? a worldwide civilization?—took place in a society gripped by an acute sense of racial paranoia, and it is easy to regard these episodes as evidence of how far we have come. But consider that these anxieties surfaced when whiteness was synonymous with the American mainstream, when threats to its status were largely imaginary. What happens once this is no longer the case—when the fears of Lothrop Stoddard and Tom Buchanan are realized, and white people actually become an American minority?

Whether you describe it as the dawning of a postracial age or just the end of white America, we're approaching a profound demographic tipping point. According to an August 2008 report by the U.S. Census Bureau, those groups currently categorized as racial minorities—blacks and Hispanics, East Asians and South Asians—will account for a majority of the U.S. population by the year 2042. Among Americans under the age of 18, this shift is projected to take place in 2023, which means that every child born in the United States from here on out will belong to the first post-white generation.

Obviously, steadily ascending rates of interracial marriage complicate this picture, pointing toward what Michael Lind has described as the "beiging" of America. And it's possible that "beige Americans" will self-identify as "white" in sufficient numbers to push the tipping point further into the future than the Census Bureau projects. But even if they do, whiteness will be a label adopted out of convenience and even indifference, rather than aspiration and necessity. For an earlier generation of minorities and immigrants, to be recognized as a "white American," whether you were an Italian or a Pole or a Hungarian, was to enter the mainstream of American life; to be recognized as something else, as the *Thind* case suggests, was to be permanently excluded. As Bill Imada, head of the IW Group, a prominent Asian American communications and marketing company, puts it: "I think in the 1920s, 1930s, and 1940s, [for] anyone who immigrated, the aspiration was to blend in and be as American as possible so that white America wouldn't be intimidated by them. They wanted to imitate white America as much as possible: learn English, go to church, go to the same schools."

Today, the picture is far more complex. To take the most obvious example, whiteness is no longer a precondition for entry into the highest levels of public office. The son of Indian immigrants doesn't have to become "white" in order to be elected governor of Louisiana. A half-Kenyan, half-Kansan politician can self-identify as black and be elected president of the United States.

As a purely demographic matter, then, the "white America" 10 that Lothrop Stoddard believed in so fervently may cease to exist in 2040, 2050, or 2060, or later still. But where the culture is concerned, it's already all but finished. Instead of the long-standing model of assimilation toward a common center, the culture is being remade in the image of white America's multiethnic, multicolored heirs.

For some, the disappearance of this centrifugal core heralds a future rich with promise. In 1998, President Bill Clinton, in a now-famous address to students at Portland State University, remarked:

> Today, largely because of immigration, there is no majority race in Hawaii or Houston or New York City. Within five years, there will be no majority race in our largest state, California. In a little more than 50 years, there will be no majority race in the United States. No other nation in history has gone through demographic change of this magnitude in so short a time . . . [These immigrants] are energizing our culture and broadening our vision of the world. They are renewing our most basic values and reminding us all of what it truly means to be American.

Not everyone was so enthused. Clinton's remarks caught the attention of another anxious Buchanan—Pat Buchanan, the conservative thinker. Revisiting the president's speech in his 2001 book, *The Death of the West*, Buchanan wrote: "Mr. Clinton assured us that it will be a better America when we are all minorities and realize true 'diversity.' Well, those students [at Portland State] are going to find out, for they will spend their golden years in a Third World America."

Today, the arrival of what Buchanan derided as "Third World America" is all but inevitable. What will the new mainstream of America look like, and what ideas or values might it rally around?

What will it mean to be white after "whiteness" no longer defines the mainstream? Will anyone mourn the end of white America? Will anyone try to preserve it?

Another moment from *The Great Gatsby:* as Fitzgerald's narrator and Gatsby drive across the Queensboro Bridge into Manhattan, a car passes them, and Nick Carraway notices that it is a limousine "driven by a white chauffeur, in which sat three modish negroes, two bucks and a girl." The novelty of this topsy-turvy arrangement inspires Carraway to laugh aloud and think to himself, "Anything can happen now that we've slid over this bridge, anything at all. . . ."

For a contemporary embodiment of the upheaval that this scene portended, consider Sean Combs, a hip-hop mogul and one of the most famous African Americans on the planet. Combs grew up during hip-hop's late-1970s rise, and he belongs to the first generation that could safely make a living working in the industry—as a plucky young promoter and record-label intern in the late 1980s and early 1990s, and as a fashion designer, artist, and music executive worth hundreds of millions of dollars a brief decade later.

In the late 1990s, Combs made a fascinating gesture toward New York's high society. He announced his arrival into the circles of the rich and powerful not by crashing their parties, but by inviting them into his own spectacularly over-the-top world. Combs began to stage elaborate annual parties in the Hamptons, not far from where Fitzgerald's novel takes place. These "white parties"—attendees are required to wear white—quickly became legendary for their opulence (in 2004, Combs showcased a 1776 copy of the Declaration of Independence) as well as for the cultures-colliding quality of Hamptons elites paying their respects to someone so comfortably nouveau riche. Prospective business partners angled to get close to him and praised him as a guru of the lucrative "urban" market, while grateful partygoers hailed him as a modern-day Gatsby.

"Have I read *The Great Gatsby?*" Combs said to a London newspaper in 2001. "I am the Great Gatsby."

Yet whereas Gatsby felt pressure to hide his status as an arriviste, Combs celebrated his position as an outsider-insider— someone who appropriates elements of the culture he seeks to join without attempting to assimilate outright. In a sense, Combs

Sean Combs staged opulent "white parties" in the Hamptons, where attendees were required to wear white. How do such events play with the meaning of "whiteness"?

was imitating the old WASP establishment; in another sense, he was subtly provoking it, by over-enunciating its formality and never letting his guests forget that there was something slightly off about his presence. There's a silent power to throwing parties where the best-dressed man in the room is also the one whose public profile once consisted primarily of dancing in the background of Biggie Smalls videos. ("No one would ever expect a young black man to be coming to a party with the Declaration of Independence, but I got it, and it's coming with me," Combs joked at his 2004 party, as he made the rounds with the document, promising not to spill champagne on it.)

In this regard, Combs is both a product and a hero of the new cultural mainstream, which prizes diversity above all else, and whose ultimate goal is some vague notion of racial transcendence, rather than subversion or assimilation. Although Combs's vision is far from representative—not many hip-hop stars vacation in St. Tropez with a parasol-toting manservant shading their every step—his industry lies at the heart of this new mainstream. Over the past 30 years, few changes in American culture have been as significant as the rise of hip-hop. The genre has radically reshaped the way we listen to and consume music, first by opposing the pop mainstream and then by becoming it. From its constant sampling of past styles and eras—old records, fashions, slang, anything—to its mythologization of the self-made black antihero, hip-hop is more than a musical genre: it's a philosophy, a political statement, a way of approaching and remaking culture. It's a lingua franca[2] not just among kids in America, but also among young people worldwide. And its economic impact extends beyond the music industry, to fashion, advertising, and film.

But hip-hop's deepest impact is symbolic. During popular 20 music's rise in the 20th century, white artists and producers consistently "mainstreamed" African American innovations. Hip-hop's ascension has been different. Eminem notwithstanding, hip-hop never suffered through anything like an Elvis Presley moment, in which a white artist made a musical form safe for white America. This is no dig at Elvis—the constrictive racial logic of the 1950s demanded the erasure of rock and roll's black roots, and if it hadn't been him, it would have been someone else. But hip-hop—the sound of the post-civil-rights, post-soul generation—found a global audience on its own terms.

Today, hip-hop's colonization of the global imagination, from fashion runways in Europe to dance competitions in Asia, is Disneyesque. This transformation has bred an unprecedented cultural confidence in its black originators. Whiteness is no longer a threat or an ideal: it's kitsch[3] to be appropriated, whether with gestures like Combs's "white parties" or the trickle-down epidemic of collared shirts and cuff links currently afflicting rappers. And an expansive multiculturalism is replacing the us-against-the-world bunker mentality that lent a thrilling edge to hip-hop's mid-1990s rise.

Peter Rosenberg, a self-proclaimed "nerdy Jewish kid" and radio personality on New York's Hot 97 FM—and a living example of how hip-hop has created new identities for its listen-

---

[2]*lingua franca:* any language that is widely used as a means of communication among speakers of other languages. [Editor's note.]
[3]*kitsch:* any entertainment or artifact with enormous popular appeal, but usually associated with bad taste, like sensationalism and sentimentality. [Editor's note.]

ers that don't fall neatly along lines of black and white—shares another example: "I interviewed [the St. Louis rapper] Nelly this morning, and he said it's now very cool and *in* to have multicultural friends. Like you're not really considered hip or 'you've made it' if you're rolling with all the same people."

Pop culture today rallies around an ethic of multicultural inclusion that seems to value every identity—except whiteness. "It's become harder for the blond-haired, blue-eyed commercial actor," remarks Rochelle Newman-Carrasco, of the Hispanic marketing firm Enlace. "You read casting notices, and they like to cast people with brown hair because they could be Hispanic. The language of casting notices is pretty shocking because it's so specific: 'Brown hair, brown eyes, could look Hispanic.' Or, as one notice put it: 'Ethnically ambiguous.'"

"I think white people feel like they're under siege right now—like it's not okay to be white right now, especially if you're a white male," laughs Bill Imada, of the IW Group. Imada and Newman-Carrasco are part of a movement within advertising, marketing, and communications firms to reimagine the profile of the typical American consumer. (Tellingly, every person I spoke with from these industries knew the Census Bureau's projections by heart.)

"There's a lot of fear and a lot of resentment," Newman- 25
Carrasco observes, describing the flak she caught after writing an article for a trade publication on the need for more diverse hiring practices. "I got a response from a friend—he's, like, a 60-something white male, and he's been involved with multicultural recruiting," she recalls. "And he said, 'I really feel like the hunted. It's a hard time to be a white man in America right now, because I feel like I'm being lumped in with all white males in America, and I've tried to do stuff, but it's a tough time.'"

"I always tell the white men in the room, 'We need you,'" Imada says. "We cannot talk about diversity and inclusion and engagement without you at the table. It's okay to be white!

"But people are stressed out about it. 'We used to be in control! We're losing control!'"

If they're right—if white America is indeed "losing control," and if the future will belong to people who can successfully navigate a postracial, multicultural landscape—then it's no surprise that many white Americans are eager to divest themselves of their whiteness entirely. . . .

"I get it: as a straight white male, I'm the worst thing on Earth," Christian Lander says. Lander is a Canadian-born, Los Angeles–based satirist who in January 2008 started a blog called *Stuff White People Like*, which pokes fun at the manners and mores of a specific species of young, hip, upwardly mobile whites. (He has written more than 100 entries about whites' passion for things like bottled water, "the idea of soccer," and "being the only white person around.") At its best, Lander's site is a cunningly precise distillation of the identity crisis plaguing well-meaning, well-off white kids in a post-white world.

Lander's "white people" are products of a very specific histori- 30 cal moment, raised by well-meaning Baby Boomers to reject the old ideal of white American gentility and to embrace diversity and fluidity instead. ("It's strange that we are the kids of Baby Boomers, right? How the hell do you rebel against that? Like, your parents will march against the World Trade Organization next to you. They'll have bigger white dreadlocks than you. What do you do?") But his lighthearted anthropology suggests that the multicultural harmony they were raised to worship has bred a kind of self-denial.

Matt Wray, a sociologist at Temple University who is a fan of Lander's humor, has observed that many of his white students are plagued by a racial-identity crisis: "They don't care about socioeconomics; they care about culture. And to be white is to be culturally broke. The classic thing white students say when you ask them to talk about who they are is, 'I don't have a culture.' They might be privileged, they might be loaded socioeconomically, but they feel bankrupt when it comes to culture. . . . They feel disadvantaged, and they feel marginalized. They don't have a culture that's cool or oppositional." Wray says that this feeling of being culturally bereft often prevents students from recognizing what it means to be a child of privilege—a strange irony that the first wave of whiteness-studies scholars, in the 1990s, failed to anticipate.

"The best defense is to be constantly pulling the rug out from underneath yourself," Wray remarks, describing the way self-aware whites contend with their complicated identity. "Beat people to the punch. You're forced as a white person into a sense of ironic detachment. Irony is what fuels a lot of white subcultures. You also see things like Burning Man, when a lot of white people are going into the desert and trying to invent something that is entirely new and not a form of racial mimicry. That's its own kind of flight from whiteness. We're going through a period where whites are really trying to figure out: Who are we?"

The "flight from whiteness" of urban, college-educated, liberal whites isn't the only attempt to answer this question. You can flee *into* whiteness as well. This can mean pursuing the authenticity of an imagined past: think of the deliberately white-bread world of Mormon America, where the '50s never ended, or the anachronistic WASP entitlement flaunted in books like last year's *A Privileged Life: Celebrating WASP Style*, a handsome coffee-table book compiled by Susanna Salk, depicting a world of seersucker blazers, whale pants, and deck shoes. (What the book celebrates is the "inability to be outdone," and the "self-confidence and security that comes with it," Salk tells me. "That's why I call it 'privilege.' It's this privilege of time, of heritage, of being in a place longer than anybody else.") But these enclaves of preserved-in-amber whiteness are likely to be less important to the American future than the construction of whiteness as a somewhat pissed-off minority culture. . . .

The rise of country music and auto racing took place well off the American elite's radar screen. (None of Christian Lander's white people would be caught dead at a NASCAR race.) These phenomena reflected a growing sense of cultural solidarity among lower-middle-class whites — a solidarity defined by a yearning for American "authenticity," a folksy realness that rejects the global, the urban, and the effete in favor of nostalgia for "the way things used to be."

Like other forms of identity politics, white solidarity comes 35 complete with its own folk heroes, conspiracy theories (Barack Obama is a secret Muslim! The U.S. is going to merge with Canada and Mexico!), and laundry lists of injustices. The targets and scapegoats vary — from multiculturalism and affirmative action to a loss of moral values, from immigration to an economy that no longer guarantees the American worker a fair chance — and so do the political programs they inspire. But the core grievance, in each case, has to do with cultural and socioeconomic dislocation — the sense that the system that used to guarantee the white working class some stability has gone off-kilter.

Wray is one of the founders of what has been called "white-trash studies," a field conceived as a response to the perceived elite-liberal marginalization of the white working class. He argues that the economic downturn of the 1970s was the precondition for the formation of an "oppositional" and "defiant" white-working-class sensibility—think of the rugged, anti-everything individualism of 1977's *Smokey and the Bandit*. But those anxieties took their shape from the aftershocks of the identity-based movements of the 1960s. "I think that the political space that the civil-rights movement opens up in the mid-1950s and '60s is the transformative thing," Wray observes. "Following the black-power movement, all of the other minority groups that followed took up various forms of activism, including brown power and yellow power and red power. Of course the problem is, if you try and have a 'white power' movement, it doesn't sound good."

The result is a racial pride that dares not speak its name, and that defines itself through cultural cues instead—a suspicion of intellectual elites and city dwellers, a preference for folksiness and plainness of speech (whether real or feigned), and the association of a working-class white minority with "the real America." (In the Scots-Irish belt that runs from Arkansas up through West Virginia, the most common ethnic label offered to census takers is "American.") Arguably, this white identity politics helped swing the 2000 and 2004 elections, serving as the powerful counterpunch to urban white liberals, and the McCain–Palin campaign relied on it almost to the point of absurdity (as when a McCain surrogate dismissed Northern Virginia as somehow not part of "the real Virginia") as a bulwark against the threatening multiculturalism of Barack Obama. Their strategy failed, of course, but it's possible to imagine white identity politics growing more potent and more forthright in its racial identifications in the future, as "the real America" becomes an ever-smaller portion of, well, the real America, and as the soon-to-be white minority's sense of being besieged and disdained by a multicultural majority grows apace.

At the moment, we can call this the triumph of multiculturalism, or postracialism. But just as *whiteness* has no inherent meaning—it is a vessel we fill with our hopes and anxieties—these terms may prove equally empty in the long run. Does being post-racial mean that we are past race completely, or merely that race is no longer essential to how we identify ourselves? Karl Carter, of Atlanta's youth-oriented GTM, Inc. (Guerrilla Tactics Media), suggests that marketers and advertisers would be better off focusing on matrices like "lifestyle" or "culture" rather than race or ethnicity. "You'll have crazy in-depth studies of the white consumer or the Latino consumer," he complains. "But how do skaters feel? How do hip-hoppers feel?"

The logic of online social networking points in a similar direction. The New York University sociologist Dalton Conley has written of a "network nation," in which applications like Facebook create "crosscutting social groups" and new, flexible identities that only vaguely overlap with racial identities. Perhaps this is where the future of identity after whiteness lies—in a dramatic departure from the racial logic that has defined American culture from the very beginning. What Conley, Carter, and others are describing isn't merely the displacement of whiteness from our cultural center; they're describing a social structure that treats race as just one of a seemingly infinite number of possible self-identifications.

The problem of the 20th century, W. E. B. Du Bois famously 40 predicted, would be the problem of the color line. Will this continue to be the case in the 21st century, when a black president will govern a country whose social networks increasingly cut across every conceivable line of identification? The ruling of *United States v. Bhagat Singh Thind* no longer holds weight, but its echoes have been inescapable: we aspire to be postracial, but we still live within the structures of privilege, injustice, and racial categorization that we inherited from an older order. We can talk about defining ourselves by lifestyle rather than skin color, but our lifestyle choices are still racially coded. We know, more or less, that race is a fiction that often does more harm than good, and yet it is something we cling to without fully understanding why—as a social and legal fact, a vague sense of belonging and place that we make solid through culture and speech.

But maybe this is merely how it used to be—maybe this is already an outdated way of looking at things. "You have a lot of young adults going into a more diverse world," Carter remarks. For the young Americans born in the 1980s and 1990s, culture is something to be taken apart and remade in their own image. "We came along in a generation that didn't have to follow that path of race," he goes on. "We saw something *different*." This moment was not the end of white America; it was not the end of anything. It was a bridge, and we crossed it.

For Discussion and Writing

1. **Comprehension**   According to Hsu, how is "whiteness" or the "white American" identity viewed by minorities and immigrants in America? How is this perspective different from that of earlier generations of minorities and immigrants?

2. **Critical Reading**   Hsu begins his essay by quoting a fictional character from *The Great Gatsby*. How does this introduction signal or introduce the **themes** and arguments that follow? Identify specific examples. Do you find this strategy effective? Explain your answer.

3. **Analysis**   Hsu quotes sociologist Matt Wray, who describes the "racial-identity crisis" of his white students: "They don't care about socioeconomics; they care about culture. And to be white is to be culturally broke" (par. 31). What does this mean? Why would the distinction between socioeconomics and culture be important? How can someone be "broke" culturally?

4. **Connections**   In "The N-Word Is Flourishing among Generation Hip-Hop Latinos: Why Should We Care Now?" (p. 90), Raquel Cepeda reads the Caribbean Latino identity—an ethnicity that she argues is, to Americans at least, an "ethnically ambiguous [product] of miscegenation" (par. 7)—through the lens of hip-hop. How would you read her essay in the context of "The End of White America?" For example, do you think her analysis supports Hsu's point of view? Do you think it complicates Hsu's essay or challenges it in any way? Identify specific passages to support your answer.

5. **Writing**   Hsu writes of the "new cultural mainstream, which prizes diversity above all else, and whose ultimate goal is some vague notion of racial transcendence, rather than subversion or assimilation" (par. 19). Do you agree with this characterization of the "mainstream" and its assumptions and aims? Why or why not? Hsu uses many examples from American culture to support his points. Choose your examples to make your case in a persuasive essay. You might also consider this question in light of the contrasting attitudes of Bill Clinton and Pat Buchanan (pars. 11–13).

MALCOLM GLADWELL

The Sports Taboo

A staff writer for the New Yorker, *Canadian journalist Malcolm Gladwell (b. 1963) writes about complex subjects — social psychology, statistics, economics, epidemiology — in a lively, accessible style. Before joining the* New Yorker, *Gladwell worked for the* American Spectator, Insight on the News, *and the* Washington Post. *He is the author of* The Tipping Point: How Little Things Can Make a Big Difference *(2000),* Blink: The Power of Thinking Without Thinking *(2005),* Outliers: The Story of Success *(2008), and* David and Goliath: Underdogs, Misfits, and the Art of Battling Giants *(2013). Gladwell's work often upends common assumptions. In "The Sports Taboo," published in the* New Yorker, *those assumptions include unspoken rules about discussing the racial dimensions of athleticism and the genetic differences between black and white athletes: "There is nothing particularly scary about this fact, and certainly nothing to warrant the kind of gag order on talk of racial differences which is now in place."*

As you read, *consider: Why are discussions of race and genetics unsettling or controversial? Are there any problems with framing discussions of race in this way? Do you agree with Gladwell that, in many cases, "there is a point at which it becomes foolish to deny the fact of black athletic prowess"?*

1.

The education of any athlete begins, in part, with an education in the racial taxonomy of his chosen sport — in the subtle, unwritten rules about what whites are supposed to be good at and what blacks are supposed to be good at. In football, whites play quarterback and blacks play running back; in baseball whites pitch and blacks play the outfield. I grew up in Canada, where my brother Geoffrey and I ran high-school track, and in Canada the rule of running was that anything under the quarter-mile belonged to the West Indians. This didn't mean that white people didn't run the sprints. But the expectation was that they would never win, and, sure enough, they rarely did. There was just a handful of West Indian immigrants in Ontario at that point—clustered in and around Toronto—but they owned Canadian sprinting, setting up under the stands at every major championship, cranking up the reggae on their boom boxes, and then humiliating everyone else on the track. My brother and I weren't from Toronto, so we weren't part of that scene. But our West Indian heritage meant that we got to share in the swagger. Geoffrey was a magnificent runner, with powerful legs and a barrel chest, and when he was warming up he used to do that exaggerated, slow-motion jog that the white guys would try to do and never quite pull off. I was a miler, which was a little outside the West Indian range. But, the way I figured it, the rules meant that no one should ever outkick me over the final two hundred meters of any race. And in the golden summer of my fourteenth year, when my running career prematurely peaked, no one ever did.

When I started running, there was a quarter-miler just a few years older than I was by the name of Arnold Stotz. He was a bulldog of a runner, hugely talented, and each year that he moved through the sprinting ranks he invariably broke the existing four-hundred-meter record in his age class. Stotz was white, though, and every time I saw the results of a big track meet I'd keep an eye out for his name, because I was convinced that he could not keep winning. It was as if I saw his whiteness as a degenerative disease, which would eventually claim and cripple him. I never asked him whether he felt the same anxiety, but I can't imagine that he didn't. There was only so long that anyone could defy the rules. One day, at the provincial championships, I looked up at the results board and Stotz was gone.

Talking openly about the racial dimension of sports in this way, of course, is considered unseemly. It's all right to say that blacks dominate sports because they lack opportunities elsewhere. That's the *Hoop Dreams* line, which says whites are allowed to acknowledge black athletic success as long as they feel guilty about it. What you're not supposed to say is what we were saying in my track days—that we were better because we were black, because of something intrinsic to being black. Nobody said anything like that publicly last month when Tiger Woods won the Masters or

© Bob Olsen/Getty Images

The author (right) during his high school track years: "In those days, I was whippet-thin . . . and I could skim along the ground so lightly that I barely needed to catch my breath."

when, a week later, African men claimed thirteen out of the top twenty places in the Boston Marathon. Nor is it likely to come up this month, when African Americans will make up eighty percent of the players on the floor for the N.B.A. playoffs. When the popular television sports commentator Jimmy (the Greek) Snyder did break this taboo, in 1988—infamously ruminating on the size and significance of black thighs—one prominent N.A.A.C.P. official said that his remarks "could set race relations back a hundred years." The assumption is that the whole project of trying to get us to treat each other the same will be undermined if we don't all agree that under the skin we actually are the same.

The point of this, presumably, is to put our discussion of sports on a par with legal notions of racial equality, which would be a fine idea except that civil-rights law governs matters like housing and employment and the sports taboo covers matters like what can be said about someone's jump shot. In his much heralded book *Darwin's Athletes*, the University of Texas scholar John Hoberman tries to argue that these two things are the same, that it's impossible to speak of black physical superiority without implying intellectual inferiority. But it isn't long before the argument starts to get ridiculous. "The spectacle of black athleticism," he writes, inevitably turns into "a highly public image of black retardation." Oh, really? What, exactly, about Tiger Woods's victory in the Masters resembled "a highly public image of black retardation"? Today's black athletes are multimillion-dollar corporate pitchmen, with talk shows and sneaker deals and publicity machines and almost daily media opportunities to share their thoughts with the world, and it's very hard to see how all this contrives to make them look stupid. Hoberman spends a lot of time trying to inflate the significance of sports, arguing that how we talk about events on the baseball diamond or the track has grave consequences for how we talk about race in general. Here he is, for example, on Jackie Robinson:

> The sheer volume of sentimental and intellectual energy that has been invested in the mythic sage of Jackie Robinson has discouraged further thinking about what his career did and did not accomplish. . . . Black America has paid a high and largely unacknowledged price for the extraordinary prominence given the black athlete rather than other black men of action (such as military pilots and astronauts), who represent modern aptitudes in ways that athletes cannot.

Please. Black America has paid a high and largely unacknowledged price for a long list of things, and having great athletes is far from the top of the list. Sometimes a baseball player is just a baseball player, and sometimes an observation about racial difference is just an observation about racial difference. Few object when medical scientists talk about the significant epidemiological differences between blacks and whites—the fact that blacks have a higher incidence of hypertension than whites and twice as many black males die of diabetes and prostate cancer as white males, that breast tumors appear to grow faster in black women than in white women, that black girls show signs of puberty sooner than white girls. So why aren't we allowed to say that there might be athletically significant differences between blacks and whites?

According to the medical evidence, African Americans seem to have, on the average, greater bone mass than do white Americans—a difference that suggests greater muscle mass. Black men have slightly higher circulating levels of testosterone and human-growth hormone than their white counterparts, and blacks overall tend to have proportionally slimmer hips, wider shoulders, and longer legs. In one study, the Swedish physiologist Bengt Saltin compared a group of Kenyan distance runners with a group of Swedish distance runners and found interesting differences in muscle composition: Saltin reported that the Africans appeared to have more blood-carrying capillaries and more mitochondria (the body's cellular power plant) in the fibers of their quadriceps. Another study found that, while black South African distance runners ran at the same speed as white South African runners, they were able to use more oxygen—eighty-nine percent versus eighty-one percent—over extended periods: somehow, they were able to exert themselves more. Such evidence suggested that there were physical differences in black athletes which have a bearing on activities like running and jumping, which should hardly come as a surprise to anyone who follows competitive sports.

To use track as an example—since track is probably the purest measure of athletic ability—Africans recorded fifteen out of the twenty fastest times last year in the men's ten-thousand-meter event. In the five thousand meters, eighteen out of the twenty fastest times were recorded by Africans. In the fifteen hundred meters, thirteen out of the twenty fastest times were African, and in the sprints, in the men's hundred meters, you have to go all the way down to the twenty-third place in the world rankings—to Geir Moen, of Norway—before you find a white face. There is a point at which it becomes foolish to deny the fact of black athletic prowess, and even more foolish to banish speculation on the topic. Clearly, something is going on. The question is what.

2.

If we are to decide what to make of the differences between blacks and whites, we first have to decide what to make of the word "difference," which can mean any number of things. A useful case study is to compare the ability of men and women in math. If

you give a large, representative sample of male and female students a standardized math test, their mean scores will come out
pretty much the same. But if you look at the margins, at the very
best and the very worst students, sharp differences emerge. In
the math portion of an achievement test conducted by Project
Talent—a nationwide survey of fifteen-year-olds—there were 1.3
boys for every girl in the top ten percent, 1.5 boys for every girl in
the top five percent, and seven boys for every girl in the top one
percent. In the fifty-six-year history of the Putnam Mathematical
Competition, which has been described as the Olympics of college math, all but one of the winners have been male. Conversely,
if you look at people with the very lowest math ability, you'll find
more boys than girls there, too. In other words, although the
average math ability of boys and girls is the same, the distribution isn't: there are more males than females at the bottom of the
pile, more males than females at the top of the pile, and fewer
males than females in the middle. Statisticians refer to this as a
difference in variability.

   This pattern, as it turns out, is repeated in almost every conceivable area of gender difference. Boys are more variable than girls
on the College Board entrance exam and in routine elementary-
school spelling tests. Male mortality patterns are more variable
than female patterns; that is, many more men die in early and
middle age than women, who tend to die in more of a concen-
trated clump toward the end of life. The problem is that variability differences are regularly confused with average differences. If
men had higher average math scores than women, you could say
they were better at the subject. But because they are only more
variable, the word "better" seems inappropriate.

   The same holds true for differences between the races. A racist 10
stereotype is the assertion of average difference—it's the claim
that the typical white is superior to the typical black. It allows a
white man to assume that the black man he passes on the street
is stupider than he is. By contrast, if what racists believed was
that black intelligence was simply more variable than white intelligence, then it would be impossible for them to construct a stereotype about black intelligence at all. They wouldn't be able to
generalize. If they wanted to believe that there were a lot of blacks
dumber than whites, they would also have to believe that there
were a lot of blacks smarter than they were. This distinction is

critical to understanding the relation between race and athletic performance. What are we seeing when we remark black domination of elite sporting events—an average difference between the races or merely a difference in variability?

This question has been explored by geneticists and physical anthropologists, and some of the most notable work has been conducted over the past few years by Kenneth Kidd, at Yale. Kidd and his colleagues have been taking DNA samples from two African Pygmy tribes in Zaire and the Central African Republic and comparing them with DNA samples taken from populations all over the world. What they have been looking for is variants—subtle differences between the DNA of one person and another—and what they have found is fascinating. "I would say, without a doubt, that in almost any single African population—a tribe or however you want to define it—there is more genetic variation than in all the rest of the world put together," Kidd told me. In a sample of fifty Pygmies, for example, you might find nine variants in one stretch of DNA. In a sample of hundreds of people from around the rest of the world, you might find only a total of six variants in that same stretch of DNA—and probably every one of those six variants would also be found in the Pygmies. If everyone in the world was wiped out except Africans, in other words, almost all the human genetic diversity would be preserved.

The likelihood is that these results reflect Africa's status as the homeland of Homo sapiens: since every human population outside Africa is essentially a subset of the original African population, it makes sense that everyone in such a population would be a genetic subset of Africans, too. So you can expect groups of Africans to be more variable in respect to almost anything that has a genetic component. If, for example, your genes control how you react to aspirin, you'd expect to see more Africans than whites for whom one aspirin stops a bad headache, more for whom no amount of aspirin works, more who are allergic to aspirin, and more who need to take, say, four aspirin at a time to get any benefit—but far fewer Africans for whom the standard two-aspirin dose would work well. And to the extent that running is influenced by genetic factors you would expect to see more really fast blacks—and more really slow blacks—than whites but far fewer Africans of merely average speed. Blacks are like boys. Whites are like girls.

There is nothing particularly scary about this fact, and certainly nothing to warrant the kind of gag order on talk of racial differences which is now in place. What it means is that comparing elite athletes of different races tells you very little about the races themselves. A few years ago, for example, a prominent scientist argued for black athletic supremacy by pointing out that there had never been a white Michael Jordan. True. But, as the Yale anthropologist Jonathan Marks has noted, until recently there was no black Michael Jordan, either. Michael Jordan, like Tiger Woods or Wayne Gretzky or Cal Ripken, is one of the best players in his sport not because he's like the other members of his own ethnic group but precisely because he's not like them—or like anyone else, for that matter. Elite athletes are elite athletes because, in some sense, they are on the fringes of genetic variability. As it happens, African populations seem to create more of these genetic outliers than white populations do, and this is what underpins the claim that blacks are better athletes than whites. But that's all the claim amounts to. It doesn't say anything at all about the rest of us, of all races, muddling around in the genetic middle.

3.

There is a second consideration to keep in mind when we compare blacks and whites. Take the men's hundred-meter final at the Atlanta Olympics. Every runner in that race was of either Western African or Southern African descent, as you would expect if Africans had some genetic affinity for sprinting. But suppose we forget about skin color and look just at country of origin. The eight-man final was made up of two African-Americans, two Africans (one from Namibia and one from Nigeria), a Trinidadian, a Canadian of Jamaican descent, an Englishman of Jamaican descent, and a Jamaican. The race was won by the Jamaican-Canadian, in world-record time, with the Namibian coming in second and the Trinidadian third. The sprint relay—the 4 × 100—was won by a team from Canada, consisting of the Jamaican-Canadian from the final, a Haitian-Canadian, a Trinidadian-Canadian, and another Jamaican-Canadian. Now it appears that African heritage is important as an initial determinant of sprinting ability, but also that the most important advantage of all is some kind of cultural or environmental factor associated with the Caribbean.

Or consider, in a completely different realm, the problem of 15 hypertension. Black Americans have a higher incidence of hypertension than white Americans, even after you control for every conceivable variable, including income, diet, and weight, so it's tempting to conclude that there is something about being of African descent that makes blacks prone to hypertension. But it turns out that although some Caribbean countries have a problem with hypertension, others—Jamaica, St. Kitts, and the Bahamas—don't. It also turns out that people in Liberia and Nigeria—two countries where many New World slaves came from—have similar and perhaps even lower blood-pressure rates than white North Americans, while studies of Zulus, Indians, and whites in Durban, South Africa, showed that urban white males had the highest hypertension rates and urban white females had the lowest. So it's likely that the disease has nothing at all to do with Africanness.

The same is true for the distinctive muscle characteristic observed when Kenyans were compared with Swedes. Saltin, the Swedish physiologist, subsequently found many of the same characteristics in Nordic skiers who train at high altitudes and Nordic runners who train in very hilly regions—conditions, in other words, that resemble the mountainous regions of Kenya's Rift Valley, where so many of the country's distance runners come from. The key factor seems to be Kenya, not genes.

Lots of things that seem to be genetic in origin, then, actually aren't. Similarly, lots of things that we wouldn't normally think might affect athletic ability actually do. Once again, the social-science literature on male and female math achievement is instructive. Psychologists argue that when it comes to subjects like math, boys tend to engage in what's known as ability attribution. A boy who is doing well will attribute his success to the fact that he's good at math, and if he's doing badly he'll blame his teacher or his own lack of motivation—anything but his ability. That makes it easy for him to bounce back from failure or disappointment, and gives him a lot of confidence in the face of a tough new challenge. After all, if you think you do well in math because you're good at math, what's stopping you from being good at, say, algebra, or advanced calculus? On the other hand, if you ask a girl why she is doing well in math she will say, more often than not, that she succeeds because she works hard. If she's doing poorly, she'll say she isn't smart enough. This, as should be obvious, is a self-defeating attitude. Psychologists call it "learned helplessness"—the state in which failure is perceived as insurmountable. Girls who engage in effort attribution learn helplessness because in the face of a more difficult task like algebra or advanced calculus they can conceive of no solution. They're convinced that they can't work harder, because they think they're working as hard as they can, and that they can't rely on their intelligence, because they never thought they were that smart to begin with. In fact, one of the fascinating findings of attribution research is that the smarter girls are, the more likely they are to fall into this trap. High achievers are sometimes the most helpless. Here, surely, is part of the explanation for greater math variability among males. The female math whizzes, the ones who should be competing in the top one and two percent with their male counterparts, are the ones most often paralyzed by a lack of confidence in their own aptitude. They think they belong only in the intellectual middle.

The striking thing about these descriptions of male and female stereotyping in math, though, is how similar they are to black and white stereotyping in athletics—to the unwritten rules holding that blacks achieve through natural ability and whites through effort. Here's how *Sports Illustrated* described, in a recent article, the white basketball player Steve Kerr, who plays alongside Michael Jordan for the Chicago Bulls. According to the magazine, Kerr is a "hard-working overachiever," distinguished by his "work ethic and heady play" and by a shooting style "born of a million practice shots." Bear in mind that Kerr is one of the best shooters in basketball today, and a key player on what is arguably one of the finest basketball teams in history. Bear in mind, too, that there is no evidence that Kerr works any harder than his teammates, least of all Jordan himself, whose work habits are legendary. But you'd never guess that from the article. It concludes, "All over America, whenever quicker, stronger gym rats see Kerr in action, they must wonder, How can that guy be out there instead of me?"

There are real consequences to this stereotyping. As the psychologists Carol Dweck and Barbara Licht write of high-achieving schoolgirls, "[They] may view themselves as so motivated and well disciplined that they cannot entertain the possibility that they did poorly on an academic task because of insufficient effort. Since blaming the teacher would also be out of character, blaming their abilities when they confront difficulty may seem like the most reasonable option." If you substitute the words "white athletes" for "girls" and "coach" for "teacher," I think you have part of the reason that so many white athletes are underrepresented at the highest levels of professional sports. Whites have been saddled with the athletic equivalent of learned helplessness—the idea that it is all but fruitless to try and compete at the highest levels, because they have only effort on their side. The causes of athletic and gender discrimination may be diverse, but its effects are not. Once again, blacks are like boys, and whites are like girls.

4.

When I was in college, I once met an old acquaintance from my high-school running days. Both of us had long since quit track, and we talked about a recurrent fantasy we found we'd both had for getting back into shape. It was that we would go away somewhere remote for a year and do nothing but train, so that when the year was up we might finally know how good we were. Neither of us had any intention of doing this, though, which is why it was a fantasy. In adolescence, athletic excess has a certain appeal—during high school, I happily spent Sunday afternoons running up and down snow-covered sandhills—but with most of us that obsessiveness soon begins to fade. Athletic success depends on having the right genes and on a self-reinforcing belief in one's own ability. But it also depends on a rare form of tunnel vision. To be a great athlete, you have to care, and what was obvious to us both was that neither of us cared anymore. This is the last piece of the puzzle about what we mean when we say one group is better at something than another: sometimes different groups care about different things. Of the seven hundred men who play major-league baseball, for example, eighty-six come from either the Dominican Republic or Puerto Rico, even though those two islands have a combined population of only eleven million. But then baseball is something that Dominicans and Puerto

Ricans care about—and you can say the same thing about African-Americans and basketball, West Indians and sprinting, Canadians and hockey, and Russians and chess. Desire is the great intangible in performance, and unlike genes or psychological affect we can't measure it and trace its implications. This is the problem, in the end, with the question of whether blacks are better at sports than whites. It's not that **it's** offensive, or that it leads to discrimination. It's that, in some sense, it's not a terribly interesting question; "better" promises a tidier explanation than can ever be provided.

I quit competitive running when I was sixteen—just after the summer I had qualified for the Ontario track team in my age class. Late that August, we had travelled to St. John's, Newfoundland, for the Canadian championships. In those days, I was whippet-thin, as milers often are, five feet six and not more than a hundred pounds, and I could skim along the ground so lightly that I barely needed to catch my breath. I had two white friends on that team, both distance runners, too, and both, improbably, even smaller and lighter than I was. Every morning, the three of us would run through the streets of St. John's, charging up the hills and flying down the other side. One of these friends went on to have a distinguished college running career, the other became a world-class miler; that summer, I myself was the Canadian record holder in the fifteen hundred meters for my age class. We were almost terrifyingly competitive, without a shred of doubt in our ability, and as we raced along we never stopped talking and joking, just to prove how absurdly easy we found running to be. I thought of us all as equals. Then, on the last day of our stay in St. John's, we ran to the bottom of Signal Hill, which is the town's principal geographical landmark—an abrupt outcrop as steep as anything in San Francisco. We stopped at the base, and the two of them turned to me and announced that we were all going to run straight up Signal Hill backward. I don't know whether I had more running ability than those two or whether my Africanness gave me any genetic advantage over their whiteness. What I do know is that such questions were irrelevant, because, as I realized, they were willing to go to far greater lengths to develop their talent. They ran up the hill backward. I ran home.

For Discussion and Writing

1. **Comprehension** Gladwell writes that, as a younger runner, he always tracked the progress of an older "quarter-miler" who "moved through the sprinting ranks" (par. 2). Why did Gladwell keep an eye on this runner? How does this anecdote support his main point?

2. **Critical Reading** What point does Gladwell emphasize in his **conclusion**? How might it affect our interpretation of his essay as a whole?

3. **Analysis** For Gladwell, racial and genetic dispositions toward athletic talent are similar to racial dispositions toward diabetes and hypertension. Do you find this analogy persuasive? Why or why not?

4. **Connections** In this essay, Gladwell writes about race in terms of genetics and "innate" qualities. How is his approach different from the conception of race and racial identity in Hua Hsu's "The End of White America" (p. 96)?

5. **Writing** According to Gladwell, "there are real consequences to . . . stereotyping" (par. 19). He explores a variety of stereotypes, including perceptions based on gender. Have you ever been stereotyped, either positively or negatively? What was the basis for the stereotype? Did it have consequences for you? Write a narrative essay that answers these questions. Alternately, you could present your narrative as a blog post and place it in the context of a wider, online conversation.

DANAH BOYD

Impression Management in a Networked Setting

Writer danah boyd earned an undergraduate degree from Brown University, a master's degree from MIT, and a Ph.D. in information management and systems from the University of California, Berkeley. She is a principal researcher at Microsoft Research, a professor at New York University, and a fellow at Harvard University's Berkman Center for Internet and Society. boyd is the author of It's Complicated: The Social Lives of Networked Teens *(2014). Her work has appeared in many academic journals, as well as publications such as* Psychology Today, *the* Los Angeles Times, Wired, *and the* Guardian. *In this excerpt from her book, boyd writes about the difficulties of shaping and controlling one's identity online. As she writes, teenagers are "grappling with battles that adults face, but they are doing so while under constant surveillance and without a firm grasp of who they are."*

As you read, *reflect on the ways identity can be mediated by technology. What makes the presentation of personal identity difficult in a "networked setting"? How is identity contextual rather than innate? How do you manage these complex issues in your own life?*

In *The Presentation of Self in Everyday Life*, sociologist Erving Goffman describes the social rituals involved in self-presentation as "impression management." He argues that the impressions we make on others are a product of what is *given* and what is *given off*. In other words, what we convey to others is a matter of what we choose to share in order to make a good impression and also what we unintentionally reveal as a byproduct of who we are and how we react to others. The norms, cultural dynamics, and institutions where giving and giving off happen help define the broader context of how these performances are understood.

When interpreting others' self-presentations, we read the explicit content that is conveyed in light of the implicit information that is given off and the context in which everything takes place. The tension between the explicit and implicit signals allows us to obtain much richer information about individuals' attempts to shape how they're perceived. Of course, our reactions to their attempts to impress us enable them to adjust what they give in an attempt to convey what they think is best.

Based on their understanding of the social situation—including the context and the audience—people make decisions about what to share in order to act appropriately for the situation and to be perceived in the best light. When young people are trying to get a sense of the context in which they're operating, they're doing so in order to navigate the social situation in front of them. They may want to be seen as cool among their peers, even if adults would deem their behavior inappropriate. Teens may be trying to determine if someone they're attracted to is interested in them without embarrassing themselves. Or they may wish to be viewed as confident and happy, even when they're facing serious depression or anxiety. Whatever they're trying to convey, they must first get a grasp of the situation and the boundaries of the context. When contexts collapse or when information is taken out of context, teens can fail to make their intended impression.

Self-presentations are never constructed in a void. Goffman writes at length about the role individuals play in shaping their self-presentations, but he also highlights ways in which individuals are part of broader collectives that convey impressions about the whole group. In discussing the importance of "teams" for impression management, he points out that people work together to shape impressions, often relying on shared familiarity to help define any given situation in a mutually agreeable manner. He also argues that "any member of the team has the power to give the show away or to disrupt it by inappropriate conduct." When teens create profiles online, they're both individuals and part of a collective. Their self-representation is constructed through what they explicitly provide, through what their friends share, and as a product of how other people respond to them. When Alice's friend Bob comments on her profile, he's affecting her self-presentation. Even the photo that Bob chooses as his primary photo affects

Alice because it might be shown on Alice's profile when he leaves a comment. Impression management online and off is not just an individual act; it's a social process.

Part of what makes impression management in a networked setting so tricky is that the contexts in which teens are operating are also networked. Contexts don't just collapse accidentally; they collapse because individuals have a different sense of where the boundaries exist and how their decisions affect others. In North Carolina, I briefly chatted with a black high school senior who was gunning for a soccer scholarship at a Division One school. When recruiters and coaches from different schools asked to be his friend on Facebook, he immediately said yes. He had always treated Facebook like a résumé, using the site to position himself as a thoughtful, compassionate, all-American young man. But he was often concerned about what his friends posted on Facebook, and for good reason.

A few days later, I was talking casually with Matthew, one of   5
the soccer player's classmates with whom he was friends on Facebook. Unlike the all-American athlete persona his classmate had crafted, Matthew's profile was filled with crass comments and humor that could easily be misinterpreted. I asked Matthew, a white seventeen-year-old, about his decision to post these items on his profile with a particular eye to how they might get misinterpreted if read by a stranger. Matthew told me that he wasn't friends with anyone who didn't know him and wouldn't understand that he was joking around. I pointed out that his privacy settings meant that his profile could be viewed by friends-of-friends. When he didn't get my point, I showed him that his classmate had chosen to connect with many coaches and other representatives from schools to which he had applied for admission. Matthew's stunned response was simple: "But why would he do that?" Matthew and his classmate had very different ideas of how to use Facebook and who their imagined audiences might be, but their online presence was interconnected because of the technical affordances of Facebook. They were each affecting the other's attempts at self-presentation, and their sharing and friending norms created unexpected conflicts.

Even when teens have a coherent sense of what they deem to be appropriate in a particular setting, their friends and peers do not necessarily share their sense of decorum and norms. Resolving the networked nature of social contexts is complicated. The "solution" that is most frequently offered is that people should not try to engage in context-dependent impression management. Indeed, Mark Zuckerberg, the founder of Facebook, is quoted as having said, "Having two identities for yourself is an example of a lack of integrity." Teens who try to manage context collapses by segregating information often suffer when that information crosses boundaries. This is particularly true when teens are forced to contend with radically different social contexts that are not mutually resolvable. What makes this especially tricky for teens is that people who hold power over them often believe that they have the right to look, judge, and share, even when their interpretations may be constructed wholly out of context.

In 2010, the American Civil Liberties Union received a complaint from a student at a small, rural high school that sheds light on this issue. At a school assembly, in order to set an example, a campus police officer had shown a photo of one of the students holding a beer. The picture was not on that girl's Facebook profile; it was posted by a friend of hers and tagged. The purpose of the assembly was to teach teenagers about privacy, but the students were outraged. Because of the police officer's attempt to shame students into behaving by adult standards, the student exposed with a beer feared that she would not receive a local scholarship or might face other serious consequences. To complicate matters, she had not chosen to present herself in that light; her friend had done this for her. In choosing to upload and tag this photo, her friend undermined the self-image that the girl wished to present. Some may argue that this girl was at fault for being at a party holding a beer in the first place. She may indeed have been drinking the beer—72 percent of students in high school report having had alcohol at least once—but she may also just have been holding the beer for a friend or simply trying to fit in by appearing to drink. This girl certainly did not think that her decision to attend that party would result in such public shaming, nor is it clear that the punishment fit the crime. In situations like this, teens are blamed for not thinking while adults assert the right to define the context in which young people interact. They take content out of context to interpret it through the lens of adults' values and feel as though they have the right to shame youth because that content was available in the first place. In doing so, they ignore teens' privacy while undermining their struggles to manage their identity.

One might reasonably argue that the girl holding the beer was lucky not to have been arrested, since alcohol consumption by minors is illegal. Yet it is important to note that the same shaming tactics that adults use to pressure teens to conform to adult standards are also used by both teens and adults to ostracize and punish youth whose identities, values, or experiences are not widely accepted. I met plenty of teens who wanted to keep secrets from their parents or teachers, but the teens who struggled the most with the challenges of collapsed contexts were those who were trying to make sense of their sexual identity or who otherwise saw themselves as outcasts in their community. Some, like Hunter—a boy from DC who was trying to navigate his "ghetto" family alongside his educationally minded friends—were simply frustrated and annoyed. Others, like teen girls who are the subject of "slut shaming," were significantly embarrassed and emotionally distraught after photos taken in the context of an intimate relationship were widely shared to shame them by using their sexuality as a weapon. Still others, like the lesbian, gay, bisexual, and transgender (LGBT) teens I met from religious and conservative backgrounds, were outright scared of what would happen if the contexts in which they were trying to operate collapsed.

In Iowa, I ended up casually chatting with a teen girl who was working through her sexuality. She had found a community of other queer girls in a chatroom, and even though she believed that some of them weren't who they said they were, she found their anonymous advice to be helpful. They gave her pointers to useful websites about coming out, offered stories from their own experiences, and gave her the number of an LGBT-oriented hotline if she ran into any difficulty coming out to her conservative parents. Although she relished the support and validation these strangers gave her she wasn't ready to come out yet, and she was petrified that her parents might come across her online chats. She was also concerned that some of her friends from school might find out and tell her parents. She had learned that her computer recorded her browser history in middle school when her parents had used her digital traces to punish her for visiting inappropriate sites. Thus, she carefully erased her history after each visit to the chatroom. She didn't understand how Facebook seemed to follow her around the web, but she was afraid that somehow the company would find out and post the sites she visited to her Facebook page. In an attempt to deal with this, she used Internet

Explorer to visit the chatroom or anything that was LGBT-related while turning to the Chrome browser for maintaining her straight, school-friendly persona. But still, she was afraid that she'd mess up and collapse her different social contexts, accidentally coming out before she was ready. She wanted to maintain discrete contexts but found it extraordinarily difficult to do so. This tension comes up over and over again, particularly with youth who are struggling to make sense of who they are and how they fit into the broader world.

As teens struggle to make sense of different social contexts and present themselves appropriately, one thing becomes clear: the internet has not evolved into an idyllic zone in which people are free from the limitations of the embodied world. Teens are struggling to make sense of who they are and how they fit into society in an environment in which contexts are networked and collapsed, audiences are invisible, and anything they say or do can easily be taken out of context. They are grappling with battles that adults face, but they are doing so while under constant surveillance and without a firm grasp of who they are. In short, they're navigating one heck of a cultural labyrinth.

For Discussion and Writing

1. **Comprehension** According to boyd, what teens "struggled the most with the challenges of collapsed contexts" (par. 8)?

2. **Critical Reading** Who is boyd's primary **audience**? What clues in the text indicate boyd's sense of her readers?

3. **Analysis** In this excerpt, boyd writes about a high school soccer player "gunning for a scholarship" and one of the soccer player's classmates (pars. 4–5). How does this narrative account support her overall argument? Do you find the example effective and persuasive?

4. **Connections** Boyd begins by explaining the theory of sociologist Erving Goffman. How might you apply this intellectual framework to Liz Armstrong's "An Argument for Being a Poser" (p. 85)? For example, how do Armstrong's ideas about identity correlate to Goffman's (and boyd's) ideas about impression management, social contexts, and identity as a function of "teams"?

5. **Writing** What principles, if any, guide your online behavior and engage in "impression management"? Write a response to boyd's text that draws on your own experiences, observations, and perspectives. You may also respond online (on a class discussion board, a blog, a social media site) and solicit the responses of others.

ARIEL LEVY

Women and the Rise of Raunch Culture

A staff writer for the New Yorker *magazine since 2008, Ariel Levy (b. 1974) is perhaps best known for her book* Female Chauvinist Pigs: Women and the Rise of Raunch Culture *(2005). She has also written for the* Washington Post, Vogue, Slate, *and other publications. In this excerpt from* Female Chauvinist Pigs, *Levy considers the way "post-feminist" women participate in a "tawdry, tarty, cartoonlike version of female sexuality." But as she notes, "'Raunchy' and 'liberated' are not synonymous."*

As you read, *consider the following questions: What is Levy's thesis? How does she use examples to support her main point? Can her examples and evidence be interpreted in an alternative way—one that supports a different thesis than Levy proposes in this selection?*

I first noticed it several years ago. I would turn on the television and find strippers in pasties explaining how best to lap dance a man to orgasm. I would flip the channel and see babes in tight, tiny uniforms bouncing up and down on trampolines. Britney Spears was becoming increasingly popular and increasingly unclothed, and her undulating body ultimately became so familiar to me I felt like we used to go out.

Charlie's Angels, the film remake of the quintessential jiggle show, opened at number one in 2000 and made $125 million in theaters nationally, reinvigorating the interest of men and women alike in leggy crime fighting. Its stars, who kept talking about "strong women" and "empowerment," were dressed in alternating soft-porn styles—as massage parlor geishas, dominatrixes, yodeling Heidis in alpine bustiers. (The summer sequel in 2003—in which the Angels' perilous mission required them to perform stripteases—pulled in another $100 million domestically.) In my own industry, magazines, a porny new genre called the Lad Mag, which included titles like *Maxim*, *FHM*, and *Stuff*, was hitting the stands and becoming a huge success by delivering what *Playboy* had only occasionally managed to capture: greased celebrities in little scraps of fabric humping the floor.

This didn't end when I switched off the radio or the television or closed the magazines. I'd walk down the street and see teens and young women—and the occasional wild fifty-year-old—wearing jeans cut so low they exposed what came to be known as butt cleavage paired with miniature tops that showed off breast implants and pierced navels alike. Sometimes, in case the overall message of the outfit was too subtle, the shirts would be emblazoned with the *Playboy* bunny or say PORN STAR across the chest.

Some odd things were happening in my social life, too. People I knew (female people) liked going to strip clubs (female strippers). It was sexy and fun, they explained; it was liberating and rebellious. My best friend from college, who used to go to Take Back the Night marches on campus, had become captivated by porn stars. She would point them out to me in music videos and watch their (topless) interviews on *Howard Stern*. As for me, I wasn't going to strip clubs or buying *Hustler* T-shirts, but I was starting to show signs of impact all the same. It had only been a few years since I'd graduated from Wesleyan University, a place where you could pretty much get expelled for saying "girl" instead of "woman," but somewhere along the line I'd started saying "chick." And, like most chicks I knew, I'd taken to wearing thongs.

What was going on? My mother, a shiatsu masseuse who 5 attended weekly women's consciousness-raising groups for twenty-four years, didn't own makeup. My father, whom she met as a student radical at the University of Wisconsin, Madison, in the sixties was a consultant for Planned Parenthood, NARAL, and NOW. Only thirty years (my lifetime) ago, our mothers were "burning their bras" and picketing *Playboy*, and suddenly we were getting implants and wearing the bunny logo as supposed symbols of our liberation. How had the culture shifted so drastically in such a short period of time?

What was almost more surprising than the change itself were the responses I got when I started interviewing the men and—often—women who edit magazines like *Maxim* and make programs like *The Man Show* and *Girls Gone Wild*. This new raunch culture

Clothing on display at Urban Outfitters. Is this feminism, "raunch culture," or both?

didn't mark the death of feminism, they told me; it was evidence that the feminist project had already been achieved. We'd *earned* the right to look at *Playboy;* we were *empowered* enough to get Brazilian bikini waxes. Women had come so far, I learned, we no longer needed to worry about objectification or misogyny. Instead, it was time for us to join the frat party of pop culture, where men had been enjoying themselves all along. If Male Chauvinist Pigs were men who regarded women as pieces of meat, we would outdo them and be Female Chauvinist Pigs: women who make sex objects of other women and of ourselves.

When I asked female viewers and readers what they got out of raunch culture, I heard similar things about empowering mini-skirts and feminist strippers, and so on, but I also heard something else. They wanted to be "one of the guys"; they hoped to be experienced "like a man." Going to strip clubs or talking about porn stars was a way of showing themselves and the men around them that they weren't "prissy little women" or "girly-girls." Besides, they told me, it was all in fun, all tongue-in-cheek, and for me to regard this bacchanal as problematic would be old-school and uncool.

I tried to get with the program, but I could never make the argument add up in my head. How is resurrecting every stereotype of female sexuality that feminism endeavored to banish *good* for women? Why is laboring to look like Pamela Anderson empowering? And how is imitating a stripper or a porn star—a woman whose *job* is to imitate arousal in the first place—going to render us sexually liberated?

Despite the rising power of Evangelical Christianity and the political right in the United States, this trend has only grown more extreme and more pervasive in the years that have passed since I first became aware of it. A tawdry, tarty, cartoonlike version of female sexuality has become so ubiquitous, it no longer seems particular. What we once regarded as a *kind* of sexual expression we now view *as* sexuality. As former adult film star Traci Lords put it to a reporter a few days before her memoir hit the bestseller list in 2003, "When I was in porn, it was like a back-alley thing. Now it's everywhere." Spectacles of naked ladies have moved from seedy side streets to center stage, where everyone— men and women—can watch them in broad daylight. *Playboy* and its ilk are being "embraced by young women in a curious way in a postfeminist world," to borrow the words of Hugh Hefner.

But just because we are post doesn't automatically mean we are 10 feminists. There is a widespread assumption that simply because my generation of women has the good fortune to live in a world touched by the feminist movement, that means everything we do is magically imbued with its agenda. It doesn't work that way. "Raunchy" and "liberated" are not synonyms. It is worth asking ourselves if this bawdy world of boobs and gams we have resurrected reflects how far we've come, or how far we have left to go.

For Discussion and Writing

1. **Comprehension** What is Levy's definition of a "female chauvinist pig" (par. 6)?

2. **Critical Reading** Levy uses anecdotal **evidence** and personal observations in the essay, including some "odd things" that were happening in her social life (par. 4). What odd things did she notice? How are these instances related to her **thesis**?

3. *Analysis*   In writing about a shift in popular culture and attitudes about women, Levy writes: "What we once regarded as a *kind* of sexual expression we now view *as* sexuality" (par. 9). What does she mean by this? Why is this distinction important for her argument?

4. *Connections*   In "Pop Culture's Transgender Moment" (p. 133), Sonali Kohli writes about a new openness to the stories of complex, transgender characters. As *Transparent* associate producer Rhys Ernst says, "It's become normal to see lesbian and gay characters on TV, so this is the next step" (par. 9). How is this apparent trend toward openness and tolerance related to the "raunch culture" phenomenon described by Levy? Are they both part of the same "moment"? Why or why not?

5. *Writing*   Levy interviews women who claim that the "new raunch culture" was evidence that the "feminist project had already been achieved" (par. 6). Levy disagrees. What is your position on this issue? Can raunchiness be "empowering" (par. 7)? Levy asserts that "'raunchy' and 'liberated' are not synonyms" (par. 10). Are the two terms mutually exclusive? Write an argumentative response to "Women and the Rise of Raunch Culture" that addresses these questions, and support your claims with specific examples from pop culture.

SONALI KOHLI

Pop Culture's Transgender Moment: Why Online TV Is Leading the Way

Often focused on education and diversity issues, Sonali Kohli is an Atlantic Media Fellow and reporter for Quartz, *a Web-based business publication created by the Atlantic Media Company. Kohli has also been a reporter for the* Los Angeles Times, *and she is a graduate of UCLA. In this article from the* Atlantic, *Kohli discusses an "increase in awareness of transgender issues" unfolding online, particularly on Netflix's series* Orange Is the New Black *and Amazon's* Transparent.

As you read, consider Kohli's argument and her evidence: Do you find it convincing? Why are popular culture representations of marginalized individuals and communities important? Why do you think these shows are being shown online rather than on, say, network television?

Amazon's new show *Transparent* stars Jeffrey Tambor as a transgender woman who is transitioning late in life. The show follows Netflix's *Orange Is the New Black,* which features Laverne Cox as a transgender prisoner—the first truly multidimensional transgender character on American television.

Transgender portrayals on TV, when they show up at all, tend to render the characters as victims or villains. Or they are portrayed as sex workers: GLAAD found that from 2002 to 2012, one in five transgender TV characters was a sex worker. More nuanced stories of gender transition by adults, especially when that adult is one of the show's stars, haven't been told.

So Netflix was breaking ground with Cox's Sophia, a prisoner with a wife and son. She was arrested for financial fraud. Her character, and now Tambor's in *Transparent*, are adults with full backstories. Cox earned an Emmy nomination for her portrayal, making her the first openly transgender actress in the category, and both *Orange* and *Transparent* have received critical approval for their treatment of transgender characters. Why are Amazon and Netflix, both new online studios, the only ones producing these stories?

Amazon and Netflix are young, and that's an advantage. "They have no historical boundaries in which to butt their heads against," British comedian Claire Parker tells *Quartz*. Parker was the project manager of the Trans Comedy Award, which has yielded a romantic comedy series for BBC Two,[1] *Boy Meets Girl*, that will start filming next year and features a transgender woman as one of the main characters. Parker says working on the project was difficult at times because the network continuously told them to keep their expectations low, and at each level of bureaucracy, there's less of an emphasis on the reason for the show, which is to represent a story about a transgender character in a full and responsible way.

Transparent creator Jill Soloway says she was able to stay true   5
to the characters and to a strong transgender portrayal because Amazon didn't strictly oversee the project. Rhys Ernst, an associate producer and transgender man who worked as a consultant on the show, says he was able to make adjustments without executive interference. "On a bigger studio production there would have been a lot more executives around the monitor," he says.

The increase in awareness of transgender issues and the move for increased rights has largely taken place online, among young people who see that the transgender community is far behind the lesbian and gay communities in terms of rights, says Matt Kane, GLAAD director of entertainment media. Amazon and Netflix are building a loyal audience of young, web-savvy people by investing in shows that address what they want to see in TV. The shows "reflect a very modern awareness of identity in our culture, and . . . the challenges of it, but also the unexpected emotion and humor that can come out of it," Kane says.

Successful portrayals of transgender characters include storylines beyond the fact that they are transgender. *Transparent* focuses not just on Maura (Tambor's character) but on her family, which includes three selfish children who have their own internal struggles with gender and sexual identity. Laverne Cox's role in

---

[1]*BBC Two:* a television channel operated by the British Broadcasting Corporation that trends toward prestige television programming. [Editor's note.]

Laverne Cox as Sophia Burset in *Orange Is the New Black*: "Successful portrayals of transgender characters include storylines beyond the fact that they are transgender."

Orange is similar in its depth: She is an adult with a wife and child from when she was biologically male, and her personal storyline centers around those relationships, rather than the fact or science of being transgender. *Orange* is at its very base a show about women in a prison, and one of them happens to be transgender. *Transparent* is a show about a family reacting to change.

It's important to note that there have been occasionally awareness-raising or complex portrayals of teen transgender and gender identity stories—*Glee* and *House of Lies* come to mind. What sets *Orange* and *Transparent* apart from those is that they address a population of transgender people that's sizable and absent from the media—those who transition later in life.

Transgender stories are also being told in these online spaces for the most obvious reason: They haven't yet been told on TV. Amazon and Netflix need to set themselves apart from traditional media and prove their worth as original content providers, and the way to do this is through framings that are new. Transgender characters, outside of the tropes described above, are close to invisible in TV and movies. It's become normal to see lesbian and gay characters on TV, so this is the next step, Ernst says.

Because the new online studios have less bureaucracy and can 10
turn shows around quickly, they can stay with the pulse of the
trans movement. "Trans people are becoming galvanized and out-
spoken," Ernst says. "And not accepting disparaging or unfair
portrayals anymore."

For Discussion and Writing

1. **Comprehension**   According to Kohli, what is the "most obvious
   reason" (par. 9) that these transgender stories are being told online?

2. **Critical Reading**   In its discussion of *Transparent* and *Orange Is the
   New Black*, as well as its interviews with other sources, Kohli's article
   suggests that these shows are part of a larger, broader trend or
   cultural shift. Do you find her **thesis** persuasive? Why or why not?
   Does she provide enough **evidence**?

3. **Analysis**   Kohli acknowledges that television shows have provided
   representations of transgender individuals in the past. But she
   argues that the characters on *Transparent* and *Orange Is the New
   Black* are new and distinctive. How do you understand this difference? What makes for a "realistic" or authentic character or even
   "good" dramatic television writing? Do you agree with her standards? Why or why not?

4. **Connections**   Both Kohli and Ariel Levy ("Women and the Rise of
   Raunch Culture," p. 128) discuss the power, influence, and importance of media images and representations on our ideas of gender
   and sexuality. How can such images affect society in a positive way?
   In what ways can they have a negative effect?

5. **Writing**   How do you see the relationship between fictional, popular culture representations of groups and real-world rights? For
   example, do you think there are causal connections between images
   of gay individuals or the gay community on television shows and
   the social acceptance—or rejection—of gay people? Write an essay
   that analyzes—examines, breaks down, explores—the relationship
   between media representations of a particular group and its real-
   world implications or consequences.

CHAPTER 3

Technology
How do new devices and apps transform experience?

In "The Judgment of Thamus" (included in this section), media critic Neil Postman provides a pointed and sobering appraisal of technological advancement. He argues that every technology is "both a burden and a blessing; not either-or, but this-and-that." For Postman, such innovations are never merely additions or points along a linear course of "progress." Instead, technologies such as the book, the steam engine, and the computer are transformative. They redefine "'freedom,' 'truth,' 'intelligence,' 'fact,' 'wisdom,' 'memory,' 'history'—all the words we live by."

Americans tend to be optimistic about technology and progress: We are more likely to quote the oracular pronouncements of Facebook's Mark Zuckerberg than remember the cautionary words of a critic like Postman. That idealism shapes contemporary life in innumerable ways, from the convenience of our consumer products and the limitless information of our Internet search engines, to our relationships with friends, money, education, jobs, and culture. Increasingly our lives are mediated through technology. Even America's sense of national identity is shaped by technological achievement—and a perpetual anxiety that the rest of the world is catching up. In his 2011 State of the Union address, President Barack Obama said, "In a single generation, revolutions in technology have transformed the way we live, work, and do business. . . . Meanwhile, nations like China and India realized that with some changes of their own, they could compete in this new world."

In "Wall of Sound: The iPod Has Changed the Way We Listen to Music," Nikil Saval draws on the history of listening and the work of theorist Theodor Adorno to illuminate the meaning of music in a "Shuffled world." Postman's "The Judgment of Thamus" encourages us to view that "new world" with open eyes: Technological innovations giveth, but they also taketh away. In contrast, Clay Shirky's "Gin, Television, and Social Surplus" provides a (mostly) optimistic view of a society stumbling through the process of technological transformation. All the essays here wrestle with these trade-offs, as well as other questions: What does technology mean? *How* does it mean? In what ways does it alter human psychology, relationships, privacy, culture, and entertainment? For example, Jennifer Bleyer's "Love the One You're Near" surveys a range of mobile dating and "hookup" apps and wonders "whether long-term partners can be found by flicking through a river of pictures on a smartphone."

The paired readings address how technology complicates distinctions between the public and the private, the virtual and the "real." In "You Are What You Click," David Auerbach looks at the ways in which companies like Google and Facebook profile consumers and "define down" our notions of "privacy" and "anonymity." Nathan Jurgenson ("The IRL Fetish") argues against the conventional wisdom that technology is undermining our sense of what happens "in real life" (IRL); in his view, our hyperconnected and digitized lives only heighten our appreciation for the "offline" and the "physical." In the process, he argues against "digital dualism": the idea that there is a hard distinction between online life and IRL.

As you read, try to identify and consider the apparent paradoxes of technology:

- How does technology offer opportunities for connection, even as it may lead to disconnection?
- In what ways do technologies bring us closer to—or enhance—reality, even as they seduce us with the appeal of the virtual or unreal?
- Are the challenges we face in understanding new technology today different from the ones we faced in the past? Or are they the same timeless questions and opportunities that technological progress has always raised?

NIKIL SAVAL

Wall of Sound:
The iPod Has Changed the
Way We Listen to Music

Nikil Saval (b. 1982) is an editor at the literary magazine n+1. *His writing has appeared in the* London Review of Books, *the* New York Times, *the* New Statesman, *and other publications. He is the author of* Cubed: A Secret History of the Workplace *(2014). In this essay, which was adapted from a longer* n+1 *article and published in* Slate, *Saval considers how the iPod changed the way we listen to—and consume—music. He draws on the history of Western music, from Beethoven, jazz, and Jimi Hendrix to countless subgenres of hip-hop and heavy metal. He also frames his argument using the opposing theories of German-born philosopher Theodor Adorno (1903–1969) and the French sociologist Pierre Bourdieu (1930–2002). In the process, Saval highlights the various ways that we use music, whether we are hearing it in the background of our shopping or relying on it to help us "swallow an unpalatable life."*

As you read, *notice how Saval uses a theoretical framework to ground his argument. Do you find this approach accessible and effective? Think about the ways you listen to music and your reasons for doing so. Do you agree with Saval that we live in a dystopian "counterfeit heaven where music plays all the time"?*

At the nadir of the financial crisis, the urban sociologist Sudhir Venkatesh wondered aloud in the *New York Times* why no mass protests had arisen against what was clearly a criminal coup by the banks. Where were the pitchforks, the tar, the feathers? Where, more importantly, were the crowds? Venkatesh's answer was the iPod: "In public spaces, serendipitous interaction is needed to create the 'mob mentality.' Most iPod-like devices separate citizens from one another; you can't join someone in a movement if you can't hear the participants. Congrats Mr. Jobs for impeding social change." Venkatesh's suggestion was glib, tossed off—yet it was also a rare reminder, from the quasi-left, of how urban life has been changed by recording technologies.

The concern that recorded music promotes solipsism and isolation isn't new. Before the invention of the record and the gramophone (1887), the only form of listening people knew was social; the closest thing to a private musical experience was playing an instrument for yourself, or silently looking over a score. More often, if you had the means, you got to sit in the panopticon of the concert hall, seeing and being seen to the accompaniment of Verdi—an experience most fully described by Edith Wharton in the opening scene of *The Age of Innocence* (1920), just as it was going out of style. With mechanical reproduction came the hitherto unimaginable phenomenon of listening to multi-instrumental music by *yourself*. How, a contributor to *Gramophone* magazine asked in 1923, would you react if you stumbled upon somebody in the midst of this private rapture? It would be "as if you had discovered your friend sniffing cocaine, emptying a bottle of whisky, or plaiting straws in his hair. People, we think, should not do things 'to themselves,' however much they may enjoy doing them in company."

But it wasn't only solitary hyper-listening that recording facilitated. By 1960, recorded popular music had begun, in mysterious ways, to promote new social movements. Former Black Panther[1] Bobby Seale recounts in his memoir how Huey Newton developed an elaborate reading of Dylan's "Ballad of a Thin Man" as an allegory of race: "This song Bobby Dylan was singing became a very big part of that whole publishing operation of the Black Panther paper. And in the background, while we were putting this paper out, this record came up and I guess a number of papers were published, and many times we would play that record." The song wasn't overtly political but its mood of stately menace seems to have insinuated itself into the politics of the Panthers.

The '60s were a decade of both mass protests and mass concerts, and this was more than a coincidence. Barbara Ehrenreich

---

[1]*Black Panthers:* a revolutionary leftist and black nationalist organization founded in the 1960s. [Editor's note.]

has suggested that the roots of second-wave feminism could be found in the tens of thousands of shrieking girls who filled arenas and ballparks at the Beatles' American stops, from the Hollywood Bowl to Shea. These girls, unladylike, insistent, were going to scream for what they wanted. Social change drove musical experimentation, and—more remarkably—vice versa.

The music of this era was—it's worth repeating—an incitement to social change. It was the sound of not going reflexively to war, of mingling across class and racial lines, of thinking it might be all right to sleep around a little, of wanting to work a job that didn't suck.

Of course the radical hopes of the '60s collapsed. The highest-rated YouTube comment on a video of Joan Baez singing "We Shall Overcome" manages to be both smug and glum: "Though we obviously failed, I am so glad that I am of a generation that believed we could make a difference." By the early '70s, popular music had more or less forfeited its capacity to promote social movements. From then on its different varieties would be associated with defining lifestyle niches, consumer habits, and subcultural affiliations. In this way the make-it-new modernist imperative, which seized pop music several decades late, came to seem little different from the program of advertisers launching fresh product lines. Jadedness swept pop music enthusiasts, many of whom, heartbroken by their brief glimpse of collective life, would discount the whole era of the '60s as history's cunning preparation for a descent into hellish consumerism. Welcome to dystopia, a counterfeit heaven where music plays all the time.

The first to ring the alarm about the omnipresence of recorded music were classical music snobs who, as part of their contracted duties as university professors, had to spend time on college campuses. "This is being written in a study in a college of one of the great American universities," wrote George Steiner[2] in 1974. "The walls are throbbing gently to the beat of music coming from one near and several more distant amplifiers. The walls quiver to the ear or to the touch roughly eighteen hours per day, sometimes twenty-four." Allan Bloom[3] picked up the beat in *The Closing of*

---

[2]*George Steiner* (b. 1929): French-born literary critic, philosopher, and novelist. [Editor's note.]

[3]*Allan Bloom* (1930–1992): American philosopher and classicist. [Editor's note.]

the American Mind (1987): "Though students do not have books, they most emphatically do have music. . . . Nothing is more singular about this generation than its addiction to music." Steiner: "It matters little whether it is that of pop, folk, or rock. What counts is the all-pervasive pulsation, morning to night and into the night, made indiscriminate by the cool burn of electronic timbre." The only historical analogy Bloom could think of was to the Wagner cult of the late 19th century. Yet even world-conquering Wagner appealed to a limited class, who could only hear his works in opera houses. By contrast the music of the late-20th-century world was truly ubiquitous. Steiner: "When a young man walks down a street in Vladivostok or Cincinnati with his transistor blaring, when a car passes with its radio on at full blast, the resulting sound-capsule encloses the individual." Bloom: "There is the stereo in the home, in the car; there are concerts; there are music videos, with special channels devoted to them, on the air, nonstop; there are the Walkmans so that no place—not public transportation, not the library—prevents students from communing with the Muse, even while studying." Steiner: "What tissues of sensibility are being numbed or exacerbated?"

Yadda, yadda. Yet Bloom and Steiner were right! In fact they had no idea how right they would become. If the spread of home stereo equipment in the 1970s, followed by that of portable devices (the boom box, the Walkman, briefly the Discman), brought music to the masses in a new way, digitization and the iPod have made recorded music even more plentiful and ubiquitous. The fears in Bloom's time that cassette tapes would bring down the music industry are quaint now, in the face of trillions of bytes of music traded brazenly over the Internet every minute. So, too, does the disc mania of record collectors pale in the face of digital collections measured in weeks of music. A DJ's crate of 100 LPs amounts to about three days of straight listening; your standard 60-gigabyte iPod, 50 days. Has anyone these days listened to all of their music, even once through?

Nobody knows how much music we listen to, since so often we're not even listening. The American Time Use Survey, performed every year by the Bureau of Labor Statistics, throws up its hands. Does music playing in the background at a café count? Music in a film? Music played to drown out other music? Music played while reading, writing, cleaning, exercising, eating, sleeping—all

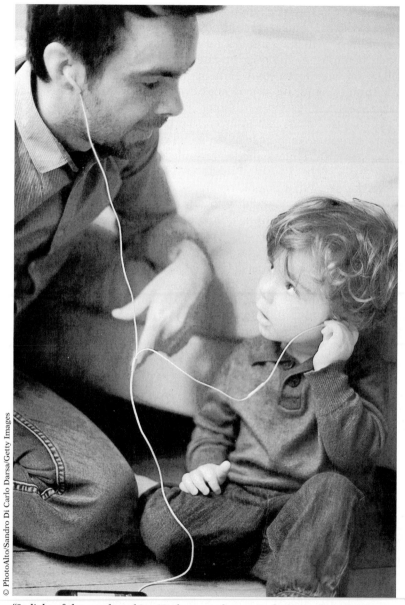

"In light of the epoch-making iPod, we need a way to find out what all this music listening is doing to us, or what we're doing with it." Do portable music devices encourage human connection—or isolation and solipsism?

of this has to count in some way. Stumbling into a college dorm now to ask the kids to turn it down, Steiner would find them all earmuffed with headphones as they stare at their computers, each listening to his own private playlist while something else plays on the stereo loud enough for a communal spirit to be maintained. And this is true not only of colleges but the world at large.

If it's easier than ever to listen to other people's music, it's also more tempting than ever to do so all alone. Walkman listening never lost the stigma of the juvenile; the sophistication—and expense—of the iPod have made adulthood safe for solipsism as never before. What does it mean for us, on the listening end, as we pad around the world with our iPods, trying to keep those shitty white earbuds from falling out of our ears? Public music criticism—a wasteland—isn't much help. It mainly focuses on individual works or single performances, when it isn't giving us drooling profiles of artists. This has nothing to do with our current mode of listening, which only rarely obsesses on particular works or genres, let alone worships particular figures. In light of the epoch-making iPod, we need a way to find out what all this music listening is doing to us, or what we're doing with it.

In the 20th century, the two most considered attempts to connect music and society were those of the philosopher Theodor Adorno and the sociologist Pierre Bourdieu.

Among the main philosophers of Western music—Schopenhauer, Nietzsche, Kierkegaard—Adorno knew the most about music and worked hardest to figure out its relationship to history. For Adorno, it wasn't just that historical forces circumscribed the production and reception of musical works; it was that historical conflicts appeared in music in mediated form. Thus a seemingly autonomous, nonrepresentational, and nonlinguistic art transfigured the world and returned it to the listener in a way that oriented him ideologically. The huge melodic conflicts animating Beethoven's symphonies and the brassy, thumping triumphs with which they concluded announced the era of bourgeois ascendancy after the French Revolution. The "emancipation of dissonance" in the atonal works of Schoenberg suggested a crisis of the bourgeoisie in which the self-evidence of tonality, like that of human progress, began to crack up.

Infamously, when society began to produce new forms of music that accompanied unrest by workers and students, the old Marxist turned a deaf ear. His essays on jazz and pop music are notorious classics of "bad" Adorno. The syncopations of bebop were only a mirage of liberty, and the relentless repetitiveness of rock and roll a virtual embodiment of a reified, historyless, mythological consciousness. The problem here was not exactly snobbism or even unconscious racism. It's that Adorno seemed only to understand and accept a model of listening in which music solicits and rewards the listener's whole attention. This is a musical sociology of the concert hall and the study, not the street, store, workplace, block party, or demonstration. From its standpoint, contemporary music of less-than-Schoenbergian melodic complexity can only seem simple, in the sense of dumb.

Bourdieu was a kind of anti-Adorno, his sociology a negation of the traditional aesthetics Adorno had mastered. Bourdieu practiced a deliberate and heroic philistinism. He seemed to know virtually nothing about music; it's not even clear he liked it. "Music is the 'pure' art par excellence," he wrote in *Distinction*. "It says nothing and it has *nothing to say*." Adorno would have recognized this ostensibly timeless aperçu as a historically specific statement, the product of a whole century (the 19th) of debate over precisely this question: What and how does music communicate? Yet out of this falsehood Bourdieu came to a startling conclusion, the truth of which we've all had to concede: "Nothing more clearly affirms one's 'class,' nothing more infallibly classifies, than tastes in music." In the mid-1960s, he conducted a giant survey of French musical tastes, and what do you know? The haute bourgeoisie loved *The Well-Tempered Clavier*; the upwardly mobile got high on "jazzy" classics like "Rhapsody in Blue"; while the working class dug what the higher reaches thought of as schmaltzy trash, the "Blue Danube" waltz and Petula Clark.[4] Bourdieu drew the conclusion that judgments of taste reinforce forms of social inequality, as individuals imagine themselves to possess superior or inferior spirit and perceptiveness, when really they just like what their class inheritance has taught them to. *Distinction* appeared in English in 1984, cresting the high tide of the

---

[4]*Petula Clark* (b. 1932): British singer of many popular songs in the 1960s. [Editor's note.]

culture wars about to hit the universities. Adorno had felt that advanced art-music was doing the work of revolution. *Are you kidding, Herr Professor?* might have been Bourdieu's response. And thus was Adorno dethroned, all his passionate arguments about history as expressed in musical form recast as moves in the game of taste, while his dismissal of jazz became practically the most famous cultural mistake of the 20th century.

In Adorno and Bourdieu we have two radically different perspec-   15 tives, inhabiting each other's blind spots, with a convergence in both authors' political sympathy with socialism. We can agree with Adorno that music has immanent, formal properties that are connected, somehow, to large-scale historical forces. And we can agree with Bourdieu that musical taste is an instrument in the legitimation of class hierarchies.

So Bourdieu is helpful when we ask what the iPod has wrought in the realm of musical classification. The social world of opera-going may be headed the way of polar bears and ice caps, but *society* hasn't disappeared. A hierarchical social world has managed to absorb the omnipresence of music pretty effortlessly. You can see this in the violent intragenre squabbling that animates indie rock circles, and in the savage takedowns of avant-garde opera performances in art-music magazines. Meanwhile the proliferation of genre names represents an ever finer process of social differentiation, each genre's acolytes determining (as Serge Gainsbourg[5] put it) *qui est* "in," *qui est* "out." The rise of generic distinctions has lately reached a climax of absurdity, such that we can name off the top of our heads: house, witch house, dub, dub-step, hardstep, dancehall, dance-floor, punk, post-punk, noise, "Noise," new wave, nu wave, No Wave, emo, post-emo, hip-hop, conscious hip-hop, alternative hip-hop, jazz hip-hop, hardcore hip-hop, nerd-core hip-hop, Christian hip-hop, crunk, crunkcore, metal, doom metal, black metal, speed metal, thrash metal, death metal, Christian death metal, and, of course, shoe-gazing, among others. (Meanwhile, 1,000 years of European art music is filed under "classical.") Some people listen to some of these; others, to only one; and others still, to nearly all. And this accomplishes a

[5]*Serge Gainsbourg* (1928–1991): popular French singer, songwriter, actor, and director. [Editor's note.]

lot of handy social sorting, especially among the young, whenever music is talked about or played so that more than one person can hear it.

At the same time, modes of listening seem to be moving toward the (apparent) opposite of micro-differentiation: a total pluralism of taste. This has become the most celebrated feature of the iPod era. "I have seen the future," Alex Ross, music critic of the *New Yorker*, wrote in 2004, "and it is called the Shuffle—the setting on the iPod that skips randomly from one track to another." Here the iPod, or the digitization of musical life it represents, promises emancipation from questions of taste. Differences in what people listen to, in a Shuffled world, may have less and less to do with social class and purchasing power. Or, better yet, taste won't correlate to class distinction: The absence of taste will. As certain foodies score points by having eaten everything— blowfish, yak milk tea, haggis, hot dogs—so the person who knows and likes all music achieves a curious sophistication-through-indiscriminateness.

Adorno would be more at home analyzing the uses to which the omnipresence of music has been put in the service of "the administered life"—the background Musak and easy listening, the somehow consolingly melancholy shopping pop, that we hear in malls and supermarkets almost without noticing. "I do love a new purchase!" says the Gang of Four outright—while all the other songs merely insinuate it. Around the holidays, Banana Republic will alternate familiar hits like George Michael's "Last Christmas" with pounding C-grade techno, lulling you into a state of sickly nostalgia before ramping up your heart rate—a perfect way to goose you into an impulse buy. So, too, as Adorno would have been unsurprised to find out, has music become a common way for people to get through the workday. Your local café's barista may literally depend on Bon Iver's reedy lugubriousness to palliate a dreary job as you depend on coffee.

On the other hand, Adorno's prejudice against empirical research—as Brecht[6] said, Adorno "never took a trip in order to see"—meant that he never understood how music could be used for different purposes by the very people it was supposed to manage and administer. People not only use music to help them

---

[6]*Bertolt Brecht* (1898–1956): German playwright and poet. [Editor's note.]

swallow an unpalatable life, but to enhance and enlarge their capacities for action. If a bass line of a standard 12-bar blues, repeating with machinelike regularity, keeps you clicking through the data entry sheet, a sharp post-punk squall can move you to sabotage and revolt, and vice versa. Of course music can also move you in less obviously political ways, filling you with romantic enthusiasm or unshakable sorrow. Then there are all the uses of music that are beneath good and evil, that neither shore up nor undermine the system. In utopia, as under late capitalism, there will still be a lot of cooking and cleaning to do, as well as long drives to take in our electric cars. These slightly boring parts of life are made less so by listening to slightly boring music.

If Adorno, in his emphasis on the immanent unfolding of musi- 20 cal works as cognition, didn't understand the mixed uses of distracted listening, Bourdieu missed something even more important. His empiricism blinded him to the utopian potential in music. You would never guess, to read his books, that they were published *after* the '60s, an extraordinary period that demonstrated the capacity of musical taste to break down as well as reinforce social boundaries. Shoveled at us now as commodities played ad nauseam on Clear Channel, the "classic rock" of the '60s no longer discloses its role in the social movements of that time. And yet—Hendrix, Joplin; Coltrane, Davis, Coleman; the Stones, the Beatles; and Riley, Young, Reich—even if they didn't sing a single revolutionary word, even if they chastised you for "carrying pictures of Chairman Mao," they were all either directly involved with social movements or deeply implicated in them.

The great 1990s magazine the *Baffler* spent its first half-decade analyzing how the culture industry managed, with increasing success, to recognize new musical trends and package them and sell them back at a markup to the people who'd pioneered them. The *Baffler* looked back to the punk scene of the early '80s for inspiration; it spoke up for small labels that sold music to local constituencies. If you couldn't get what you wanted on the radio, you would have to find it left of the dial—and keep looking over your shoulder for the man.

The danger now is different. The man no longer needs a monopoly on musical taste. He just wants a few cents on the dollar of every song you download, he doesn't care what that song says.

Other times he doesn't even care if you pay that dollar, as long as you listen to your stolen music on his portable MP3 player, store it on his Apple computer, send it to your friends through his Verizon network. To paraphrase Yeltsin's[7] famous offer to the Chechens, take as much free music as you can stomach. We'll see where it gets you.

If recording and mechanical reproduction opened up the world of musical pluralism—of listening to other people's music until you and they became other people yourselves—digital reproduction expanded that pluralism to the point where it reversed itself. You have all the world's music on your iPod, in your earphones. Now it's "other people's music"—which should be very exciting to encounter—as played in cafés and stores that is the problem. In any public setting, it acquires a coercive aspect. The iPod is the thing you have to buy in order not to be defenseless against the increasingly sucky music played to make you buy things.

One radical option remains: abnegation—some "Great Refusal" to obey the obscure social injunction that condemns us to a lifetime of listening. *Silence*: The word suggests the torture of enforced isolation, or a particularly monkish kind of social death. But it was the tremendously congenial avant-garde gadabout John Cage[8] who showed, just as the avalanche of recorded music was starting to bury us, how there was "no such thing as silence," that listening to an absence of listener-directed sounds represented a profounder and far more heroic submission than the regular attitude adopted in concert halls—a willingness to "let sounds be," as he put it. Such were Cage's restrictions that he needed to herd everyone into their seats in order to make his point—an authoritarian gesture toward an anarchic result. But now in conditions of relative freedom we can listen to 4'33" on record, or on our iPods, and the change in attention it demands is exactly the opposite of our endless contemporary communing with music, our neurotic search for the right sound, the exact note that never comes. What if we tried to listen to nothing? Silence is the feature of our buzzing sound-world we enjoy least, whose very existence we threaten

---

[7]*Boris Yeltsin* (1931–2007): first president of the Russian Federation (1991–1999) after the fall of the Soviet Union. [Editor's note.]

[8]*John Cage* (1912–1992): American composer, music theorist, and artist. [Editor's note.]

to pave over track by track. Silence is the most endangered musical experience in our time. Turning it up, we might figure out what all our music listening is meant to drown out, the thing we can't bear to hear.

For Discussion and Writing

1. **Comprehension**   What is a "Shuffled world," according to Saval (par. 17)? What effect does randomized listening have on people's listening habits and musical tastes?
2. **Critical Reading**   Who is Saval's **audience** for this essay? How can you tell?
3. **Analysis**   While Saval writes broadly about contemporary music and musical history, including many references to specific composers and artists, he offers no real close analysis of specific songs, performers, or genres. Why do you think he avoids doing so? Would his essay be stronger if he included more attention to particular songs and individual artists? Why or why not?
4. **Connections**   In "The Art of Immersion: Fear of Fiction" (p. 409), Frank Rose writes about immersive entertainment, which (some argue) can be addictive and cut us off from authenticity, reality, and real human connections. He traces this anxiety back to early novels and up through film, television, video games, and the Internet. Is his analysis applicable to Saval's "Wall of Sound"? Can music be immersive? How do you think Rose would respond to Saval's essay? Are Saval's anxieties about the omnipresence of music — even as it isolates listeners — unfounded or overstated? Why or why not?
5. **Writing**   Pierre Bourdieu argues that "nothing more clearly affirms one's 'class,' nothing more infallibly classifies, than tastes in music" (par. 14). Saval concurs, writing that musical choices "accomplis[h] a lot of handy social sorting, especially among the young" (par. 16). How do your musical preferences indicate or affirm your identity — socioeconomically, culturally, ethnically, or otherwise? Do you use music for "social sorting," or for establishing relationships and communities? You may answer these questions in an essay, or you may address them in a multimodal presentation or composition that uses sound clips.

NEIL POSTMAN

The Judgment of Thamus

Neil Postman (1931–2003) was an American media theorist, cultural critic, and educator. He also founded the graduate program in Media Ecology at New York University's Steinhart School of Education, where he taught for many years. Postman is best known for his sharp and witty criticism of technology and the media. His books include Teaching as a Subversive Activity *(1969), cowritten with Charles Weingartner;* Amusing Ourselves to Death: Public Discourse in the Age of Show Business *(1985); and* The End of Education: Redefining the Value of School *(1995). The following essay, from his 1992 book* Technopoly: The Surrender of Culture to Technology, *brings together several of Postman's recurrent themes and preoccupations, especially the meaning of technological progress: "Every technology is both a burden and a blessing; not either-or, but this-and-that." He grounds his argument in Plato's dialogue* Phaedrus, *an ancient story that proves prescient and relevant to contemporary debates about technology.*

***As you read,** notice how Postman integrates a broad range of sources into his essay—not merely to support his argument, but to place it in the context of a broader conversation. Consider, also, technological "progress" during the last two decades. What technologies does Postman write about? How have developments like the Internet, smartphones, and iPods affected our culture and society in light of Postman's analysis? Do his questions and concerns still seem relevant?*

You will find in Plato's *Phaedrus* a story about Thamus, the king of a great city of Upper Egypt. For people such as ourselves, who are inclined (in Thoreau's phrase) to be tools of our tools, few legends are more instructive than his. The story, as Socrates tells it to his friend Phaedrus, unfolds in the following way: Thamus once entertained the god Theuth, who was the inventor of many things, including number, calculation, geometry, astronomy, and writing. Theuth exhibited his inventions to King Thamus, claiming that they should be made widely known and available to Egyptians. Socrates continues:

> Thamus inquired into the use of each of them, and as Theuth went through them expressed approval or disapproval, according as he judged Theuth's claims to be well or ill founded. It would take too long to go through all that Thamus is reported to have said for and against each of Theuth's inventions. But when it came to writing, Theuth declared, "Here is an accomplishment, my lord the King, which will improve both the wisdom and the memory of the Egyptians. I have discovered a sure receipt for memory and wisdom." To this, Thamus replied, "Theuth, my paragon of inventors, the discoverer of an art is not the best judge of the good or harm which will accrue to those who practice it. So it is in this; you, who are the father of writing, have out of fondness for your off-spring attributed to it quite the opposite of its real function. Those who acquire it will cease to exercise their memory and become forgetful; they will rely on writing to bring things to their remembrance by external signs instead of by their own internal resources. What you have discovered is a receipt for recollection, not for memory. And as for wisdom, your pupils will have the reputation for it without the reality: they will receive a quantity of information without proper instruction, and in consequence be thought very knowledgeable when they are for the most part quite ignorant. And because they are filled with the conceit of wisdom instead of real wisdom they will be a burden to society."[1]

I begin . . . with this legend because in Thamus' response there are several sound principles from which we may begin to learn how to think with wise circumspection about a technological society. In fact, there is even one error in the judgment of Thamus, from which we may also learn something of importance. The error is not in his claim that writing will damage memory and create false wisdom. It is demonstrable that writing has had such an effect. Thamus' error is in his believing that writing will be a burden to society and *nothing but a burden*. For all his wisdom, he fails to imagine what writing's benefits might be, which, as we know, have been considerable. We may learn from this that it is a mistake to suppose that any technological innovation has a one-sided effect. Every technology is both a burden and a blessing; not either-or, but this-and-that.

[1]Plato, *Phaedrus and Letters VII and VIII* (New York: Penguin Classics, 1973), p. 96.

Nothing could be more obvious, of course, especially to those who have given more than two minutes of thought to the matter. Nonetheless, we are currently surrounded by throngs of zealous Theuths, one-eyed prophets who see only what new technologies can do and are incapable of imagining what they will *undo*. We might call such people Technophiles. They gaze on technology as a lover does on his beloved, seeing it as without blemish and entertaining no apprehension for the future. They are therefore dangerous and are to be approached cautiously. On the other hand, some one-eyed prophets, such as I (or so I am accused), are inclined to speak only of burdens (in the manner of Thamus) and are silent about the opportunities that new technologies make possible. The Technophiles must speak for themselves, and do so all over the place. My defense is that a dissenting voice is sometimes needed to moderate the din made by the enthusiastic multitudes. If one is to err, it is better to err on the side of Thamusian skepticism. But it is an error nonetheless. And I might note that, with the exception of his judgment on writing, Thamus does not repeat this error. You might notice on rereading the legend that he gives arguments *for* and *against* each of Theuth's inventions. For it is inescapable that every culture must negotiate with technology, whether it does so intelligently or not. A bargain is struck in which technology giveth and technology taketh away. The wise know this well, and are rarely impressed by dramatic technological changes, and never overjoyed. Here, for example, is Freud on the matter, from his doleful *Civilization and Its Discontents*:

> One would like to ask: is there, then, no positive gain in pleasure, no unequivocal increase in my feeling of happiness, if I can, as often as I please, hear the voice of a child of mine who is living hundreds of miles away or if I can learn in the shortest possible time after a friend has reached his destination that he has come through the long and difficult voyage unharmed? Does it mean nothing that medicine has succeeded in enormously reducing infant mortality and the danger of infection for women in childbirth, and, indeed, in considerably lengthening the average life of a civilized man?

Freud knew full well that technical and scientific advances are not to be taken lightly, which is why he begins this passage by acknowledging them. But he ends it by reminding us of what they have undone:

If there had been no railway to conquer distances, my child would never have left his native town and I should need no telephone to hear his voice; if traveling across the ocean by ship had not been introduced, my friend would not have embarked on his sea-voyage and I should not need a cable to relieve my anxiety about him. What is the use of reducing infantile mortality when it is precisely that reduction which imposes the greatest restraint on us in the begetting of children, so that, taken all round, we nevertheless rear no more children than in the days before the reign of hygiene, while at the same time we have created difficult conditions for our sexual life in marriage. . . . And, finally, what good to us is a long life if it is difficult and barren of joys, and if it is so full of misery that we can only welcome death as a deliverer?[2]

In tabulating the cost of technological progress, Freud takes a rather depressing line, that of a man who agrees with Thoreau's remark that our inventions are but improved means to an unimproved end. The Technophile would surely answer Freud by saying that life has always been barren of joys and full of misery but that the telephone, ocean liners, and especially the reign of hygiene have not only lengthened life but made it a more agreeable proposition. That is certainly an argument I would make (thus proving I am no one-eyed Technophobe), but it is not necessary at this point to pursue it. I have brought Freud into the conversation only to show that a wise man—even one of such a woeful countenance—must begin his critique of technology by acknowledging its successes. Had King Thamus been as wise as reputed, he would not have forgotten to include in his judgment a prophecy about the powers that writing would enlarge. There is a calculus of technological change that requires a measure of evenhandedness.

So much for Thamus' error of omission. There is another omission worthy of note, but it is no error. Thamus simply takes for granted—and therefore does not feel it necessary to say—that writing is not a neutral technology whose good or harm depends on the uses made of it. He knows that the uses made of any technology are largely determined by the structure of the technology itself—that is, that its functions follow from its form. This is why Thamus is concerned not with *what* people will write; he is concerned *that* people will write. It is absurd to imagine Thamus 5

[2]Sigmund Freud, *Civilization and Its Discontents* (New York: W. W. Norton, 1961), pp. 38–39.

advising, in the manner of today's standard-brand Technophiles, that, if only writing would be used for the production of certain kinds of texts and not others (let us say, for dramatic literature but not for history or philosophy), its disruptions could be minimized. He would regard such a counsel as extreme naïveté. He would allow, I imagine, that a technology may be barred entry to a culture. But we may learn from Thamus the following: once a technology is admitted, it plays out its hand; it does what it is designed to do. Our task is to understand what that design is— that is to say, when we admit a new technology to the culture, we must do so with our eyes wide open.

All of this we may infer from Thamus' silence. But we may learn even more from what he does say than from what he doesn't. He points out, for example, that writing will change what is meant by the words "memory" and "wisdom." He fears that memory will be confused with what he disdainfully calls "recollection," and he worries that wisdom will become indistinguishable from mere knowledge. This judgment we must take to heart, for it is a certainty that radical technologies create new definitions of old terms, and that this process takes place without our being fully conscious of it. Thus, it is insidious and dangerous, quite different from the process whereby new technologies introduce new terms to the language. In our own time, we have consciously added to our language thousands of new words and phrases having to do with new technologies—"VCR," "binary digit," "software," "front-wheel drive," "window of opportunity," "Walkman," etc. We are not taken by surprise at this. New things require new words. But new things also modify old words, words that have deep-rooted meanings. The telegraph and the penny press changed what we once meant by "information." Television changes what we once meant by the terms "political debate," "news," and "public opinion." The computer changes "information" once again. Writing changed what we once meant by "truth" and "law"; printing changed them again, and now television and the computer change them once more. Such changes occur quickly, surely, and, in a sense, silently. Lexicographers hold no plebiscites on the matter. No manuals are written to explain what is happening, and the schools are oblivious to it. The old words still look the same, are still used in the same kinds of sentences. But they do not have the same meanings; in some cases, they have opposite meanings.

Library of Congress/World Telegram & Sun photo by Herman Hiller

A man prepares a Univac computer to predict a winning horse (1959). "To a man with a pencil, everything looks like a list. To a man with a camera, everything looks like an image. To a man with a computer, everything looks like data."

And this is what Thamus wishes to teach us—that technology imperiously commandeers our most important terminology. It redefines "freedom," "truth," "intelligence," "fact," "wisdom," "memory," "history"—all the words we live by. And it does not pause to tell us. And we do not pause to ask.

. . . There are several more principles to be mined from the judgment of Thamus that require mentioning because they presage all I will write about. For instance, Thamus warns that the pupils of Theuth will develop an undeserved reputation for wisdom. He means to say that those who cultivate competence in the use of a new technology become an elite group that are granted undeserved authority and prestige by those who have no such competence. There are different ways of expressing the interesting implications of this fact. Harold Innis, the father of modern communication studies, repeatedly spoke of the "knowledge monopolies" created by important technologies. He meant precisely what Thamus had in mind: those who have control over the workings of a particular technology accumulate power and inevitably form a kind of conspiracy against those who have no access to the specialized knowledge made available by the technology. In his book *The Bias of Communication,* Innis provides many historical examples of how a new technology "busted up" a traditional knowledge monopoly and created a new one presided over by a different group. Another way of saying this is that the benefits and deficits of a new technology are not distributed equally. There are, as it were, winners and losers. It is both puzzling and poignant that on many occasions the losers, out of ignorance, have actually cheered the winners, and some still do.

Let us take as an example the case of television. In the United States, where television has taken hold more deeply than anywhere else, many people find it a blessing, not least those who have achieved high-paying, gratifying careers in television as executives, technicians, newscasters, and entertainers. It should surprise no one that such people, forming as they do a new knowledge monopoly, should cheer themselves and defend and promote television technology. On the other hand and in the long run, television may bring a gradual end to the careers of schoolteachers, since school was an invention of the printing press and must stand or fall on the issue of how much importance the printed word has. For four hundred years, schoolteachers have been part of the knowledge monopoly created by printing, and they are now witnessing the breakup of that monopoly. It appears as if they can do little to prevent that breakup, but surely there is something perverse about schoolteachers being enthusiastic about what is happening. Such enthusiasm always calls to my mind an image of some turn-of-the-century blacksmith who not only sings the praises of the automobile but also believes that his business will be enhanced by it. We know now that his business was not enhanced by it; it was rendered obsolete by it, as perhaps the clearheaded blacksmiths knew. What could they have done? Weep, if nothing else.

We have a similar situation in the development and spread of computer technology, for here too there are winners and losers. There can be no disputing that the computer has increased the power of large-scale organizations like the armed forces, or airline companies or banks or tax-collecting agencies. And it is equally clear that the computer is now indispensable to high-level researchers in physics and other natural sciences. But to what extent has computer technology been an advantage to the masses of people? To steelworkers, vegetable-store owners, teachers, garage mechanics, musicians, bricklayers, dentists, and most of the rest into whose lives the computer now intrudes? Their private matters have been made more accessible to powerful institutions. They are more easily tracked and controlled; are subjected to more examinations; are increasingly mystified by the decisions made about them; are often reduced to mere numerical objects. They are inundated by junk mail. They are easy targets for advertising agencies and political organizations. The schools teach their children to operate computerized systems instead of teaching things that are more valuable to children. In a word, almost nothing that they need happens to the losers. Which is why they are losers.

It is to be expected that the winners will encourage the losers 10 to be enthusiastic about computer technology. That is the way of winners, and so they sometimes tell the losers that with personal computers the average person can balance a checkbook more neatly, keep better track of recipes, and make more logical shopping lists. They also tell them that their lives will be conducted more efficiently. But discreetly they neglect to say from whose point of view the efficiency is warranted or what might be its costs. Should the losers grow skeptical, the winners dazzle them with the wondrous feats of computers, almost all of which have only marginal relevance to the quality of the losers' lives but which are nonetheless impressive. Eventually, the losers succumb, in part because they believe, as Thamus prophesied, that the specialized knowledge of the masters of a new technology is a form of wisdom. The masters come to believe this as well, as Thamus also prophesied. The result is that certain questions do not arise. For example, to whom will the technology give greater power and freedom? And whose power and freedom will be reduced by it?

I have perhaps made all of this sound like a well-planned conspiracy, as if the winners know all too well what is being won and what lost. But this is not quite how it happens. For one thing, in cultures that have a democratic ethos, relatively weak traditions, and a high receptivity to new technologies, everyone is inclined to be enthusiastic about technological change, believing that its benefits will eventually spread evenly among the entire population. Especially in the United States, where the lust for what is new has no bounds, do we find this childlike conviction most widely held. Indeed, in America, social change of any kind is rarely seen as resulting in winners and losers, a condition that stems in part from Americans' much-documented optimism. As for change brought on by technology, this native optimism is exploited by entrepreneurs, who work hard to infuse the population with a unity of improbable hope, for they know that it is economically unwise to reveal the price to be paid for technological change. One might say, then, that, if there is a conspiracy of any kind, it is that of a culture conspiring against itself.

In addition to this, and more important, it is not always clear, at least in the early stages of a technology's intrusion into a culture, who will gain most by it and who will lose most. This is because the changes wrought by technology are subtle if not downright mysterious, one might even say wildly unpredictable. Among the most unpredictable are those that might be labeled ideological. This is the sort of change Thamus had in mind when he warned that writers will come to rely on external signs instead of their own internal resources, and that they will receive quantities of information without proper instruction. He meant that new technologies change what we mean by "knowing" and "truth"; they alter those deeply embedded habits of thought which give to a culture its sense of what the world is like—a sense of what is the natural order of things, of what is reasonable, of what is necessary, of what is inevitable, of what is real. Since such changes are expressed in changed meanings of old words, I will hold off . . . discussing the massive ideological transformation now occurring in the United States. Here, I should like to give only one example of how technology creates new conceptions of what is real and, in the process, undermines older conceptions. I refer to the seemingly harmless practice of assigning marks or grades to the answers students give on examinations. This procedure seems so natural to most of us that we are hardly aware of its significance. We may even find it difficult to imagine that the number or letter is a tool or, if you will, a technology; still less that, when we use such a technology to judge someone's behavior, we have done something peculiar. In point of fact, the first instance of grading students' papers occurred at Cambridge University in 1792 at the suggestion of a tutor named William Farish.[3] No one knows much about William Farish; not more than a handful have ever heard of him. And yet his idea that a quantitative value should be assigned to human thoughts was a major step toward constructing a mathematical concept of reality. If a number can be given to the quality of a thought, then a number can be given to the qualities of mercy, love, hate, beauty, creativity, intelligence, even sanity itself. When Galileo said that the language of nature is written in mathematics, he did not mean to include human feeling or accomplishment or insight. But most of us are now inclined to make these inclusions. Our psychologists, sociologists, and educators find it quite impossible to do their work without numbers. They believe that without numbers they cannot acquire or express authentic knowledge.

I shall not argue here that this is a stupid or dangerous idea, only that it is peculiar. What is even more peculiar is that so many of us do not find the idea peculiar. To say that someone should be doing better work because he has an IQ of 134, or that someone is a 7.2 on a sensitivity scale, or that this man's essay on the rise of capitalism is an A—and that man's is a C+—would have sounded like gibberish to Galileo or Shakespeare or Thomas Jefferson. If it makes sense to us, that is because our minds have been conditioned by the technology of numbers so that we see the world differently than they did. Our understanding of what is real is different. Which is another way of saying that embedded in every tool is an ideological bias, a predisposition to construct the world as one thing rather than another, to value one thing over another, to amplify one sense or skill or attitude more loudly than another.

[3]This fact is documented in Keith Hoskin's "The Examination, Disciplinary Power and Rational Schooling," in *History of Education*, vol. VIII, no. 2 (1979), pp. 135–46. Professor Hoskin provides the following story about Farish: Farish was a professor of engineering at Cambridge and designed and installed a movable partition wall in his Cambridge home. The wall moved on pulleys between downstairs and upstairs. One night, while working late downstairs and feeling cold, Farish pulled down the partition. This is not much of a story, and history fails to disclose what happened next. All of which shows how little is known of William Farish.

This is what Marshall McLuhan[4] meant by his famous aphorism "The medium is the message." This is what Marx meant when he said, "Technology discloses man's mode of dealing with nature" and creates the "conditions of intercourse" by which we relate to each other. It is what Wittgenstein meant when, in referring to our most fundamental technology, he said that language is not merely a vehicle of thought but also the driver. And it is what Thamus wished the inventor Theuth to see. This is, in short, an ancient and persistent piece of wisdom, perhaps most simply expressed in the old adage that, to a man with a hammer, everything looks like a nail. Without being too literal, we may extend the truism: To a man with a pencil, everything looks like a list. To a man with a camera, everything looks like an image. To a man with a computer, everything looks like data. And to a man with a grade sheet, everything looks like a number.

But such prejudices are not always apparent at the start of a 15 technology's journey, which is why no one can safely conspire to be a winner in technological change. Who would have imagined, for example, whose interests and what worldview would be ultimately advanced by the invention of the mechanical clock? The clock had its origins in the Benedictine monasteries of the twelfth and thirteenth centuries. The impetus behind the invention was to provide a more or less precise regularity to the routines of the monasteries, which required, among other things, seven periods of devotion during the course of the day. The bells of the monastery were to be rung to signal the canonical hours; the mechanical clock was the technology that could provide precision to these rituals of devotion. And indeed it did. But what the monks did not foresee was that the clock is a means not merely of keeping track of the hours but also of synchronizing and controlling the actions of men. And thus, by the middle of the fourteenth century, the clock had moved outside the walls of the monastery, and brought a new and precise regularity to the life of the workman and the merchant. "The mechanical clock," as Lewis Mumford wrote, "made possible the idea of regular production, regular working hours and a standardized product." In short, without the clock,

---

[4]*Marshall McLuhan* (1911–1980): Canadian communications theorist and literary and media critic. [Editor's note.]

capitalism would have been quite impossible.[5] The paradox, the surprise, and the wonder are that the clock was invented by men who wanted to devote themselves more rigorously to God; it ended as the technology of greatest use to men who wished to devote themselves to the accumulation of money. In the eternal struggle between God and Mammon, the clock quite unpredictably favored the latter.

Unforeseen consequences stand in the way of all those who think they see clearly the direction in which a new technology will take us. Not even those who invent a technology can be assumed to be reliable prophets, as Thamus warned. Gutenberg, for example, was by all accounts a devout Catholic who would have been horrified to hear that accursed heretic Luther describe printing as "God's highest act of grace, whereby the business of the Gospel is driven forward." Luther understood, as Gutenberg did not, that the mass-produced book, by placing the Word of God on every kitchen table, makes each Christian his own theologian—one might even say his own priest, or, better, from Luther's point of view, his own pope. In the struggle between unity and diversity of religious belief, the press favored the latter, and we can assume that this possibility never occurred to Gutenberg.

Thamus understood well the limitations of inventors in grasping the social and psychological—that is, ideological—bias of their own inventions. We can imagine him addressing Gutenberg in the following way: "Gutenberg, my paragon of inventors, the discoverer of an art is not the best judge of the good or harm which will accrue to those who practice it. So it is in this; you, who are the father of printing, have out of fondness for your offspring come to believe it will advance the cause of the Holy Roman See, whereas in fact it will sow discord among believers; it will destroy the authenticity of your beloved Church and destroy its monopoly."

We can imagine that Thamus would also have pointed out to Gutenberg, as he did to Theuth, that the new invention would create a vast population of readers who "will receive a quantity of information without proper instruction . . . [who will be] filled with the conceit of wisdom instead of real wisdom"; that reading,

---

[5]For a detailed exposition of Mumford's position on the impact of the mechanical clock, see his *Technics and Civilization* (New York: Harcourt Brace, 1934).

in other words, will compete with older forms of learning. This is yet another principle of technological change we may infer from the judgment of Thamus: new technologies compete with old ones—for time, for attention, for money, for prestige, but mostly for dominance of their worldview. This competition is implicit once we acknowledge that a medium contains an ideological bias. And it is a fierce competition, as only ideological competitions can be. It is not merely a matter of tool against tool—the alphabet attacking ideographic writing, the printing press attacking the illuminated manuscript, the photograph attacking the art of painting, television attacking the printed word. When media make war against each other, it is a case of worldviews in collision.

In the United States, we can see such collisions everywhere—in politics, in religion, in commerce—but we see them most clearly in the schools, where two great technologies confront each other in uncompromising aspect for the control of students' minds. On the one hand, there is the world of the printed word with its emphasis on logic, sequence, history, exposition, objectivity, detachment, and discipline. On the other, there is the world of television with its emphasis on imagery, narrative, presentness, simultaneity, intimacy, immediate gratification, and quick emotional response. Children come to school having been deeply conditioned by the biases of television. There, they encounter the world of the printed word. A sort of psychic battle takes place, and there are many casualties—children who can't learn to read or won't, children who cannot organize their thought into logical structure even in a simple paragraph, children who cannot attend to lectures or oral explanations for more than a few minutes at a time. They are failures, but not because they are stupid. They are failures because there is a media war going on, and they are on the wrong side—at least for the moment. Who knows what schools will be like twenty-five years from now? Or fifty? In time, the type of student who is currently a failure may be considered a success. The type who is now successful may be regarded as a handicapped learner—slow to respond, far too detached, lacking in emotion, inadequate in creating mental pictures of reality. Consider: What Thamus called the "conceit of wisdom"—the unreal knowledge acquired through the written word—eventually became the preeminent form of knowledge valued by the schools. There is no reason to suppose that such a form of knowledge must always remain so highly valued.

To take another example: In introducing the personal com- 20 puter to the classroom, we shall be breaking a four-hundred-year-old truce between the gregariousness and openness fostered by orality and the introspection and isolation fostered by the printed word. Orality stresses group learning, cooperation, and a sense of social responsibility, which is the context within which Thamus believed proper instruction and real knowledge must be communicated. Print stresses individualized learning, competition, and personal autonomy. Over four centuries, teachers, while emphasizing print, have allowed orality its place in the classroom, and have therefore achieved a kind of pedagogical peace between these two forms of learning, so that what is valuable in each can be maximized. Now comes the computer, carrying anew the banner of private learning and individual problem-solving. Will the widespread use of computers in the classroom defeat once and for all the claims of communal speech? Will the computer raise egocentrism to the status of a virtue?

These are the kinds of questions that technological change brings to mind when one grasps, as Thamus did, that technological competition ignites total war, which means it is not possible to contain the effects of a new technology to a limited sphere of human activity. If this metaphor puts the matter too brutally, we may try a gentler, kinder one: Technological change is neither additive nor subtractive. It is ecological. I mean "ecological" in the same sense as the word is used by environmental scientists. One significant change generates total change. If you remove the caterpillars from a given habitat, you are not left with the same environment minus caterpillars: You have a new environment, and you have reconstituted the conditions of survival; the same is true if you add caterpillars to an environment that has had none. This is how the ecology of media works as well. A new technology does not add or subtract something. It changes everything. In the year 1500, fifty years after the printing press was invented, we did not have old Europe plus the printing press. We had a different Europe. After television, the United States was not America plus television; television gave a new coloration to every political campaign, to every home, to every school, to every church, to every industry. And that is why the competition among media is so fierce. Surrounding every technology are institutions whose organization—not to mention their reason for being—reflects the worldview promoted by the technology. Therefore, when an old technology is assaulted by a new one, institutions are threatened. When institutions are threatened, a culture finds itself in crisis. This is serious business, which is why we learn nothing when educators ask, Will students learn mathematics better by computers than by textbooks? Or when businessmen ask, Through which medium can we sell more products? Or when preachers ask, Can we reach more people through television than through radio? Or when politicians ask, How effective are messages sent through different media? Such questions have an immediate, practical value to those who ask them, but they are diversionary. They direct our attention away from the serious social, intellectual, and institutional crises that new media foster.

Perhaps an analogy here will help to underline the point. In speaking of the meaning of a poem, T. S. Eliot[6] remarked that the chief use of the overt content of poetry is "to satisfy one habit of the reader, to keep his mind diverted and quiet, while the poem does its work upon him: much as the imaginary burglar is always provided with a bit of nice meat for the house-dog." In other words, in asking their practical questions, educators, entrepreneurs, preachers, and politicians are like the house-dog munching peacefully on the meat while the house is looted. Perhaps some of them know this and do not especially care. After all, a nice piece of meat, offered graciously, does take care of the problem of where the next meal will come from. But for the rest of us, it cannot be acceptable to have the house invaded without protest or at least awareness.

What we need to consider about the computer has nothing to do with its efficiency as a teaching tool. We need to know in what ways it is altering our conception of learning, and how, in conjunction with television, it undermines the old idea of school. Who cares how many boxes of cereal can be sold via television? We need to know if television changes our conception of reality, the relationship of the rich to the poor, the idea of happiness itself. A preacher who confines himself to considering how a medium can increase his audience will miss the significant question: In what sense do new media alter what is meant by religion,

---

[6]*T. S. Eliot* (1888–1965): American and British poet, literary critic, and playwright. [Editor's note.]

by church, even by God? And if the politician cannot think beyond the next election, then *we* must wonder about what new media do to the idea of political organization and to the conception of citizenship.

To help us do this, we have the judgment of Thamus, who, in the way of legends, teaches us what Harold Innis, in his way, tried to. New technologies alter the structure of our interests: the things we think *about*. They alter the character of our symbols: the things we think *with*. And they alter the nature of community: the arena in which thoughts develop. As Thamus spoke to Innis across the centuries, it is essential that we listen to their conversation, join in it, revitalize it. For something has happened in America that is strange and dangerous, and there is only a dull and even stupid awareness of what it is—in part because it has no name. I call it Technopoly.

For Discussion and Writing

1. **Comprehension**   Postman argues that Thamus's response to Theuth contains an instructive error. What is the error? How is the mistake related to Postman's main point?

2. **Critical Reading**   "The Judgment of Thamus" includes many references to other texts and writers. What different purposes do these references serve? Consider a specific quotation in Postman's essay, and explain how Postman uses the quotation. For example, does the quotation allow him to explain or illustrate an idea? Does it enable him to draw a contrast?

3. **Analysis**   Although Postman concedes the value of technological progress, he proposes that in judging technology, "it is better to err on the side of Thamusian skepticism" (par. 3) than on the side of the "Technophiles." Does his argument hold up when applied to today's technological advances?

4. **Connections**   For Postman, every technology is both a blessing and a curse. Compare his point of view with Clay Shirky's in "Gin, Television, and Social Surplus" (p. 167). Do Shirky's arguments support or align with Postman's? How? Where do the authors differ?

5. **Writing**   Writing before the popularity of the Internet, Postman asks skeptically, "But to what extent has computer technology been an advantage to the masses of people?" (par. 9). How would you answer that question now? In an argumentative essay or digital presentation (using the very technology about which Postman is skeptical), try to answer Postman's question.

CLAY SHIRKY

Gin, Television, and Social Surplus

Clay Shirky (b. 1964) is a writer, social critic, and consultant. Shirky also teaches at New York University, where he is an associate professor both at the Arthur L. Carter Journalism Institute and in the Interactive Telecommunications Program. He has written for the New York Times, *the* Wall Street Journal, Wired, *and other publications. He is also the author of several books, including* Here Comes Everybody: The Power of Organizing Without Organizations *(2008) and* Cognitive Surplus: Creativity and Generosity in a Connected Age *(2010). As its style indicates, Shirky's "Gin, Television, and Social Surplus" originated as a speech; the talk was given at the 2008 Web 2.0 conference, an annual event featuring discussions of the World Wide Web. This selection touches on several key themes for Shirky, including the collaborative nature of the Internet and the idea of a "cognitive surplus."*

As you read, *think about the writer's use of analogy. What analogies underlie his main point? How do they support his thesis? Do they seem like valid connections and comparisons?*

I was recently reminded of some reading I did in college, way back in the last century, by a British historian arguing that the critical technology, for the early phase of the Industrial Revolution, was gin.

The transformation from rural to urban life was so sudden, and so wrenching, that the only thing society could do to manage was to drink itself into a stupor for a generation. The stories from that era are amazing—there were gin pushcarts working their way through the streets of London.

And it wasn't until society woke up from that collective bender that we actually started to get the institutional structures that we associate with the Industrial Revolution today. Things like public libraries and museums, increasingly broad education for children, elected leaders—a lot of things we like—didn't happen until having all of those people together stopped seeming like a crisis and started seeming like an asset.

It wasn't until people started thinking of this as a vast civic surplus, one they could design for rather than just dissipate, that we started to get what we think of now as an industrial society.

If I had to pick the critical technology for the twentieth cen- 5 tury, the bit of social lubricant without which the wheels would've come off the whole enterprise, I'd say it was the sitcom. Starting with the Second World War, a whole series of things happened— rising GDP per capita, rising educational attainment, rising life expectancy and, critically, a rising number of people who were working five-day work weeks. For the first time, society forced onto an enormous number of its citizens the requirement to manage something they had never had to manage before—free time.

And what did we do with that free time? Well, mostly we spent it watching TV.

We did that for decades. We watched *I Love Lucy*. We watched *Gilligan's Island*. We watch *Malcolm in the Middle*. We watch *Desperate Housewives*. *Desperate Housewives* essentially functioned as a kind of cognitive heat sink, dissipating thinking that might otherwise have built up and caused society to overheat.

And it's only now, as we're waking up from that collective bender, that we're starting to see the cognitive surplus as an asset rather than as a crisis. We're seeing things being designed to take advantage of that surplus, to deploy it in ways more engaging than just having a TV in everybody's basement.

This hit me in a conversation I had about two months ago. . . . I've finished a book called *Here Comes Everybody*, which has recently come out, and this recognition came out of a conversation I had about the book. I was being interviewed by a TV producer to see whether I should be on her show, and she asked me, "What are you seeing out there that's interesting?"

I started telling her about the *Wikipedia* article on Pluto. You 10 may remember that Pluto got kicked out of the planet club a couple of years ago, so all of a sudden there was all of this activity on *Wikipedia*. The talk pages light up, people are editing the article like mad, and the whole community is in a ruckus—"How should we characterize this change in Pluto's status?" And a little bit at a time they move the article—fighting offstage all the while—from

"Pluto is the ninth planet" to "Pluto is an odd-shaped rock with an odd-shaped orbit at the edge of the solar system."

So I tell her all this stuff, and I think, "Okay, we're going to have a conversation about authority or social construction or whatever." That wasn't her question. She heard this story, and shook her head and said, "Where do people find the time?" That was her question. And I just kind of snapped. And I said, "No one who works in TV gets to ask that question. You know where the time comes from. It comes from the cognitive surplus you've been masking for fifty years."

So how big is that surplus? So if you take *Wikipedia* as a kind of unit, all of *Wikipedia*, the whole project—every page, every edit, every talk page, every line of code, in every language that *Wikipedia* exists in—that represents something like the cumulation of 100 million hours of human thought. I worked this out with Martin Wattenberg at IBM; it's a back-of-the-envelope calculation, but it's the right order of magnitude, about 100 million hours of thought.

And television watching? Two hundred billion hours, in the U.S. alone, every year. Put another way, now that we have a unit, that's 2,000 *Wikipedia* projects a year spent watching television. Or put still another way, in the U.S., we spend 100 million hours every weekend, just watching the ads. This is a pretty big surplus. People asking, "Where do they find the time?" when they're looking at things like *Wikipedia* don't understand how tiny that entire project is, as a carve-out of this asset that's finally being dragged into what Tim calls an architecture of participation.

Now, the interesting thing about a surplus like that is that society doesn't know what to do with it at first—hence the gin, hence the sitcoms. Because if people knew what to do with a surplus with reference to the existing social institutions, then it wouldn't be a surplus, would it? It's precisely when no one has any idea how to deploy something that people have to start experimenting with it, in order for the surplus to get integrated, and the course of that integration can transform society.

The early phase for taking advantage of this cognitive surplus, 15 the phase I think we're still in, is all special cases. The physics of participation is much more like the physics of weather than it is like the physics of gravity. We know all the forces that combine to make these kinds of things work: there's an interesting community over here, there's an interesting sharing model over there, those people are collaborating on open source software. But despite knowing the inputs, we can't predict the outputs yet because there's so much complexity.

The way you explore complex ecosystems is you just try lots and lots of things, and you hope that everybody who fails fails informatively so that you can at least find a skull on a pike-staff near where you're going. That's the phase we're in now.

Just to pick one example, one I'm in love with, but it's tiny. A couple of weeks ago one of my students at ITP forwarded me a project started by a professor in Brazil, in Fortaleza, named Vasco Furtado. It's a Wiki Map for crime in Brazil. If there's an assault, if there's a burglary, if there's a mugging, a robbery, a rape, a murder, you can go and put a push-pin on a Google Map, and you can characterize the assault, and you start to see a map of where these crimes are occurring.

Now, this already exists as tacit information. Anybody who knows a town has some sense of "Don't go there. That street corner is dangerous. Don't go in this neighborhood. Be careful there after dark." But it's something society knows without society really knowing it, which is to say there's no public source where you can take advantage of it. And the cops, if they have that information, they're certainly not sharing. In fact, one of the things Furtado says in starting the Wiki crime map was, "This information may or may not exist some place in society, but it's actually easier for me to try to rebuild it from scratch than to try and get it from the authorities who might have it now."

Maybe this will succeed or maybe it will fail. The normal case of social software is still failure; most of these experiments don't pan out. But the ones that do are quite incredible, and I hope that this one succeeds, obviously. But even if it doesn't, it's illustrated the point already, which is that someone working alone, with really cheap tools, has a reasonable hope of carving out enough of the cognitive surplus, enough of the desire to participate, enough of the collective goodwill of the citizens, to create a resource you couldn't have imagined existing even five years ago.

So that's the answer to the question, "Where do they find the time?" Or, rather, that's the numerical answer. But beneath that question was another thought, this one not a question but an observation. In this same conversation with the TV producer, I was talking about *World of Warcraft* guilds, and as I was talking, I could sort of see what she was thinking: "Losers. Grown men sitting in their basement pretending to be elves."

At least they're doing something.

Did you ever see that episode of *Gilligan's Island* where they almost get off the island and then Gilligan messes up and then they don't? I saw that one. I saw that one a lot when I was growing up. And every half-hour that I watched, that was a half an hour I wasn't posting at my blog or editing *Wikipedia* or contributing to a mailing list. Now, I had an ironclad excuse for not doing those things, which is none of those things existed then. I was forced into the channel of media the way it was because it was the only option. Now it's not, and that's the big surprise. However lousy it is to sit in your basement and pretend to be an elf, I can tell you from personal experience it's worse to sit in your basement and try to figure if Ginger or Mary Ann is cuter.

And I'm willing to raise that to a general principle. It's better to do something than to do nothing. Even lolcats, even cute pictures of kittens made even cuter with the addition of cute captions, hold out an invitation to participation. When you see a lolcat, one of the things it says to the viewer is, "If you have some sans-serif fonts on your computer, you can play this game, too." And that message—I can do that, too—is a big change.

This is something that people in the media world don't understand. Media in the twentieth century was run as a single race—consumption. How much can we produce? How much can you consume? Can we produce more and you'll consume more? And the answer to that question has generally been yes. But media is actually a triathlon, it's three different events. People like to consume, but they also like to produce, and they like to share.

And what's astonished people who were committed to the 25 structure of the previous society, prior to trying to take this surplus and do something interesting, is that they're discovering that when you offer people the opportunity to produce and to share, they'll take you up on that offer. It doesn't mean that we'll never sit around mindlessly watching *Scrubs* on the couch. It just means we'll do it less.

And this is the other thing about the size of the cognitive surplus we're talking about. It's so large that even a small change could have huge ramifications. Let's say that everything stays 99 percent the same, that people watch 99 percent as much television as they used to, but 1 percent of that is carved out for producing and for sharing. The Internet-connected population watches roughly a trillion hours of TV a year. That's about five times the size of the annual U.S. consumption. One percent of that is 100 *Wikipedia* projects per year worth of participation.

I think that's going to be a big deal. Don't you?

Well, the TV producer did not think this was going to be a big deal; she was not digging this line of thought. And her final question to me was essentially, "Isn't this all just a fad?" You know, sort of the flagpole-sitting of the early twenty-first century? It's fun to go out and produce and share a little bit, but then people are going to eventually realize, "This isn't as good as doing what I was doing before," and settle down. And I made a spirited argument that no, this wasn't the case, that this was in fact a big one-time shift, more analogous to the Industrial Revolution than to flagpole-sitting.

I was arguing that this isn't the sort of thing society grows out of. It's the sort of thing that society grows into. But I'm not sure she believed me, in part because she didn't want to believe me, but also in part because I didn't have the right story yet. And now I do.

I was having dinner with a group of friends about a month ago, 30 and one of them was talking about sitting with his four-year-old daughter watching a DVD. And in the middle of the movie, apropos of nothing, she jumps up off the couch and runs around behind the screen. That seems like a cute moment. Maybe she's going back there to see if Dora is really back there or whatever. But that wasn't what she was doing. She started rooting around in the cables. And her dad said, "What you doing?" And she stuck her head out from behind the screen and said, "Looking for the mouse."

Here's something four-year-olds know: A screen that ships without a mouse ships broken. Here's something four-year-olds know: Media that's targeted at you but doesn't include you may not be worth sitting still for. Those are things that make me believe that this is a one-way change. Because four-year-olds, the people who are soaking most deeply in the current environment, who won't have to go through the trauma that I have to go through of trying to unlearn a childhood spent watching *Gilligan's Island*, they just assume that media includes consuming, producing, and sharing.

It's also become my motto, when people ask me what we're doing—and when I say "we," I mean the larger society trying to figure out how to deploy this cognitive surplus, but I also mean we, especially, the people in this room, the people who are working hammer and tongs at figuring out the next good idea. From now on, that's what I'm going to tell them: We're looking for the mouse. We're going to look at every place that a reader or a listener or a viewer or a user has been locked out, has been served up passive or a fixed or a canned experience, and ask ourselves, "If we carve out a little bit of the cognitive surplus and deploy it here, could we make a good thing happen?" And I'm betting the answer is yes.

For Discussion and Writing

1. **Comprehension** Shirky sees the Internet functioning similarly to other manifestations of cognitive surplus, such as gin and television. At the same time, the Internet is distinct in a crucial way. What makes the Internet so different from television, according to the writer?

2. **Critical Reading** How does Shirky incorporate **evidence**, including numbers and statistics, into his argument? Do you find these calculations and claims credible and easy to understand? Are they sufficiently rigorous for his purpose? Do they help his argument? Why or why not?

3. **Analysis** Writing about a "big one-time shift" in contemporary society, culture, and technology, Shirky claims, "this isn't the sort of thing society grows out of. It's the sort of thing that society grows into" (par. 29). What do you think he means by this assertion? In what ways does society "grow into" such shifts?

4. **Connections** Shirky tells a story about talking to a television producer. As he describes "guilds" for the video game *World of Warcraft*, he notes: "I could sort of see what she was thinking: 'Losers. Grown men sitting in their basement pretending to be elves'" (par. 20). In contrast, Shirky sees this phenomenon in a positive light: "At least they're doing something" (par. 21). How do you think Nathan Jurgenson ("The IRL Fetish," p. 191) would respond to this image of "grown men" in the basement "pretending to be elves"? Would he agree with Shirky? Why or why not?

5. **Writing** Shirky incorporates several personal anecdotes to illustrate different points throughout the essay. In paragraph 29, he even refers to finding the "right story" to make a particular argument. Choose a specific anecdote or experience from your life; then, in a brief essay, use it to illustrate a point about your own—or our society's—relationship to technology. What does your story reveal?

JENNIFER BLEYER

Love the One You're Near

A graduate of Columbia University, Jennifer Bleyer is an editor at Psychology Today. *Her work has appeared in the* New York Times, Slate, Salon, *the* Christian Science Monitor, *and other publications. In this article, from* Psychology Today, *Bleyer writes about a refinement in the flourishing world of online dating: GPS-enabled dating apps that encourage "location-based liaisons." These apps may help make online dating more spontaneous and fun. But they may also reinforce the downsides of this "vast and dehumanizing virtual marketplace."*

As you read, *consider: Does the article take a stand on whether these apps are "good" or "bad"? Do you think technological developments have led to "shifts" in the "landscape of love-seeking"? Would you consider using one of these apps?*

In the beginning there was online dating, with carefully curated profiles detailing everything from education level to favorite movies and providing earnest answers to questions like "What's the first thing people notice about you?"

Then came the smartphone and, with it, mobile dating apps that can make online dating seem downright quaint. Forget personality: proximity and pouty lips are the new landmarks in the quest for love. Consider the popular "geosocial" app Tinder: You're shown a succession of user photographs, along with people's first name, age, and distance from you at the moment. There may be, at most, a line or two of personal description ("Always down to binge on Netflix," "I say YES to life!"). You swipe left to reject and move on to the next photo, or swipe right to express a liking, at which point you message the other or "keep playing," in the app's gamelike jargon. And thanks to the GPS connection, you know instantly if that guy with the come-hither eyes or the girl with the plunging neckline is just a block away.

Proximity is a helpful parameter for those interested mainly in casual sex, the original purpose of mobile dating. It all began with Grindr, a geosocial app for gay men. Launched in 2007 and still largely used for hookups (or as some winkingly call them, "short-short-short-term relationships"). Grindr claims six million gay users worldwide and has become so entrenched in the cultural firmament that it's been namechecked on *Saturday Night Live* and *Glee*.

Location-based liaisons have surged well beyond their hookup origins, however. A 2011 report by Flurry, a mobile app analytics firm, found that the number of dating app users grew 150 percent between 2010 and 2011—including mobile add-ons to established online dating sites such as Match.com and OKCupid. In fact, 2011 was the first year that people spent more time on dating apps than on dating websites. The ascendance of mobile dating is expected to continue as host devices flourish: The Pew Research Internet Project reports that 58 percent of Americans now own smartphones, up from only 11 percent in 2008; the number is projected to hit 80 percent by 2018.

As the landscape of love-seeking shifts, many experts question   5
whether long-term partners can be found by flicking through a river of pictures on a smartphone. With little to go on except appearance and location, mobile dating may be changing what people are looking for—a perfect 10 and nothing less—as well as what they're missing.

"You get into this mode of screening that sculpts a kind of superficiality and coldness," says Ken Page, a New York–based therapist and author of the forthcoming *Deeper Dating: How to Drop the Games of Seduction and Discover the Power of Intimacy*. "It's the opposite of giving somebody a chance. When you swipe really quickly—no, no, no—you're going to screen out most of the people in the midlevel of your attraction spectrum, which is a very fruitful place to look."

Even when people do agree to link up in person, the casual medium of the mobile app often becomes the message. Meeting through a vast and dehumanizing virtual marketplace, Page says, encourages people to see each other more as products and less as people, and to not afford each other common courtesy, let alone the focused attention it takes to forge a real, intimate connection.

"There's a culture of unkindness because meeting has become so easy and cheap," Page observes. Clients tell him that some people keep their geosocial apps open and pinging on their smartphones while on dates, peering at their screens to see who else might be interested and available. "Having only a picture and a few words to go on leads people to be cool and casual, not warm. It's created a lot more micro-jerkiness in early-stage dating than there has ever been before."

Many mobile dating apps build in text messaging, a feature that can set up unrealistic expectations about communication IRL (in real life, that is). Jesse Fox, an assistant professor of communication at Ohio State University who studies the role of social media in romantic relationships, notes that people are often let down when they meet, because the wit and personality projected through texting isn't mirrored in person.

"It's easy to sound as if you're awesome through text messages," she says. Texting allows just enough time for crafting the perfect witty retort or quickly Googling something about a band you've never heard of just to appear in the know. "Because we're so used to cultivating such false images of ourselves through texting, meeting is awkward. It's not perfect, it's not flawless, it's not like a rom-com. There are going to be uncomfortable silences. That's the nature of human communication." 10

Which isn't to say that mobile dating apps are useless. They can infuse the spontaneity of real-world dating into online dating. Eli Finkel, a professor of social psychology at Northwestern University who studies online dating and romantic relationships, contends that prolonged periods of computer-mediated conversation can actually be a detriment to new relationships since there's always such a wide gulf between how we present ourselves online and who we are in person. Geosocial apps, Finkel says, tend to minimize online banter and lead quickly to an offline meeting, which is the only way to see if there's real promise.

"Rather than slowly crafting a series of email exchanges over the course of days or weeks, you can get a cup of coffee or a beer with the person in 10 minutes," he says. "In many cases, that's way better."

Even Ken Page welcomes geosocial apps as a kind of virtual "wink across the room," the first step to seeing if there's a spark. Instead of discouraging singles from using mobile dating apps

LOCATING LOVERS

Here's a rundown of some of the most popular smartphone dating apps that aim to help users locate mates for life . . . or just for a night.

TINDER A popular app that makes appraising people seem like a game, Tinder presents a succession of potential dates based on gender and age preferences as well as GPS coordinates. Industry analysts estimated it to have 4.2 million active daily users in April [2014], although the verdict is still out on whether it's for serious dating or just entertainment.

GRINDR The original blockbuster hookup app, Grindr uses GPS to help men liaison with other men whose proximity is bluntly expressed in feet (a beefcake named Tom, for instance, might be identified as 32 years old and 25 feet away). It's also used as digital gaydar for gay and bisexual men, an asset for those in more remote areas.

BLENDER An app introduced by the creators of Grindr to let women in on the game, Blender operates in much the same way as its progenitor but prompts a critical question: How likely are women to be looking for casual, immediate sex nearby? The answer seems to be: not very.

OKCUPID LOCALS The online dating favorite jumped on the geosocial bandwagon by adding GPS capability to its existing smartphone app. Some users seem to like it, but many see it as negating the point of OKCupid, which is to have matches suggested based on deep personal questions, not location.

HINGE Unlike other apps, Hinge doesn't use GPS at all. Instead, it pulls from users' Facebook profiles to connect them to single friends of their own friends, considering points of common interest and revealing their social connections. It's like being set up on an old-fashioned blind date, but with an algorithm as matchmaker.

because they spur depersonalization, he encourages people to use the programs in kinder, wiser ways. Turning on a geosocial app at a music festival or a professional conference, for instance, as opposed to on a street corner, adds a layer of filtering beyond the blunt factor of geographical proximity, indicating a common interest and an actual basis to meet.

"There's no reason not to have a sense of fun with this stuff," Page says. "But the huge, huge thing is to come out as quickly as you can from the screen of anonymity and meet the person. That's really everything."

For Discussion and Writing

1. **Comprehension**   According to the article, how can these apps lead to superficiality and a "culture of unkindness" (par. 8)? How do they encourage their users to view one another?

2. **Critical Reading**   How would you describe Bleyer's **purpose** in this article? Is she writing to persuade? Inform? Express?

3. **Analysis**   Bleyer writes, "Even when people do agree to link up in person, the casual medium of the mobile app often becomes the message" (par. 7). What do you think she means by this claim? What does it suggest about the way users of these apps might view each other and interact?

4. **Connections**   In "The Judgment of Thamus" (p. 151), Neil Postman argues that every tool or technology brings with it "an ideological bias, a predisposition to construct the world as one thing rather than another, to value one thing over another, to amplify one sense or skill or attitude more loudly than another" (par. 13). How can Postman's claim be applied to the apps Bleyer describes—and online dating, generally? For example, what "things" does an app like Tinder privilege or amplify? How might it construct, condition, or change its users' understandings of "romance," "relationships," or "love"?

5. **Writing**   According to communications professor Jesse Fox, social media and technological communication can lead to inauthenticity: "Because we're so used to cultivating such false images of ourselves through texting, meeting is awkward" (par. 10). Do you agree that people generally cultivate "false images" of themselves, whether they are texting or using other social media? Or do you think that people generally use these technologies to express their "true" selves and identities? Write a response that takes a clear position on this question, and support it with specific examples.

DAVID AUERBACH

You Are What You Click

David Auerbach is a writer as well as a software engineer who has worked for Microsoft and Google. He is a graduate of Yale University. His work has appeared in Slate, *the* Nation, n+1, *and other publications. In this article from the* Nation, *Auerbach writes about the ways in which we are "stalked" online by corporations "in the pursuit of marketing optimization." Implicitly, he reminds us that our privacy concerns should not be limited to fears about intrusive government departments, like the National Security Agency or the FBI. Private interests are tracking us and surveilling us, too — particularly as our digital footprints get larger and the efficacy of traditional advertising diminishes.*

As you read, *consider Auerbach's purpose. To what degree is he trying to correct misunderstandings about Internet privacy and anonymity? What common misconceptions do people have about the Web, according to the writer? Will this article change your attitude about the Internet — or even change your online behavior?*

Every few months there's a headline story about privacy violations committed by a high-profile online company, and the violations usually span the spectrum. Google was recently slapped with two fines: $22.5 million for tracking users of Apple's Safari browser, and $25,000 for impeding an FCC probe into a bizarre episode of alleged wireless data "sniffing." For some years now, the privacy policies of Facebook have been under investigation in Germany and the United States.

What's always missing from these stories is context. Accounts of privacy violations bubble through the news and stir public outrage, which is often followed by a backlash and occasionally a fine. But these stories rarely reveal the porous privacy lines of the digital realm, or whether other types of violations are being committed

179

online, by companies other than the household names. The outrage is selective and the enforcements ad hoc. News stories about hacking, data sniffing, and the like have become red herrings. They provide false assurances that, in the normal course of things, our privacy is not being invaded on the Internet, that our personal data is safe, and that we are anonymous in our online — and offline — activities.

But we aren't. "Privacy" and "anonymity" are being defined down, and single violations of individual privacy like hacking and identity theft, while aggravating, are trivial compared with efforts toward the comprehensive accumulation of data on every single consumer. The marketing industry is attempting to profile and classify us all, so that advertising can be customized and targeted as precisely as possible. Google, Facebook, Apple, and thousands of lesser-known companies are making it their policy and business to profile us in detail, all in the hopes of crafting better sales pitches. For these companies, your value is expressed most often when you click on an ad, signaling that you're interested in the product being sold. But will you buy it? For those paying for the ads, your value depends on other factors: your socioeconomic class, your credit, your purchasing record.

The sort of consumer profiling that has become increasingly necessary for targeted marketing has yet to generate significant increases in revenue. However, even the modest success of "micro-targeting" has been enough to encourage the collection of vast quantities of consumer data, which is cheap and easy to do with today's technology. There is no incentive to stop this activity; no law prohibits it, and the growing electronic data board will be very difficult to expunge. Big Brother is watching you, but he's no longer a dictator; instead, he's a desperate and persistent door-to-door salesman. Call him Big Salesman.

Big Salesman is engineering a far grosser violation of our privacy than most people suspect — not a single incident, but a slow, unstoppable process of profiling who we are and what we do, to be sold to advertisers and marketing companies. Information that we reveal about ourselves constantly every day in our online and offline actions has become valuable to those who collect and amass it. Because the value does not lie in any one piece of data but in its unification and aggregation, the data in sum is worth far more than its individual parts. Ticketmaster may know which   5 concerts I've attended and Amazon may know which albums I've bought, but each company would benefit if it had the other's file on me. It's a slow death by a thousand clicks: thousands of people see you on the street every day and it does not feel like an invasion of privacy, but if one person follows you everywhere as you work, read, watch movies, and do myriad other things, it becomes stalking. And so we are stalked in the pursuit of marketing optimization.

WHERE THE MONEY IS

The key data lesson of the Internet age is that the amount of data one possesses is just as important as the type. With enough data, it becomes possible to see patterns that one could never guess in isolation. Consider two contrasting examples: toothpaste and the flu.

Google Flu Trends is an example of apparently beneficent data aggregation. By tracking when and where people are searching Google for terms related to the flu, flu symptoms, and flu treatments, Google has been able to predict outbreaks of influenza before government agencies do, and has made it easier to track the path of a flu virus. In many First World countries, Google's predictions have correlated reasonably closely with subsequent government data. Only an entity with access to an enormous plurality of all Internet searches could achieve such accuracy in prediction.

The same goes for consumer data. If a marketer sees me buy toothpaste at a drugstore, that is not tremendously valuable information by itself. But if he knows my entire history of toothpaste purchases, including which brands I buy and how often, he can predict when I might need to buy toothpaste again, and whether I might be inclined to click on an ad directing me to a lower-cost brand, or to a store selling my usual brand at a cheaper price. If my dental insurer knew my toothpaste purchases, it could classify me as higher or lower risk and adjust my premiums and payments accordingly.

Google Flu Trends gauges collective tendencies among many people, but market research is oriented toward the individual. Targeting the right set of consumers has always been at the heart of advertising, but when web ads first appeared in the 1990s, their click-through rates quickly plummeted as users wised up; people stopped clicking on even the brightest banner ads. The revolution in Internet advertising did not come until 2000, when Google introduced its AdWords program, which allows anyone to bid for placement on ad spots that appear in response to searches for keywords. Google's system collected little to no data about a user; the ads were displayed based merely on the search query itself. Searching for "watches" generates watch ads, searching for "asbestos" generates ads for tort lawyers. The advertising model fortuitously avoided many of the privacy concerns that are emerging today, because the very nature of Google's business ensured that it would find out exactly what consumers wanted at the exact moment they wanted it: during the search.

Yet Google's system was dependent on its having a search   10
engine—*the* search engine, in fact. Click-through rates for online ads not generated by search engines are considerably lower, and Google's success in search ads has not been replicated anywhere else. For comparison, consider that Google's gross revenue was $37.9 billion in 2011 (96 percent of it from advertising), while Facebook's was merely $3.7 billion. And search continues to make up nearly half of all Internet advertising revenues, with Google dominating its competitors. Thus the social revolution precipitated by Facebook has not yet amounted to a shift in advertising effectiveness—one possible reason for Facebook's drastic decline in share price following its IPO in May 2012.

Internet marketing companies that aren't Google can't observe people at the moment of search, but knowing more about their lives might help refine targeted advertising. And so it has: while microtargeting hasn't come close to matching Google's success, it appears to have increased click-through rates sufficiently that several industries have sprung up around profiling and targeting consumers for advertising.

OBSERVATION

Whenever you browse the web, you leave a permanent trace of your activity. Every machine and device connected to the Internet has an IP address. The IP address does not identify you, but neither is it wholly anonymous. Blocks of IP addresses are associated with particular Internet service providers (ISPs), and most are geographically specific. This information is public: by visiting a website, you enable the website owner to learn where you are located. An ISP may assign you a different IP address over time, but frequently the address remains the same, so repeat visits can also be tracked.

Cookies are little pieces of data that websites ask your web browser to store. They can contain almost any data, but they're frequently used for remembering user preferences: the language you speak, for example, or your login and password. They also provide an easy way to tell when the same user is returning to a site. Browsers will send cookies back only to the site that sent them, and there are few limitations on what the site does with that knowledge, such as sell it to any or many other companies.

Companies like BlueCava have figured out a way to track online behavior without cookies. BlueCava's device identification platform attempted to identify individual users based on which browser and device they were using, information that is sent along with every request to a web server. (BlueCava now describes the service it provides as "multi-screen identification capabilities," presumably because it's harder to decipher what that actually means.) This is one of the reasons privacy remedies focused on particular technical mechanisms, such as the (mostly ignored) "do not track" header or third-party cookies, cannot suffice on their own.

The situation is different with sites like Facebook and Twitter, 15 which require users to sign up for an account that they are encouraged to remain logged in to. Unless you micromanage your web privacy settings and browser activity, these sites have the ability to track you across the web. Every time you go to a site that has a Facebook "like" button or a Twitter "tweet" button or a Google "+1" button, or a site that lets you comment with your Facebook or Twitter or Google account, those companies know that you've visited the site, whether or not you click on the button. And every time you click the "like" button or authorize an application, Facebook eagerly hands over your data to the online gaming company Zynga, and to newspapers and publishing companies. Sharing your information with a third-party application on Facebook is akin to poking a hole in a water balloon: only one prick is needed for everything to leak out.

COLLECTION

The lie of the web is that each page is a discrete entity. This was true a generation ago, when pages were merely formatted text, but now that they host all sorts of code and cookies, it's more accurate to think of web pages as collages of content, advertisements, federated services, and tracking mechanisms that can talk to one another to a lesser or greater degree depending on your browser's privacy settings. The web is becoming a tightly connected mass of trackers and bugs, a single beast with a million eyes pointing in every direction.

If you're logged in to Facebook, Twitter, Google, or Amazon, it's safe to say these sites are tracking and retaining everything you're doing on their sites and on any other sites that host their scripts and widgets. It's how they make recommendations: for friends, products, events. Advertising targeters like Acxiom, Turn, and BlueKai are tracking users in a different though equally invasive way. A newspaper's website may know all the visitors to its site, but it knows nothing about their activities elsewhere. Its advertisers might, however, and Google Analytics certainly does: it offers a wide array of services to websites, tracking where users are coming from and what they search for before arriving at a page, all behind a slick interface. In exchange, Google gets to see the entire history of a site's access logs. Google Analytics and similar services like Quantcast and comScore are so ubiquitous that most of your web browsing is likely captured by one or more of these companies. They don't have your name, but they have your IP address, rough physical location, and a good chunk of your activity online.

AGGREGATION AND MICROTARGETING

With so many entities collecting data and amassing consumer profiles, the profiles are often incomplete or even inaccurate. Acxiom may slot you, without your name, into a particular demographic: upscale young single male, suburban mom in a rich county, or one of many other categories. But for targeting coupons, a company needs far more than just a demographic. It needs to know which products you buy, the brands you like, when you buy and how.

This is the world of microtargeting. It has been used and refined over the last decade by political parties to determine where their voters are, so they don't mistakenly encourage the wrong people to get out and vote on Election Day. In 2012, the Obama campaign took a huge leap forward in microtargeting; its technology was unmatched by that of the inept Romney campaign, giving Obama's team a crucial edge in its ground game.

But identifying political affiliation is low-tech compared with advertising targeting, which needs to predict far more than one kind of behavior. Last June, the *New York Times* published a long article by Natasha Singer on Acxiom, which claims to have profiled 500 million consumers and offers its data in aggregated form to anyone who will pay for it, from websites to banks to insurance companies, and even to a US Army contractor. In the name of "multichannel marketing"—which is code for tracking a consumer in all her activities, from web browsing to television advertising to mail-order catalogs—Acxiom has been aggregating consumer data since its founding in 1969, and the explosion of data in the Internet age has been a big boon to it.

Acxiom offers a lengthy and confusing form to opt out of its database, as well as the ability to see some of the data it has collected on you, though not for free: "Access to information about you in our directory and our fraud detection and prevention products will be provided in the form of a Reference Report that is available for a processing fee of $5."

To compensate for the limitations of their data sets, smaller sites are increasingly turning over their advertising operations to exchanges. An advertising exchange determines the user's identity and targeted demographic and then offers that knowledge to advertisers, who bid in real time for the opportunity to show the user their ad. The consumer may be identified generally as a member of a particular microdemographic, but because these "segments" are very small, they can be linked to personally identifiable information with ease. The exchange knows exactly who you are.

FALSE PROMISES OF PRIVACY

Promises of anonymity are misleading and far from absolute. In a famous 2000 study, Latanya Sweeney determined that a voter list could be correlated with medical records at a rate of 87 percent

How familiar are you with the privacy policies of companies such as Google?

based not on any personal information but on three pieces of demographic data: sex, ZIP code, and birth date. This allowed the "anonymized" medical data to be linked to a particular name.

But it is not just those three pieces of data: enough anonymous data of any form allows for a positive identification. In 2006, Netflix offered up a huge, seemingly anonymous data set of the complete video ratings of nearly half a million members. In their 2008 paper "Robust De-anonymization of Large Sparse Datasets," computer scientists Arvind Narayanan and Vitaly Shmatikov showed that very little knowledge was required to correlate one of the anonymous lists with an Internet Movie Database account: an overlap of even a half-dozen films between Netflix's list and an IMDb account could suffice to make a highly likely positive match. Because many IMDb accounts use people's real names and other identifying information, they provide a foothold for obtaining a person's entire viewing history.

A Netflix user history may seem like a fairly harmless example 25 of "reidentification." Other data sets that are released "anonymously," including consumer purchases, website visits, health information, and basic demographic information, appear more menacing. When AOL Research released a large data set of Internet searches for 650,000 users of AOL's search engine in 2006, the *New York Times* and others were immediately able to identify some of the users by finding personal information in the search queries. AOL admitted its error, but the data remains out there for anyone to view. Notoriously, there was User 927, whose searches included "beauty and the beast disney porn," "intersexed genitals," and "oh i like that baby. I put on my robe and wizards hat."

Reidentification is a key aspect of giving value to data. It frequently has its value in the absence of total reidentification—marketers do not need to know your name or your Social Security number to show you ads. But if the value of the data goes up for credit bureaus and others that can determine your true identity, there is a strong incentive for them to do exactly that.

Hence, many privacy policies today give a false sense of security. Parsing the language of these policies is not easy, and because the information's value changes depending on how much other data it is collated with, such guarantees are at best naïve and at worst disingenuous.

As for subscription services, such as those offered by Apple, Google, and Facebook, anonymity doesn't really exist. These companies already know who you are. Ex-Google CEO Eric Schmidt described the Google+ social network as fundamentally an "identity service" providing a verifiable "strong identity" for its users—one that requires you to use your real name. Needless to say, actions performed while logged in to this identity are far less anonymous than those performed under a pseudonym or when not signed in. . . .

FIGHTING THE FUTURE

Given the choice, most consumers would prefer that their information not be collected and aggregated. And so advertisers and data aggregators have treated them like the proverbial boiling frog: enticing them into an indispensible social or technological network, then slowly eliminating their choices. Regulations and advocacy have been consistently losing ground against the advertising behemoth.

Most resistance to this kind of aggregation has been purely 30 reactive and not particularly effective. When the resistance has had any effect, it has played on momentary consumer outrage. Consider the case of Facebook Beacon, launched in 2007: the concept was that companies partnering with Facebook, which included eBay, Yelp, the *New York Times*, and Blockbuster, would allow it to put an invisible "web bug" on their sites that would enable Facebook to see everything its users did on the partner sites and associate that activity with their Facebook accounts, whether or not they were logged in. If I purchased shoes from Zappos, for example, Facebook would post that information to my wall automatically, saying, "David just bought shoes from Zappos!" Facebook users were "opted" in to Beacon without being asked and had to manually turn it off.

There was a public outcry: Facebook users did not want their online activity automatically advertised to their friends. MoveOn started a petition, and a class-action suit was filed against Facebook and several partners. Facebook quickly made Beacon optional for users, requiring an explicit opt-in, and subsequently allowed people to turn it off completely. Two years later, in 2009, it shut down Beacon altogether because, when given a choice, very few people wanted to opt in to such a program.

But Facebook didn't abandon the goals of Beacon. Rather, it learned from its mistake, grasping that what frightened people most about Beacon was seeing their online behavior publicized without their consent. Through the use of "like" buttons, comment registration, and third-party cookies, Facebook still monitors a large percentage of the online activity that Beacon was supposed to capture. It just doesn't publicize its actions.

This kind of two-step, where data is collected but the consumer is not notified, has become the norm in Internet commerce. The two-step works in other ways. Facebook has drastically weakened its privacy policies several times, most notably in 2009, 2010, and 2012, each time attempting to make more user information less private by default. (A brief timeline is available from the Electronic Frontier Foundation, which has worked diligently to raise consumer awareness.) Whenever there was a strong public protest, Facebook retreated, but not to its original position, thereby cooling critics' ire while still managing to raise the flame under the frog.

Facebook's case is an unusually visible one. Most companies have not had their data collection practices scrutinized so closely, if at all. Natasha Singer's *Times* article about Acxiom raised eyebrows in Congress and at the FTC, but no action has been forthcoming: "self-policing" seems to be the order of the day, which is to say there's no order at all. Because consumers remain mostly in the dark about the activities of companies like Acxiom, there is far less pressure on them than there has been on Facebook—and even there, the pressure hardly seems to have made a difference. The Obama administration's Consumer Privacy Bill of Rights, issued in February 2012, sets out vague guidelines for control and transparency that are wholly out of touch with reality: corporations have so far yielded nothing to it, and the government has not pressed the point.

Legislatively, there are very few existing guidelines, partly 35 owing to the difficulty in quantifying exactly what should be illegal: companies have been collecting this sort of data for years, so how would one justify criminalizing the collection of more of it? In *Steinberg v. CVS*, decided last year, CVS successfully fought off a Pennsylvania lawsuit over giving "anonymized" data to pharmacy companies and data brokers, because no legal protections were in place beyond the requirement of scrubbing people's names from the data. The concept of reidentification has not yet entered the legal domain—nor has the inevitability that the data will be combined with other data.

There are many legal issues to resolve, and the only impetus for change appears to be consumer education and outrage. But given the complexity and obscurity of data aggregation today, outrage occurs only when a company makes a public relations gaffe that's big, simple, and visible enough for the media to latch on to. Even then, few people end up leaving Facebook. All of your friends are there, being watched and anonymized as they "friend" and watch you, all of them doing, in the words of Joseph Turow, "free labor in the interest of corporate profits."

For Discussion and Writing

1. **Comprehension**   According to Auerbach, what is the "key data lesson of the Internet age" (par. 6)?

2. **Critical Reading**   At several points in the article, Auerbach tries to correct common misconceptions about Internet anonymity and privacy. How does he accomplish this? Point to a specific example, and describe the writer's strategy.

3. **Analysis**   Auerbach provides a thorough examination of microtargeting and the ways in which corporations continue to "to raise the flame under the frog" (par. 33). Does his article suggest any course of action to combat these invasions of privacy? Do you think it should? Explain your answer.

4. **Connections**   In "The IRL Fetish" (p. 191), Nathan Jurgenson writes about a "backlash" against connectivity and life online, including complaints that the "logic" of the Internet "has burrowed far into our consciousness" (pars. 2–3). How do you think Jurgenson would respond to Auerbach's article? For example, do you think he would accuse Auerbach of misguided "digital dualism" (par. 12)? Is Jurgenson's argument compatible with Auerbach's? Why or why not?

5. **Writing**   According to Auerbach, "most consumers would prefer that their information not be collected and aggregated" (par. 29). How do you respond to this, and to other generalizations about online users in the article? Do they apply to you? How do you understand notions of "privacy" and "anonymity" online? Will this article change your online behavior in any way? In a brief explanatory essay, lay out your own views of—and guidelines for managing—your online privacy.

NATHAN JURGENSON

The IRL Fetish

A doctoral candidate in sociology, Nathan Jurgenson researches and writes in the areas of social theory and the Internet. Jurgenson's work has appeared in Salon, *the* Atlantic, Omni, *and many other publications and academic journals, and he is a contributing editor at the* New Inquiry, *where this essay appeared in 2012. In the essay, Jurgenson addresses the now-common complaint that digital connectivity has disconnected us from "real life"—and that we have "logged on and checked out." But perhaps the relationship between the virtual, online world and "IRL" is not as simple as many presume.*

As you read, *notice how the writer embeds his argument into a wider conversation. Do you agree with his thesis? Where does Jurgenson address those with opposing points of view? How would you describe the style and tone of his writing?*

The deep infiltration of digital information into our lives has created a fervor around the supposed corresponding loss of logged-off *real life*. Each moment is oversaturated with digital potential: Texts, status updates, photos, check-ins, tweets, and emails are just a few taps away or pushed directly to your buzzing and chirping pocket computer—anachronistically still called a "phone." Count the folks using their devices on the train or bus or walking down the sidewalk or, worse, crossing the street oblivious to drivers who themselves are bouncing back and forth between the road and their digital distractor. Hanging out with friends and family increasingly means also hanging out with their technology. While eating, defecating, or resting in our beds, we are rubbing on our glowing rectangles, seemingly lost within the infostream.

If the hardware has spread virally within physical space, the software is even more insidious. Thoughts, ideas, locations, photos, identities, friendships, memories, politics, and almost everything else are finding their way to social media. The power of "social" is not just a matter of the time we're spending checking apps, nor is it the data that for-profit media companies are gathering; it's also that the *logic* of the sites has burrowed far into our consciousness. Smartphones and their symbiotic social media give us a surfeit of options to tell the truth about who we are and what we are doing, and an audience for it all, reshaping norms around mass exhibitionism and voyeurism. Twitter lips and Instagram eyes: Social media is part of ourselves; the Facebook source code becomes our own code.

Predictably, this intrusion has created a backlash. Critics complain that people, especially young people, have logged on and checked out. Given the addictive appeal of the infostream, the masses have traded real connection for the virtual. They have traded human friends for Facebook friends. Instead of being present at the dinner table, they are lost in their phones. Writer after writer laments the loss of a sense of disconnection, of boredom (now redeemed as a respite from anxious info-cravings), of sensory peace in this age of always-on information, omnipresent illuminated screens, and near-constant self-documentation. Most famously, there is Sherry Turkle, who is amassing fame for decrying the loss of real, offline connection. In the *New York Times*, Turkle writes that "in our rush to connect, we flee from solitude . . . we seem almost willing to dispense with people altogether." She goes on:

> I spend the summers at a cottage on Cape Cod, and for decades I walked the same dunes that Thoreau once walked. Not too long ago, people walked with their heads up, looking at the water, the sky, the sand, and at one another, talking. Now they often walk with their heads down, typing. Even when they are with friends, partners, children, everyone is on their own devices. So I say, look up, look at one another.

While the Cape Cod example is Kerry/Romney-level unrelatable, we can grasp her point: Without a device, we are heads up, eyes to the sky, left to ponder and appreciate. Turkle leads the chorus that insists that taking time out is becoming dangerously difficult and that we need to follow their lead and log off.

This refrain is repeated just about any time someone is forced to detether from a digital appendage. Forgetting one's phone causes a sort of existential crisis. Having to navigate without a

© haveseen/Shutterstock

"Nothing has contributed more to our collective appreciation for being logged off and technologically disconnected than the very technologies of connection." Has technology heightened the value of IRL, or diminished it?

maps app, eating a delicious lunch and not being able to post a photograph, having a witty thought without being able to tweet forces reflection on how different our modern lives really are. To spend a moment of boredom without a glowing screen, perhaps while waiting in line at the grocery store, can propel people into a *This American Life*[1]–worthy self-exploration about how profound the experience was.

Fueled by such insights into our lost "reality," we've been told to resist technological intrusions and aspire to consume less information: turn off your phones, log off social media, and learn to reconnect offline. Books like Turkle's *Alone Together*, William Powers's *Hamlet's Blackberry*, and the whole Digital Sabbath movement plead with us to close the Facebook tab so we can

5

---

[1]*This American Life:* a journalistic public radio program that features nonfiction short stories and essays. It is affiliated with National Public Radio (NPR) and hosted by Ira Glass. [Editor's note]

focus on one task undistracted. We should go out into the "real" world, lift our chins, and breathe deep the wonders of the offline (which, presumably, smells of Cape Cod).

But as the proliferation of such essays and books suggests, we are far from forgetting about the offline; rather we have become obsessed with being offline more than ever before. We have never appreciated a solitary stroll, a camping trip, a face-to-face chat with friends, or even our boredom better than we do now. Nothing has contributed more to our collective appreciation for being logged off and technologically disconnected than the very technologies of connection. The ease of digital distraction has made us appreciate solitude with a new intensity. We savor being face-to-face with a small group of friends or family in one place and one time far more thanks to the digital sociality that so fluidly rearranges the rules of time and space. In short, we've never cherished being alone, valued introspection, and treasured information disconnection more than we do now. Never has being disconnected—even if for just a moment—felt so profound.

The current obsession with the analog, the vintage, and the retro has everything to do with this fetishization of the offline. The rise of the mp3 has been coupled with a resurgence in vinyl. Vintage cameras and typewriters dot the apartments of Millennials. Digital photos are cast with the soft glow, paper borders, and scratches of Instagram's faux-vintage filters. The ease and speed of the digital photo resists itself, creating a new appreciation for slow film photography. "Decay porn" has become a thing.

Many of us, indeed, have always been quite happy to occasionally log off and appreciate stretches of boredom or ponder printed books—even though books themselves were regarded as a deleterious distraction as they became more prevalent. But our immense self-satisfaction in disconnection is new. How proud of ourselves we are for fighting against the long reach of mobile and social technologies! One of our new hobbies is patting ourselves on the back by demonstrating how much we *don't* go on Facebook. People boast about not having a profile. We have started to congratulate ourselves for keeping our phones in our pockets and fetishizing the offline as something more real to be nostalgic for. While the offline is said to be increasingly difficult to access, it is simultaneously easily obtained—if, of course, you are the "right" type of person.

Every other time I go out to eat with a group, be it family, friends, or acquaintances of whatever age, conversation routinely plunges into a discussion of when it is appropriate to pull out a phone. People boast about their self-control over not checking their device, and the table usually reaches a self-congratulatory consensus that we should all just keep it in our pants. The pinnacle of such abstinence-only smartphone education is a game that is popular to talk about (though I've never actually seen it played) wherein the first person at the dinner table to pull out their device has to pay the tab. Everyone usually agrees this is awesome.

What a ridiculous state of affairs this is. To obsess over the offline and deny all the ways we routinely remain disconnected is to fetishize this disconnection. Author after author pretends to be a lone voice, taking a courageous stand in support of the offline in precisely the moment it has proliferated and become over-valorized. For many, maintaining the fiction of the collective loss of the offline *for everyone else* is merely an attempt to construct their own personal time-outs as more special, as allowing them to rise above those social forces of distraction that have ensnared the masses. "I am real. I am the thoughtful human. You are the automaton." I am reminded of a line from a recent essay by Sarah Nicole Prickett: that we are "so obsessed with the real that it's unrealistic, atavistic, and just silly." How have we come to make the error of collectively mourning the loss of that which is proliferating?

In great part, the reason is that we have been taught to mistakenly view *online* as meaning *not offline*. The notion of the offline as real and authentic is a recent invention, corresponding with the rise of the online. If we can fix this false separation and view the digital and physical as enmeshed, we will understand that what we do while connected is inseparable from what we do when disconnected. That is, disconnection from the smartphone and social media isn't really disconnection at all: The logic of social media follows us long after we log out. There was and is no offline; it is a lusted-after fetish object that some claim special ability to attain, and it has always been a phantom.

Digital information has long been portrayed as an elsewhere, a new and different cyberspace, a tendency I have coined the term "digital dualism" to describe: the habit of viewing the online and offline as largely distinct. The common (mis)understanding is

[that] experience is zero-sum: time spent online means less spent offline. We are either jacked into the Matrix or not; we are either looking at our devices or not. When camping, I have service or not, and when out to eat, my friend is either texting or not. The smartphone has come to be "the perfect symbol" of leaving the here and now for something digital, some other, *cyber*, space.[2]

But this idea that we are trading the offline for the online, though it dominates how we think of the digital and the physical, is myopic. It fails to capture the plain fact that our lived reality is the result of the constant interpenetration of the online and offline. That is, we live in an augmented reality that exists at the intersection of materiality and information, physicality and digitality, bodies and technology, atoms and bits, the off and the online. It is wrong to say "IRL" to mean offline: *Facebook is real life.*

Facebook doesn't curtail the offline but depends on it. What is most crucial to our time spent logged on is what happened when logged off; it is the fuel that runs the engine of social media. The photos posted, the opinions expressed, the check-ins that fill our streams are often anchored by what happens when disconnected and logged-off. The Web has everything to do with reality; it comprises real people with real bodies, histories, and politics. It is the fetish objects of the offline and the disconnected that are not real.

Those who mourn the loss of the offline are blind to its prominence online. When Turkle was walking Cape Cod, she breathed in the air, felt the breeze, and watched the waves with Facebook in mind. The appreciation of this moment of so-called disconnection was, in part, a product of online connection.[3] The stroll ultimately was understood as and came to be fodder for her op-ed, just as our own time spent not looking at Facebook becomes the status updates and photos we will post later. 15

---

[2]To be clear, the digital and physical *are not the same*, but we should aim to better understand the relationship of different combinations of information, be they analog or digital, whether using the technologies of stones, transistors, or flesh and blood. Also, technically, bits *are* atoms, but the language can still be conceptually useful.

[3]Turkle takes for granted not only her Cape Cod cottage but also her access to high-profile op-ed space, blinding her to others' similar need for media to declare how meaningful our lives are.

The clear distinction between the on and offline, between human and technology, is queered beyond tenability. It's not real unless it's on Google; pics or it didn't happen. We aren't friends until we are Facebook friends. We have come to understand more and more of our lives through the logic of digital connection. Social media is more than something we log into; it is something we carry within us. We can't log off.

Solving this digital dualism also solves the contradiction: We may never fully log off, but this in no way implies the loss of the face-to-face, the slow, the analog, the deep introspection, the long walks, or the subtle appreciation of life sans screen. We enjoy all of this more than ever before. Let's not pretend we are in some special, elite group with access to the pure offline, turning the real into a fetish and regarding everyone else as a little less real and a little less human.

For Discussion and Writing

1. *Comprehension*   How would you restate Jurgenson's **thesis** in your own words?

2. *Critical Reading*   What is the **purpose** of the first six paragraphs of this essay? Why do you think the writer structured his argument in this way? How else could he have organized it?

3. *Analysis*   Jurgenson argues that the "current obsession with the analog, the vintage, and the retro has everything to do with this fetishization of the offline" (par. 7). What does he mean by this, specifically? Do you agree with the causal connection he proposes here? Why or why not?

4. *Connections*   In both Jurgenson's essay and David Auerbach's "You Are What You Click" (p. 179), the writers generalize about how most people interact with the Internet. How would you compare and contrast their two characterizations of online users? For example, Auerbach uses the word "consumers" to describe them, while Jurgenson does not. What does that (or other details) reveal about their different views?

5. *Writing*   According to Jurgenson, we have "never cherished being alone, valued introspection, and treasured information disconnection more than we do now" (par. 6). Do you agree that connectivity and immersion in technology has made us more appreciate and sensitive to "real life"? Or do you identify with the technological "backlash," and see problems with his argument? Write an argumentative response to Jurgenson that takes a position on one or more of these questions.

CHAPTER 4

Music
How does popular music reflect and express our identities?

Popular culture may be America's greatest—and most influential—domestic product and global export, everything from our movies and television shows to our fashion and music. When we consider the country's singular cultural icons, American popular music might be its most distinctive legacy. Musical traditions and genres such as jazz, blues, rock 'n' roll, and hip-hop are accepted by most cultural critics as exemplars of indigenous American art. Of course, that was not always the case. Now embraced in concert halls and composition courses at prestigious music colleges, jazz spent most of the early twentieth century as a disreputable, vulgar, "popular" form associated with rebellion and licentious sexuality. Its African American origins and associations only compounded the worst suspicions of its detractors. European classical music was "respectable," said the great jazz bandleader Duke Ellington, while "jazz has always been like the kind of man you wouldn't want your daughter to associate with." We can trace the same trajectory for other popular musical forms. In 1957, the singer Frank Sinatra—himself an avatar of an earlier popular music genre gone "respectable"—lashed out at rock 'n' roll as a "vicious" and "degenerate" idiom that was "sung, played, and written for the most part by cretinous goons and by means of its almost imbecilic reiterations and sly, lewd—in plain fact dirty—lyrics." From our perspective, of course, rock 'n' roll long ago entered the respectable American mainstream as a form lauded for its authenticity, complexity, and power. The same story arc is true for hip-hop and country music.

198

That "respectability" has brought praise and acceptance, along with academic and scholarly attention. No doubt, the analysis of popular music can provide insight into our culture, society, and politics—perhaps more than its sophisticated, esoteric, or "serious" counterparts. For example, we would likely learn more about the social and cultural mood of 1967 from that year's hit pop songs, like Buffalo Springfield's "For What It's Worth"; Aretha Franklin's "Respect"; Sam and Dave's "Soul Man"; or the Jefferson Airplane's "White Rabbit," than we would from the "serious" composer Aaron Copeland's demanding 1967 work *Inscape,* an orchestral homage to the work of nineteenth-century English poet Gerald Manley Hopkins. That is, those popular hits are probably more indicative of the everyday tastes of ordinary people—especially younger people—as well as more overtly representative of cultural preoccupations and themes like rebellion, feminism, race, and social change. "Respectability" may have a downside as well, as formerly rebellious or subversive forms lose their dangerous edges and become safe for mass consumption. But whether the writers in this chapter are focusing on a megastar like Taylor Swift or a niche indie rock band like Neutral Milk Hotel, all of them demonstrate that popular music makes a powerful conduit for vital, revealing, and contentious conversations about art, authenticity, identity, technology, spirituality, politics, and America.

In "'Elevate My Mind': Identities for Women in Hip-Hop Love Songs," Pamela Hollander uses the tools of discourse theory to analyze feminine identity and gender relationships in hip-hop and contemporary rhythm and blues. Will Wilkinson analyzes the connections between personality, political ideology, and country music in "Country Music, Openness to Experience, and the Psychology of Culture War." In "Seduced by 'Perfect' Pitch: How Auto-Tune Conquered Pop Music," Lessley Anderson reports—and reflects—on one of the most commonly reviled and commonly used pieces of musical technology: the audio-processing device, Auto-Tune. In "Riffs of Passage," Tina Vasquez mixes personal narrative and cultural analysis to paint a revealing portrait of a Latino musical subculture in Los Angeles.

The paired readings offer two distinct but overlapping perspectives on contemporary pop and indie rock. Saul Austerlitz ("The Pernicious Rise of Poptimism") challenges pop-music writing's dominant "mode of critical thought": "poptimism," which privileges artificiality and sheer popularity over more traditional aesthetic standards. In the process, it "diminishes the glory of music," according to Austerlitz. In "Concerning the Spiritual in Indie Rock," Judy Berman explores a particular kind of musical glory: spirituality. Considering bands like Animal Collective and Arcade Fire in a secular age, she suggests the possibility that their music can "reawake[n] our collective memory of what faith and worship feel like."

As you read, notice that while all these writers write about music, they are also exploring larger themes and topics like identity, spirituality, technology, and economic inequality.

- How do your own musical preferences and interests overlap with these, and other, more general issues?
- Does popular music serve any purpose beyond fun and entertainment? Should it?
- How do these writers move from reflecting on their personal experiences and musical preferences to analyzing more general questions and issues?

PAMELA HOLLANDER

"Elevate My Mind": Identities for Women in Hip-Hop Love Songs

Pamela Hollander is an assistant professor in the education depart-ment at Worcester State University. She earned a B.A. from Bingham-ton University, an M.Ed. from Rutgers University, and an Ed.D. from the University of Massachusetts. Her research focuses on the connec-tions between popular culture and learning, both inside and outside the classroom. In this scholarly article from the journal Studies in Popu-lar Culture, *Hollander uses Critical Discourse Analysis, which ana-lyzes the details of spoken and written language to show how discourse reveals social and political power relationships—especially around issues of dominance and control. Hollander examines various types of female identity as they are constructed in songs by hip-hop and R&B artists like Ms. Dynamite, Beyoncé, and Eve.*

As you read, notice how Hollander uses classification to organize her analysis. What categories of identity does she establish? Do you find Hollander's theoretical framework a useful way of exploring this topic? What insights does her argument give into representations of women—and gender roles—in hip-hop?

In hip hop within the category of "confessional" songs, love can be a viable topic. LL Cool J's "I Need Love," which explores what happens when a young man outgrows superficial dalliances, came out in 1987 and is considered an early example of a commercially successful hip hop love song (Pough 164). Although there have continued to be rap songs about love, identities in hip hop love songs are constrained by the pressure to fit already existing iden-tities for men and women in hip hop, as well as by music indus-try demands (Long par. 4, Pough 165). In her essay "Love as the

201

Practice of Freedom," bell hooks speaks about the importance of love for social justice work. She describes how popular culture often "mocks" the idea of real love and says, "To choose love is to go against the prevailing values of the culture" (293). She quotes Scott Peck's definition of love from his self-help book *The Road Less Traveled* as the basis for her "ethic of love." Peck says love is "the will to extend one's self for the purpose of nurturing one's own or another's spiritual growth" (qtd. in hooks 293). Through my teaching of a class called The Culture and Language of Hip Hop, I began to notice some recent hip hop love songs which seemed to push against the accepted identities for women in hip hop and point toward love as involving "nurturing" and "spiritual growth." This essay is an examination of those love songs.

IDENTITY AND WRITING

Theories of language which concern themselves with the reflexive nature of language and reality are helpful for looking at rap lyrics. These theories talk about language as being made up of discourses, ways of seeing the world, which position the language user as well as the receiver, and influence the individual and collective understanding of self and reality (Pahl and Rowsell). These discourses wield different amounts of power and influence, depending on their cultural dominance at any one moment in time. Discourses and associated identities vie for power in the open market of culture.

The notion of discourses is particularly exciting for the study of language such as rap lyrics because 1) discourses and their associated identities tell a great deal about the values of an individual or culture when analyzed, and 2) discourses' and identities' influential and dynamic nature means that if enough people use a discourse, it can make a change in people's thinking, identities, and the language itself. Discourse theory, which posits that discourses offer people identities (often called subjectivities or subject positions) to be taken up, gives reason to hope for the raising of consciousness and for positive change through a person's adoption of these identities (Ivanic 1–55). An example of this would be the rise of the "Conscious Rap" or "Conscience Rap" Discourse, which has spread because of rappers like Talib Qweli, Mos Def, Common, and others associated with exploring intellectual and political issues in their songs, while eschewing to some degree commercial success. The Conscious Hip Hop discourse offers new identities to take up as "someone who cares about political issues and is intellectually involved." These new identities did not exist in quite the same way before the rise of this discourse.

The importance of applying such discourse theory to writing, like rap songs, lies in its ability to show connections between what is said and particular identities and the underlying values and ideologies of their associated discourses. Hip hop artists can create new identities through their identification with particular discourses, and that in itself is exciting, but the real potential here is in how these discourses and identities make new identities available to the countless listeners and consumers of hip hop culture. Listeners of hip hop may be influenced to take up discourses and identities they gain access to through the songs.

To get at these connections between the micro-level (what is said) and the macro-level (particular identities and underlying values and ideologies of their associated discourses), I will use the New Literacy Studies method of Critical Discourse Analysis. This method consists of coding songs for particular identities. In this case I will be looking for the alternative identities connected to "nurturing" and "spiritual growth" which I mentioned earlier, as well as more traditional identities, such as "angry," "feminist" or "ride or die," which will be discussed later.

While reproduction of existing discourses and identities is most common, the possibility for resistance always exists. Resistance typically occurs when a new discourse/identity is created. One way new identities are created is through hybridity. Hybrid identities are created when different identities and discourses are blended together to form something which is more than a sum of its parts. I will be looking for instances of hybridity between different, potentially conflicting identities for women in hip hop.

WOMEN AND HIP HOP

Women have struggled to be heard in hip hop since the beginning. Much has been written about the difficulties women have had breaking into this male-dominated area. Early women in hip hop often reacted against male versions of reality. As women railed against male stereotypes of women, they took up a variety of new and stereotypical identities themselves. Cheryl Keyes, in her article "Empowering Self, Making Choices, Creating Spaces," talks about four images of black womanhood introduced to hip hop by women rappers: Queen Mother, Fly Girl, Sista With Attitude, and Lesbian. While female rappers responded to male versions of reality with their own versions, like Queen Latifah's feminist, Queen persona, female rappers often mirrored traditionally male personas as well. For example, although MC Lyte rapped feminist lyrics, she portrayed herself in some of her videos similarly to male rappers, wearing masculine clothing and posturing as a male rapper might. Salt n Pepa surprised audiences with their refreshing woman-centered views of sexual relations with men, although they could be considered Fly Girls: they sometimes wore tight-fitting and low-cut clothing, seemingly playing into stereotypes of women as sex objects. (Queen Latifah, MC Lyte, and Salt n Pepa all flourished as rappers in the late 1980s and early 1990s.) The identities that women took up in hip hop were complex from the beginning. Women gained acceptance and power in hip hop through imitation of a male style of rapping as well as through introducing their own unique identities and styles.

HIP HOP AND LOVE

Love is one topic of many that female and male rappers have rapped about. However, both sexes have been constrained in their expressions about love. Nathan Long writes about how male rappers have only been able to rap about love in ways that allow them to take up certain identities acceptable in the black urban community (par. 1). According to Long, males rapping about love must present their tale in a way that does not show their sensitivity as a weakness (par. 5). Male rappers have dexterously worked to create hybrid identities which include love and acceptable identities related to the "cool pose," so they can rap about love.

Women rappers are under constraints as well when it comes to rapping about love. Dominant identities available include those related to questioning male love or those affirming male versions of love. Additionally, women rappers have often represented a less "romanticized" love than other forms of music, as they represent a grittier working-class view of relationships (Pough 186–187).

The identity of "feminist" has been taken up by women in relation to love. "Feminism" might be thought of in association with Queen Mothers or Feminists, but is just [as] likely to be taken up by Sistas With Attitude, Fly Girls, R&B/Neo Soul, or category-defying artists. This identity has mainly been associated with a posture of defense against male neglect and abuse in relationships with women. Many women rappers have devoted much of their time responding to male versions of sexuality, relationships, and other aspects of reality (Weiner par. 4), from Roxanne ("Roxanne Roxanne") to Queen Latifah ("Ladies First") to Lauryn Hill ("That Thing"). In Eve's 1999 song "Love Is Blind," she rails against her friend's abusive boyfriend: "I don't even know you and I'd kill you myself / You played wit her like a doll and put her back on the shelf." She gets more specific: "Wouldn't let her go to school and better herself / She had a baby by your ass and you ain't giving no help." Eve paints the abusive relationship: "Uh-huh big time hustler, snake mother fucker / One's born everyday and everyday she was your sucker." Eve's discussion of abuse places her among feminists.

Another identity women in hip hop take up in relation to love is a Ride or Die (stand by your man) identity. This identity is also more widespread than might be assumed, being found not only among those taking on a female Thug identity or a Sista With Attitude identity, but also among Fly Girls and others when they want to represent themselves, in the hip hop tradition, as loyal to the end. While romanticized love, according to Pough, is more of a topic for women in R&B and pop music, hip hop represents a less romantic view of love connected to a working-class view of life:

> Women of rap address issues pertinent to black working-class and ghetto culture in a manner unlike other black women artists in jazz, rhythm and blues, and contemporary pop song styles. While other black women singers deal with topics that conform to the traditional or mainstream idealization of romantic love, women in rap approach love themes and other topics from a viewpoint that is meaningful to black working-class women. Women in rap are more closely allied to the women blues singers, known as classic blues singers, of the 1920s. (186–187)

10

© Myrna Suarez/Getty Images

"The Ride or Die imagery is obvious in the references to Bonnie and Clyde, and both Jay-Z and Beyoncé say several times that they would give their lives for each other." How does this image support Hollander's analysis?

Working-class women's representation of love may take the shape of concerns such as incarcerated men, money problems, and ghetto life. A good example of this would be M.I.A. X's 1995 song about waiting for her boyfriend to get out of jail, "Wanna Be With You": "For 15 months this heat in here has been locked up / My Man Fell has been away; he fell right through the system." M.I.A. X stands by her man, taking up a traditional Ride or Die identity which has been around in hip hop at least since the rise of gangsta rap in the early 1990s: "Although he's been gone I've had to stay true / 'Cause you got to be down if your man is down for you." This Ride or Die identity, which is connected to hip hop's obsession with Bonnie and Clyde, can be seen in many songs, including Ice Cube and Yo-Yo's "Bonnie and Clyde Theme" and "Bonnie & Clyde II," Ja Rule's "Down Ass Bitch" (Pough 189), and many others. In all of these songs the theme is that the woman will stay by the man's side through anything—will give her life for him. The pact that Ride or Die represents is not only a pact to stand by each other, but has an element of the gangster life. So each member of the couple will watch each other's backs because there may be danger everywhere.

Although there are constraints, the influence of R&B and Neo-Soul on hip hop allows for a dialogue between men and women that moves toward the sort of love that Mary J. Blige talks about in "Real Love" and a move toward concern with intellectual and emotional needs of the self and a romantic partner. R&B and Neo-Soul seem to provide broader possibilities for love in hip hop in two ways. First, using R&B and Neo-Soul hooks/choruses opened "more possibilities for women's voices and issues to be heard" (Pough 172). Second, as R&B and Neo-Soul singers began to sing whole songs with hip hop sensibilities, women and men were able to maintain their identities as singers who sing about love while also showing their connection to hip hop. Their identities became hybrid, and this hybridity allowed for new ideas to come through. I will look at some of these new identities next.

"NURTURING" AND "SPIRITUAL GROWTH" IDENTITIES

My analysis of identities for women in hip hop love songs began with mostly mainstream hip hop, hip hop/R&B, and mainstream hip hop/Neo-Soul hybrid songs that were about "relationships." I looked at Nelly's (feat. Kelly Rowland) "Dilemma," Lil' Flip's (feat. Lea) "Sunshine," J. Lo and Ja Rule's "I'm Real," Ne-Yo's "Miss Independent," Jay-Z and Beyoncé's "'03 [2003] Bonnie & Clyde," and Erykah Badu and Common's "Love of My Life." I found a range of identities available for women in these songs, often multiple identities in the same songs, from a "friend with benefits" with no strings attached in Lil' Flip's declaration that he can't promise anything long term, "But when my plane touch down, pick me up at 8:00, don't be late" ("Sunshine") to the more serious declarations of long-term commitment couched in the gritty "I'll die for you" sentiment of "'03 Bonnie & Clyde." I did not find commitment and intimacy portrayed in most of these songs, except for Jay-Z and Beyoncé's duet. After this exploration I became more selective, really homing in on my search for the commitment and intimacy associated with the reality of, or search for, "love" as opposed to just a relationship. I was particularly interested in how women portrayed themselves in their own songs. I searched through many women's songs to find ones which talked about "nurturing" and "spiritual development." The songs that I found were Jill Scott's "A Long Walk," Jean Grae's "Give It Up," Ms. Dynamite's "Fall in Love Again," Da Brat and Cherish's "In Love Wit Chu," and Erykah Badu's (featuring Common) "Love of My Life." I then looked at some men's songs and duets which made identities associated with "nurturing" and "spiritual development" available, including Fabulous and Ne-Yo's

"Make Me Better," Common's "The Light," Black Thought and Erykah Badu's "You Got Me," and Common's (featuring Mary J. Blige) "Come Close." I also took a second look at Jay-Z and Beyoncé's "'03 Bonnie & Clyde."

FINDINGS

Intellectual Connection

An alternative identity that comes through in relation to love in these songs is "intellectual." As I alluded to earlier, women in hip hop have occupied the identity of "intellectual," drawing on the Queen Mother position and on the sort of identities Perry talks about in relation to men: "preacher," "intellectual" (157, 132). In the case of love songs, this intellectualism is directed toward love. These women are experiencing or looking for love which includes a meeting of the minds. Sharing poetry, talking about ideas, and appreciating each other's intellect become an important part of a relationship.

It is fitting that one intellectual connection given importance 15 has to do with "words" and "writing." "Love of My Life" traces a lifelong relationship between a woman and man and begins, "I met him when I was a little girl. He gave me poetry and he was my first." "He gave me poetry" suggests that he inspired her intellectually. Jean Grae pairs sex and words in these lines from "Give It Up": "I wanna Rock a fella so bad, oh man. Note pad filled with all the ink his soul had visions of us kissin' the whole nine." Grae fears losing her friendship with this man if they take their relationship to a physical level: "But I can't sleep, I risk the chance of losin' everything. / A friendship is more important than a wedding ring." And she adds, "I'm in this universal problem. Y'all can probably relate, y'all follow then, so do I give my lovin' to him? Or would that just ruin everything that we're about?" These words show her enjoyment of his intellect. Women and men in these songs are enjoying each other's ideas and intellectual company. Jill Scott lays out many delicious possibilities for time spent together: "Find a spot for us to spark conversation, verbal elation, stimulations. Share our situation, temptations, education, relaxations, elevations, maybe we can talk about Surah 31.18. . . . Or maybe we can see a play on Saturday, or maybe we can . . . feel the breeze and listen to a symphony" ("A Long Walk"). Da Brat raps that she "Finally found somebody who see me instead what's on the outside" ("In Love Wit Chu") and Ms. Dynamite refers to intellectual connection when she says she is looking for a man who will "Elevate my mind and stimulate my soul" ("Fall in Love Again").

Intimacy and Nurturing

The intimacy and nurturing I found in women's love songs draw on identities made available through R&B and Neo-Soul songs and performances, as opposed to those made available through hip hop. The blurring of lines between the music genres has helped to bring this intimacy into women's hip hop love songs.

All of these songs referred to intimacy, making an "intimate" identity available. Intimacy was referred to in terms of how the men make the women feel loved and cared for, and how the women feel around the men in general. These lyrics talk about closeness and meaningful times they spend together. The women rap about how they know they will feel safe and adored when close to the men they are with or want to be with. Da Brat raps about how her boyfriend "adores" her and Jean Grae says the man she loves "knows the way I am" ("In Love Wit Chu"; "Give It Up"). Trina, thinking about the guy she has "a thang for," says, "Just hold me tightly up in your arms / And tell me (everyday) that you ain eva gon leave me heartbroke" ("I Got a Thang for You").

A love that helps both parties grow was a theme in many of these songs, making the identity available of someone who is nurtured by a relationship and can nurture in return. Da Brat expresses the feeling that she has found someone who makes her feel even better about herself. She raps, "My self esteem is even higher when I'm walking with you" ("In Love Wit Chu"). Ms. Dynamite captures this sentiment when she says, "Love me much and he ain't afraid to let it show and help me grow, and he's honest" ("Fall in Love Again"). She paints her fantasy love as someone who will help her "achieve things." Jill Scott's song "A Long Walk," about spending the day "sparking" each other's thoughts, portrays a relationship based on the idea that she and her boyfriend will nurture and encourage each other's intellectual and spiritual growth with positivity (and see above on intellectual connection).

Complications

Nonetheless, many of these songs did not belie problems and issues with love. Ms. Dynamite's "Fall in Love Again" is actually an echo of Mary J. Blige's song "Real Love" in that it is about what she wishes she had, not what she has. In that song she points out some problems she has faced in relationships in the past: "He was too insecure and immature / I was open, my heart got broken." Even in the songs that are about relationships that are positive, concerns arise. Throughout Jean Grae's song "A Long Walk," she is contemplating whether she should move forward with a romantic relationship: "Hey boy, you know sometimes when two people are in love / They just can't see to get it together / And that's how I feel about you / But he's different though I feel him mo / Can't fuck up the friendship for those dimples, Nope!" She worries continually about "ruining" the friendship they have by having a physical relationship with this man. The whole of Badu's song "Love of My Life" is about two people who care about each other and have a bond, but don't get together for a long time.

DISCUSSION

The range of possible identities available for women in hip hop love songs seems to be widened by identities associated with intellectual connection, intimacy, and growth. Men seem to draw on these identities as well, although in some cases I saw hybridity between these identities and the Ride or Die identity. I found duets that made available the identities associated with intellectual connection, intimacy, and growth, but duets do not always represent a dialogue between the sexes. Sometimes there is dialogue, and other times the female part is simply an extension of the male's thoughts, as in the case of "'03 Bonnie & Clyde," when Beyoncé [simply] agrees with what Jay-Z has outlined. It should be said that in terms of the amount of singing or rhyming, most of the duets that I found are dominated by the male artist.

Nevertheless, intellectual, intimacy, and growth identities represent resistance to more traditional hip hop Ride or Die identities. Some of the artists themselves point out the contrast between other less intellectual and intimate types of love. Jean Grae thinks about her previous experiences with the "rules" of romance in comparison to this more serious kind of love: "He's not a bad boy, never sampled his type before" ("Give It Up"). Jay-Z points out that his love for his girlfriend goes against the way that other men treat women—men who "treat the one that you lovin' with the same respect that you treat the one that you humpin'" ("'03 Bonnie and Clyde"). Da Brat compares her intimate love with other available approaches when she says, "Finally found somebody who see me instead what's on the outside" ("In Love Wit Chu"). And finally, Common says, "I will never call you my bitch or even my boo. There's so much in a name and so much more in you," acknowledging the demeaning "bitch" and pet name "boo" which is often associated with a Ride or Die identity in hip hop ("The Light"). Intellectual, intimate, and nurturing identities widen possibilities for women and men when it comes to love.

CONCLUSION

Love is not the dominant focus of hip hop, but rap love songs provide an interesting look into the ways women and men are identifying themselves and relating to each other. "Watching each other's backs" may be a real and practical concern, but it is joined by and in some cases replaced by mutual respect, admiration, and intimacy.

The kind of new identities associated with women that I saw in relation to love—intellectual commitment, intimacy, and growth— were ones associated with a mature view of relationships. These are the sorts of songs a rapper might pen after earlier years of writing about clubbing. P Diddy, for example, didn't contribute the song about commitment titled "I Need a Girl" until he had done a lot of rapping about being a "player." Jean Grae's song "Give It Up," seen within her other work, shows a serious, introspective woman who has a certain maturity beyond hanging out in clubs. Rappers who now might not be including these kinds of mature love identities, might, at some future date.

bell hooks writes that "Without love, our efforts to liberate ourselves and our world community from oppression and exploitation are doomed" (289). hooks feels that an "ethic of love" needs to be present for forward movement away from domination. She often writes and speaks about pop culture and the importance of critically studying pop culture, and realizing the impact it has on our culture, in addition to enjoying it.

Love, according to hooks, needs to be worked on and improved 25 actively. Improvements in the representation of love in hip hop will have far-reaching effects.

Works Cited

Badu, Erykah (featuring Common). "Love of My Life (An Ode to Hip Hop)." *Music From the Motion Picture Soundtrack Brown Sugar*. MCA, 2002. CD.

Common (featuring Mary J. Blige). "Come Close." *Electric Circus*. MCA/Universal, 2002. CD.

Common. "The Light." *Like Water for Chocolate*. MCA, 2000. CD.

Da Brat (featuring Cherish). "In Love Wit Chu." *Limelight, Luv and Nightclubz*. Arista, 2003. CD.

Eve. "Love Is Blind." *Ruff Ryder's First Lady*. Interscope Records, 1999. CD.

Grae, Jean. "Give It Up." *This Week*. Babygrande/Orchestral, 2004. CD.

hooks, bell. *Outlaw Culture*. New York: Routledge, 1994. Print.

Ivanic, Roz. *Writing and Identity*. Philadelphia: John Benjamins, 1998. Print.

Jay-Z (feat. Beyoncé Knowles). "'03 Bonnie & Clyde." *Blueprint 2.1*. Rock-A-Fella Records, 20 Sony Urban Music/Sucka Free Records/Columbia, 2004. CD.

Keyes, Cheryl L. "Empowering Self, Making Choices, Creating Spaces: Black Female Identity via Rap Music Performance." *That's the Joint!: The Hip-Hop Studies Reader*. Eds. Murray Forman and Mark Anthony Neal. New York: Routledge, 2004. Print.

Lil' Flip (featuring Lea). "Sunshine." *U Gotta Feel Me*. Sony Urban Music/Sucka Free Records/Columbia, 2004. CD.

Long, Nathaniel. "Hip-Hop Love Songs and the Construction of Socially Acceptable Urban Identities." N.d. Hiphoplinguistics .com. Nathaniel Long. Rpt. Articles3K.com. N.p. Web. 19 July 2013.

M.I.A.X. "Wanna Be With You." *Good Girl Gone Bad*. Priority Records, 1995. CD.

Ms. Dynamite. "Fall in Love Again." *Judgement Days*. Polydor Ltd., 2005. CD.

Ne-Yo. "Miss Independent." *Year of the Gentleman*. Def Jam, 2008. CD.

Pahl, Kate, and Jennifer Rowsell. *Literacy and Education: Understanding the New Literacy Studies in the Classroom*. London: Sage / Paul Chapman Educational, 2005. Print.

Perry, Imani. *Prophets of the Hood*. London: Duke UP, 2004. Print.

Pough, Gwendolyn D. *Check It While I Wreck It*. Boston: Northeastern UP, 2004. Print.

Roots (featuring Erykah Badu). "You Got Me." MCA America, 1999. CD.

Scott, Jill. "A Long Walk." *Who Is Jill Scott, Vol. I*. Hidden Beach/ Sony Music Entertainment, 2000. CD.

Weiner, Jonah. "Ladies! I Can't Hear You! No, Really, I Can't Hear You!: Where Did All the Female Rappers Go?" *Slate Magazine*. Nov. 6, 2008. Web. 18 July, 2013.

For Discussion and Writing

1. **Comprehension**   According to Hollander, why is studying discourses "exciting" as an approach to rap lyrics (par. 3)?

2. **Critical Reading**   Who is the **audience** for this article? What does the writer assume about her readers? Considering where it was published, do you think that "Elevate My Mind" is reasonably accessible for general readers? Why or why not?

3. **Analysis**   From the perspective of Hollander's analysis, how do "intellectual," "intimacy," and "growth" identities "represent resistance to more traditional hip-hop Ride or Die identities" (par. 21)?

4. **Connections**   Both Pamela Hollander and Ariel Levy (p. 128) write about representations of female identity in the context of popular culture. Considering the same cultural time period as Hollander, Levy analyzes the tendency for women to enact a "tawdry, tarty, cartoonlike version of female sexuality" (par. 9). What topical or thematic overlap do you find between Hollander's article and Levy's? How might the subtext of racial and cultural identity explain some of the differences between the two analyses?

5. **Writing**   Hollander focuses her analysis mostly on "mainstream hip-hop, hip-hop/R&B, and mainstream hip-hop/Neo-Soul hybrid songs that were about 'relationships'" (par. 13). In an essay that follows Hollander's strategy—closely reading lyrics and interpreting the song's themes and implications for female identity—analyze a song or multiple songs by an artist of singer in the same genre. Does your example (or examples) support Hollander's categorical and theoretical framework? Does your analysis complicate or problematize her conclusions, or show the limitations of her approach? Explain your answer to these questions as part of your essay.

WILL WILKINSON

Country Music, Openness to Experience, and the Psychology of Culture War

Writer Will Wilkinson grew up in Iowa and graduated from the University of Northern Iowa. He has an M.A. in philosophy from Northern Illinois University. Wilkinson has held positions at the libertarian Cato Institute, George Washington University's Mercatus Center, and the Institute for Humane Studies. His work has appeared in the Atlantic, *the* Economist, Slate, Reason, *and many other outlets. Currently, he is working on his M.F.A. in creative writing at the University of Houston. In this article, which appeared online at BigThink, he connects the powerful appeal of country music to listeners with specific temperamental tendencies, cognitive styles, and political convictions.*

As you read, note the writer's own perspective on country music: Is he a fan? Do his musical preferences and his personality align with the main point of his essay? In what ways does country music serve as a "bulwark against cultural change"?

In the car, I listen to country music. Country has an ideology. Not to say country has a position on abortion, exactly. But country music, taken as a whole, has a position on life, taken as a whole. Small towns. Dirt roads. Love at first sight. Hot-blooded kids havin' a good ol' time. Gettin' hitched. America! Raisin' up ruddy-cheeked scamps who you will surely one day worry are having too good a hot-blooded time. Showing up for Church. Venturing confused into the big wide world only to come back to Alabama forever since there ain't a damn single thing out there in the Orient or Paris, France, what compares to that spot by the river under the trembling willows where first you kissed the girl you've known in your heart since second grade is the only girl you would ever truly love. Fishin'! How grandpa, who fought in two wars, worked three jobs, raised four kids, and never once complained, can't hardly wait to join grandma up in heaven, cuz life just ain't no good without her delicious pies.

Last night, on my way to fetch bok choy, I heard Collin Raye's classic "One Boy, One Girl," a song that takes the already suffocating sentimentality of the FM-country weltanschauung and turns it up to fourteen. The overwhelming force of this song's manufactured emotion led me unexpectedly to a conjecture about conservative psychology and the stakes of the "culture wars."

Now, conservatives and liberals really do differ psychologically. Allow me to drop some science:

> Applying a theory of ideology as motivated social cognition and a "Big Five" framework, we find that two traits, Openness to New Experiences and Conscientiousness, parsimoniously capture many of the ways in which individual differences underlying political orientation have been conceptualized. . . .
>
> We obtained consistent and converging evidence that personality differences between liberals and conservatives are robust, replicable, and behaviorally significant, especially with respect to social (vs. economic) dimensions of ideology. In general, liberals are more open-minded, creative, curious, and novelty seeking, whereas conservatives are more orderly, conventional, and better organized. (Carney et al. 807)

Full disclosure: I score very high in "openness to experience" and worryingly low in "conscientiousness." (When I was first diagnosed with ADD, my very concerned psychiatrist asked, "Do you have a hard time keeping jobs?") This predicts that I'm extremely liberal, that my desk is a total mess, and that my bedroom is cluttered with books, art supplies, and "cultural memorabilia." It's all true.

Is country music really conservative music? It's obvious if you 5
listen to it: Peter Rentfrow and Samuel Gosling's fascinating paper "The Do Re Mi's of Everyday Life: The Structure and Personality Correlates of Music Preferences" helps identify country as the most "upbeat and conventional" genre of music. A preference for "upbeat and conventional" music is negatively correlated with "openness" and positively correlated with "conscientiousness," and so, as you would then expect, self-described conservatives tend to like "upbeat and conventional" music (more than

any other kind), while self-described liberals tend to like everything else better.

Again, those low in "openness" are less likely to visit other countries, try new kinds of food, take drugs, or buck conventional norms generally. This would suggest that most conservatives aren't going to seek and find much intense and meaningful emotion in exotic travel, hallucinogenic ecstasy, sexual experimentation, or challenging aesthetic experience. The emotional highlights of the low-openness life are going to be the type celebrated in "One Boy, One Girl": the moment of falling in love with "the one," the wedding day, the birth [of] one's children (though I guess the song is about a surprising ultrasound). More generally, country music comes again and again to the marvel of advancing through life's stations, and finds delight in experiencing traditional familial and social relationships from both sides. Once I was a girl with a mother, now I'm a mother with a girl. My parents took care of me, and now I take care of them. I was once a teenage boy threatened by a girl's gun-loving father, now I'm a gun-loving father threatening my girl's teenage boy. And country is full of assurances that the pleasures of simple, rooted, small-town, lives of faith are deeper and more abiding than the alternatives.

My conjecture, then, is that country music functions in part to reinforce in low-openness individuals the idea that life's most powerful, meaningful emotional experiences are precisely those to which conservative personalities living conventional lives are most likely to have access. And it functions as a device to coordinate members of conservative-minded communities on the incomparable emotional weight of traditional milestone experiences.

Yesterday's *Washington Post* features a classic "conservatives in the mist" piece on the conservative denizens of Washington, OK, and their sense that their values are under attack. Consider this passage about fellow named Mark Tague:

> "I want my kids to grow up with values and ways of life that I had and my parents had," he says, so his youngest son tools around the garage on a Big Wheel, and his oldest daughter keeps her riding horse at the family barn built in 1907, and they buy their drinking milk from Braun's because he always has. "Why look for change?" he says. "I like to know that what you see is what you get." (Saslow)

Country music is for this guy.

"Yeah this is right where you belong/This is country music."—Brad Paisley, "This Is Country Music" (2010).

But why would you want your kids to grow up with the same 10 way of life as you and your grandparents? My best guess (and let me stress *guess*) is that those low in openness depend emotionally on a sense of enchantment of the everyday and the profundity of ritual. Even a little change, like your kids playing with different toys than you did, comes as a small reminder of the instability of life over generations and the contingency of our emotional attachments. This is a reminder low-openness conservatives would prefer to avoid, if possible. What high-openness liberals feel as *mere* nostalgia, low-openness conservatives feel as the baseline emotional tone of a recognizably decent life. If your kids don't experience the same meaningful things in the same way that you experienced them, then it may seem that their lives will be deprived of meaning, which would be tragic. And even if you're able to see that your kids will find plenty of meaning, but in different things and in different ways, you might well worry about the possibility of ever really understanding and relating to them. The inability to bond over profound common experience would itself constitute a grave loss of meaning for both generations. So when the culture redefines a major life milestone, such as marriage, it trivializes one's own milestone experience by imbuing it [with] a sense of contingency, threatens to deprive one's children of the same experience, and thus threatens to make the generations strangers to one another. And what kind of monster would want that?

Country music is a bulwark against cultural change, a reminder that "what you see is what you get," a means of keeping the charge of enchantment in "the little things" that make up the texture of the everyday, and a way of literally broadcasting the emotional and cultural centrality of the conventional big-ticket experiences that make a life a life.

A lot of country music these days *is* culture war, but it's more bomb shelter than bomb.

Works Cited

Carney, Dana, et al. "The Secret Lives of Liberals and Conservatives: Personality Profiles, Interaction Styles, and the Things They Leave Behind." *Political Psychology* 29.6 (2008): 807–40. Print.

Rentfrow, Peter J., and Samuel D. Gosling. "The Do Re Mi's of Everyday Life: The Structure and Personality Correlates of Music Preferences." *Journal of Psychology and Social Psychology* 84.6 (2003): 1236–56. Print.

Saslow, Eli. "To Residents of Another Washington, Their Cherished Values Are Under Assault." *Washington Post* 1 Mar. 2012. Web. 29 Dec. 2014.

For Discussion and Writing

1. ***Comprehension***   According to Wilkinson, what "emotional highlights of the low-openness life" (par. 6) does country music celebrate?

2. ***Critical Reading***   In the **introduction**, Wilkinson uses a series of sentence fragments. Why do you think he chooses this **style**? Do you find it effective? Why or why not?

3. ***Analysis***   Wilkinson writes, "A lot of country music these days *is* culture war, but it's more bomb shelter than bomb" (par. 12). What do you think he means by this? How does this metaphor tie into his main point?

4. ***Connections***   While Wilkinson focuses primarily on the ideological orientations of country music and the individual fan, he also writes that the genre "functions as a device to coordinate members of conservative-minded communities on the incomparable emotional

weight of traditional milestone experiences" (par. 7). In "Riffs of Passage" (p. 232), Tina Vasquez writes about the connections between music and community identities as well. For example, one person she interviews sees music as a "tool to share our stories and communicate our struggles and successes as a people" (par. 18). Do you think music serves a similar purpose in the community that Wilkinson writes about? How are the communities in Vasquez's essay similar to—and different from—the ones Wilkinson discusses?

5. **Writing** Wilkinson's essay explores the connections between personality, musical preference, and political ideology. Do his categories and claims apply to your own experiences, tastes, and views? Do they apply to your observations of other people? In an essay, blog post, or multimedia presentation, respond to his article by making your own connections between personality, music, and cultural or political orientation. Wilkinson claims that "country has an ideology" (par. 1); does the music you listen to have an "ideology"?

LESSLEY ANDERSON

Seduced by "Perfect" Pitch: How Auto-Tune Conquered Pop Music

A graduate of Vassar College, Lessley Anderson is a San Francisco–based writer whose work has appeared in SFGate, Fast Company, Vanity Fair, *the* New York Times, *and other publications. In this article from the* Verge, *a Web site and network devoted to technology news, Anderson writes about the prevalence of the audio-processing effect Auto-Tune. But her discussion raises larger questions about music, technology, and authenticity: "What happens when an entire industry decides it's safer to bet on the robot? Will we start to hate the sound of our own voices?"*

As you read, *notice how Anderson's analysis deepens and complicates the issues around Auto-Tune rather than simplifying or reducing them. What are the range of attitudes toward Auto-Tune presented in the article? What kinds of sources does Anderson rely on in her reporting? Does her own attitude about Auto-Tune change by the end of the article?*

In January of 2010 Kesha Sebert, known as "Ke$ha," debuted at number one on Billboard with her album, *Animal*. Her style is electro pop-y dance music: she alternates between rapping and singing, the choruses of her songs are typically melodic party hooks that bore deep into your brain: "Your love, your love, your love, is my drug!" And at times, her voice is so heavily processed that it sounds like a cross between a girl and a synthesizer. Much of her sound is due to the pitch correction software, Auto-Tune.

Sebert, whose label did not respond to a request for an interview, has built a persona as a badass wastoid, who told *Rolling*

Stone that all male visitors to her tour bus had to submit to being photographed with their pants down. Even the bus drivers.

Yet this past November on the *Today Show*, the 25-year-old Sebert looked vulnerable, standing awkwardly in her skimpy purple, gold, and green unitard. She was there to promote her new album, *Warrior*, which was supposed to reveal the *authentic* her.

"Was it really important to let your voice to be heard?" asked the host, Savannah Guthrie.

"Absolutely," Sebert said, gripping the mic nervously in her fin-   5
gerless black gloves.

"People think they've heard the Auto-Tune, they've heard the dance hits, but you really have a great voice, too," said Guthrie, helpfully.

"No, I got, like, bummed out when I heard that," said Sebert, sadly. "Because I really can sing. It's one of the few things I can do."

Warrior starts with a shredding electrical static noise, then comes her voice, sounding like what the *Guardian* called "a robo squawk devoid of all emotion."

"That's pitch correction software for sure," wrote Drew Waters, Head of Studio Operations at Capitol Records, in an email. "She may be able to sing, but she or the producer chose to put her voice through Auto-Tune or a similar plug-in as an aesthetic choice." So much for showing the world the authentic Ke$ha.

Since rising to fame as the weird techno-warble effect in the   10
chorus of Cher's 1998 song, "Believe," Auto-Tune has become bitchy shorthand for saying somebody can't sing. But the diss isn't fair, because everybody's using it. For every T-Pain—the R&B art- ist who uses Auto-Tune as an over-the-top aesthetic choice—there are 100 artists who are Auto-Tuned in subtler ways. Fix a little backing harmony here, bump a flat note up to diva-worthy heights there: smooth everything over so that it's perfect. You can even use Auto-Tune live, so an artist can sing totally out of tune in concert and be corrected before their flaws ever reach the ears of an audi- ence. (On season 7 of the UK *X-Factor*, it was used so excessively on contestants' auditions that viewers got wise, and protested.)

Indeed, finding out that all the singers we listen to have been Auto-Tuned does feel like someone's messing with us. As humans, we crave connection, not perfection. But we're not the ones pull- ing the levers. What happens when an entire industry decides it's safer to bet on the robot? Will we start to hate the sound of our own voices?

Cher's late '90s comeback and makeover as a gay icon can entirely be attributed to Auto-Tune, though the song's producers claimed for years that it was a Digitech Talker vocoder pedal effect. In 1998, she released the single "Believe," which featured a strange, robotic vocal effect on the chorus that felt fresh. It was created with Auto-Tune. The technology, which debuted in 1997 as a plug-in for Pro Tools (the industry standard recording software), works like this: you select the key the song is in, and then Auto-Tune analyzes the singer's vocal line, moving "wrong" notes up or down to what it guesses is the intended pitch. You can control the time it takes for the program to move the pitch: slower is more natural, faster makes the jump sudden and inhuman sounding. Cher's producers chose the fastest possible setting, the so-called "zero" setting, for maximum pop.

"Believe" was a huge hit, but among music nerds, it was polarizing. Indie rock producer Steve Albini, who's recorded bands like the Pixies and Nirvana, has said he thought the song was mind-numbingly awful, and was aghast to see people he respected seduced by Auto-Tune. "One by one, I could see that my friends had gone zombie. This horrible piece of music with this ugly soon-to-be cliché was now being discussed as something that was awesome. It made my heart fall," he told the *Onion AV Club* in November of 2012.

The Auto-Tune effect spread like a slow burn through the industry, especially within the R&B and dance music communities. T-Pain began Cher-style Auto-Tuning all his vocals, and a decade later, he's still doing it. "It's makin' me money, so I ain't about to stop!" T-Pain told DJ Skee in 2008.

Kanye West did an album with it. Lady Gaga uses it. Madonna, too. Maroon 5. Even the artistically high-minded Bon Iver has dabbled. A YouTube series where TV news clips were Auto-Tuned, "Auto-Tune the News," went viral. The glitchy Auto-Tune mode seems destined to be remembered as the "sound" of the 2000s, the way the gated snare (that dense, big, reverb-y drum sound on, say, Phil Collins songs) is now remembered as the sound of the '80s.

Auto-Tune certainly isn't the only robot voice effect to have wormed its way into pop music. In the '70s and early '80s, voice synthesizer effects units became popular with a lot of bands. Most famous is the Vocoder, originally invented in the 1930s to send encoded Allied messages during WWII. Prototechno groups like New Order and Kraftwerk (i.e., "Computer World") embraced it. So did American early funk and hip-hop groups like the Jonzun Crew. '70s rockers gravitated towards another effect, the talk box. Peter Frampton (listen for it on "Do You Feel Like We Do") and Joe Walsh (used it on "Rocky Mountain Way") liked its similar-to-a-vocoder sound. The talk box was easier to rig up than the Vocoder—you operate it via a rubber mouth tube when applying it to vocals. But it produces massive amounts of slobber. In Dave Tompkins' book, *How to Wreck a Nice Beach*, about the history of synthesized speech machines in the music industry, he writes that Frampton's roadies sanitized his talk box in Remy Martin Cognac between gigs.

The use of showy effects usually has a backlash. And in the case of the Auto-Tune warble, Jay-Z struck back with the 2009 single, "D.O.A.," or "Death of Auto-Tune":

> I know we facing a recession
> But the music y'all making going make it the great depression
> All y'all lack aggression
> Put your skirt back down, grow a set man
> Nigga this shit violent
> This is death of Auto-Tune, moment of silence

That same year, the band Death Cab for Cutie showed up at the Grammys wearing blue ribbons to raise awareness, they told MTV, about "rampant Auto-Tune abuse." The protests came too late, though. The lid to Pandora's box had been lifted. Music producers everywhere were installing the software.

"I'll be in a studio and hear a singer down the hall and she's clearly out of tune, and she'll do one take," says Drew Waters of Capitol Records. That's all she needs. Because they can fix it later, in Auto-Tune.

There is much speculation online about who does—or doesn't— use Auto-Tune. Taylor Swift is a key target, as her terribly off-key 20 duet with Stevie Nicks at the 2010 Grammys suggests she's tone deaf. (Label reps said at the time something was wrong with her earpiece.) But such speculation is naïve, say the producers I talked to. "Everybody uses it," says Filip Nikolic, singer in the LA-based band Poolside and a freelance music producer and studio engineer. "It saves a ton of time."

On one end of the spectrum are people who dial up Auto-Tune to the max, a la Cher/T-Pain. On the other end are people who use it occasionally and sparingly. You can use Auto-Tune not only to pitch-correct vocals, but other instruments too, and light users will tweak a note here and there if a guitar is, say, rubbing up against a vocal in a weird way. "I'll massage a note every once in a while, and often I won't even tell the artist," says Eric Drew Feldman, a San Francisco–based musician and producer who's worked with The Polyphonic Spree and Frank Black. But between those two extremes, you have the synthetic middle, where Auto-Tune is used to correct nearly every note, as one integral brick in a thick wall of digitally processed sound. From Justin Bieber to One Direction, from The Weeknd to Chris Brown, most pop music produced today has a slick, synth-y tone that's partly a result of pitch correction.

However, good luck getting anybody to cop to it. Big producers like Max Marlin and Dr. Luke, responsible for mega hits from artists like Ke$ha, Pink, and Kelly Clarkson, either turned me down or didn't respond to interview requests. And you can't really blame them. "Do you want to talk about that effect you probably use that people equate with your client being talentless?" Um, no thanks.

In 2009, an online petition went around protesting the overuse of Auto-Tune on the show *Glee*. Those producers turned down an interview, too. The artists and producers who would talk were conflicted. One indie band, The Stepkids, had long eschewed Auto-Tune and most other modern recording technologies to make what they call "experimental soul music." But the band recently did an about-face, and Auto-Tuned their vocal harmonies on their forthcoming single, "Fading Star."

Were they using Auto-Tune ironically or seriously? Co-frontman Jeff Gitelman said, "Both. For a long time we fought it, and we still are to a certain degree. But attention spans are a certain way, and that's how it is . . . we just wanted it to have a clean, modern sound."

Hanging above the toilet in San Francisco's Different Fur 25 recording studios—where artists like the Alabama Shakes and Bobby Brown have recorded—is a clipping from *Tape Op* magazine that reads: "Don't admit to Auto-Tune use or editing of drums, unless asked directly. Then admit to half as much as you really did." Different Fur's producer/engineer/owner, Patrick Brown, who hung the clipping there, has recorded acts like the Morning Benders, and says many indie rock bands "come in, and first thing they say is, 'We don't tune anything,'" he says. Brown is up for ditching Auto-Tune if the client really wants to, but he says most of the time, they don't really want to. "Let's face it, most bands are not genius." He'll feel them out by saying, with a wink-wink-nod-nod: "Man, that note's really out of tune, *but that was a great take.*" And a lot of times they'll tell him, go ahead, Auto-Tune it.

Marc Griffin is in the RCA-signed band 2AM Club, which has both an emcee and a singer (Griffin's the singer). He first got Auto-Tuned in 2008, when he recorded a demo with producer Jerry Harrison, the former keyboardist and guitarist for the Talking Heads. "I sang the lead, then we were in the control room with the engineer, and he put 'tune on it. Just a little. And I had perfect pitch vocals. It sounded amazing. Then we started stacking vocals on top of it, and *that* sounded amazing," says Griffin. Now, Griffin sometimes records with Auto-Tune on in real time, rather than having it applied to his vocals in post-production, a trend producers say is not unusual. This means that the artist hears the tuned version of his or her voice coming out of the monitors while singing. "Every time you sing a note that's not perfect, you can hear the frequencies battle with each other," Griffin says, which sounds kind of awful, but he insists it "helps you hear what it will really sound like."

Singer/songwriter Neko Case kvetched about these developments in an interview with online music magazine *Pitchfork*. "I'm not a perfect note hitter either but I'm not going to cover it up with auto tune. Everybody uses it, too. I once asked a studio guy in Toronto, 'How many people don't use Auto-Tune?' and he said, 'You and Nelly Furtado are the only two people who've never used it in here.' Even though I'm not into Nelly Furtado, it kind of made me respect her. It's cool that she has some integrity."

That was 2006. In September of 2012, Nelly Furtado released the album *The Spirit Indestructible*. Its lead single is doused in massive levels of Auto-Tune.

Somebody once wrote on an online message board that the guy who created Auto-Tune must "hate music." That could not be further from the truth. Its creator, Dr. Andy Hildebrand, AKA Dr. Andy, is a classically trained flautist who spent most of his youth playing professionally, in orchestras. Despite the fact that the 66-year-old only recently lopped off a long, gray ponytail, he's no hippie. He never listened to rock music of his generation. "I was too busy practicing," he says. "It warped me." The only post-Debussy artist he's ever gotten into is Patsy Cline.

Hildebrand's company—Antares—nestled in an anonymous-looking office park in the mountains between Silicon Valley and the Pacific Coast, has only ten employees. Hildebrand invents all the products (Antares recently came out with Auto-Tune for Guitar). His wife is the CFO. Hildebrand started his career as a geophysicist, programming digital signal-processing software which helped oil companies find drilling spots. After going back to school for music composition at age 40, he discovered he could use those same algorithms for the seamless looping of digital music samples, and later for pitch correction. Auto-Tune, and Antares, were born. Auto-Tune isn't the only pitch correction software, of course. Its closest competitor, Melodyne, is reputed to be more "natural" sounding. But Auto-Tune is, in the words of one producer, "the go-to if you just want to set-it-and-forget-it."

In interviews, Hildebrand handles the question of "Is Auto-Tune evil?" with characteristic dry wit. His stock answer is, "My wife wears makeup. Does that make her evil?" But on the day I asked him, he answered, "I just make the car. I don't drive it down the wrong side of the road."

The T-Pains and Chers of the world are the crazy drivers, in Hildebrand's analogy. The artists that tune with subtlety are like his wife, tasteful people looking to put their best foot forward. Another way you could answer the question: recorded music is, by definition, artificial. The band is not singing live in your living room. Microphones project sound. Mixing, overdubbing, and multi-tracking allow instruments and voices to be recorded, edited, and manipulated separately. There are multitudes of effects, like compression, which brings down loud sounds and amplifies quiet ones, so you can hear an artist taking a breath in between words. Reverb and delay create echo effects, which can make vocals sound fuller and rounder.

When recording went from tape to digital, there were even more opportunities for effects and manipulation, and Auto-Tune is just one of many of the new tools available. Nonetheless, there are some who feel it's a different thing. At best, unnecessary. At worst, pernicious. "The thing is, reverb and delay always existed in the real world, by placing the artist in unique environments, so [those effects are] just mimicking reality," says Larry Crane, the editor of music recording magazine *Tape Op* and a producer who's recorded Elliott Smith and The Decemberists. If you sang in a cave, or some other really echo-y chamber, you'd sound like early Elvis, too. "There is nothing in the natural world that Auto-Tune is mimicking, therefore any use of it should be carefully considered."

"I'd rather just turn the reverb up on the Fender Twin in the troubling place," says Arizona indie rock pioneer Howe Gelb, of the band Giant Sand. He describes Auto-Tune and other correction plug-ins as "foul" in a way he can't quite put his finger on. "There's something embedded in the track that tends to push my ear away."

Lee Alexander, one-time boyfriend of Norah Jones and bass 35 player and producer for her country side project, The Little Willies, used no Auto-Tune on their two records, and says he doesn't even own the program. "Stuff is out of tune everywhere . . . that to me is the beauty of music," he wrote in an email.

In 2000, Matt Kadane of the band The New Year and his brother, Bubba, covered Cher's "Believe," complete with Auto-Tune. They did it in their former Texas Slo-Core band, Bedhead. Kadane told me [he] hated the original "Believe," and had to be talked into covering it, but had surprisingly found that putting Auto-Tune on his vocals "added emotional weight." He hasn't, however, used Auto-Tune since. "It's one thing to make a statement with hollow, disaffected vocals, but it's another if this is the way we're communicating with each other," he says. For some people, I said, it seems that Auto-Tune is a lot like dudes and fake boobs. Some dudes see fake boobs, they know they're fake, but they get an erection anyway. They can't help themselves. Kadane agreed that it "can serve that function. . . . But at some point you'd say' 'That's fucked up that I have an erection from fake boobs!, And in the midst of experiencing that, I think ideally you have a moment that reminds you that authenticity is still possible. And thank *God* not everything in the world is Auto-Tuned."

The concept of pitch needing to be "correct" is a somewhat recent construct. Cue up the Rolling Stones' *Exile on Main St.*, and listen to what Mick Jagger does on "Sweet Virginia." There are a lot of flat and sharp notes, because, well, that's characteristic of blues singing, which is at the roots of rock and roll. "When a (blues) singer is 'flat' it's not because he's doing it because he doesn't know any better. It's for inflection!" says Victor Coelho, Professor of Music at Boston University. Blues singers have traditionally played with pitch to express feelings like longing or yearning, to punch up a nastier lyric, or make it feel dirty, he says. "The music is not just about hitting the pitch." Of course that style of vocal wouldn't fly in Auto-Tune. It would get corrected. Neil Young, Bob Dylan, many of the classic artists whose voices are less than pitch perfect—they probably would be pitch corrected if they started out today.

John Parish, the UK-based producer who's worked with PJ Harvey and Sparklehorse, says that though he uses Auto-Tune on rare occasions, he is no fan. Many of the singers he works with, Harvey in particular, have eccentric vocal styles—he describes them as "character singers." Using pitch correction software on them would be like trying to get Jackson Pollock to stay inside the lines.

"I can listen to something that can be really quite out of tune, and enjoy it," says Parish. But is he a dying breed?

"That's the kind of music that takes five listens to get really 40 into," says Nikolic, of Poolside. "That's not really an option if you want to make it in pop music today. You find a really catchy hook and a production that is in no way challenging, and you just *gear it up!*"

If you're of the generation raised on technology-enabled perfect pitch, does your brain get rewired to expect it? So-called "supertasters" are people who are genetically more sensitive to bitter flavors than the rest of us, and therefore can't appreciate delicious bitter things like IPAs and arugula. Is the Auto-Tune generation likewise more sensitive to off-key-ness, and thus less able to appreciate it? Some troubling signs point to "yes." "I was listening to some young people in a studio a few years ago, and they were like, 'I don't think The Beatles were so good,'" says producer Eric Drew Feldman. They were discussing the song "Paperback Writer." "They're going, 'They were so sloppy! The harmonies are so flat!'"

John Lennon famously hated his singing voice. He thought it sounded too thin, and was constantly futzing with vocal effects, like the overdriven sound on "I Am the Walrus." I can relate. I love to sing, and in my head, I hear a soulful, husky, alto. What comes out, however, is a cross between a child in the musical *Annie*, and Gretchen Wilson: nasal, reedy, about as soulful as a mosquito. I'm in a band and I write all the songs, but I'm not the singer. I wouldn't subject people to that.

Producer and editor Larry Crane says he thinks lots of artists are basically insecure about their voices, and use Auto-Tune as a kind of protective shield. "I've had people come in and say I *want* Auto-Tune, and I say, 'Let's spend some time, let's do five vocal takes and compile the best take. Let's put down a piano guide track. There's a million ways to coach a vocal. Let's try those things first,'" he says.

Recently, I went over to a couple-friend's house with my husband, to play with Auto-Tune. The husband of the couple, Mike, had the software on his home computer—he dabbles in music production—and the idea was that we'd record a song together, then Auto-Tune it. We looked for something with four-part harmony, so we could all sing, and for a song where the backing instrumental was available online. We settled on Boyz II Men's "End of the Road." One by one we went into the bedroom to record our parts, with a mix of shame and titillation not unlike taking turns with a prostitute.

When we were finished, Mike played back the finished piece, 45 without Auto-Tune. It was nerve-wracking to listen to, I felt like my entire body was cringing. Although I hit the notes OK, there was something tentative and childlike about my delivery. Thank God these are my good friends, I thought. Of course they were probably all thinking the same thing about their performances, too, but in my mind, *my* voice was the most annoying of all, so wheedling and prissy sounding. Then Mike Auto-Tuned two versions of our Boys II Men song: one with Cher/T-Pain style glitchy Auto-Tune, the other with "natural" sounding Auto-Tune. The exaggerated one was hilariously awesome—it sounded just like a generic R&B song. But the second one shocked me. It sounded like us, for sure. But an idealized version of us. My husband's gritty vocal attack was still there, but he was singing on key. And something about fine-tuning my vocals had made them sound more confident, like smoothing out a tremble in one's speech.

The Auto-Tune or not Auto-Tune debate always seems to turn into a moralistic one, like somehow you have more integrity if you don't use it, or only use it occasionally. But seeing how really innocuous-yet-lovely it could be, made me rethink. If I were a professional musician, would I reject the opportunity to sound, what I consider to be, "my best," out of principle?

The answer to that is probably no. But then it gets you wondering. How many insecure artists with "annoying" voices will retune themselves before you ever have a chance to fall in love?

For Discussion and Writing

1. **Comprehension**   Near the end of her article, Anderson narrates an account of having her own vocals Auto-Tuned. What happens? Describe her experience.

2. **Critical Reading**   The writer begins her article with a story about the recording artist Ke$ha. What is the point of the story? How does it support Anderson's **thesis**?

3. **Analysis**   Anderson claims that the "Auto-Tune or not Auto-Tune debate always seems to turn into a moralistic one . . ." (par. 46). How and why would the topic of musical processing effects become a "moralistic" debate? What moral issues—if any—are at stake in this context?

4. **Connections**   The writer cites indie rock producer Steve Albini, who (according to Anderson) thinks Auto-Tune is "mind-numbingly awful" (par. 13). She quotes an interview in which Albini compares the use of the effect to "going zombie." How might a "poptimist" critic, as described in Saul Austerlitz's "The Pernicious Rise of Poptimism" (p. 240), respond to Albini? How might a poptimist view the use of Auto-Tune, generally?

5. **Writing** Anderson asserts the inherent artificiality of *all* recorded music: "The band is not singing live in your living room" (par. 32). Is Auto-Tune merely one more artificial effect in a largely artificial experience? Is it unfairly maligned by its critics? Or do you find it annoying or even "mind-numbingly awful"? Do you think there is a moral issue or question at stake in its use? Present your own view of Auto-Tune in a brief argumentative essay. You may defend it, criticize it, or provide a more nuanced view of the device. To support your points, you might consider locating two different versions of a song (Auto-Tuned vs. not Auto-Tuned, original vs. remastered, etc.) and comparing and contrasting the effects.

TINA VASQUEZ

Riffs of Passage

*Tina Vasquez is a queer-identified, Los Angeles–based freelance writer
and editor. She is a staff blogger at the pop culture and politics site* In
the Fray, *the West Coast editor of* Black Girl Dangerous, *and the writer
of* CultureStrike's *weekly comic* Liberty for All. *Vasquez is currently
working on her first book,* Growing Up Girl (Or How to Take a Sea-
soned Punch). *In this essay from* Bitch *magazine, Vasquez combines a
musical memoir with a discussion of Latino musical subculture,
immigrant identity, and feminism in Los Angeles. Her personal survey
of the city's venerable and vital Latino punk scene reveals how its artists use music to communicate their struggles and create a sense of
community.*

As you read, *notice how the distinctions between the "musical," the
"personal," and the "political" become blurry or disappear altogether.
Why is Vasquez attracted to the music of artists like Pilar Díaz, La
Santa Cecilia, and Las Cafeteras? How does she combine narrative
with analysis? Does the essay endorse a particular view of immigration
or immigration policy?*

In 2005, Julio Salgado was a budding artist, I was a fledgling
writer, and we were both broke college students living near Los
Angeles. We met working on a student newspaper and quickly
bonded over our mutual love of women-fronted punk and alternative bands. We had a lot in common since we were both raised
in traditional Mexican households, but had one considerable difference: I was an American citizen, and Ensenada-born Salgado
was undocumented.

Los Angeles is a diverse city—white people are a minority and
Latinos make up more than half the population. Still, music that
reflected our bicultural identities was hard to come by. But on
Friday nights, we worshipped at the stage of Los Abandoned, a

multicultural, bilingual, postpunk, alt-rock band considered home-town heroes by the sweaty, moshing fans who religiously attended their shows at The Echo. The tiny club on Sunset Boulevard was one of the few in the area to accept Salgado's Mexican consulate–issued *matrícula*; it was his only form of identification.

Other Latina-fronted bands seemed few and far between, though you could draw a straight line from East L.A.'s punk pio-neer Alice Bag to Pilar Díaz, the ukulele-strumming frontwoman of Los Abandoned. Sporting sparkly majorette uniforms with Reebok Freestyle high-tops from the '80s, Díaz went by "Lady P" and spoke and sang in Spanglish, covering Selena and Blondie in equal measure. We didn't know that growing up, her parents were undocumented and her folk-musician father earned money for her piano lessons by singing at weddings dressed as a *huaso*, a Chilean cowboy.

Along with Los Abandoned, we also followed La Santa Cecilia, whose frontwoman Marisol "La Marisoul" Hernandez had a voice as colorful as her clothing. Hernandez wore cat-eye glasses, neon tutus, striped tights, and hand-painted Mary Janes, with acces-sories informed by both traditional and classic Latina street style—flowers in her hair, a *rebozo*, and hoop earrings. We were in awe, and in a few short years, the rest of the country would be too. La Santa Cecilia would go on to be nominated for Grammy Awards and eventually make it onto the radar of Elvis Costello, who appeared on a duet with Hernandez for the song "Losing Game" on La Santa Cecilia's 2013 album *Treinta Días*.

In 2011, at a downtown L.A. bar, Salgado introduced me to the   5
music of Las Cafeteras, who blend hip hop, folk, traditional, and spoken word for a sound that could only be born in the streets of Los Angeles by the children of immigrants. Three of Las Cafe-teras' seven members are women who play traditional instru-ments: Annette Torres plays the *marimbol*, vocalist Denise Carlos plays the *jarana*, and Leah Rose Gallegos plays the *quijada*, a per-cussion instrument made from an equine jawbone. The band's music is steeped in tradition, but each member comes from an activist background and, according to Carlos, the band applies a feminist framework to its approach.

Díaz, Hernandez, and Carlos have paved the way for Latinas in the Los Angeles music scene and provided a soundtrack for life in the city that actually reflects its roots and honors the bicultural identities of so many of its residents and transplants. These women have come to mean so much to fans and have offered powerful representations of Los Angeles to the rest of the country. Their stories as musicians coming of age in Los Angeles, however, reveal a bigger narrative about the beauty and brutality of migration.

Leading bilingual bands "was never an intentional thing—it just was," says Díaz, who was born in Chile. "When my family came to the States it was very important to my parents that I keep my culture and language alive. I was living in this bicultural world, half English and half Spanish; two countries were my home. So when writing songs, it just came naturally."

In Los Abandoned, Díaz's songs never overtly touched on her experience as an immigrant or as the child of immigrants, but her powerful presence and the band's Spanglish love songs left a lasting impression on the local music scene. When the band announced its breakup in 2007, Gustavo Arellano, editor of the *OC Weekly* and writer of the syndicated column "Ask a Mexican!," wrote that Los Abandoned embodied a "postmodern Latino experience" and that their denouement signified more than just a band's breakup; it hinted "at the end of rock *en español* itself."

Díaz now performs as a solo artist. Her first self-titled album was released in 2009 and her latest, *Songs + Canciones* (2013), was under the new moniker María del Pilar. Her 2010 song "Ilegal en Estyle" was inspired by many things, but primarily by touring with artists like Zoé, Café Tacuba, Julieta Venegas, Molotov, and Aterciopelados while fronting Los Abandoned.

"We'd play in these small towns in the Southwest and our audi- 10
ences were Latino immigrants and the people were so proud," Díaz says. "We played with bands whose members didn't have papers and they weren't ashamed—and no one should be. In a way, 'Ilegal en Estyle' fucks with stereotypes about people who are seen as illegal. In my song, they're not swimming in a river; they're swimming in pools in hotels. They're fully-formed people who aren't limited by their status. I say fuck it, celebrate who you are. Your status in the U.S. doesn't make you less of a person. People aren't illegal; no one is illegal."

The inspiration for the song is also deeply personal. Upon first coming to the States, Díaz's parents were undocumented. "The

© Rebecca Blackwell/AP Images

"I just wanted to be free, to do my own thing. And if being a brown, fat, curly-haired, crazy-dressed girl singing her heart out is feminist, then that's what I am."—Marisol Hernandez of the band La Santa Cecilia, pictured here.

fear of deportation was very real to me. I can still remember the stories my dad would tell of being so nervous visiting the immigration office that he threw up in the elevator. Immigration, deportation—those issues have been huge parts of my life and I wanted to address [them] in my music, even if it's in an abstract or playful way."

From an early age, words like "deportation" and "illegal" would strike fear in Hernandez as well. The La Santa Cecilia frontwoman was born in the United States, though her parents came with visas. Other members of La Santa Cecilia are also immigrants and the children of immigrants. When the band participated in the Not One More Deportation campaign, which fosters collaboration between organizations and artists to expose and confront unjust immigration laws, La Santa Cecilia was suddenly labeled a "political band"—and the release of the video for their song "El Hielo" underscored their activism. The song is about ICE (Immigration and Customs Enforcement), and is told from the perspectives of several undocumented immigrants, and the video features undocumented activists and organizers.

"It's not 'political' when it's your life," Hernandez said. "Our bandmate Pepe is undocumented, so when we were asked to play in Mexico, he couldn't go. When we went to certain places in the country with really severe anti-immigration laws, he wouldn't go. When writing 'El Hielo,' we never thought about politics. Fuck politics, it was personal. It was about love and dreams. It's about what we feel; it's the story of what happens to our friends and family and to us. Saying 'not one more deportation' isn't political."

Hernandez says that even though she and her bandmates are Mexican, they proudly claim Los Angeles as their home. "Los Angeles isn't La-La Land. It's not Beverly Hills or Paris Hilton or rich people or movies. There is real culture and history here. I have a deep love for this place and La Santa Cecilia is proud to rep it. When we were nominated for a Latin Grammy, we dedicated it to our city," she says.

In turn, the frontwoman is inspiring the young Latinas who go 15 to her shows wearing flowers in their hair and brightly-colored tutus, just like their favorite singer. But Hernandez says she has never given much thought to being a role model as a woman leading a band.

"I grew up singing in bands with dudes, not really giving a fuck what anyone thought. I just wanted to be free, to do my own thing. And if being a brown, fat, curly-haired, crazy-dressed girl singing her heart out is feminist, then that's what I am," Hernandez says. "And if me being who I am inspires other women to be who they want to be? That's awesome."

Unlike La Santa Cecilia, Las Cafeteras aim to be overtly political. Community-focused from the get-go, some of the band members met while studying the Afro-Mexican folk music from Veracruz known as *son jarocho* at El Sereno's Eastside Café. Others met at the 2006 protests against the eviction of the farmers of the South Central Farm, which was once considered the largest urban farm in the country before it was bulldozed and turned into an empty lot. Before some of the members considered themselves musicians, they bonded over their passion for community organizing and their love of son jarocho, which would give their band its distinctive sound.

"We're all very proud of being from East L.A. and of our Chicano identities. How we portray this identity in Las Cafeteras is very different than the representation you see in the media," Carlos says. "There's an East L.A. music renaissance happening right now and a lot of us are using music as a tool to share our stories and communicate our struggles and successes as a people."

The fear of *la Migra* coming to take her parents was an everyday reality for Carlos, like it continues to be for so many. "It's a privilege to have certain paperwork so you can obtain a license, a job, an education," Carlos says. "I have so much empathy for those who are undocumented. My parents became citizens in the '90s. They came here because they wanted to give us a different life and that's never an easy decision to make, especially when your existence in the U.S. is criminalized. This idea that people are 'illegal' because they've crossed an invisible line built on corruption has got to stop."

One song that catapulted Las Cafeteras onto the national stage 20 was the Chicano anthem "La Bamba Rebelde," a radical version of "La Bamba" that appeared on their 2012 album *It's Time*. The song tells the story of Latinos migrating and growing up in the United States. Lyrics include, *"Yo no creo en fronteras, yo no creo en fronteras / Yo cruzaré, yo cruzaré!"* (I don't believe in borders, I don't believe in borders / I will cross, I will cross!)

Often, Las Cafeteras are invited to perform in spaces that champion similar politics, but in other parts of the country they've been told not to be "too political" and instead, to just be a "fun band." Carlos takes issue when this happens, saying the essence of what the band does is political.

"For us, it's important to use our platform to talk about challenging the status quo and discussing the issues that affect people of color and undocumented people. You can't separate that from our music; they're fully integrated. We can't turn off the lens we see the world through as Chicanos," Carlos says.

Even the band's name can be construed as political. Despite comprising of more men than women, the band feminized its name by choosing Las Cafeteras, rather than Los Cafeteros. Carlos says she and her bandmates proudly claim the "feminist" label, with the caveat that their feminism and the feminism of other women of color is different because of the roles their culture and families play in their lives.

"My dad wouldn't want credit for this, but he raised two daughters to be very independent. He told us to go to college, buy our own houses, and make and manage our own money. The message was to be independent, but we also weren't allowed to go out after

certain hours, we served guests their meals, and if we wore something he didn't like, he'd go, 'What will the neighbors say?' Some
feminists may not get that because it seems contradictory. Many
of us are raised in a way that has us adhering to traditional gender roles while also being instilled with pretty radical messages
about the importance of working hard to be seen and heard and
to operate independently. Maybe it only makes sense if you grew
up Chicana," Carlos says.

She and her bandmates are deeply invested in gender equality 25
and Carlos says they will continue to write songs like "Mujer Soy,"
which discusses the femicides that have been taking place in Ciu-
dad Juárez since the early '90s.

"So much of who we are as a band is a reflection of our lived
experiences as Chicanos in L.A.," Carlos says. "Our people have to
overcome so much, while also having so much to celebrate. I
hope our music reflects all of that longing and joy."

Three years after we met, Salgado and I were coming into consciousness in very different ways. I was on the cusp of dropping
out of college for good and he was working under the table to pay
his tuition. At the time, the California Development, Relief, and
Education for Alien Minors (DREAM) Act did not exist, so when
he came up short on tuition he called on those around him for
help. A fundraiser was thrown and five bucks got you admission
into the Salgado family living room where couches were pushed
aside to make room for La Santa Cecilia. It would be our first of
many lessons in what it means to have a community.

Crowded into the living room that night, Hernandez's voice
struck a chord in so many of us, though at the time there was no
way of knowing how each of the band members' lives had been
shaped by migration and impacted by unjust laws that criminalized their—our—communities. There was no way to know; we
just knew their music felt like home.

For Discussion and Writing

1. **Comprehension**   In the essay, Denise Carlos, a member of the band
   Las Cafeteras, refers to an aspect of her identity and background
   that may seem "contradictory" (par. 24) to feminists. What is this
   apparent contradiction?

2. **Critical Reading**   How does Vasquez's **introduction** lay out
   important themes in her essay? Explain.

3. ***Analysis***   Discussing her band's music, Marisol Hernandez of La Santa Cecilia asserts, "It's not 'political' when it's your life" (par. 13). What does she mean in the context of Vasquez's essay? What distinction is she challenging?

4. ***Connections***   As Vasquez does in "Riffs of Passage," Liz Armstrong explores the connections between identity and musical subcultures in "An Argument for Being a Poser" (p. 85). How are these two essays similar in their themes? In what ways are they different? How important are the differences?

5. ***Writing***   Vasquez writes that when Las Cafeteras play in other parts of the United States, "they've been told not to be 'too political' and instead, to just be a 'fun band'" (par. 21). How do you understand the opposition between "political" and "fun"? Do you listen to music that is explicitly "political"? Do you think political messaging or advocacy is compatible with art, entertainment, and fun, or are these purposes antithetical? Using specific examples to support your claims, write a personal essay that explores and explains the relationship between popular music and politics.

SAUL AUSTERLITZ

The Pernicious Rise of Poptimism

Writer and critic Saul Austerlitz graduated from Yale University. He is the author of Money for Nothing: A History of the Music Video from the Beatles to the White Stripes *(2007),* Another Fine Mess: A History of American Film Comedy *(2010), and* Sitcom: A History in 24 Episodes from I Love Lucy to Community (2014). *His written work has appeared in the* Village Voice, Rolling Stone, Spin, *and many other publications. In this article from the* New York Times, *Austerlitz identifies a trend in contemporary music criticism he calls "poptimism": an aesthetic that "demands devotion to pop idols" and shouts down those "who might not be equally enamored of pop music."*

As you read, *notice how Austerlitz begins building his argument by defining his term and by observing specific examples of "poptimism." What are the goals of poptimist critics? What factors led to its dominance? Why does Austerlitz find it so problematic as a critical approach to popular music?*

Not too long ago, I completed the annual music geek's ritual of filling out my ballot for the *Village Voice*'s vaunted Pazz & Jop poll. During the past 40 years, the *Voice* has surveyed critics on their favorite albums and singles in an effort to create something approaching a consensus. In scrambling to put together a Top 10 list that I could live with, I poked through my iTunes playlists, looked at other critics' 10-bests (it's allowed!), and flipped through essays by everyone from the *New Yorker*'s Sasha Frere-Jones to the tastemakers at *Pitchfork*. My survey of 2013's critical landscape only reinforced something I've suspected for some time now: Music criticism has gotten really weird.

The *New Yorker* devotes pages to praising the comeback album by Britney Spears. Eight of the 12 essays in last year's *Slate* Music Club focused primarily on the kinds of artists normally found on the Billboard Hot 100. (One was actually *about* the Billboard Hot 100 itself.) The higher reaches of the 2013 Pazz & Jop singles list were dominated by artists like Lorde, Robin Thicke, and Icona Pop. The fourth-best album was Beyoncé's December surprise, which had already prompted a near-avalanche of 140-character hosannas and substantially longer think pieces.

A *Grantland* article published a few months ago was illustrative of this new mode of critical thought. The author described being disappointed with the new Beyoncé album after having listened to it some 20 times, before eventually changing his mind and pleading guilty to deviations from orthodoxy. "I was wrong to say that I didn't like the Beyoncé album after two days," he wrote, eventually concluding by admonishing any others who had not yet seen the light: "If you don't like the new Beyoncé album, reevaluate what you want out of music."

The reigning style of music criticism today is called "poptimism," or "popism," and it comes complete with a series of trap doors through which the unsuspecting skeptic may tumble. Prefer Queens of the Stone Age to Rihanna? Perhaps you are a "rockist," still salivating over your old Led Zeppelin records and insisting that no musical performer not equipped with a serious case of self-seriousness and, probably, a guitar, bass, and drums is worthy of consideration. Find Lady Gaga's bargain basement David Bowie routine a snooze? You, my friend, are fatally out of touch with the mainstream, with the pop idols of the present. You are, in short, an old person. Contemporary music criticism is a minefield rife with nasty, ad hominem attacks, and the most popular target, in recent years, has been those professing inadequate fealty to pop.

Poptimism is a studied reaction to the musical past. It is, to 5 paraphrase a summary offered by Kelefa Sanneh some years ago in the *New York Times* in an article on the perils of "rockism": disco, not punk; pop, not rock; synthesizers, not guitars; the music video, not the live show. It is to privilege the deliriously artificial over the artificially genuine. It developed as an ideology to counteract rockism, the stance held by the sort of critic who, in Sanneh's words, whines "about a pop landscape dominated by big-budget spectacles and high-concept photo shoots" and reminisces "about a time when the charts were packed with people who had something to say, and meant it, even if that time never actually existed."

© NBC/Photofest

© Photofest/CBS

According to Austerlitz, poptimism is a "studied reaction to the musical past," as well as a response to "rockism." Why would a poptimist prefer Taylor Swift to Bruce Springsteen?

Poptimism wants to be in touch with the taste of average music fans, to speak to the rush that comes from hearing a great single on the radio, or YouTube, and to value it no differently from a song with more "serious" artistic intent. It's a laudable goal, emerging in part from the identity politics of the 1990s and in part from a desire to undo the original sin of rock 'n' roll: white male performers' co-opting of established styles and undeservedly receiving credit as musical innovators. Jody Rosen, a music critic I admire greatly, admitted as much in *Slate* in 2006, writing that "many of my colleagues, like me, have embraced the anti-rockist critique with particular fervor as a kind of penance, atoning for past rockist misdeeds—for the party line we'd swallowed whole in our formative years and maybe even parroted under our bylines."

Rosen is describing poptimism as a reaction to what I think of as "Rolling Stone disease," whereby Bob Dylan and Bruce Springsteen were treated as geniuses and the likes of Marvin Gaye and Madonna as mere pop singers. Obviously there should be no test of race or gender in musical immortality. But now the reaction has swamped the initial problem and created a wildly distorted version of the music world in 2014, as reflected in the way it's covered.

Poptimism now not only demands devotion to pop idols; it has instigated an increasingly shrill shouting match with those who might not be equally enamored of pop music. Disliking Taylor Swift or Beyoncé is not just to proffer a musical opinion, but to reveal potential proof of bias. Hardly a week goes by in music-critic land without such accusations flying to and fro. In one particularly ugly contretemps a few years back, led by prominent critics, the indie hero Stephin Merritt of the Magnetic Fields was accused of being a racist for expressing his appreciation for the song "Zip-a-Dee-Doo-Dah," from the (actually racist) Disney musical *Song of the South*, and his general dislike of hip-hop.

The music historian Ted Gioia recently argued in a pointed *Daily Beast* article that "music criticism has turned into lifestyle reporting," more interested in breakups and arrests than in-depth musical analysis. He has a point, although the culprit is not rampant musical illiteracy on the part of critics or the fact that not everyone is Lester Bangs reincarnate, as he suggests. The problem may very well be that music criticism has become so staunchly descriptivist.

I spend most of my time, professionally speaking, writing about 10 movies and books, and during quiet moments, I like to entertain myself by imagining what might happen if the equivalent of poptimism were to transform those other disciplines. A significant subset of book reviewers would turn up their noses at every mention of Jhumpa Lahiri and James Salter as representatives of snobbish, boring novels for the elite and argue that to be a worthy critic, engaged with mass culture, you would have to direct the bulk of your critical attention to the likes of Dan Brown and Stephenie Meyer. Movie critics would be enjoined from devoting too much of their time to *12 Years a Slave* (box-office take: $56 million) or *The Great Beauty* ($2.7 million), lest they fail to adequately analyze the majesty that is *Thor: The Dark World* ($206.2 million). What if New York food critics insisted on banging on about the virtues of Wendy's Spicy Chipotle Jr. Cheeseburger? No matter the field, a critic's job is to argue and plead for the underappreciated, not just to cheer on the winners.

The issue is not attention—any critic who ignored mass taste entirely would be doing his or her readers a disservice—so much as it is proportion. Music critics are as snobbish as any other variety of critic, but lately, their snobbishness has been devoted to demonstrating just how unsnobbish they are. Given Katy Perry's string of No. 1 hits, a well-honed argument about her appeal is a welcome addition to the musical conversation. But should gainfully employed adults whose job is to listen to music thoughtfully really agree so regularly with the taste of 13-year-olds?

Poptimism has become a cudgel with which to selectively club music that aims for something other than the whoosh of an indelibly catchy riff. Its Kryptonite is indie rock, subjected to repeated assaults for its self-seriousness and rockist fervor. Bands? With guitars? And sometimes with beards? Don't ever tell a poptimist critic that you love the Strokes' later albums or think the National are geniuses (guilty on both counts). "Rock music," *Slate*'s Carl Wilson sniffed when reviewing the National's most recent album, "has died and gone to graduate school."

So why is music criticism more or less alone in this affectation? Unlike those other disciplines, it has had to wrestle with the fact that music is now effectively free. Music criticism's former priority—telling consumers what to purchase—has been rendered null and void for most fans. In its stead, I believe, many critics have become cheerleaders for pop stars.

It is no accident that poptimism is an Internet-era permutation. Obsessive coverage of stars like Drake and Justin Bieber drives Web traffic in a way that more judicious, varied coverage of the likes of, say, the Tuareg guitar wizard Bombino generally cannot. Once, we learned about new music by listening to the radio, reading *Spin*, or watching MTV. Today MTV is largely a reality-TV channel, and most people prefer their iPods or Spotify playlists or Pandora stations to fusty radio programming.

In this way, poptimism embraces the familiar as a means of 15 keeping music criticism relevant. Click culture creates a closed system in which popular acts get more coverage, thus becoming more popular, thus getting more coverage. But criticism is supposed to challenge readers on occasion, not only provide seals of approval.

In this light, poptimism can be seen as an attempt to resuscitate the unified cultural experience of the past, when we were all, at least in theory, listening together to *Sgt. Pepper's* or *Thriller*. The dissolution of a shared musical mainstream means that my Speedy Ortiz or Ka may be gobbledygook to someone whose musical hero is Sky Ferreira. But the splintering of tastes should be celebrated, not treated as further cause for doubling down on our focus on a few familiar stars or sounds. Let a thousand Haims bloom!

In the guise of open-mindedness and inclusivity, poptimism gives critics—and by extension, fans—carte blanche to be less adventurous. If we are all talking about Miley Cyrus, then we do not need to wrestle with knottier music that might require some effort to appreciate. And so jazz and world music and regional American genres are shunted off to specialized reviewers, or entirely ignored. If this sounds like a fundamental challenge of the contemporary world—preserving complexity and nuance in a world devoted to bite-size nuggets of easy-to-swallow, predigested information—it should.

Poptimism diminishes the glory of music by declaring, repeatedly and insistently, that this is all it can do. But there is always more to the story. Critics of all stripes have the privilege of devoting their professional lives to hacking a path through the thicket of cultural abundance. There is, now more than ever, too much to listen to, too much to watch, too much to read. All we can do is point out some highlights of our journey. Criticism matters because its virtues are profoundly human ones: honesty, curiosity, diligence, pluralism. We should never sacrifice any of those in the name of an artificial consensus.

For Discussion and Writing

1. **Comprehension**   Define "poptimism" and explain its difference from "rockism" in your own words.
2. **Critical Reading**   Where in the essay does the writer examine cause-and-effect relationships? Where does he argue using analogies? Point to specific examples of each strategy and explain how the author uses the strategies to support his **main points**.
3. **Analysis**   According to Austerlitz, poptimism is, in a way, a populist phenomenon that "wants to be in touch with the taste of average music fans" (par. 6). At the same time, music critics are "as snobbish as any other variety of critic" (par. 11). How does poptimism allow critics to be both "snobbish" *and* devoted to "mass taste"? Explain this paradox.

4. **Connections**   How might a poptimist critic respond to Judy Berman's "Concerning the Spiritual in Indie Rock" (p. 247)? How do you think Austerlitz would view Berman's article, given what we know about his views of music criticism? Explain your answers.

5. **Writing**   As part of his argument, Austerlitz reflects on the importance of criticism and the privileged role of the critic. "Criticism matters," he writes, "because its virtues are profoundly human ones: honesty, curiosity, diligence, pluralism" (par. 18). Do you agree with him? Do you read, watch, or listen to reviews and criticism (of books, movies, music, television shows, or video games) from professional critics? Why or why not? What should critics and criticism try to accomplish? Explain your answer in a brief essay that proposes and defines the role of a critic.

JUDY BERMAN

Concerning the Spiritual
in Indie Rock

Judy Berman is the editor-in-chief of Flavorwire, *a pop culture Web site. Her work has appeared in* Slate, *the* Atlantic, *the* Los Angeles Times, *and other publications. A former editor at* Salon, *she coedits (with Niina Pollari)* It's Complicated, *a 'zine that features feminist writers writing about the "artists whose misogynist work we love." In this essay from the* Believer, *Berman reflects on the spiritual preoccupations of bands such as Animal Collective, Neutral Milk Hotel, and Arcade Fire. For Berman, indie rock has a complex "metaphysical fixation" that seems to "grab for our souls."*

As you read, *be mindful of Berman's implied notions of audience: What does she assume about her readers' range of reference? How does she use specific examples to support her general claims? What does she imply about the purpose—and power—of music to affect its listeners?*

In his strange, dazzling 1911 essay "Concerning the Spiritual in Art," Wassily Kandinsky wrote, "Music has been for some centuries the art which has devoted itself not to the reproduction of natural phenomena but rather to the expression of the artist's soul." As he saw it, analyzing earthly minutiae that would soon become irrelevant was less important than pushing against the boundaries of consciousness and expanding the scope of mankind's experience. "Literature, music and art are the first and most sensitive spheres in which this spiritual revolution makes itself felt," as artists "turn away from the soulless life of the present towards those substances and ideas which give free scope to the non-material strivings of the soul." By "spiritual," Kandinsky meant both the universal and the emotional—accessing both the enormity of the cosmos and the bottomless depths of the human psyche.

Kandinsky's is an uncompromising standard. But what does it tell us about Animal Collective's latest single?

Among the immediate forerunners of indie rock's current metaphysical fixation, Neutral Milk Hotel's 1998 *In the Aeroplane Over the Sea* is perhaps the most widely cherished. The album combines Middle Eastern and South Asian devotional music and Christian prayer, sometimes within the same song, to conjure the dream-story of the singer's mournful, soul-consuming obsession with Anne Frank.

This potentially disastrous conceit somehow yields a mysterious, ruminative, and profoundly affecting album. Hundreds of years of history melt together in a feverish heap of images. Without ever mentioning Frank's full name, Neutral Milk Hotel's singer and songwriter, Jeff Mangum, projects onto her ghostly figure a lifetime of anxieties about youth and aging, love and sex, birth and death and rebirth. We see his heroine buried alive only weeks before her liberators would have come, and then reincarnated as a "little boy in Spain playing pianos filled with flames." Mangum idealizes childhood and its chaste, innocent love affairs. Adult sexuality, with its insidious reminders of mortality, both attracts and repels him; the album bursts at the seams with bodily fluids and putrefying flesh.

Mangum's lyrics are strong enough that they could work on the 5
page as poetry, but it's the arrangements that propel the songs heavenward. Violently plucked folk guitar amplifies the singer's ardor, and the antiquated instruments of rural musicians—banjo, singing saw, flugelhorn—get caught in the swells of miniature symphonies. Tapes, radios, and filters add another dimension, as layers of sound swell and then fade into the distance. Mangum's vocal cords are the most expressive instruments of all, allowing him to embody the roles of lover, child, and mystic. At moments he sounds messy and frantic, a holy fool receiving revelations in the desert; his voice stretches and quivers as he sings funeral dirges for his lost love. On "King of Carrot Flowers Pts. Two & Three," Mangum strains to reach a higher register, chanting, "I love you, Jesus Christ"—in nasal tones reminiscent of a Muslim call to prayer.

As if to cement *Aeroplane*'s mythic impact, the cryptic and fragile Mangum abandoned his band before Neutral Milk Hotel could begin to lead a movement. Today's cadre of spiritually oriented musicians finds its de facto leadership in Animal Collective, a group that has spent nearly a decade chipping away at the barrier between earth and heaven. The incantatory single "My Girls," from the band's newest album, *Merriweather Post Pavilion*, is a glittering whirlpool of synthetic sound. Harmonic elements merge, divide, and disappear like cells gone wild, only to resurface, transformed, a verse or two later.

Animal Collective is only one of many bands striving for something more resonant than a catchy melody. At their most potent, these artists make big, constantly evolving sounds that redraw the universe around us in deep Kandinsky colors. Harmonies build, choruses climax with eye-dilating intensity, and, if we're lucky, time and space get disrupted.

In "My Girls," Animal Collective's chanted vocals become mantra-like, as the repetition itself becomes more important than the words being uttered. And while repetition is a hallmark of just about all popular music, the particular ways in which these musicians use it recall Zen meditation more than Top 40 choruses. Drone, a technique derived from southwest Asian music in which a single sound remains constant throughout a composition, permeates the album. Although it has been a hallmark of Western experimental music for decades, from La Monte Young's minimalist classical pieces to the shrieking violin compositions of Burning Star Core's C. Spencer Yeh, drone is fairly new to indie rock. Dirty Projectors bassist and vocalist Angel Deradoorian,[1] who uses it on her recent solo EP, *Mind Raft*, has become fascinated with the way drone lends itself to subtle variations on a fixed theme.

Music may also make a grab for our souls by recalling the sounds or harmonic structures of devotional songs, thus reawakening our collective memory of what faith and worship feel like. Arcade Fire's *Neon Bible* (2007) was recorded for the most part in a converted church and reverberates with the deep groan of organs. Ezra Buchla of Gowns[2] believes that his band's brittle harmonies have a similar effect to gospel music. ("If people have

---

[1]*Angel Deradoorian* (b.1986): a musician who works primarily as a solo artist. She worked with the Dirty Projectors from 2007–2008. [Editor's note.]
[2]Gowns broke up in 2010. [Editor's note.]

Montreal's Arcade Fire perform at St. John's Church in London. How does the staging in this image emphasize Berman's claims?

souls, that's the way to activate them," he says.) The band's 2007 album, *Red State*, shaped by layers of drone, amplifier static, and vocals that range from soft and dejected to harried and screaming, doesn't sound like church-choir material. But the tension between these elements sets up its own kind of call-and-response pattern; the feedback becomes a voracious chorus, always threatening to devour the soloist.

If many of these bands traffic in twenty-first-century head music, another contingent thrives on a polymorphously perverse brand of physical rapture. The title of Ponytail's[3] most recent album, *Ice Cream Spiritual* (2008), perfectly captures the band's sugar-high, wonder-stricken noise-punk. Singer Molly Siegel's high-pitched shrieks and her bandmates' wild, experimental take on the classic guitar-bass-drum combination recall nothing more than childhood playtime. For Siegel, childhood and spirituality are about both exploding boundaries between ourselves and the universe and the "ecstasy in losing yourself" that creates. Such moments are explicitly communal for Los Angeles spazz-core outfit the Mae Shi,[4] who build to moments of regressive, holy-rolling exhilaration, complete with contagious hand claps and delirious screams. And Ponytail's friend and fellow Baltimorean Dan Deacon shapes the sounds of childhood (video games, cartoons) into ebullient electronic music that's been dubbed "future shock."

Deacon often begins shows by asking everyone to grab their neighbors' hands and repeat a nonsensical chant ("Ethan Hawke, Ethan Hawke") whose only purpose is to transform groups of strangers into a united, if temporary, gathering of friends. Seeking to eliminate the I–thou relationship between musician and fan, he insists on setting up his array of neon-accented keyboards, sound mixers, and microphones in the middle of the audience. Ponytail's performances conjure the group-wide fervor of Easter Sunday at an evangelical church where both minister and congregation are hyperactive preschoolers. Band and audience members fuse into an army of true believers, baptized in sweat and whinnying in tongues.

Rather than break a performance's spell, Animal Collective and a handful of like-minded bands seamlessly segue from one song

---

[3]*Ponytail:* artrock/noise pop band active from 2005–2011. [Editor's note.]
[4]*The Mae Shi:* experimental rock band active from 2002–2010. [Editor's note.]

to the next. Their sets often include moments of quiet, but the absence of complete silence means there is no designated time for applause. Instead of clapping politely as the rock stars onstage indulge in inane banter that breaks the spell of a good concert, we cheer when Animal Collective's music soars to its all-consuming zenith. Rather than detracting from the power of the moment, this nearly involuntary applause intensifies it.

Devotional lyrics can't redeem a spiritually lifeless track, but, like those that fill *In the Aeroplane Over the Sea*, they can focus our reveries. Set in the harsh, natural world of the Dakotas in winter, Gowns' *Red State* summons its visual power from what Erika Anderson and Buchla call "visions." Like recurring, waking dreams, these vivid images—of a soldier's empty basement bedroom, of the American flag hanging in its window—meld together on the album with memories of characters and scenes from Anderson's rural youth. Rather than elevating us to beatitude, *Red State* envelops us in its stark desolation. We don't just empathize with the spiritual hunger that comes from living in the middle of nowhere, with no one around to listen but God; we feel it gnawing at our own stomachs, in Anderson's and Buchla's searching voices and static snowdrifts ten feet high.

Gowns' lyrics brim with Christian imagery, oscillating between an earthly hell—chained-up dogs and teenage rapists who huff gasoline—and distant glimpses of heaven. On "Fargo," Anderson lists the pharmaceuticals her narrator has been consuming, then makes a sudden, echo-laden break for the transcendent: The sun shines through the window, and the days ahead reach out to eternity. Images of light from above become glimmers of hope trailing the album's characters. A savior slides down the mountainside. "I've seen the sound of angels," sings Anderson. "I've heard the sound, their wings / He said that I was judgment / You know I'm everything."

A few artists, such as Sufjan Stevens and Danielson's Daniel 15 Smith (who sometimes performs dressed as a tree bearing the nine fruits of the Holy Spirit), are outspokenly Christian, and often weave their faith into lyrics and song titles. But many others, like ex-Catholic Anderson and lifelong nonbeliever Buchla, have more complicated relationships to religion. Deradoorian, the Dirty Projectors bassist and vocalist, has an ongoing fascination with religion that began in junior high, when she was "born again" in a youth-group parking lot. A few years later, she rejected fundamentalist Christianity and began practicing a nondenominational form of meditation. Members of the Mae Shi have wildly divergent takes on religion. While some have never believed in God, others are devout Christians. The songs on last year's *HLLLYH* (pronounced "hell yeah," or "hallelujah") fuse biblical imagery with *Dawn of the Dead* gore. But because the songwriters' standpoints clash, the tracks careen from fire and brimstone to deep-seated doubt.

Some bands are even leery of secular spirituality. Yeasayer's 2007 debut, *All Hour Cymbals*, traces its influences to a complex, global web of secular and devotional music. Haunting Middle Eastern psychedelia crosses paths with Bollywood soundtracks and African chants in a heady, hypnotic collage that only distantly resembles any one of its forebears. Critics pegged their music as cosmic and even "tribal," but the band members are avowed skeptics who understand mysticism's potential to mislead and anesthetize. Chris Keating, who sings and plays keyboards, calls *All Hour Cymbals* a nonbeliever's attempt to understand what devotion and awe might feel like. The album, he says, strives to awaken through art the feelings others go to church seeking.

These days, mainstream religion feels largely divorced from metaphysics. The language of good and evil has been co-opted in the service of countless holy wars, and Christian leaders spend more time railing against gay marriage than debating the nature of the human soul. Those of us who can't buy into these crusades must find other marvels to contemplate. As Keating recognizes, art may help to fill a void left by organized religion: Indie rock's predominantly young, urban, and irreligious audience kneels to worship at the foot of a stage. Bible study is replaced by ritualistic listening and re-listening to tease out the meaning or simply bask in the bliss of favorite albums.

Perhaps this is why Kandinsky exhorted artists to turn their attentions away from the sordidness of life on earth toward the "nonmaterial" realm. But these musicians are not as detached as he prescribed. In fact, many bring spirituality to bear on the physical realm. The mantra that pervades Animal Collective's "My Girls" has nothing to do with God or redemption. Noah

"Panda Bear" Lennox sings—in words so sincere and conversational they are almost embarrassing—about wanting to protect his wife and daughter: "I don't mean to seem like I care about material things like a social status / I just want four walls and adobe slats for my girls." And Gowns uses religious imagery to talk about politics; Anderson goes so far as to say that the carefully titled *Red State* was a protest album, lamenting everything from rural poverty and drug dependence to South Dakota's proposed abortion ban.

From the very first listen, *In the Aeroplane Over the Sea* hooks us with its blaring horn section, singing saw solos, and Mangum's yowls. But what keeps us up at night, as our minds obsess over snatches of lyrics, is the mournful longing at the album's core, the way it makes Anne Frank and the horrors that befell her resonate. Kandinsky saw the spiritual and the earthly as opposites, but for indie rock's spiritual explorers, they are inextricably linked. This music doesn't suffer from the communion but originates in the space where they meet.

For Discussion and Writing

1. **Comprehension**   According to the Berman, how do Animal Collective stage shows differ from the performances of typical "rock stars"? How does this difference affect the reactions of the band's audience?

2. **Critical Reading**   Why do you think Berman begins an essay about contemporary indie rock with a discussion about Wassily Kandinsky's essay? How is the opening paragraph related to both her writing **purpose** and her **thesis**?

3. **Analysis**   Berman discusses a member of the band Ponytail, who seeks to "eliminate the I–thou relationship between musician and fan . . ." (par. 11). What do you think that means? How would doing so suggest a "spiritual" purpose?

4. **Connections**   In "The Pernicious Rise of Poptimism" (p. 240), Saul Austerlitz writes that indie rock, with its "self-seriousness," is poptimism's "Kryptonite" (par. 12). Certainly, Berman's serious essay about indie rock considers (in Austerlitz's words) "knottier music that might require some effort to appreciate" (par. 17). In contrast, poptimism celebrates the accessible pleasures of popular hit songs. After reading both essays, which sensibility do you find more appealing—and which view of music best describes your own?

5. ***Writing*** Berman suggests that rock music can aspire to the highest aspirations of art and spirituality. According to her, it may even "help to fill a void left by organized religion" (par. 17). Do you expect your own favorite bands to be "spiritual explorers" (par. 19)? Or do you want something else from the music you love? What music genres, listening experiences, bands, or individual artists fulfill that purpose for you? Do you see other patterns or tendencies that unite the music you listen to and care about? Write an essay that addresses these questions. Use specific examples of musical artists or songs to support your points, as Berman does. You may want use her title as your template: "Concerning the _____ in _____."

CHAPTER 5

Television

Are we living in a Golden Age of television?

Over the last sixty years, no pop culture medium has done more to shape American life than television. To take just one facet of society, consider its effects on U.S. politics, from Joseph McCarthy's televised congressional hearings, the first televised presidential debate between John Kennedy and Richard Nixon, and news images from the Vietnam War, to today's cable news channel shoutfests. Indeed, TV has provided the space and occasion for national public discourse. But the medium's social and cultural influence goes much deeper. Clay Shirky, whose essay "Gin, Television, and Social Surplus" appears in Chapter 3 of this book (p. 167), sees twentieth-century American TV as a "cognitive heat sink, dissipating thinking that might otherwise have built up and caused society to overheat." In other words, TV became one way for Americans to process the tensions and potential dangers of technological and social transformation. We should consider what Americans have been thinking about while watching all that television: national greatness and human progress with the broadcast of the 1969 moon landing; bigotry and intergenerational struggle on *All in the Family*; concerns about nuclear war in *The Day After*; idyllic family lives on *The Waltons* and *Happy Days*; a new image of the affluent African American family on *The Cosby Show*; criminal lives on *The Wire* and *Breaking Bad*. To talk about American popular culture is, almost axiomatically, to talk about television. And television programming over the years provides capsule summaries of American concerns, hopes, and enthusiasms: American history by way of *TV Guide*.

Although experimental television had existed since the late 1920s, the RCA corporation introduced the new medium to the American public at the 1939 World's Fair. A writer for the *New York Times* responded dubiously: "The problem with television is that people must sit and keep their eyes glued on a screen; the average American family hasn't time for it." But the average family made time: Within two decades, over forty million American families owned television sets. TV has always had its idealistic boosters and skeptical critics, of course. Newton Minow, former chairman of the Federal Communications Commission, embodied both sides of this debate in a famous 1961 speech: "When television is good, nothing—not the theater, not the magazines or newspapers—nothing is better. But when television is bad, nothing is worse. I invite each of you to sit down in front of your own television set when your station goes on the air and stay there, for a day, without a book, without a magazine, without a newspaper, without a profit and loss sheet or a rating book to distract you. Keep your eyes glued to that set until the station signs off. I can assure you that what you will observe is a vast wasteland."

All of the following essays engage this dichotomy of good and bad television in one way or another. In "Television Addiction Is No Mere Metaphor," Robert Kubey and Mihaly Csikszentmihalyi examine the term "TV addiction" and discover that it "captures the essence of a very real phenomenon." In "Girls, Girls, Girls," Roxane Gay dissects Lena Dunham's HBO series *Girls*, illuminating the show's strengths and weaknesses, along with its cultural cachet: "We have so many expectations for this show because *Girls* is a significant shift in what we normally see about girls and women." Paul A. Cantor's "The Apocalyptic Strain in Popular Culture: The American Nightmare Becomes the American Dream" suggests that post-apocalyptic shows like *The Walking Dead* affirm America's libertarian ideals of "independence and self-reliance." Ken Auletta focuses on how television's influence is changing because of the medium itself in "Netflix and the Future of Television," as television "is undergoing a digital revolution."

In the paired readings, David Charpentier ("Story or Spectacle? Why Television Is Better Than the Movies") and Jake Flanagin ("Stay Unlikable—for the Good of TV") explore the ways in which quality television has turned into a vehicle for presenting increasingly complex and satisfying characters.

As you read, consider the centrality of television to American popular culture:

- How do television shows reflect our culture and its preoccupations?
- What aesthetic qualities determine "good" television programming from "bad"?
- How is the medium of television—and our relationship with it—changing?

ROBERT KUBEY AND
MIHALY CSIKSZENTMIHALYI

Television Addiction
Is No Mere Metaphor

*Robert Kubey (b. 1952) is the director of the Center for Media Studies
and professor of journalism and media studies at Rutgers University.
He is the author of several books, including* Television and the Quality
of Life: How Viewing Shapes Everyday Experience *(1990) and* Creating Television: Conversations with the People behind 50 Years of
American TV *(2003). Kubey has written for the* New York Times, *Scientific* American, *and other publications. Mihaly Csikszentmihalyi
(b. 1934) is the C.S. and D. J. Davidson Professor of Psychology and
Management at Claremont University's graduate school of management.
Csikszentmihalyi is best known for his theory of "flow": a state of concentration and absorption in an activity associated with productivity
and satisfaction. His books include* Flow: The Psychology of Optimal
Experience *(1990) and* Good Business: Leadership, Flow, and the
Making of Meaning *(2003). People often use the term "addiction" in its
metaphorical or colloquial sense, particularly regarding the pleasures,
habits, and leisure activities of their day-to-day lives. In the following
article from* Scientific American, *Kubey and Csikszentmihalyi argue
that television can be addictive in a clinical sense, causing physiological
responses commonly associated with drugs like alcohol and cigarettes.*

*As you read, note Kubey and Csikszentmihalyi's purpose. Are they
trying to inform? Analyze? Persuade? Warn? How do they distinguish
healthy, harmless television viewing from television addiction? How do
you make such distinctions in your own life, whether about television
or other media?*

Perhaps the most ironic aspect of the struggle for survival is
how easily organisms can be harmed by that which they desire.
The trout is caught by the fisherman's lure, the mouse by cheese.

259

But at least those creatures have the excuse that bait and cheese look like sustenance. Humans seldom have that consolation. The temptations that can disrupt their lives are often pure indulgences. No one has to drink alcohol, for example. Realizing when a diversion has gotten out of control is one of the great challenges of life.

Excessive cravings do not necessarily involve physical substances. Gambling can become compulsive; sex can become obsessive. One activity, however, stands out for its prominence and ubiquity—the world's most popular leisure pastime, television. Most people admit to having a love–hate relationship with it. They complain about the "boob tube" and "couch potatoes," then they settle into their sofas and grab the remote control. Parents commonly fret about their children's viewing (if not their own). Even researchers who study TV for a living marvel at the medium's hold on them personally. Percy Tannenbaum of the University of California at Berkeley has written: "Among life's more embarrassing moments have been countless occasions when I am engaged in conversation in a room while a TV set is on, and I cannot for the life of me stop from periodically glancing over to the screen. This occurs not only during dull conversations but during reasonably interesting ones just as well."

Scientists have been studying the effects of television for decades, generally focusing on whether watching violence on TV correlates with being violent in real life (see "The Effects of Observing Violence," by Leonard Berkowitz; *Scientific American*, February 1964; and "Communication and Social Environment," by George Gerber, September 1972). Less attention has been paid to the basic allure of the small screen—the medium, as opposed to the message.

The term "TV addiction" is imprecise and laden with value judgments, but it captures the essence of a very real phenomenon. Psychologists and psychiatrists formally define substance dependence as a disorder characterized by criteria that include spending a great deal of time using the substance; using it more often than one intends; thinking about reducing use or making repeated unsuccessful efforts to reduce use; giving up important social, family, or occupational activities to use it; and reporting withdrawal symptoms when one stops using it.

All these criteria can apply to people who watch a lot of television. That does not mean that watching television, per se, is   5 problematic. Television can teach and amuse; it can reach aesthetic heights; it can provide much-needed distraction and escape. The difficulty arises when people strongly sense that they ought not to watch as much as they do and yet find themselves strangely unable to reduce their viewing. Some knowledge of how the medium exerts its pull may help heavy viewers gain better control over their lives.

A BODY AT REST TENDS TO STAY AT REST

The amount of time people spend watching television is astonishing. On average, individuals in the industrialized world devote three hours a day to the pursuit—fully half of their leisure time, and more than on any single activity save work and sleep. At this rate, someone who lives to seventy-five would spend nine years in front of the tube. To some commentators, this devotion means simply that people enjoy TV and make a conscious decision to watch it. But if that is the whole story, why do so many people experience misgivings about how much they view? In Gallup polls in 1992 and 1999, two out of five adult respondents and seven out of ten teenagers said they spent too much time watching TV. Other surveys have consistently shown that roughly 10 percent of adults call themselves TV addicts.

To study people's reactions to TV, researchers have undertaken laboratory experiments in which they have monitored the brain waves (using an electroencephalograph, or EEG), skin resistance, or heart rate of people watching television. To track behavior and emotion in the normal course of life, as opposed to the artificial conditions of the lab, we have used the Experience Sampling Method (ESM). Participants carried a beeper, and we signaled them six to eight times a day, at random, over the period of a week; whenever they heard the beep, they wrote down what they were doing and how they were feeling using a standardized scorecard.

As one might expect, people who were watching TV when we beeped them reported feeling relaxed and passive. The EEG studies similarly show less mental stimulation, as measured by alpha brain-wave production, during viewing than during reading.

What is more surprising is that the sense of relaxation ends when the set is turned off, but the feelings of passivity and lowered alertness continue. Survey participants commonly reflect that television has somehow absorbed or sucked out their energy, leaving them depleted. They say they have more difficulty concentrating after viewing than before. In contrast, they rarely indicate such difficulty after reading. After playing sports or engaging in hobbies, people report improvements in mood. After watching TV, people's moods are about the same or worse than before.

Within moments of sitting or lying down and pushing the 10 "power" button, viewers report feeling more relaxed. Because the relaxation occurs quickly, people are conditioned to associate viewing with rest and lack of tension. The association is positively reinforced because viewers remain relaxed throughout viewing, and it is negatively reinforced via the stress and dysphoric rumination that occurs once the screen goes blank again.

Habit-forming drugs work in similar ways. A tranquilizer that leaves the body rapidly is much more likely to cause dependence than one that leaves the body slowly, precisely because the user is more aware that the drug's effects are wearing off. Similarly, viewers' vague learned sense that they will feel less relaxed if they stop viewing may be a significant factor in not turning the set off. Viewing begets more viewing.

Thus, the irony of TV: people watch a great deal longer than they plan to, even though prolonged viewing is less rewarding. In our ESM studies the longer people sat in front of the set, the less satisfaction they said they derived from it. When signaled, heavy viewers (those who consistently watch more than four hours a day) tended to report on their ESM sheets that they enjoy TV less than light viewers did (less than two hours a day). For some, a twinge of unease or guilt that they aren't doing something more productive may also accompany and depreciate the enjoyment of prolonged viewing. Researchers in Japan, the U.K., and the U.S. have found that this guilt occurs much more among middle-class viewers than among less affluent ones.

GRABBING YOUR ATTENTION

What is it about TV that has such a hold on us? In part, the attraction seems to spring from our biological "orienting response." First described by Ivan Pavlov in 1927, the orienting response is our instinctive visual or auditory reaction to any sudden or novel stimulus. It is part of our evolutionary heritage, a built-in sensitivity to movement and potential predatory threats. Typical orienting reactions include dilation of the blood vessels to the brain, slowing of the heart, and constriction of blood vessels to major muscle groups. Alpha waves are blocked for a few seconds before returning to their baseline level, which is determined by the general level of mental arousal. The brain focuses its attention on gathering more information while the rest of the body quiets.

In 1986, Byron Reeves of Stanford University, Esther Thorson of the University of Missouri, and their colleagues began to study whether the simple formal features of television — cuts, edits, zooms, pans, sudden noises — activate the orienting response, thereby keeping attention on the screen. By watching how brain waves were affected by formal features, the researchers concluded that these stylistic tricks can indeed trigger involuntary responses and "derive their attentional value through the evolutionary significance of detecting movement. . . . It is the form, not the content, of television that is unique."

The orienting response may partly explain common viewer remarks such as: "If a television is on, I just can't keep my eyes off it," "I don't want to watch as much as I do, but I can't help it," and "I feel hypnotized when I watch television." In the years since Reeves and Thorson published their pioneering work, researchers have delved deeper. Annie Lang's research team at Indiana University has shown that heart rate decreases for four to six seconds after an orienting stimulus. In ads, action sequences, and music videos, formal features frequently come at a rate of one per second, thus activating the orienting response continuously.

Lang and her colleagues have also investigated whether formal features affect people's memory of what they have seen. In one of their studies, participants watched a program and then filled out a score sheet. Increasing the frequency of edits — defined here as a change from one camera angle to another in the same visual scene — improved memory recognition, presumably because it focused attention on the screen. Increasing the frequency of cuts — changes to a new visual scene — had a similar effect but only up to a point. If the number of cuts exceeded ten in two minutes, recognition dropped off sharply.

Producers of educational television for children have found that formal features can help learning. But increasing the rate of cuts and edits eventually overloads the brain. Music videos and

© Howard Kingsnorth/Getty Images

"The irony of TV: people watch a great deal longer than they plan to, even though prolonged viewing is less rewarding." How do the viewers in this image compare with your own experiences with television and computer use?

commercials that use rapid intercutting of unrelated scenes are designed to hold attention more than they are to convey information. People may remember the name of the product or band, but the details of the ad itself float in one ear and out the other. The orienting response is overworked. Viewers still attend to the screen, but they feel tired and worn out, with little compensating psychological reward. Our ESM findings show much the same thing.

Sometimes the memory of the product is very subtle. Many ads today are deliberately oblique: they have an engaging story line, but it is hard to tell what they are trying to sell. Afterward you may not remember the product consciously. Yet advertisers believe that if they have gotten your attention, when you later go to the store you will feel better or more comfortable with a given product because you have a vague recollection of having heard of it.

The natural attraction to television's sound and light starts very early in life. Dafna Lemish of Tel Aviv University has described babies at six to eight weeks attending to television. We have observed slightly older infants who, when lying on their backs on the floor, crane their necks around 180 degrees to catch what light through yonder window breaks. This inclination suggests how deeply rooted the orienting response is.

"TV IS PART OF THEM"

That said, we need to be careful about overreacting. Little evi- 20
dence suggests that adults or children should stop watching TV altogether. The problems come from heavy or prolonged viewing.

The Experience Sampling Method permitted us to look closely at most every domain of everyday life: working, eating, reading, talking to friends, playing a sport, and so on. We wondered whether heavy viewers might experience life differently than light viewers do. Do they dislike being with people more? Are they more alienated from work? What we found nearly leaped off the page at us. Heavy viewers report feeling significantly more anxious and less happy than light viewers do in unstructured situations, such as doing nothing, daydreaming, or waiting in line. The difference widens when the viewer is alone.

Subsequently, Robert D. McIlwraith of the University of Manitoba extensively studied those who called themselves TV addicts on surveys. On a measure called the Short Imaginal Processes Inventory (SIPI), he found that the self-described addicts are more easily bored and distracted and have poorer attentional control than the nonaddicts. The addicts said they used TV to distract themselves from unpleasant thoughts and to fill time. Other studies over the years have shown that heavy viewers are less likely to participate in community activities and sports and are more likely to be obese than moderate viewers or nonviewers.

The question that naturally arises is: In which direction does the correlation go? Do people turn to TV because of boredom and loneliness, or does TV viewing make people more susceptible to boredom and loneliness? We and most other researchers argue that the former is generally the case, but it is not a simple case of either/or. Jerome L. and Dorothy Singer of Yale University, among others, have suggested that more viewing may contribute to a shorter attention span, diminished self-restraint, and less patience with the normal delays of daily life. More than twenty-five years ago, psychologist Tannis M. MacBeth Williams of the University of British Columbia studied a mountain community that had no television until cable finally arrived. Over time, both adults and children in the town became less creative in problem solving, less able to persevere at tasks, and less tolerant of unstructured time.

To some researchers, the most convincing parallel between TV and addictive drugs is that people experience withdrawal symptoms when they cut back on viewing. Nearly forty years ago, Gary A. Steiner of the University of Chicago collected fascinating individual accounts of families whose set had broken—this back in the days when households generally had only one set: "The family walked around like a chicken without a head." "It was terrible. We did nothing—my husband and I talked." "Screamed constantly. Children bothered me, and my nerves were on edge. Tried to interest them in games, but impossible. TV is part of them."

In experiments, families have volunteered or been paid to stop viewing, typically for a week or a month. Many could not complete the period of abstinence. Some fought, verbally and physically. Anecdotal reports from some families that have tried the annual "TV turn-off" week in the U.S. tell a similar story. 25

If a family has been spending the lion's share of its free time watching television, reconfiguring itself around a new set of activities is no easy task. Of course, that does not mean it cannot be done or that all families implode when deprived of their set. In a review of these cold-turkey studies, Charles Winick of the City University of New York concluded: "The first three or four days for most persons were the worst, even in many homes where viewing was minimal and where there were other ongoing activities. In over half of all the households, during these first few days of loss, the regular routines were disrupted, family members had difficulties in dealing with the newly available time, anxiety and aggressions were expressed. . . . People living alone tended to be bored and irritated. . . . By the second week, a move toward adaptation to the situation was common." Unfortunately, researchers have yet to flesh out these anecdotes; no one has systematically gathered statistics on the prevalence of these withdrawal symptoms.

Even though TV does seem to meet the criteria for substance dependence, not all researchers would go so far as to call TV addictive. McIlwraith said in 1998 that "displacement of other activities by television may be socially significant but still fall short of the clinical requirement of significant impairment." He argued that a new category of "TV addiction" may not be necessary if heavy viewing stems from conditions such as depression and social phobia. Nevertheless, whether or not we formally diagnose someone as TV-dependent, millions of people sense that they cannot readily control the amount of television they watch.

SLAVE TO THE COMPUTER SCREEN

Although much less research has been done on video games and computer use, the same principles often apply. The games offer escape and distraction; players quickly learn that they feel better when playing; and so a kind of reinforcement loop develops. The obvious difference from television, however, is the interactivity. Many video and computer games minutely increase in difficulty along with the increasing ability of the player. One can search for months to find another tennis or chess player of comparable ability, but programmed games can immediately provide a near-perfect match of challenge to skill. They offer the psychic pleasure—what one of us (Csikszentmihalyi) has called "flow"—that accompanies increased mastery of most any human endeavor. On the other hand, prolonged activation of the orienting response can wear players out. Kids report feeling tired, dizzy, and nauseated after long sessions.

In 1997, in the most extreme medium-effects case on record, 700 Japanese children were rushed to the hospital, many suffering from "optically stimulated epileptic seizures" caused by viewing bright flashing lights in a Pokémon video game broadcast on Japanese TV. Seizures and other untoward effects of video games are significant enough that software companies and platform manufacturers now routinely include warnings in their instruction booklets. Parents have reported to us that rapid movement on the screen has caused motion sickness in their young children after just fifteen minutes of play. Many youngsters, lacking self-control and experience (and often supervision), continue to play despite these symptoms.

Lang and Shyam Sundar of Pennsylvania State University have 30 been studying how people respond to Web sites. Sundar has shown people multiple versions of the same Web page, identical except for the number of links. Users reported that more links conferred a greater sense of control and engagement. At some point, however, the number of links reached saturation, and adding more of them simply turned people off. As with video games, the ability of Web sites to hold the user's attention seems to depend less on formal features than on interactivity.

For growing numbers of people, the life they lead online may often seem more important, more immediate, and more intense than the life they lead face-to-face. Maintaining control over one's media habits is more of a challenge today than it has ever been. TV sets and computers are everywhere. But the small screen and the Internet need not interfere with the quality of the rest of one's life. In its easy provision of relaxation and escape, television can be beneficial in limited doses. Yet when the habit interferes with the ability to grow, to learn new things, to lead an active life, then it does constitute a kind of dependence and should be taken seriously.

For Discussion and Writing

1. **Comprehension**   What is the "orienting response" (par. 13)? How is it related to television viewing and addiction?

2. **Critical Reading**   What kinds of **evidence** do Kubey and Csikszentmihalyi use to support their argument? Is it clearly presented and effective? How do they integrate it into their essay?

3. **Analysis**   Kubey and Csikszentmihalyi concede that television has benefits as well as drawbacks: "Television can teach and amuse; it can reach aesthetic heights; it can provide much-needed distraction and escape" (par. 5). Do you find these concessions convincing in the context of the writers' overall argument? What attitude toward television do Kubey and Csikszentmihalyi want their readers to adopt?

4. **Connections**   How might Frank Rose ("The Art of Immersion: Fear of Fiction," p. 409) respond to Kubey and Csikszentmihalyi's argument? Is "Television Addiction Is No Mere Metaphor" merely another example of immersive media arousing "fear" and "hostility"? Or are Kubey and Csikszentmihalyi writing about a phenomenon that is distinct from the "transporting power of narrative" (par. 37)?

5. **Writing**   The authors write, "Maintaining control over one's media habits is more of a challenge today than it has ever been" (par. 31). Do you have any misgivings over your television viewing, online activity, video-game playing, or any other similar activities? Do you find them addictive? How do you maintain control over your behavior? In a brief essay or blog post, enumerate a brief guide or set of rules to govern your "media habits."

ROXANE GAY

Girls, Girls, Girls

*Roxane Gay is a novelist, blogger, editor, and cultural critic. She teaches
English at Purdue University. Her work has appeared in* McSweeney's,
the Los Angeles Times, *the* Nation, *and* Salon.com, *among many other
publications, and she is the editor of "The Butter" vertical on the* Toast,
*a feminist general interest Web site. She is the author of bestselling
books, including* An Untamed State *(2014) and* Bad Feminist *(2014).
She is also the coeditor of the literary magazine* PANK. *In this essay
from* Bad Feminist, Gay *reflects on the television show* Girls *to analyze
the intersection of "girlhood" and popular culture, as well as the pressures faced by women and people of color when they become creators
of popular culture.*

As you read, *consider Gay's larger view of popular culture: Do her
expectations about the quality of popular culture seem too high—or
too low? How does she incorporate personal experience and observation into her criticism of television shows like* Girls? *Do you identify
with her longing to recognize herself in popular culture?*

A television show about my twenties would follow the life of a girl
who is lost, literally and figuratively. There wouldn't be a laugh
track. The show would open deep in my *lost year*—the year I drop
out of college and disappear. With no ability to cope and no way
to ask for help, the main character—me—is completely crazy.
She makes a spectacular mess.

A lot happens in the pilot. About ten days before the start of
junior year, my character gets on a plane and abandons everything. She runs away to Arizona by way of a trip to San Francisco
with a much older man she has only corresponded with via the
Internet. We're talking about the old-fashioned Internet, in
1994—a 2400-baud modem or some such. It is a small miracle

270

she isn't killed. She cuts off all contact with her family, her friends, or anyone who thought they knew her. She has no money, no plan, a suitcase, and a complete lack of self-regard. It is real drama.

The rest of that first season is equally dramatic. Before long, she finds a seedy job doing about the only thing she's qualified to do, working from midnight to eight in a nondescript office building. She sits in a little, windowless booth and talks to strangers on the phone. She drinks diet soda from a plastic cup, sometimes with vodka, and does crossword puzzles. It is so easy to talk to strangers. She loves the job until she doesn't.

There is an interesting cast. Her coworkers are girls who are also messy. They are different races, from different places, but all lost together. They give themselves names like China and Bubbles and Misty, and at the end of a long shift they hardly remember who belongs to which name. My character has many different names. She wakes up and says, "Tonight, I'm Delilah, Morgan, Becky." She wants to be anyone else.

This is late-night television. Cable. China does heroin in the   5
bathroom at work. Sometimes, she leaves a burnt strip of tinfoil on the counter. The manager calls them all into her office and yells. The girls will never rat China out. Bubbles has baby daddy problems. Sometimes, her man drops her off at work and girls smoking in the parking lot watch as Bubbles and her man yell at each other, terrible things. In another episode, the baby daddy drops Bubbles off and they practically fuck in the front seat. Misty has been on her own since she was sixteen. She is very skinny and has scabs all over her arms and never seems to wash her hair. After most shifts, the girls go to Jack in the Box and then lie out by the pool of the house where my character is staying. The girls tell my character how lucky she is to live in a house with air-conditioning. They have swamp coolers and live in crappy apartments. My character stares up at the sun from the diving board where she loves to stretch out and thinks, bitterly, *Yes, I am so fucking lucky*. She is too young to realize that compared to them she is lucky. She ran away but still has something to run back to when she is ready. My character doesn't come to this realization until the season finale.

Every woman has a series of episodes about her twenties, her girlhood, and how she came out of it. Rarely are those episodes so neatly encapsulated as an episode of, say, *Friends,* or a romantic comedy about boy meeting girl.

Girls have been written and represented in popular culture in many different ways. Most of these representations have been largely unsatisfying because they never get girlhood quite right. It is not possible for girlhood to be represented wholly—girlhood is too vast and too individual an experience. We can only try to represent girlhood in ways that are varied and recognizable. All too often, however, this doesn't happen.

We put a lot of responsibility on popular culture, particularly when some pop artifact somehow distinguishes itself as not terrible. In the months and weeks leading up to the release of *Bridesmaids,*[1] for example, there was a great deal of breathless talk about the new ground the movie was breaking, how yes, indeed, women *are* funny. Can you believe it? There was a lot of pressure on that movie. *Bridesmaids* had to be good if any other women-driven comedies had any hope of being produced. This is the state of affairs for women in entertainment—everything hangs in the balance all the time.

Why do we put so much responsibility on movies like *Bridesmaids*? How do we get to a place where a movie, one movie, can be considered revolutionary for women?

There's another woman-oriented pop artifact being asked to 10 shoulder a great deal of responsibility these days: Lena Dunham's *Girls,* a television series on HBO. The show debuted to a lot of hype. Critics almost universally embraced Dunham's vision and the way she chronicles the lives of four twenty-something girls navigating that interstitial time between graduating from college and growing up.

I am not the target audience for *Girls*. I was not particularly enthralled by the first three episodes or the first two seasons, but the show gave me a great deal to think about. That counts for something. The writing is often smart and clever. I laughed a few times during each episode and recognize the ways in which this show is breaking new ground. I admire how Dunham's character, Hannah Horvath, doesn't have the typical body we normally see

---

[1]*Bridesmaids* (2011): a film directed by Paul Feig, produced by Judd Apatow, and starred Kristen Wiig and Maya Rudolph. [Editor's note.]

Gay writes that Lena Dunham's *Girls* "is a fine example of someone writing what she knows and the painful limitations of doing so." Why do viewers and critics expect so much of Dunham's show?

on television. There is some solidity to her. We see her eat, enthusiastically. We see her fuck. We see her endure the petty humiliations so many young women have to endure. We see the life of one kind of real girl and that is important.

It's awesome that a twenty-five-year-old woman gets to write, direct, and star in her own show for a network like HBO. It's just as sad that this is so *revolutionary* it deserves mention.

A generation is a group of individuals born and living contemporaneously. In the pilot, Hannah Horvath is explaining to her parents why she needs them to keep supporting her financially. She says, "I think I might be the voice of my generation. Or at least, a generation . . . somewhere." We have so many expectations; we're so thirsty for authentic representations of girls that we only hear the first half of that statement. We hear that *Girls* is supposed to speak for all of us.

At times, I find *Girls* and the overall premise to be forced. Amidst all the cleverness, I want the show to have a stronger emotional tone. I want to feel something genuine, and rarely has the show given me that opportunity. Too many of the characters seem like caricatures, where more nuance would better serve both the characters and their story lines. In the first season, for example, Hannah's not-boyfriend, Adam, is a depressing, disgusting composite of every asshole every woman in her twenties has ever dated. We would get the point if he were even half the asshole. The pedophile fantasy Adam shares at the beginning of the "Vagina Panic" episode is cringe-worthy. The ironic rape joke Hannah makes during her job interview in that same episode is cringe-worthy. It all feels very "Look at me! I am edgy!" Maybe that's the point. I cannot be sure. More often than not, the show is trying too hard to do too much, but that's okay. This show should not have to be perfect.

Girls reminds me of how terrible my twenties were—being lost 15 and awkward, having terrible sex with terrible people, being perpetually broke, eating ramen. I am not nostalgic for that time. I had no money and no hope. Like the girls in *Girls,* I was never really on the verge of destitution but I lived a generally crappy life. There was nothing romantic about the experience. I understand why many young women find the show so relatable, but watching the show makes me slightly nauseated and exceptionally grateful to be in my thirties.

As you might expect, the discourse surrounding *Girls* has been remarkably extensive and vigorous—nepotism, privilege, race. Dunham has given us a veritable trifecta of reasons to dissect her show.

Lena Dunham is, indeed, the daughter of a well-known artist, and the principal cast comprises the daughters of other well-known figures like Brian Williams and David Mamet. People resent nepotism because it reminds us that sometimes success really is whom you know. This nepotism is mildly annoying, but it is not new or remarkable. Many people in Hollywood make entire careers out of hiring their friends for every single project. Adam Sandler has done it for years. Judd Apatow does it with such regularity you don't need to consult IMDb to know whom he will cast in his projects.

Girls also represents a very privileged existence—one where young women's New York lifestyles can be subsidized by their parents, where these young women can think about art and unpaid internships and finding themselves and writing memoirs at twenty-four. Many people are privileged, and again, it's easy to resent that because the level of privilege expressed in the show reminds us that sometimes, success really starts with where you come from. *Girls* is a fine example of someone writing what she knows and the painful limitations of doing so.

One of the most significant critiques of *Girls* is the relative absence of race. The New York where *Girls* takes place is much like the New York where *Sex and the City* was set—a mythical city completely void of the rich diversity of the very real New York. The critique is legitimate, and people across many publications have written deeply felt essays about why it is damaging for a show like *Girls* to completely negate certain experiences and realities. In the second season, *Girls* tried and failed to bring race into the show in a relevant way. During the premiere, Hannah has a black boyfriend and it's handled fairly well. The boyfriend, Sandy, is conservative, and there's a clever moment in which Hannah claims she doesn't see race, thereby exposing that she is not nearly as evolved as she might believe. The episode is smart, but not smart enough because it misses the point—clever defiance does not a diversity problem address.

Every girl or once-was-girl has a show that would be best for her. In *Girls* we finally have a television show about girls who are awkward and say terribly inappropriate things, are ill equipped to set boundaries for themselves, and have no idea who they're going to be in a few years. We have so many expectations for this show because *Girls* is a significant shift in what we normally see about girls and women. While critics, in their lavish attention, have said Dunham's show is speaking to an entire generation of girls, there are many of us who recognize that the show is only speaking to a narrow demographic within a generation.

Maybe the narrowness of *Girls* is fine. Maybe it's also fine that Dunham's vision of coming-of-age is limited to the kinds of girls she knows. Maybe, though, Dunham is a product of the artistic culture that created her—one that is largely myopic and unwilling to think about diversity critically.

We all have ideas about the way the world should be, and sometimes we forget how the world is. The absence of race in

Girls is an uncomfortable reminder of how many people lead lives segregated by race and class. The stark whiteness of the cast, their upper-middle-class milieu, and the New York where they live force us to interrogate our own lives and the diversity, or lack thereof, in our social, artistic, and professional circles.

Don't get me wrong. The stark whiteness of *Girls* disturbs and disappoints me. During the first season, I wondered why Hannah and her friends didn't have at least one blipster friend or why Hannah's boss at the publishing house or one or more of the girls' love interests couldn't be an actor of color. The show is so damn literal. Still, *Girls* is not the first show to commit this transgression, and it certainly won't be the last. It is unreasonable to expect Dunham to somehow solve the race and representation problem on television while crafting her twenty-something witticisms and appalling us with sex scenes so uncomfortable they defy imagination.

In recent years, I have enjoyed looking at pictures from literary events, across the country, wondering if I will see a person of color. It's a game I play that I generally win. Whether the event takes place in Los Angeles or New York City or Austin or Portland, more often than not, the audiences at these events are completely white. Sometimes, there will be one or two black people, perhaps an Asian. At most of these literary events I attend, I am generally the only spot of color, even at a large writers' conference like Association of Writers & Writing Programs events. It's not that people of color are deliberately excluded but that they are not included because most communities, literary or otherwise, are largely insular and populated by people who know the people they know. This is the uncomfortable truth of our community, and it is disingenuous to be pointing the finger at *Girls* when the show is a pretty accurate reflection of many artistic communities.

There's more, though, to this intense focus on privilege and 25 race and *Girls*. Why is this show being held to the higher standard when there are so many television shows that have long ignored race and class or have flagrantly transgressed in these areas?

There are so many terrible shows on television representing women in sexist, stupid, silly ways. Movies are even worse. Movies take one or two anemic ideas about women, caricature them, and shove those caricatures down our throats. The moment we

see a pop artifact offering even a sliver of something different—
say, a woman who isn't a size zero or who doesn't treat a man as
the center of the universe—we cling to it desperately because
that representation is all we have. There are all kinds of television
shows and movies about women but how many of them make
women recognizable?

There are few opportunities for people of color to recognize
themselves in literature, in theater, on television, and in movies.
It's depressingly easy for women of color to feel entirely left out
when watching a show like *Girls*. It is rare that we ever see ourselves as anything but the *sassy* black friend or the nanny or the
secretary or the district attorney or the magical negro—roles relegated to the background and completely lacking in authenticity,
depth, or complexity.

Women of color come of age and have the same experiences
Dunham depicts in her shows, but we rarely see those stories
because they don't fit the popular imagination's rendering of
Other girlhood, which is generally nonexistent in popular culture.
At least there have been a few shows for black women to recognize themselves—*Girlfriends, Living Single, A Different World, The
Cosby Show*. What about other women of color? For Hispanic
and Latina women, Indian women, Middle Eastern women, Asian
women, their absence in popular culture is even more pronounced, their need for relief just as palpable and desperate.

The incredible problem *Girls* faces is that all we want is everything from each movie or television show or book that promises
to offer a new voice, a relatable voice, an important voice. We
want, and rightly so, to believe our lives deserve to be new, relatable, and important. We want to see more complex, nuanced
depictions of what it really means to be whoever we are or were
or hope to be. We just want so much. We just need so much.

I'm more interested in a show called *Grown Women* about a 30
group of friends who finally have great jobs and pay all their bills
in a timely manner but don't have any savings and still deal with
sloppy love lives and hangovers on Monday morning at work.
That show doesn't exist, though, because stability holds little
allure for the popular imagination and Hollywood rarely acknowledges women of a certain age. Until that show comes along or I
decide to write it, we have to deal with what we have.

For Discussion and Writing

1. **Comprehension**   What does Gay admire about the presentation of the character Hannah Horvath on *Girls*?

2. **Critical Reading**   The first section of Gay's essay is a long description of a hypothetical television show about her life in her twenties. Why do you think she wrote her introduction this way? How does it support her claims about pop-culture representations of girls and women?

3. **Analysis**   Gay claims, "We have so many expectations for this show because *Girls* is a significant shift in what we normally see about girls and women" (par. 20). Are her expectations of the show realistic, from your point of view? Do Gay's criticisms, such as her claim that the show lacks diversity, seem reasonable and valid?

4. **Connections**   In "Stay Unlikable — for the Good of TV" (p. 315), Jake Flanagin writes about Lena Dunham and *Girls*, noting that "viewers are split on the issue of liking or disliking Hannah Horvath" (par. 14). Do you think that Gay would agree with Flanagin's thesis that television needs more "unlikable" women characters? Why or why not?

5. **Writing**   Gay writes, "While critics . . . have said Dunham's show is speaking to an entire generation of girls, there are many of us who recognize that the show is only speaking to a narrow demographic within a generation" (par. 20). What — if any — television shows today speak to your "generation" — or even a "narrow demographic" within your generation? Do you think television, as a pop-culture medium, is still capable of connecting with younger viewers in ways that speak to their experiences, ideals, hopes, and fears? Are other media more effective? Explain your answer in an essay or in a project developed in the medium that you think best represents your generation.

PAUL A. CANTOR

The Apocalyptic Strain in Popular Culture: The American Nightmare Becomes the American Dream

Paul A. Cantor (b. 1949) is the Clifton Waller Barrett Professor of English at the University of Virginia. He earned his B.A. and Ph.D. at Harvard University. He has written on a wide range of subjects, including Shakespeare, Nietzsche, Romanticism, film, economics, and popular culture. His books include Gilligan Unbound: Pop Culture in the Age of Globalization *(2001),* Literature and the Economics of Liberty *(2009), and* The Invisible Hand in Popular Culture *(2012). In this essay, which originally appeared in the* Hedgehog Review, *Cantor suggests that postapocalyptic fantasies such as* The Walking Dead *reimagine the American dream—and perhaps embody a collective desire to live more deliberate, individualistic lives outside of large government or corporate institutions.*

***As you read,** notice how Cantor provides historical and cultural context for his claims. What conventional version of the American dream anchors his argument? Do you agree with Cantor that there is a "disenchantment with the mid-twentieth-century formulation of the American dream"? How does the writer make his analysis of two television shows accessible and meaningful even to readers who have not seen* Falling Skies *or* The Walking Dead?

We seem to have survived the Mayan apocalypse predicted for December 21, 2012, but maybe we should not get too cocky. American popular culture is overflowing with doomsday prophecies and end-of-the-world scenarios. According to film and television, vampires, werewolves, and zombies are storming across our landscape, and alien invaders, asteroids, and airborne toxic events threaten us from the skies. We might as well be living in the late

Middle Ages. Our films and television shows seem locked into a perpetual and ever-more-frenzied Dance of Death. Whatever happened to the popular culture that used to offer up charming images of the American dream? Where are the happy households—the Andersons, the Nelsons, the Cleavers, the Petries—when we need them? Film and television today are more likely to present images of the American nightmare: our entire civilization reduced to rubble and the few survivors forced to live a primitive existence in terror of monstrous forces unleashed throughout the land. Has the American nightmare paradoxically become the new American dream? Is there some weird kind of wish-fulfillment at work in all these visions of near-universal death and destruction?

THE DREAM AND THE NIGHTMARE

To explore these questions, we need to examine one standard notion of the American dream. There are, of course, as many versions of the American dream as there are Americans, but by the middle of the twentieth century, one common pattern emerged. This dream was very much embodied in material terms—a family happily ensconced in a spacious house, preferably in the suburbs, with the most up-to-date appliances and two or three cars in the garage. This dream was founded on faith in modern science and technology, which seemed to be continually improving the human condition. The path to achieving this American dream was clearly laid out. One got a good education in order to land a good job, which might or might not be fulfilling in itself but would in any case provide the financial means of buying all the material components that seemed essential to the American dream. As usually envisioned, the job—in order to pay enough—would be in one of the professions, chiefly law or medicine, or in some kind of business, probably a corporate position that would provide financial security. The notion of security was integral to this version of the American dream. One would find a job for life that included solid medical and retirement benefits. This model of happiness was often on view in film and television in the 1950s and 60s, supplying the framework for television situation comedies, for example, or providing the happy endings in many Hollywood movies.

This vision of the American dream was bound up with trust in American institutions. The goal of long-term security rested on faith in financial institutions, such as banks, insurance companies, and the stock market. Medical institutions, such as hospitals, clinics, and the pharmaceutical industry, were supposed to keep extending our life expectancy. Americans also looked up to their educational institutions, from primary schools to universities. After all, they were relying on their schools to prepare them for the careers that would underwrite their financial prosperity. In short, Americans relied on their institutions to shape them properly in the first place; in many cases they looked forward to being employed by institutions such as corporations and the professions; and they trusted these institutions in turn to work for their benefit, providing, for example, health care and financial security.

Overarching all these institutions was the grandest institution of them all, American government: local, state, and above all the federal government. Especially during the Cold War era, Americans looked up to the Washington establishment because it was protecting them from foreign and domestic enemies. Given the widespread faith in technical expertise after World War II, Americans generally trusted their government to regulate the economy and produce the prosperity that would make the American dream possible. In the second half of the twentieth century, the American government kept expanding its scope as a welfare state, with the goal of insuring the security of all aspects of its citizens' lives. Moreover, the federal government steadily increased its role in financially supporting and regulating the various institutions that were woven into the fabric of the American dream, especially educational and medical institutions. In sum, for decades the American dream came boxed in an institutional framework, and most Americans, without thinking much about it, assumed that they could not realize their dreams without these institutions.

But even at the peak of this conception of the American dream   5
in the 1950s, this faith in institutions did not go unchallenged. Dissenting voices charged that Americans were being increasingly "institutionalized," sacrificing their freedom in their quest for comfort and security. Talk of the "organization man" (the title of a 1956 book by William Whyte) reflected fears that Americans were selling their souls to corporations, giving up their individuality and autonomy to work in bureaucratic organizations. Skeptics also voiced concerns that the standard conception of the

American dream might be self-defeating. In the course of trying to provide material benefits to their families, men—and later women—were losing touch with the very spouses and children they claimed to cherish. The notion of the happy, close-knit family was at the core of the American dream, and yet career values often seemed to conflict with family values. Working hard at the office left men—and later women—with little or no time for their children. And everywhere institutions seemed to be coming between people, preventing them from interacting in face-to-face situations. The very institutions that Americans had turned to in order to achieve and secure their dreams seemed to have trapped them in a vast impersonal system that by its nature was inimical to personal fulfillment.

These anxieties about the American dream sometimes surfaced in popular culture in the middle of the twentieth century. Movies such as the 1957 *The Man in the Gray Flannel Suit* portrayed corporate life as empty and stultifying. And the immense popularity of Westerns during this era signaled a dissatisfaction with comfortable suburban life. Dramas set in the Wild West provided an imaginative escape from the safe and boring world of modern institutions—an image of a rugged, frontier existence, in which earlier Americans, especially men, were on their own and could act heroically in their struggle with hostile and dangerous environments.

Disenchantment with the mid-twentieth-century formulation of the American dream gradually increased and became widespread at the turn of the twenty-first century, as people lost their confidence in American institutions. A series of bubbles and meltdowns led people to doubt the fundamental honesty and integrity of financial institutions, above all, their ability to provide long-term economic security. Confidence in the competence and caring nature of the medical establishment began to erode, as witness the alternative medicine movement, the return to traditional home remedies, and skepticism about vaccination programs. Whether these doubts are scientifically justified is irrelevant to the larger cultural issue. The fact is that doctors and the medical profession in general are no longer held in the high esteem they once enjoyed in America. Educational institutions are also being challenged on a wide range of fronts, with critics complaining that they fail to deliver on their promises and charge exorbitant rates in the process. The home schooling movement offers concrete proof that many Americans have become disillusioned with the educational establishment. As for government institutions, with one "-gate" scandal after another, polling suggests that Americans' faith in institutions such as Congress and the Presidency is at an all-time low. Looking at the world around them, Americans may be excused for concluding that the financial-medical-educational-government complex that was supposed to help them achieve their dreams has failed them. At this point, it becomes tempting for Americans to wish away their banks, their hospitals, their schools, and their government. Perhaps life might be easier and more fulfilling without them.

Popular culture has stepped forward to offer Americans a chance to explore these possibilities imaginatively and to rethink the American dream. Films and television shows have allowed Americans to imagine what life would be like without all the institutions they had been told they need, but which they now suspect may be thwarting their self-fulfillment. We are dealing with a wide variety of fantasies here, mainly in the horror or science fiction genres, but the pattern is quite consistent and striking, cutting across generic distinctions. In the television show *Revolution*,[1] for example, some mysterious event causes all electrical devices around the world to cease functioning. The result is catastrophic and involves a huge loss of life, as airborne planes crash to earth, for example. All social institutions dissolve, and people are forced to rely only on their personal survival skills. Governments around the world collapse, and the United States divides up into a number of smaller political units. This development runs contrary to everything we have been taught to believe about "one nation, indivisible." Yet it is characteristic of almost all these shows that the federal government is among the first casualties of the apocalyptic event, and—strange as it may at first sound—there is a strong element of wish fulfillment in this event. The thrust of these end-of-the-world scenarios is precisely for government to grow smaller or to disappear entirely. These shows seem to reflect a sense that government has grown too big and too remote from the concerns of ordinary citizens and unresponsive to their needs and demands. If Congress and the president are

---

[1]*Revolution* aired on NBC 2012–2014. [Editor's note.]

unable to shrink the size of government, perhaps a plague or cosmic catastrophe can do some real budget cutting for a change.

One might even describe these shows as "federalist" in spirit. The aim seems to be to reduce the size of government radically and thereby to bring it closer to the people. Cut back to regional or local units, government becomes manageable again and ordinary people get to participate in it actively, recovering a say in the decisions that affect their lives. In cases where the apocalyptic event dissolves all government, these shows in effect return people to what political theorists call the state of nature. As if we were reading Thomas Hobbes, John Locke, or Jean-Jacques Rousseau, we get to see how people form a social contract. No longer locked into institutions already in place, the public gets to assess their value and see if it really needs them or might be better off under other arrangements or perhaps no government at all.

THE RETURN OF THE MINUTEMEN

In the television show *Falling Skies*,[2] invading aliens destroy civilization as we know it, and they are quick to eliminate governments around the world. Set in and around Boston, the show revives the tradition of the New England town meeting, as the characters get to deliberate on their own affairs and debate courses of action in the absence of any higher political authority. The characters have been left to their own devices because, in a decisive blow to civilization, the aliens have destroyed communication circuits and in particular the Internet. The Internet is a perfect example of the kind of technological advance that has usually been featured in the formulation of the American dream. The characters in *Falling Skies* of course miss the Internet, but they learn to live without it and develop more intimate, and perhaps more satisfactory, modes of communication. The loss of modern technology is characteristic of all these apocalyptic scenarios and reflects Americans' love–hate relationship with their machines, appliances, and devices. These shows display an ambivalent attitude toward modernity in general, perhaps a gen-

10

---

[2]*Falling Skies* aired on TNT 2011–2014. [Editor's note.]

uine disillusionment with it, a sense that all the technological progress upon which we pride ourselves has not made us happier and may, on the contrary, have made us miserable by depersonalizing our relationships and limiting our freedom.

To be sure, the characters in *Falling Skies* regret the loss of the benefits of modern civilization. Many of them wish they still had access to the advanced medical technology that used to be available in Boston's world-class hospitals. Several of the episodes take place in an abandoned school, which points to the loss of modern educational institutions. But the show portrays major compensations for the destruction of modern medical and educational facilities. The featured band of survivors includes a female pediatrician. As she herself admits, she cannot provide the services of a big-city, hospital-based physician, but she makes up for her lack of scientific expertise with her personal concern for the welfare of her patients, who are also her friends. Deprived of urban hospitals, our survivors now have access to a genuine family doctor and what is in effect home health care (their doctor lives right among them). Similarly, all the children are now home-schooled. Their teachers are their parents, and in the absence of professional educators, the students seem to thrive, actually enjoying their lessons for a change because they are now being taught by people who know them and care about them as individuals. Perhaps there is something dreamlike about this nightmare after all.

The way the relationships between parents and children have changed in light of the apocalyptic events goes right to the emotional core of *Falling Skies*. The characters have lost everything that used to make up the American dream—all their material possessions, their social status, their professional careers, and of course their three-bedroom houses. But that means that they can now focus on each other. Careers no longer distract them from their family obligations. For the adults, parenting becomes their full-time job. They used to put their careers ahead of their family life; now they will sacrifice anything for the sake of their children. The main character is a father who gets to bond with his sons in a way that was not possible when he was pursuing his career as a history professor at Boston University. Now he spends all his time with his sons at his side and gets to watch them grow up under his guidance. This logic takes us to the heart of these end-of-the-world narratives. The characters have lost everything that used to make their lives seem worthwhile, but they discover that those elements of the American dream were at best distractions from, and at worst obstacles to, their true happiness and sense of fulfillment. Liberated from material concerns and impersonal institutions, the characters have the opportunity to search for what makes life truly meaningful, and that turns out to be devotion to friends and especially family.

With its setting in Massachusetts and its main character a history professor, *Falling Skies* frequently refers to the American Revolution. The names of Lexington and Concord keep coming up, and our heroes become latter-day Minutemen. Their resistance to the alien invaders is repeatedly compared to the American colonists' resistance to British tyranny. The Spirit of '76 thus comes to prevail in *Falling Skies*. The characters have lost their material possessions and the security that institutions used to give them, but they have regained their independence and self-reliance. In the midst of a nightmarish existence, an older conception of the American dream comes back to life. The characters grow in self-respect because they learn that they can rely on their own resources to deal with the challenges they face. They do not need a whole network of impersonal institutions to preserve their lives and to take care of their welfare—and in particular they do not need the federal government. In the spirit of the American Revolution, they form militias and become citizen-soldiers, defending themselves. As do many of these apocalyptic narratives, *Falling Skies* features boys who have to grow quickly into men, a process epitomized by their learning to use weapons and thus assuming the adult role of protecting their loved ones. Taking pride in their maturation, these boys reveal what these shows stand for—they champion people who assume responsibility for their lives, rather than passively accepting a role as wards of institutions or the state.

THE ZOMBIES ARE COMING

If alien invaders are temporarily unavailable, fortunately American pop culture can supply us with all the zombies we need to reexamine the meaning of our lives. In the television show *The*

Walking Dead,[3] a zombie plague has quickly spread around the world, annihilating all but a remnant of the human population. In all these end-of-the-world scenarios, whatever triggers the apocalypse tends to affect the entire Earth more or less simultaneously. The fear of modernity in all these narratives is specifically a fear of global modernity. What upsets people is the sense that they are losing control of their lives in a world of impersonal and unresponsive institutions, and the fact that all this is happening on a global scale is especially unnerving.

Among their many meanings, zombies have come to symbolize the force of globalization. National borders cannot stop the zombie plague from spreading, and it evidently dissolves all cultural distinctions. The zombies lose their individuality, freedom of will, and everything that makes them human beings. With their herd mentality, they are precisely the kind of mass-men that impersonal institutions seek to produce, and in a curious way they represent the docile subjects that governments secretly—or not so secretly—desire. Zombification is a powerful image of what governments try to do to their citizens—to create a uniform, homogenous population, incapable of acting independently. It is no accident that zombies sometimes are portrayed as the products of scientific experiments and specifically of government projects gone awry (or gone all too well).

In *The Walking Dead,* it is not clear what produced the zombies, but in any event they set off the typical end-of-the-world scenario. Governments have fallen everywhere, and in the power vacuum that results, the characters are plunged back into the state of nature, with a decidedly Hobbesian emphasis on the war of all against all. Chased by relentless if plodding zombies and also by marauding gangs of the remaining humans, the main characters at first think of turning to traditional authorities to protect them. Coming from semi-rural Georgia, they head for Atlanta, assuming that a big city will have the resources to keep them safe. But the city, with its concentration of zombies, proves to be even more dangerous than the countryside. The characters keep thinking of the federal government as their ultimate protector. Pinning their hopes on the military, they talk about going to

[3]*The Walking Dead* began its run on AMC in 2010. [Editor's note.]

Fort Benning for security, although they never get there and are warned away from it by other human fugitives they encounter.

Season One of the series culminates in a quest to find safety with a famous federal agency, the Centers for Disease Control, conveniently located in Atlanta and a seemingly ideal refuge from a plague. Viewing the CDC as their salvation, our band of survivors finds instead that it is a source of destruction. The gleaming modernistic edifice is a deathtrap, run by a sole survivor, who seems borderline sane and fast approaching a pop culture stereotype of the mad scientist. Far from finding a cure for the zombie plague, the CDC may be the source of the infection. We learn in the sixth episode that the CDC weaponized smallpox. It is holding so many deadly germs and viruses that the building is programmed to self-destruct once its generators fail. Our heroes and heroines barely have time to escape before the building blows up, taking the last of the CDC scientists with it. If the CDC functions as a symbol of the federal government in *The Walking Dead*, then the medical-military-industrial complex proves to be a dangerous and self-destructive force.[4]

In the second season of *The Walking Dead*, the characters find a refuge, but it is in an isolated farmhouse, presided over by a sort of biblical patriarch. The answer seems to be to get as far away as possible from the modern world and all its complex interrelations. Retreating into the narrow realm of the nuclear family, the survivors find a momentary peace and even a degree of safety. Given the primitive conditions under which they live, it is almost

---

[4]Given the way the CDC is portrayed in *The Walking Dead*, it may be difficult to believe that the real CDC has a section called "Zombie Preparedness" on its official Web site, but check out www.cdc.gov/phpr/zombies.htm. According to this site, if you are "looking for an entertaining way to introduce emergency preparedness," you should read the CDC's own zombie novella. Unsurprisingly, in the CDC novella, the CDC responds quickly and effectively to the zombie plague, although readers might not be fully reassured by the doctors' claim: "We're using the same type of vaccine that we use for the seasonal flu." In general, the CDC's version of a zombie apocalypse is the exact opposite of what we see in popular culture—and much cheerier. In response to the plague, government institutions at all levels function perfectly and are credited with saving the ordinary Americans in the story, who would apparently be helpless if left to their own devices. And, as far as I can tell, no zombies were injured in the making of the CDC novella. Even when being overrun by zombies, the soldiers in the story say: "We can't just shoot them. These are our fellow citizens."

as if they have journeyed back in time to the simpler and happier age of nineteenth-century America, when living on a self-contained farm was the typical way of life. As in *Falling Skies,* the characters miss modern medicine and often have to go scavenging in cities for stores of drugs and other medical supplies. But when a boy named Carl is shot, they look to the patriarch, Hershel, to save him. To their shock, Hershel turns out to be a veterinarian, not a board-certified surgeon. But as in *Falling Skies,* the fact that the old man genuinely cares about his patient and is willing to sit up with him all night by his bedside trumps his lack of medical expertise. Once again home medicine beats the big city hospital. In fact, we see in flashbacks that when the main hero, Sheriff's Deputy Rick Grimes, wakes up from a coma, he finds himself in a hospital at its most hideous, portrayed as a prison-like containment facility for zombies being slaughtered by military forces. In *The Walking Dead,* public health institutions seem to be devoted to imprisoning and annihilating their patients, not curing them.

Zombies eventually overrun the pastoral retreat at the end of Season Two of *The Walking Dead,* and in Season Three the band of survivors finds a new refuge—this time in a prison. An institution originally designed to keep criminals in turns into the best way to keep the zombies out. Season Three deals with various efforts to move beyond the nuclear family and restore order to society, but they are not portrayed in positive terms. At the end of the second season, Grimes ominously proclaims, "This isn't a democracy anymore," and the specter of autocracy haunts the third season. A prison is obviously not an attractive model of social order; it suggests that the overriding concern for security requires locking down everything and allowing no scope for freedom. Later in Season Three, we encounter an alternate model of order, the town of Woodbury, presided over by a character named simply the Governor. At first Woodbury seems nice enough, indeed the very model of small-town America, almost a re-creation of Andy Griffith's Mayberry. In the third episode of the third season, the Governor says with some pride: "People here have homes, medical care, kids go to school. . . . And people here have jobs. It's a sense of purpose. We have community." It sounds as if government institutions have been reconstituted to good effect. But we soon discover that Woodbury is a gated community in the bad sense of the term, basically just a prison with a Main Street, U.S.A. façade. The armed guards posted to keep the zombies out are also tasked with keeping Woodbury's citizens in, thus maintaining their subjugation to the Governor's arbitrary commands. Once again the price of security is freedom, and the more we learn about the Governor, the more he appears to be a tyrant and a crazed one at that.

All attempts to turn to institutions to solve problems in *The* 20 *Walking Dead* seem to fail. The show suggests that its characters must ultimately rely on themselves and their own resources. In various flashbacks, we learn that, prior to the zombie plague, the characters had all sorts of problems in their relationships. The husbands and wives were generally unhappy in their marriages, with soap opera consequences. Again as in *Falling Skies,* a disaster in material terms proves to have some good results in emotional terms. Under the pressure of the zombie threat, family bonds grow tighter, and people learn who their real friends are. On one level, the zombies represent the absence of true humanity, a mass of beings who are braindead. They go through the mere motions of living, but their existence is completely meaningless. By contrast, life has become meaningful for the surviving human beings. As shown in several episodes, they have had to make conscious choices to go on living and thereby recover a strong sense of purpose in their struggle for survival.

Given the survivalist ethic in all these end-of-the-world shows, they are probably not popular with gun control advocates. One of the most striking motifs they have in common—evident in *Revolution, Falling Skies, The Walking Dead,* and many other such shows—is the loving care with which they depict an astonishing array of weaponry. *The Walking Dead* features an Amazon warrior, who is adept with a samurai sword, as well as a southern redneck, who specializes in a crossbow. The dwindling supply of ammunition puts a premium on weapons that do not require bullets. That is not to say, however, that *The Walking Dead* has no place for modern firearms and indeed the very latest in automatic weapons. Both the heroes and the villains in the series—difficult to tell apart in this respect—are as well-armed as the typical municipal SWAT team in contemporary America.

Being able to use a weapon is the chief marker of status in *The Walking Dead*. At first the need to go armed restores the men to positions of unchallenged leadership, overcoming feminist tendencies in the pre-apocalyptic world (suggested in several flashbacks). In a throwback in human evolution, the men again become the hunter-gatherers, while the women return to household chores. But the gun is actually a great equalizer and is particularly effective in overcoming women's disadvantage in physical strength vis-à-vis men. A character named Andrea starts off as a stereotypically weak, dependent woman, but once she learns to shoot—more specifically to *kill* zombies—she is completely transformed into a powerful figure, who can take command in difficult situations, even over aggressive males. Andrea is emblematic of the overall tendency of *The Walking Dead* to show ordinary people moving from situations of dependence (relying on institutions to save them) to genuine independence (relying only on themselves and each other).

Amazingly, this tendency applies even to children in *The Walking Dead* (as it also does in *Falling Skies*). The young boy Carl wants nothing more than to learn how to shoot a gun, and, although his mother and father are at first hesitant, they allow a family friend to initiate the young boy into the company of trained marksmen. Carl graduates from shooting zombies to taking out fellow human beings, and, in one of the more shocking developments in a series that thrives on shock value, the youngster eventually reaches an elite plateau of cold-bloodedness when he shoots his own mother, rather than let her turn into a zombie. Carl is the ultimate example of how the characters in *The Walking Dead* must toughen up or fall by the wayside.

HOME ON THE RANGE

Carl's father is Rick Grimes, and earlier in the series he gives the boy his lawman's hat. In the February 17, 2013, episode of *The Talking Dead,* a fan discussion show that follows the weekly broadcasts of *The Walking Dead* on AMC, actor–director Kevin Smith cleverly referred to Carl as "Wyatt Twerp." Smith's evocation of a classic Western hero is right on the mark. Beneath all the horror-story gore in *The Walking Dead* beats the heart of a good old-fashioned Western. The show transposes the Wild West to a contemporary setting, reviving the spirit of rugged individualism that Westerns promoted as an antidote to the comfortable version of the American dream in the middle of the twentieth century. By stripping away all the institutions that constitute modern civilization, *The Walking Dead* gives us what the Western used to provide in American pop culture—an image of frontier existence, of living on the edge, of seeing what it is like to manage without a settled government, of facing the challenge of protecting oneself and one's family on one's own, of learning the meaning of independence and self-reliance.

The zombies play the role traditionally assigned to Indians in 25
Westerns—the barbarian hordes lurking on the borders of the civilized community and threatening to annihilate it. Just like the Indians in many Westerns, the zombies are nameless and virtually faceless, they never speak, and they may be killed off indiscriminately, with their genocide being the apparent goal. The odyssey of the characters in *The Walking Dead* through the shattered landscape of Georgia resembles the wagon trains of Westerns, navigating through one danger after another, fighting or negotiating with rival groups, troubled by dwindling supplies, searching in vain for refuge in military outposts that turn out to have been overrun and abandoned, slowed down by stragglers and delayed by searches for lost comrades, torn by disputes over their destination and other challenges to their leaders, dealing with childbirth or other medical emergencies on the fly—the list of parallels goes on and on. People have been lamenting the closing of the frontier throughout American history. Zombie tales and other apocalyptic scenarios turn out to be a way of imaginatively reopening the frontier in twenty-first-century popular culture.

In general, all these end-of-the-world shows are re-creations of that most basic of American genres, the Western. A character in *Falling Skies* says of the postapocalyptic environment: "It's the Wild West out there." The 2011 film *Cowboys and Aliens* explicitly unites the Western and the alien invasion narrative. Once we realize that contemporary end-of-the-world scenarios share with Westerns the goal of imaginatively returning their characters to the state of nature, we can see how the American nightmare can turn into the American dream when rampaging aliens or zombies descend upon a quiet American suburb. The dream of material prosperity and security is shattered, but a different ideal comes back to life—the all-American ideal of rugged individualism, the spirit of freedom, independence, and self-reliance.

For Discussion and Writing

1. **Comprehension** According to Cantor, postapocalyptic shows like *The Walking Dead* are "re-creations" of the "most basic of American genres" (par. 26). What is that genre? What purpose does this genre fulfill for Americans?

2. **Critical Reading** How and why does Cantor use rhetorical questions in his **introduction** to set up his argument and his analysis?

3. **Analysis** Cantor provides a specific explanation for the meaning, function, and appeal of "these end-of-the-world shows" (par. 26). For Cantor, they suggest the desire for an ideal of liberty, individualism, and self-reliance. Do you agree with his interpretation? What other meaning or significance might these shows have? What other fears and ideals could they represent?

4. **Connections** Both Cantor and Chuck Klosterman ("My Zombie, Myself," p. 422) propose allegorical or symbolic interpretations of zombies in popular culture. For example, Cantor writes that "zombies have come to symbolize the force of globalization" (par. 15), among their other meanings. Which interpretation do you find more persuasive and why? Are the two arguments compatible with each other, or mutually exclusive?

5. **Writing** Cantor writes, "Popular culture has stepped forward to offer Americans a chance to explore . . . and to rethink the American dream" (par. 8). He analyzes two shows in particular. Choose one or two television shows and write an essay that illustrates how these programs explore, imagine, rethink, or challenge the American dream—or another ideology. As Cantor does, try to place your analysis in the current social, political, or cultural context. For example, how does a show address or illuminate contemporary anxieties or ideals?

KEN AULETTA

Netflix and the Future of Television

A graduate of State University of New York at Oswego, Ken Auletta (b. 1942) is a journalist and media critic for the New Yorker *magazine. Previously, he wrote for the* New York Post, *the* Village Voice, *the* New York Daily News, *and* New York *magazine. He is also the author of several books, including* World War 3.0: Microsoft and Its Enemies *(2001) and* Googled: The End of the World As We Know It *(2009). In this "Annals of Communications" column from the* New Yorker, *Auletta tells the story of Netflix; in the process, he shows how Netflix (and several other companies) are changing television—and changing how we watch it.*

As you read, *notice how Auletta incorporates narrative into his essay. What are the key events in the story of Netflix? What is Auletta's writing purpose? How does the story intersect with your own television viewing preferences?*

In the spring of 2000, Reed Hastings, the C.E.O. of Netflix, hired a private plane and flew from San Jose to Dallas for a summit meeting with Blockbuster, the video-rental giant that had 7,700 stores worldwide handling mostly VCR tapes. Three years earlier, Hastings, then a thirty-six-year-old Silicon Valley engineer, had co-founded Netflix around a pair of emerging technologies: DVDs, and a Web site from which to order them. Now, for twenty dollars a month, the site's subscribers could rent an unlimited number of DVDs, one at a time, for as long as they wished; the disks arrived in the mail, in distinctive red envelopes. Eventually, Hastings was convinced, movies would be rented even more cheaply and conveniently by streaming them over the Internet, and popular films would always be in stock. But in 2000 Netflix had only about three hundred thousand subscribers and relied on the U.S. Postal Service to deliver its DVDs; the company was losing money. Hastings proposed an alliance.

"We offered to sell a 49 percent stake and take the name Block-buster.com," Hastings told me recently. "We'd be their online service." Hastings, now fifty-three, has a trimmed, graying goatee and a slow, soft voice. As he spoke, he was drinking Prosecco at an outdoor table at Nick's on Main, a favorite Italian restaurant of his, in Los Gatos, an affluent community in the foothills of the Santa Cruz Mountains. The sounds of Sinatra carried across the patio.

Blockbuster wasn't interested. The dot-com bubble[1] had burst, and some film and television executives, like those in publishing and music, did not yet see a threat from digital media. Hastings flew home and set to work promoting Netflix to the public as the friendly rental underdog. By the time Blockbuster got around to offering its own online subscription service, in 2004, it was too late. "If they had launched two years earlier, they would have killed us," Hastings said. By 2005, Netflix had 4.2 million subscribers, and its membership was growing steadily. Hastings had rented a house outside Rome for a year with his wife, Patty Quillin, and two children and was commuting to his Silicon Valley[2] office two weeks each month. Hollywood studios began offering the company more movies to rent; the licensing arrangements presented a new way to make money from their libraries and provided leverage against Blockbuster.

By 2007, when Netflix began streaming movies and TV shows directly to personal computers, it had all but won the rental war. Last November, Blockbuster said that it was going out of business; the previous month, Netflix had announced that it had thirty-one million subscribers in the United States, three million more than HBO, and that its stock was at an all-time high. In 2013, it launched an original-programming series, *House of Cards,* which became a critical hit. During peak hours, Netflix accounts for more than 30 percent of all Internet down-streaming traffic in North America, nearly twice that of YouTube, its closest competitor. The Netflix Web site describes the company as "the world's leading Internet television network."

[1]*Dot-com bubble:* an economic time period from about 1997–2000 when stock trading rose rapidly from investment in Internet companies and expanded online business. [Editor's note.]
[2]*Silicon Valley:* an area near San Francisco commonly referenced as the site of high-tech start-up companies. [Editor's note.]

Hastings has succeeded, in large part, by taking advantage of 5 what he calls viewers' "managed dissatisfaction" with traditional television: each hour of programming is crammed with about twenty minutes of commercials and promotional messages for other shows. Netflix carries no commercials; its revenue derives entirely from subscription fees. Viewers are happy to pay a set fee, now eight dollars a month, in order to watch, uninterrupted, their choice of films or shows, whenever they want, on whatever device they want. "Think of it as entertainment that's more like books," Hastings said. "You get to control and watch, and you get to do all the chapters of a book at the same time, because you have all the episodes."

Television is undergoing a digital revolution. Last autumn, in the company's annual "Long-Term View" report to shareholders, Netflix argued that "the linear TV experience," with its programs offered at set times, "is ripe for replacement." Hastings told me, "We are to cable networks as cable networks were to broadcast networks." But Netflix is just one of many contenders. "It's like little termites eating away," Jason Hirschhorn, an Internet entrepreneur and a former Viacom executive, told me. "I don't think the incumbents are insecure enough."

In the early days, television was both a box and the black-and-white world that issued from it: quiz shows, soaps, Ed Sullivan, Edward R. Murrow, *I Love Lucy*.[3] Until the 1980s, the vast majority of the shows were commissioned and carried by ABC, CBS, and NBC, which started out as radio networks and were granted television licenses by the F.C.C., with the expectation that they broadcast at no charge to viewers. Audiences were rapt, and broadcasters made money by selling spots to advertisers.

Today, the audience for the broadcast networks is a third what it was in the late seventies, lost to a proliferating array of viewing options. First came cable-television networks, which delivered HBO, ESPN, CNN, Nickelodeon, and dozens of other channels

---

[3]*The Ed Sullivan Show* (1948–1971): a popular variety and sketch comedy show hosted by entertainment reporter and columnist Ed Sullivan (1901–1974). *Edward R. Murrow* (1908–1965): a prominent journalist and host of the award-winning television news broadcast *See It Now* (1951–1958). *I Love Lucy* (1951–1957): a beloved sitcom starring comedian Lucille Ball and her musician husband, Desi Arnaz. [Editor's note.]

through a coaxial cable. Cable operators and networks charged monthly fees and sold ads, and even commercial-free premium networks such as HBO made money for cable operators, because they attracted subscribers. Traditional broadcasters saw their advertising income slow, but they compensated by charging cable companies for carrying their content, a "retransmission consent" fee made possible, in 1992, by the Cable Television Consumer Protection and Competition Act. Soon after, the F.C.C. relaxed rules that restricted the networks' ownership of prime-time programs, which opened a new stream of revenue from the syndication of their shows to local stations, cable networks, and other platforms.

The advent of the Internet and streaming video brought new competitors. In 2011, Amazon made its streaming-video service, Instant Video, available free to every customer who signs up for its Amazon Prime program, which, for seventy-nine dollars a year, also provides free two-day shipping. The arrangement inverts the traditional advertising model: instead of forcing you to view commercials, video is the gift you get for shopping. Amazon Prime subscribers number about twenty million, although the number of those who are Instant Video viewers is certainly smaller. Last fall, Amazon released its first original series, "Alpha House," created by Garry Trudeau. Apple, which popularized the purchase of digital music, offers video sales and rentals through iTunes. It is not expected to develop its own content.

The busiest "television" platform in the world is YouTube, 10 which is owned by Google and has a billion unique visitors watching six billion hours of video every month. Ynon Kreiz, the executive chairman of Maker Studios, the world's largest provider of online content, noted that its series *Epic Rap Battles of History*, broadcast on YouTube, and which offers comical face-offs between, say, a faux Miley Cyrus and Joan of Arc, attracts on average forty million viewers—almost four times the viewership of the finale of AMC's *Breaking Bad*. YouTube makes money through what Robert Kyncl, a vice-president at Google and the head of content and business operations at YouTube, calls "frictionless" advertising, which allows viewers to click on a True View button to skip ads and asks advertisers to pay only when viewers watch the ad. YouTube claims that 40 percent of its views are on mobile devices, a leap from just 6 percent in 2011.

"We now live in a world where every device is a television," Richard Greenfield, a media and technology analyst for the New York–based B.T.I.G., told me. "TV is just becoming video. My kids watch *Good Luck Charlie* on Netflix. To my ten-year-old, that's TV." Consumers don't care "that a show is scheduled at eight o'clock," he said. Paul Saffo, a Silicon Valley technology forecaster, says that couch potatoes have given way to "active hunters," viewers who "snack" and control what they watch and when.

Leslie Moonves, the C.E.O. of the CBS Corporation, which includes CBS and other networks, says he is untroubled. "For twenty-five years, I've been hearing that network television is dead," he told me. "We're thriving like never before." CBS has been the top-ranked network in prime time for ten of the past eleven years. On the day before we spoke, last October, the company's stock price had risen to nearly sixty dollars a share, almost twenty times higher than its lowest share price in 2009. Moonves is the most richly compensated executive in traditional media; his total compensation in 2012 was sixty-two million dollars. He insists that advertisers need a mass audience to introduce products, an audience that only a broadcast network can deliver consistently. The CBS Corporation is less dependent on commercials, which now account for just over half of its revenues. The rest comes from its overseas sales, which totalled $1.1 billion last year, and from licensing deals with cable and digital platforms such as Verizon FiOS and Netflix; Netflix pays CBS and Fox about two hundred and fifty million dollars each to let it air programs from their archives.

Other observers are more critical. The venture capitalist Marc Andreessen, who co-invented Mosaic, the first commercial Internet browser—it later became Netscape—told me, "TV in ten years is going to be 100 percent streamed. On demand. Internet Protocol. Based on computers and based on software." He said that the television industry has managed the transition to the digital age better than book publishers and music executives, but "software is going to eat television in the exact same way, ultimately, that software ate music and as it ate books."

In 2007, in an effort to combat Netflix, NBC and Fox—joined, two years later, by ABC—created Hulu, a Web site that lets viewers watch current and many past television shows but is subsidized by the same complement of commercials seen on broadcasters' Web sites. Five million viewers subscribe to Hulu Plus, which, for eight dollars per month, offers more current content and past shows, on multiple devices and with fewer commercials.

Hastings founded Netflix, in 1997, with Marc Randolph, who 15 worked for him at Pure Software. To manage the technical aspects of the Web site, he recruited Neil Hunt, another mathematician and former colleague. Hunt helped to create a "personalization" engine that would decipher what each subscriber liked to watch, based on what the subscriber had watched before, and suggest what he or she might want to see next. Similar advisory algorithms were entering the home through TiVo, the digital video recorder introduced in 1999, and Amazon's Web site. In 1999, Hastings hired Ted Sarandos, who had been the vice-president of product and marketing for West Coast Video, a Blockbuster-like company with nearly five hundred stores. Sarandos had a deep knowledge of movies and television shows and began to broaden the range of material that Netflix made available. In 2002, the company turned profitable and went public.

Hastings pressed his team to begin streaming movies and television shows over the Internet. The film industry, worried about digital piracy, initially resisted licensing its content to stream; and Netflix lacked access to recent movies, because the studios had exclusive long-term deals to sell them to HBO and other cable subscription channels such as Starz. Finally, in 2008, Netflix made a deal with Starz to stream the movies it had acquired. "We agreed to pay thirty million dollars annually," Sarandos said. "It was about three times my budget!"

Starz and other content providers realized that Netflix offered not only a new source of revenue but also a way to build audiences for current broadcast and cable shows, by allowing Netflix subscribers to watch prior seasons. The ratings for the fifth season of AMC's *Breaking Bad* were more than double those of the season before, and several times higher than those of Season One. "It seems to me close to inarguable that, when past seasons were available, people were introduced to them through on-demand services like Netflix," Josh Sapan, the president and C.E.O. of AMC Networks, told me. "They became engaged." Between 2007, when streaming began, and the end of 2009, Netflix subscriptions jumped from 7.5 million to twelve million. Media executives dismissed the notion that Netflix was a threat. In 2010, Jeff Bewkes, the C.E.O. of Time Warner, told the *Times*, "It's a little bit like, is the Albanian army going to take over the world?" adding, "I don't think so."

Hastings told me that he treated Bewkes's comment "as a badge of honor. For the next year, I wore Albanian Army dog tags around my neck. It was my rosary beads of motivation." Netflix continued to expand, making itself available on game consoles, mobile phones, tablets, and other streaming devices, such as Apple TV and Roku—and, for the first time outside the U.S., in Canada. It reached licensing agreements to air complete previous seasons of programs from ABC, NBC, Fox, CBS, and the leading cable networks.

Whatever Hastings's ambitions, he was eager not to appear to be competing with his sources of content. In its first-quarter report for 2011, Netflix declared that it was "fundamentally correct" to characterize the company as "rerun TV." But the broadcast networks would not sell Netflix the current seasons of television shows; customers had to turn to Hulu. For Hulu, the networks defensively bought the rights to popular cable programs like *The Daily Show with Jon Stewart* and *The Colbert Report,* which are not available on Netflix.

Hastings sees his main competitors as Showtime and, especially, HBO. Both have lucrative arrangements with cable providers, through which they offer a library of shows and movies to watch on demand; and both now offer apps—HBO Go and Showtime Anytime—that enable cable subscribers to watch any of those channels' programs on any device. HBO has more than two and a half times as many subscribers worldwide as Netflix—114 million—and its list of original hits, from *The Sopranos* to *Game of Thrones,* is extensive.

In the spring of 2011, Netflix announced that it was aggressively entering the business of original programming. The company spent a hundred million dollars to make the two-season, twenty-six-episode political thriller *House of Cards,* directed by David Fincher and starring Kevin Spacey. The director and the actor had approached several networks; Netflix offered to approve the project without seeing a pilot or test-marketing it with viewers. Last year, Spacey told an audience at the Guardian Edinburgh International Television Festival, "Netflix was the only network that said, 'We believe in you. We've run our data and it tells us that our audience would watch this series. We don't need you to do a pilot. How many do you wanna do?'"

Netflix tracks not only its subscribers' preferences and habits but also how quickly they watch each episode and how many episodes they watch in one night. It has organized its library into seventy-nine thousand categories—Foreign Sci-Fi & Fantasy, Dark Thrillers Based on Books—to better predict what you might want to watch next. "There's a whole lot of Ph.D.-level math and statistics involved," Hunt says. The Netflix database indicated that the original series on which *House of Cards* was based, a British production with the same name, was popular with Netflix users. So were political thrillers, Fincher's films (*Fight Club, The Social Network*), and Spacey, who has starred in a range of movies, including *Se7en* (another Fincher film) and *The Usual Suspects.*

But, in September of 2011, Hastings made a major miscalculation. Netflix's DVD rentals were falling, and the company had announced that it was splitting its subscription in two: one for DVDs by mail, a second for online streaming. Hastings then announced that the DVD rentals would now be handled by a new entity, Qwikster. Hastings had seen how companies such as AOL had been slow to replace dial-up Internet access with broadband. "I was so obsessed with not getting trapped by DVDs the way AOL got trapped, the way Kodak did, the way Blockbuster did," he told me. "We would say, 'Every business we could think of died because they were too cautious.'" Netflix's combined subscription rate rose by 60 percent, to sixteen dollars a month, and thousands of customers posted complaints on the company's Web site. Eight hundred thousand subscribers abandoned the service, and the stock price plummeted. By October, Netflix had reversed the decision to split itself into two companies.

The crisis soon faded. *House of Cards,* which appeared in February 2013, won three Emmys—the first time a nontraditional television show had won the award. In October of 2013, Netflix's stock price surpassed its all-time peak, approaching four hundred dollars per share, although the company's third-quarter net income was only thirty-two million dollars. (HBO's earnings exceeded $1.7 billion on five billion dollars in revenues.) By the end of 2013, Netflix's stock had tripled in value since the beginning of the year, and the board voted to boost Hastings's total compensation to six million dollars.

Television today faces two major threats. The first is to the adver- 25
tising model. About 50 percent of viewing households use a digital video recorder. Between half to two-thirds of those households skip the ads, and new features, such as those on the Hopper,
a DVR with the Dish satellite network, allow viewers to do so
instantly on select shows. Every viewer who skips an ad, or who
leaves a broadcast or cable channel to watch Netflix or another
ad-free service, is evidence to advertisers that television airtime
isn't worth what it once was—a conclusion that will eventually
mean less revenue for broadcast and cable networks. Sixty-six
billion dollars—four out of every ten media dollars—is spent
annually on TV commercials, according to Sir Martin Sorrell, the
chairman and C.E.O. of W.P.P., the world's second-largest advertising and marketing agency. Sorrell told me that W.P.P. has
shifted eighteen billion dollars, or 35 percent of its advertising
expenditures, to digital media since 2000.

   The second threat is existential. Starting around 2008, viewers
could stream video services through the television only by attach-
ing another device, such as a DVD player, an Xbox, a Nintendo
Wii, or an Apple TV. The streaming services are getting cheaper
and easier to use. Last July, Google released Chromecast, a device
that looks like a flash drive (you plug it into your TV's HDMI port)
and allows you to stream from such sources as Netflix, YouTube,
Hulu Plus, Google Play, or whatever you happen to be watching
on Google's Chrome Web browser. The device costs thirty-five dollars. As consumers grow more aware of such options, they are
bound to ask why they bother subscribing to cable television.

   The latest menace is Aereo; for eight or twelve dollars a month,
the service connects each customer to a remote, dime-size
antenna that allows members in almost two dozen cities to watch
over-the-air broadcasts or record shows in a cloud-based DVR.
Chet Kanojia, an engineer and the company's C.E.O., says that he
created Aereo to help spare people the cost and the waste of the
typical cable bundle. Technically, one can still watch broadcast
television using just an antenna, but people have grown accustomed to the more reliable picture, and to the DVR functions,
that cable provides; and broadcasters have come to rely on the
retransmission fees. Still, Kanojia wondered, why should viewers
have to pay an expensive cable bill if mostly what they want to
watch are the broadcast channels?

"Consumers had the right to this programming because it was free to air," Kanojia said. As he describes it, Aereo merely allows customers to connect to antennae that receive broadcast signals. (You can fast-forward past the ads when watching recorded shows.) But TV executives don't see it that way. "It's a technology that basically wants to steal our signal," Moonves said. "How do you take our signal"—and the programs that CBS has paid for—"and sell it to customers?" So far, Aereo has successfully convinced some courts that the technology is little different from the antennae that television viewers once mounted on their rooftops. The Supreme Court is expected to rule on Aereo's legitimacy by July [2014].

In 2013, at his annual investor conference, John Malone, the chairman of Liberty Media Corporation, which has investments in cable companies, said that cable executives needed to respond more creatively to these new technologies. He urged his colleagues to create an Internet-based streaming service to rival Netflix. As an example, he cited Comcast's XFinity, which, like Hulu, offers streaming video. Last week, Verizon announced plans to acquire Intel Media, the chipmaker's digital-TV division, in a further effort to make TV available anywhere and on any screen.

What Netflix and the other new platforms still can't offer is the 30 kind of appointment viewing—the Olympics, the Super Bowl, the Oscars, *American Idol*—that has been the mainstay of broadcast television and certain cable operators. The networks pay huge sums for the exclusive rights to broadcast these events. The future of traditional television, Hastings says, is in airing more live events, which attract higher advertising rates. In December 2013, NBC broadcast a live musical, *The Sound of Music*, starring Carrie Underwood. Although critics panned it, nearly nineteen million people watched it that night, the biggest NBC Thursday-night, non-sports audience in almost a decade. Among the few executives who express no concern about the shifting television terrain are those involved in sports. "The only certainty is sports," David Stern, the commissioner of the N.B.A., told me. Hastings agrees. "For a hundred million dollars," he told me, "we could get the Badminton League!"

Without commercial interruptions, Hastings argues, the viewing experience has become more immersive and sustained. When Netflix released *House of Cards*, it made the entire first season of episodes available at once, and viewers binged. Cindy Holland, Netflix's vice-president of original content, told me that the average Netflix viewer watches two and a half episodes in one sitting. The creative experience is different, too, she said; making *House of Cards* was akin to making "a thirteen-hour movie." There was no need to recap previous episodes or to insert cliffhangers. Increasingly, show creators can work without executives' notes, focus groups, concerns about ratings, and anxieties about whether advertisers will resist having their products slotted after a nude scene or one laced with obscenity.

"There's a reason why people now talk about this as the golden age of scripted drama," Michael Lynton, the C.E.O. of Sony Entertainment, told me. "You can write a character that grows over the course of thirteen hours of television. That's more attractive than a two-hour movie." The opportunities have enticed strong writers, directors, and actors. "What's happened as a result of this is a flourishing of an entirely new kind of television."

Netflix has also begun investing heavily in children's programming; last June, it signed a five-year deal with DreamWorks Animation, which will produce three hundred hours of original animated kids' shows. "We have become Netflix's single largest supplier of original kids' content," Jeffrey Katzenberg, the C.E.O. of DreamWorks Animation, said. The effort is part of a long-term strategy to train viewers to watch Netflix. "It's habit-forming," Sarandos, Netflix's chief content officer, said.

But there are other ways to consume video than those which Netflix has in mind. Brian Robbins, the founder of Awesomeness TV, a provider of YouTube channels, first gained recognition in the mid-1980s as a young actor on *Head of the Class*, an ABC sitcom. He went on to direct more than ten movies, including *Varsity Blues*, before becoming a writer and a producer for long-running children's programs on Nickelodeon. Four years ago, his agent told him about Fred, a teenager from Nebraska who had his own YouTube channel. Fred recorded short rants in a screechy voice on such topics as staying in a fancy hotel room and dreaming of being a famous actor. His real name was Lucas Cruikshank, and his hotel riff drew twenty-three million views, more than the biggest hit show on television. Fred's videos were a few minutes long, perfectly tailored to the medium. Robbins came home that night and asked his tween children, "You know who Fred is?" They did.

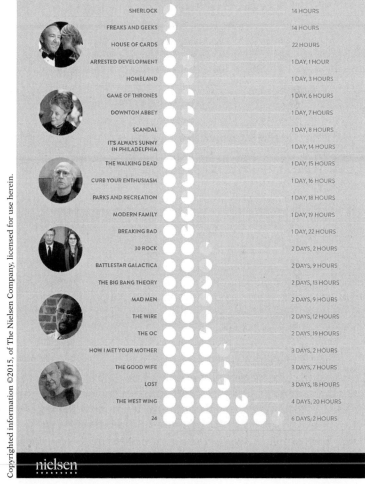

TOPTEN

HOW LONG WILL IT TAKE TO WATCH...

IF YOU WERE TO BINGE-WATCH THESE POPULAR SHOWS START TO FINISH,
HOW MUCH OF YOUR LIFE WOULD THEY CONSUME?

SHERLOCK	14 HOURS
FREAKS AND GEEKS	14 HOURS
HOUSE OF CARDS	22 HOURS
ARRESTED DEVELOPMENT	1 DAY, 1 HOUR
HOMELAND	1 DAY, 3 HOURS
GAME OF THRONES	1 DAY, 6 HOURS
DOWNTON ABBEY	1 DAY, 7 HOURS
SCANDAL	1 DAY, 8 HOURS
IT'S ALWAYS SUNNY IN PHILADELPHIA	1 DAY, 14 HOURS
THE WALKING DEAD	1 DAY, 15 HOURS
CURB YOUR ENTHUSIASM	1 DAY, 16 HOURS
PARKS AND RECREATION	1 DAY, 18 HOURS
MODERN FAMILY	1 DAY, 19 HOURS
BREAKING BAD	1 DAY, 22 HOURS
30 ROCK	2 DAYS, 2 HOURS
BATTLESTAR GALACTICA	2 DAYS, 9 HOURS
THE BIG BANG THEORY	2 DAYS, 13 HOURS
MAD MEN	2 DAYS, 9 HOURS
THE WIRE	2 DAYS, 12 HOURS
THE OC	2 DAYS, 19 HOURS
HOW I MET YOUR MOTHER	3 DAYS, 2 HOURS
THE GOOD WIFE	3 DAYS, 7 HOURS
LOST	3 DAYS, 18 HOURS
THE WEST WING	4 DAYS, 20 HOURS
24	6 DAYS, 2 HOURS

nielsen

This chart, from the Nielsen corporation, may be useful for planning
Netflix binges.

Robbins decided to make a movie with Fred. "I had a relation- 35
ship with Paramount but knew they wouldn't do it," Robbins told
me. So, in August of 2009, he put up a million dollars; four months
later, he had a ninety-minute movie, about a boy trying to get a girl
to fall in love with him. He sold *Fred: The Movie* to Nickelodeon,
and it proved so popular that two more Fred movies and a twenty-
four-episode series, *Fred: The Show*, followed. Robbins decided to
form a company, Awesomeness TV, to create content for YouTube
channels—there are more than half a billion on YouTube.com. In
the world of YouTube, not only is every device a television but
every viewer is a potential network and content provider.

Robbins works in a brick-walled office in a two-story industrial
building in West Los Angeles. He has thirty young employees, and
he roams around in jeans, a T-shirt, and shiny black sneakers.
Just before Thanksgiving in 2012, Awesomeness TV ran a promo-
tion asking subscribers, "Do you want to be the next YouTube
star?" Two hundred thousand teenagers responded, and nearly
half of them started their own YouTube channels, attracting sixty
million unique monthly visitors. Today, eighty-five thousand kids
have channels on Awesomeness TV, and thirty-one million teens
and tweens have visited the site. "When you speak to kids, the No.
1 thing they want is to be famous," Robbins said. "They don't
even know for what."

Advertisers want to reach this young demographic. Last May,
DreamWorks Animation bought Robbins's company, for thirty-
three million dollars. Katzenberg told me that "by the end of next
year, under Awesomeness TV, we could have as many daily active
users as the Disney Channel, Cartoon Network, and Nickelodeon
together."

Established executives in traditional TV are reassured by Nielsen ratings[4] suggesting that, of the forty-two hours of television
that Americans watch each week, only three hours are on portable
devices or computers. But Pat McDonough, a senior vice-president
of analysis at Nielsen, concedes that the company does not have
the capability to compile smartphone usage among very young
people. "For mobile devices, we are not measuring below age thirteen today," she said. And yet, she noted, "We think there's a lot of

---

[4]The Nielsen company evaluates and measures television audiences to produce its
Nielsen ratings. [Editor's note.]

consumption on their parents' devices." Although viewers under twenty-four watch less traditional television than ever, McDonough was confident that they would grow into the habit. "The older you get, the more you watch," she said.

Robbins disagrees: "That's like saying when color TV came in that people were going to go back to watching black-and-white television when they got older, because that's what their parents and grandparents did!" He added, "The next generation, our audience and even younger, they don't even know what live TV is. They live in an on-demand world."

For Discussion and Writing

1. **Comprehension**   Why did Netflix founder Reed Hastings spend a year wearing dog tags from the Albanian army? How does this detail fit into the story of his company's success?

2. **Critical Reading**   The writer opens his article by recounting a 2000 meeting between Reed Hastings and representatives from Blockbuster video. What does this story reveal? Why do you think Auletta chose it for the **introduction**?

3. **Analysis**   While Auletta's primary subject is Netflix, his essay raises—and explores—several different **themes**. Identify and explain one of these themes.

4. **Connections**   The article shows how newer media companies—and newer technologies—are changing television viewing habits. Hastings claims that the "viewing experience has become more immersive and sustained" (par. 31). Auletta refers to a "long-term strategy to train viewers to watch Netflix" (par. 33). How would you assess these changes using the work of Robert Kubey and Mihaly Csikszentmihalyi in "Television Addiction Is No Mere Metaphor" (p. 259)? Do these shifts encourage healthier television viewing? Will platforms like Netflix make viewers more active, engaged, and deliberate in their programming choices? Or will Netflix make viewers more prone to addictive or unhealthy media habits?

5. **Writing**   Brian Robbins, the founder of Awesomeness TV, asserts: "The next generation, our audience and even younger, they don't even know what live TV is. They live in an on-demand world" (par. 39). Do you agree? What is an "on-demand world"? Does it have implications beyond television viewing? Explain the meaning of this phrase in an essay or blog post.

DAVID CHARPENTIER

Story or Spectacle? Why Television Is Better Than the Movies

David Charpentier earned a B.A. in computer graphics and information science from the University of Rhode Island, an M.A. in architecture from the University of North Carolina, and an M.F.A. in film production from Boston University. He is a filmmaker and designer, as well as a columnist for the Web site PopMatters. *In this article from* PopMatters, *Charpentier argues that contemporary television is "better than movies" because of the advantages of a series format and the opportunity for complex character development. This represents a profound shift from the past, when it was assumed that TV could not "compete with the production values, artistry, and event status of movies."*

As you read, *note how Charpentier uses examples to build his argument. According to his timeline, what series marked the beginning of television's ascent as a superior medium for storytelling? Who is his intended audience for this essay? Do you agree with his claims about the limitations of feature-length movies? Why or why not?*

A few months ago, Steven Spielberg and George Lucas[1] put out doomsday-esque statements about the end of movies as we know them. Spielberg, almost ironically, talked about the end of the blockbuster. Budgets are too high, investments too risky, audiences too spread out or bored with the product. Film will continue on some level, no doubt—there's plenty of stories that can be told in two hours, with or without giant robots—but the idea

---

[1]*Steven Spielberg* (b. 1946): one of film's most popular directors, known for several blockbusters spanning genres, including *E.T.: The Extra-Terrestrial* (1982), *Schindler's List* (1993), and *Jurassic Park* (1993). *George Lucas* (b. 1944): director best known for creating the *Star Wars* and *Indiana Jones* franchises. [Editor's note.]

of viewed entertainment is changing. And it's television's fault. Because television is better than movies, these days.

TV's ascent has been a long time coming. Film studios were worried about television stealing their audience back in 1948. They went as far as to prohibit their movies from being shown on the small screen (until they realized they could make more money, doing that), coming up with ideas ranging from Cinemascope to the Tingler[2] to keep patrons in dark theaters instead of dark living rooms. Eventually the movie studios and television stations combined to become multimedia conglomerates, and while television provided a welcome distraction from the everyday, it could never compete with the production values, artistry, and event status of movies.

In 1998, HBO, known primarily for showing movies, debuted *The Sopranos* and television changed. *The Sopranos* was not only meant to compete with network television series, but convince the network audiences to pay extra for HBO. To do that it had to provide an experience that competed with the movies. It not only had to look like a movie, but feel like a movie. And because it was a series, it needed to sustain itself for more than two hours. It needed deep characters and great writing to suck audiences [in] and continue to pay for the privilege of watching the show.

The Sopranos was followed by *Oz, Deadwood,* and *Six Feet Under.* FX soon debuted *The Shield* and *Nip/Tuck.* Other cable and pay networks followed suit. DVDs offered the opportunity for marathon viewings, and the advent of Netflix and Internet streaming has only made that easier.

So why TV instead of movies? Actually, can what we're watching even be called just "TV" anymore? Serialized Dramas? Netflix lists its own series under "Television Shows" so I guess we'll stick with that. It's an interesting nomenclature that is apt to change over the next few years, becoming tied to the structure instead of the medium. Webseries, despite a couple getting interest from Hollywood, and a few featuring name stars like Kiefer Sutherland and Julia Stiles, are still largely viewed as being the realm of

5

---

[2]*The Cinemascope:* a lens system used in the 1950s and 1960s to film widescreen movies. *The Tingler* (1959): a horror film about fear-feeding parasites; in some theaters, vibrating devices were placed in some chairs to work in tandem with the onscreen action. [Editor's note.]

amateur filmmakers and are forced to share retail space with YouTube clips of cats and babies. Can it still be called television if there's no network? Or even no actual, physical television?

However we classify it, it all comes down to the characters. Committing to a series involves watching dozens of episodes, dozens of hours of content. To do this, a show needs deep characters. On some level we can relate to them, but on others they must remain a mystery. They can't be predictable, but they can't be total enigmas, either.

Today's TV characters embody certain elements that we both admire and despise. The Tony Sopranos, Vic Mackeys, Walter Whites, and Don Drapers of contemporary series[3] provide both interesting contrasts and insights into our own lives. Let's face it, most of us lead normal lives but want to lead extraordinary lives. These men (and it does seem to be mostly men) appear, simply by their presence on the screen, to lead extraordinary lives despite their struggle to maintain ordinary facades. This struggle between the ordinary and extraordinary, between reality and drama is what sucks us in initially.

As a good series progresses, and we continue to watch and keep watching and waste a weekend, we become more invested in the characters rooting for and against them, wondering how they will get out of this bind or whether their relationship will fail apart, or . . . well, who knows what. We spend enough time with these characters that, while we may want to see a happy ending, we won't stop watching if something bad happens. As long as it's true to the characters and the show.

Which is where movies begin to run into a problem. Two hours has long been the standard running time for films, while television shows often have twelve hours or more to tell their story. In that two-hour slot for films, a writer and director have to establish the film's world, the main characters, and their relationships, in addition to introducing plot points and explosions. Something has to give, and it's usually the relationship between characters and audience. I've come to learn that if I'm not invested in the characters, I don't care about the story.

---

[3]Names of the male protagonists of *The Sopranos* (1999), *The Shield* (2002), *Breaking Bad* (2008), and *Mad Men* (2007), respectively. [Editor's note.]

The Hulk smashing aliens to a pulp is great to watch, but the two hours preceding that point never got me to believe that any of those egotistical heroes are in grave danger and wouldn't get the job done. However, almost in spite of self-satirization, *Iron Man 3* (perhaps just by focusing on one character, and giving that character a lot to work with) provided some intense moments before it devolved into the endless-punching-explosions of the finale. Long run times are often a detriment to box offices (and induce audience rumblings—despite [their] marathoning eight episodes of *Inbetweeners*[4]), and the extra run time doesn't always make the characters or stories any more interesting or engaging.

Explosions, while awesome, give essentially the same thrill no matter the screen. Action only holds one's interest for so long, and right now the spectacle seems to be the major thing Hollywood is selling its blockbusters on—and after looking at some of this summer's returns, they aren't always selling. The structure of the typical movie follows its lead characters through a well-worn, three-act trek that sees the hero rise and fall only to rise again. While this formula has been used to tell some great stories, it's far too limiting in its service to the mechanics of plot rather than character. Series, by nature of their drawn-out form, move beyond this—and it makes watching them all the more engaging.

Following the protagonist from A to B to C in a movie takes two hours. Everything, for the most part, should be neatly wrapped up because the movie is (usually) an independent piece of work. A large amount of the secondary and all of the ancillary characters are there in service of the plot. They represent one force or another that tries to facilitate or inhibit the protagonist's inner and outer goals.

However, in a series, these characters have an opportunity for their own story lines. Series have the ability to let elements unfold slowly, like a well-structured novel. Layers of character and plot often reveal themselves instead of being forced out by the needs of the run time and story. This fleshes out the world of the story, allowing us to get into the lives of these characters, further understanding their motivations and relationships. We learn about

---

[4]*The Inbetweeners* (2008): a British TV comedy that followed the antics of four awkward teenage boys. [Editor's note.]

characters' home lives, their past, what they do when they leave the office or aren't saving the world. After fifty years, does anyone know what James Bond does on a Sunday afternoon? There's no time to learn this over the course of the movie. Forward movement comes at the expense of texture, resonance, and ambiguity.

In *Mad Men*, we are able to engage with the otherwise impenetrable Don Draper because we know about his past, how he acts differently at home, with his mistresses, or in a meeting with a client. The limited scope of plot-driven movies rarely allows for such a detailed rendering of a character. On the other hand, would anyone want to watch the slow decline of an ad executive without all the side characters?

By creating a richer, more in-depth environment, we are 15 allowed to sink into the program and draw from a deeper involvement as we approach [it] with our own worldviews and social mores, [so the program] becomes that much more personal. Through time and experience, we become invested in these characters and their fates. It's that investment [that] separates contemporary shows from their filmic counterparts and television of the past. There are times when I want to turn my mind off from my life and sink into this other world.

Getting back to the idea of structure, most mainstream movies attempt some sort of conclusion at the end of their running time. A hero (if he is, in fact, a hero) may sink further and further into the depths of despair or the evils of the underworld, but will ultimately pull free. This is rarely the case with contemporary series.

First, today's television series rarely have heroes anymore. Even the white-hatted cowboy has his hidden past. Not only does this make characters more complex, blurring the line between good and evil, but it also offers the idea that there is no neat resolution. The episode may end in five minutes, but the story line will continue on over the course of the next episode or season. Characters can get sucked down the drain and stay there.

On *Breaking Bad*, for example, Walt's dealings with the meth trade have brought to the forefront his bitterness [and] need for control. He's seized the type of authority many of us wish we had, yet he's also involved in a situation we're happy *not* to be in. It's clear that, even if he can get away with living his criminal life, his character, his person, has become nearly irredeemable in the process. *Mad Men* started at the beginning of the '60s, when Don was riding high as a star of Madison Avenue. Given the events of [the series], it's not hard to see the decade closing down upon him.

This ability to not wrap things up neatly means television or serialized dramas (and comedies and dramedies and comedramas) can take us in any direction (that reasonably fits with the characters). It leaves us with not just a "What will they think of next?" feeling. It's not merely that we can't always predict what will happen next. No, the real draw is watching the characters make choices. A character can be utterly reprehensible, but given the opportunity to engage with him/her (or in comparison with another character) to the degree that television allows, the audience may become more understanding.

A character can be both hero and villain, playing in a gray area 20 that allows the audience to root for them or against them, [depending] on the actions of other characters. *The Shield* does this incredibly well over the course of its run. From the start, we know that Vic is willing to do anything to protect his crew, and himself. Shane is his right-hand man, always there for him. In a way, he looks up to Vic, but is even more of a loose cannon.

After the shock of the initial episode, we slowly begin to appreciate Vic more when compared to the more dangerous Shane. When Shane commits an unspeakable crime, offing one of his own team, we want to see Vic get revenge. But, as Vic comes closer to getting revenge, Shane has had his own turn and tries to seek some manner of nonreligious salvation.

As these two ride along the labored path to an inevitable showdown, our initial [perceptions] of the characters change. This is an example of creating active viewing—asking the audience to constantly think about and reassess the meaning and relative morality of the characters' actions. In turn, we reevaluate the notion of heroes and villains, cops and criminals, as a whole.

So, has television finally defeated cinema? The concept of traditional television will likely fade away far earlier than movies. That being said, the appeal of today's top series amongst viewers may change the way that movies are made. And there's no reason a film and a series can't exist side by side in today's culture. Who's to say they should be defined separately at all? New forms of visual expression are constantly emerging. And as long as they maintain their quality, create great characters, and stay interesting in the name of entertainment, I'll be watching.

For Discussion and Writing

1. **Comprehension** Charpentier claims that most movie studios originally prohibited their films to be shown on television. What led them to change this policy, according to Charpentier?

2. **Critical Reading** Charpentier asks, "After fifty years, does anyone know what James Bond does on a Sunday afternoon?" (par. 13). What **main point** is Charpentier making with this rhetorical question? What role does the point serve in his larger argument?

3. **Analysis** Charpentier thinks the allure of complex, ambiguous television protagonists arises from the way they embody a "struggle between the ordinary and extraordinary, between reality and drama" (par. 7). Do you agree? Can you provide an alternate or more compelling explanation for the dramatic power of these characters?

4. **Connections** In "Stay Unlikable—for the Good of TV" (p. 315), Jake Flanagin discusses the importance of "unlikable" television characters. Similarly, Charpentier notes that today's complex television "characters embody certain elements that we both admire and despise" (par. 7). Why do you think we are drawn to "unlikable" characters, or dramatic figures who embody qualities that we "despise"? Can you think of your own specific examples?

5. **Writing** According to Charpentier, contemporary television shows are superior to contemporary films; he makes his case by comparing them in terms of character and plot. Do you agree with this thesis? Is his analysis accurate? For example, are his examples from television and movies representative of these two media forms? Write an argumentative essay that either supports and extends Charpentier's thesis with different points of comparison, or (alternately) complicates or refutes his thesis. In either case, choose specific examples to support your points.

JAKE FLANAGIN

Stay Unlikable— for the Good of TV

Jake Flanagin (b. 1991) earned his B.A. from New York University. He writes mainly about human rights and identity politics, including issues such as human trafficking and refugees. He has written for the New York Times, Quartz, *the* Los Angeles Review of Books, *and other publications. In this essay, which appeared in the* Atlantic, *Flanagin writes specifically about Mindy Kaling's popular television sitcom* The Mindy Project, *but he also provides a broader, more general meditation on the quality of "likability" in dramatic television characters, the gender politics of comedy and drama, and the idea of the endearing "antihero."*

As you read, *notice how Flanagin uses examples from a variety of television shows to place* The Mindy Project *in a wider context. What "major change" in the show is Flanagin writing about? What does he assume about his readers? Why would unlikable characters be appealing to viewers?*

The Mindy Project's main character, Dr. Mindy Lahiri, is a Princeton-educated OB-GYN, and she's the first South Asian–American character to anchor a network sitcom. She is also kind of a jerk.

She loves to gossip. She doesn't really care about climate change. Her personal spirituality extends little beyond an aesthetic appreciation for the various animal-headed Hindu gods. At times, it seems her wardrobe and love life take precedence over her career in medicine. She lies about having kids to get into trendy bars.

To review: disposed to gossip, blasé about the environment, religious when it's convenient, materialistic, often selfish, occasionally dishonest. She's not that different from many of us, if we're being honest. Yet despite her relatably human, almost *Seinfeld*-ian personality, viewers didn't warm to Mindy in her first season

315

on the air like they did other female sitcom protagonists like Leslie Knope on *Parks and Recreation* or Pam Halpert on *The Office* —
or other *Seinfeld*-style male protagonists, like Michael Bluth on
Arrested Development or *Louie*'s eponymous Louie. Ratings fluctu-
ated uneasily all season. The show was renewed for a second season, but there was something about the petite, smart-alecky M.D.
that didn't widely appeal.

Thus, when *The Mindy Project* returns tonight, there will have
been a major change to the fledgling series: Mindy Lahiri is going
to be "likable."

Office alumna Mindy Kaling, creator and star of the semi-   5
autobiographical Fox sitcom, never intended for that to happen.
Early on, she cited Larry David's self-parody on *Curb Your Enthusiasm* as inspiration for her irritating protagonist. "I just try to
make her interesting and nuanced," she told one interviewer
shortly after *The Mindy Project* premiered last September. "And if
some people think she's obnoxious sometimes, well, people are
sometimes obnoxious, and they can still be heroes."

So when she announced earlier this summer that she wanted
to make Mindy less unlikable, it came as an unwelcome surprise
to many. Her tone was resigned: "As it turns out, you shouldn't be
on TV and be like, 'I want to be unlikable,'" she said. "That's one
of the things you learn. Unfortunately, if you're a woman, there
are some things that people don't want to see."

This is worrisome. *The Mindy Project* is distinctive because it
intentionally subverts sugary rom-com tropes—something Kaling
is an expert at identifying and demolishing. Retreating to the
safety of female characterization as defined by Rachel, Monica,
and Phoebe[1] is not the way to overturn convention. If Kaling is
to stand by her original conviction—to pull off the quietly revolutionary feat of playing a funny woman who's just as nuanced
and realistically three-dimensional as a Michael Bluth or a Louis
C.K.—Mindy needs to stay obnoxious.

Why do we need more funny, nuanced women on TV? There's
a simple answer, and a complex one. The simple answer: to rectify a double standard. Jerry Seinfeld was allowed to be an obnox-

---

[1]The popular female characters on *Friends*, often referenced as types: the beautiful "it" girl, the uptight woman, and the free spirit. [Editor's note.]

The Mindy Project's Dr. Mindy Lahiri is "kind of a jerk." Are endearing male television antiheroes like Louis C.K. allowed to be selfish and obnoxious, while women protagonists are not? Why?

ious hero, but Mindy Lahiri is apparently not. (It's worth noting that, according to many, *Seinfeld* was the first show to lend a central focus to totally unlikable characters. And yes, early critics panned "the show about nothing" as insipid, even the death throes of network television. Today, though, *Seinfeld* is credited with reviving the American sitcom, setting the tone for a generation of award-winners like *Arrested Development*, *30 Rock*, and *The Office*. Flavors of *Seinfeld* are even detectable in Dunham's equally New York–centric *Girls*.)

The complex answer runs deeper: to change, ameliorate, or even eliminate the formula for women on television. Because even in the post–Liz Lemon[2] world, stereotypes that demean the intellect and emotional profundity of women pervade. Sitcoms have an oft-underestimated power to dissolve some of the more

[2]*Liz Lemon:* the protagonist on NBC's *30 Rock* (2006), portrayed by Tina Fey. [Editor's note.]

ingrained gender conventions: *The Mary Tyler Moore Show* mainstreamed the concept of working women. *Full House* introduced
America to a single dad filling traditionally maternal roles. Relax-
ing social and behavioral expectations of women in television—
allowing them to occupy a moral milieu, or just be annoying from
time to time—might have a similar, real-world impact.

The notion of an annoying hero is hardly revolutionary, espe- 10
cially to those who have followed Kaling's career. As an Emmy-
nominated writer and performer on *The Office*, she had a hand in
making hapless regional manager Michael Scott one of the most
identifiably unpleasant yet totally beloved antiheroes on American television. The episode when Michael demands sympathy for
burning his foot on a George Foreman grill he's irresponsibly
placed at his bedside? Kaling wrote that. Deliciously dark, comi-
cally self-centered characters are her specialty.

Women in many of this generation's most popular sitcoms,
though, often fall into one of two camps: "good girls" and "bad
girls." Good girls like Rachel Green (*Friends*), Ellen Morgan
(*Ellen*), Leslie Knope (*Parks and Recreation*), Pam Halpert (*The
Office*), and Jess Day (*New Girl*) are beloved for their wide-eyed
earnestness, which can cultivate a fierce protectiveness in fans
that's been known to manifest itself in entire Internet communities devoted to, say, hashing out the legitimacy of Ross and
Rachel. Bad girls like Dee Reynolds (*It's Always Sunny in Philadelphia*), Elaine Benes (*Seinfeld*), Jenna Maroney (*30 Rock*),
Lindsay Bluth-Fünke (*Arrested Development*), and even Kaling's
Kelly Kapoor (*The Office*), on the other hand, are intensely,
almost cartoonishly unlikable. They're shrill, juvenile, oblivious,
and narcissistic, but unapologetically so. And their unbridled
confidence can be instrumental in creating delectable schaden-
freude.

None of these, technically speaking, are antiheroines. These
are mostly proper heroines, mixed with a few petty villainesses
we find amusing. So Mindy, who is neither definitively good nor
bad, presents a new kind of female sitcom lead, and viewers may
not be sure what to make of a leading lady like Mindy. She's exasperating—empirically so—but also human, lovelorn, and self-
deprecating. We care about what happens to her. When her handsome, NBA-attorney boyfriend turned out to be a serial cheater

and cocaine addict, pulling former *Office* co-star Ellie Kemper into a hilarious (and violent) love triangle, audiences laughed—hard. But they also empathized. And that confluence of exasperation and endearment makes Mindy something of an antiheroine—which can be confusing, even alienating, in the context of what many thought would be a lighthearted network sitcom.

Drama is the territory of the fully formed, morally complicated antiheroine. Nancy Botwin (*Weeds*), Olivia Pope (*Scandal*), Jackie Peyton (*Nurse Jackie*), and Lady Edith Crawley (*Downton Abbey*) demonstrate a variety of character flaws complemented by sympathetic motives. Even the diabolical Cersei Lannister (*Game of Thrones*)—who framed the show's beloved, tragic hero for a crime and indirectly brought about his onscreen beheading—later showed a softer side in a heartfelt monologue on motherly love. In this way, drama accommodates a complexity of character that sitcoms traditionally have not.

Perhaps the latter has taken a cue from the former and begun to incorporate antiheroines. And perhaps viewers aren't prepared. Criticisms levied at HBO's *Girls* illustrate this: *Girls* is not lacking in quality writing, the characters are well cast, and the talent is convincing and capable. But viewers are split on the issue of liking or disliking Hannah Horvath, the show's lead character, played by series creator Lena Dunham. Hannah exhibits neuroses, selfish compulsions, and endearing idiosyncrasies in a combination arguably more complex than any female character in television history. She's messy, literally and figuratively. She repulses and allures simultaneously, a dramatic contradiction further complicated by a Woody Allen–style jocularity and self-awareness. She's a loser, but she's relatable, and maybe a little lovable.

It would be easy to dismiss disinterest in *The Mindy Project* as   15 sexism, but the likelier culprit is the same viewer apprehensiveness directed at *Girls*—which, it seems to me, may be rooted not in bigotry but in unfamiliarity. Sure, audiences may be markedly less open to antiheroic women than they are to antiheroic men; for instance, unlikable, immoral protagonists haven't jeopardized the popularity of shows like *Breaking Bad*, *The Sopranos*, *Mad Men*, and *Dexter*, among others. But it's important to also consider the infrequency with which antiheroines have appeared in a comedic context. Historically, leading ladies in sitcoms have been necessarily likable (Mary Richards, Julia Sugarbaker, Liz Lemon). Their foils—usually supporting characters—have been largely unlikable, but their actions the stuff of guilty pleasure (Phyllis Lindstrom, Suzanne Sugarbaker, Jenna Maroney).[3] The contrast between the two archetypes was stark. But the new in-between character type presented by Hannah Horvath and Mindy Lahiri is relatively foreign in sitcom settings, and viewers may just be unsure. That trepidation may not be warranted, but it's somewhat understandable.

To be fair, a restructuring of *The Mindy Project* might work to the show's advantage. A post–Season One reworking paid off for *Veep* and for *Parks and Recreation:* On the latter, Leslie Knope evolved from a warmed-over female version of Michael Scott into the peppy, breakfast food–obsessed bureaucrat audiences have grown to love, and the show became one of the most talked-about comedies on the air. It even allowed for one of the few exceptionally well-liked antiheroines in situational comedy to blossom: Aubrey Plaza's perennially deadpan April Ludgate.

Set largely in a private gynecological practice, *The Mindy Project*'s writers have thus far failed to utilize a built-in platform to discuss women's reproductive health in the way *Parks and Rec* has riffed on women in politics. The will-they-or-won't-they vibe given off by Mindy and her coworker Danny Castellano (Chris Messina) glaringly contradicts the show's anti-cliché philosophy, and should be redirected, if not scrapped entirely. The number of subplots needs to be dialed back. So it's of course fair to say that *The Mindy Project* is due for some adjustments.

Season Two's premiere presents a Mindy who has certainly changed. For better or worse? It's too soon to say. New haircut aside, she's more introspective; maybe not more "likable," but more self-aware. But by aiming to make Mindy more likable—by toning down a personality that, without which, *The Mindy Project* wouldn't exist—Kaling risks both altering the essence of the show and missing out on an opportunity to usher in a new era of sitcoms: the era of the complicated woman.

---

[3]The female protagonists and foils of *The Mary Tyler Moore Show* (1970), *Designing Women* (1986), and *30 Rock* (2006), respectively. [Editor's note.]

For Discussion and Writing

1. **Comprehension**   What television show did Kaling work on before starring in *The Mindy Project*?

2. **Critical Reading**   In paragraph 8, Flanagin asks a rhetorical question and then provides two separate answers. How is this question—and these answers—related to the **thesis** of this essay? What does this writing strategy accomplish?

3. **Analysis**   What is the difference between a "hero" and an "anti-hero"? From Flanagin's description of Mindy Kaling's character on *The Mindy Project*, does she seem like a hero or an antihero?

4. **Connections**   In "Story or Spectacle? Why Television Is Better Than the Movies" (p. 308), David Charpentier argues that contemporary television has become more satisfying and complex than films. While he focuses on drama, not comedy, do you think Mindy Kaling's character on *The Mindy Project* would provide support for his **thesis**? Why or why not?

5. **Writing**   Consider the shows and characters that interest you as a viewer. Are you drawn to characters who are annoying, ambiguous, immoral, or even villainous? Or are you drawn to more traditional, admirable, and conventional heroes and protagonists? Explain your answer in a brief compare and contrast essay that discusses at least two television characters. You may also present your analysis as a multimedia presentation using video clips to illustrate your analysis.

CHAPTER 6

Movies
Does the big screen still shape our dreams?

Hollywood has often been called a "dream factory." The anthropologist Hortense Powdermaker coined that term in her 1950 anthropological study of the movie business, titled (appropriately) *Hollywood, the Dream Factory*. As she pointed out, Hollywood is "not an exact geographical area," but rather a "state of mind." We all live within that state of mind, to some degree. Hollywood dreams inform our own dreams—our visions of romantic love, our images of glamour and success, our ideas about American history, even our sense that Hollywood itself is a "mythic" place. That place extends well beyond America's borders: Hollywood entertainment remains one of the U.S.'s largest and most enduring exports.

Of course, moviemaking is as much a matter of making money as it is a matter of making myths. Stories about the corrupting effects of the film industry or the struggles of individuals to carve meaningful art out of mass entertainment have long been fodder for Hollywood films from *Sunset Boulevard* (1950) to *Barton Fink* (1991) and *Mulholland Drive* (2001). When we consider some of the most well-known filmmakers of the last forty years, like Steven Spielberg, George Lucas, Christopher Nolan, Guillermo del Toro, Ang Lee, and Kathryn Bigelow, we see that they manufacture studio profits by manufacturing myths, uniting the two main functions of the dream factory. But the cultural influence and significance of the movie industry transcends the work of blockbuster producers, independent art-film auteurs, and any individual or corporation. Perhaps even more than they do with

322

television, Americans look to the big screen to work through their dreams and their nightmares, their ideals and their fears, and their collective sense of a cultural moment—past, present, and future. That principle applies as much to a popular, frivolous-seeming comedy as it does to the most somber Oscar contender.

The essays in this section give diverse perspectives on movies and the role of Hollywood in American culture, as well as the business—and ideology—of popular filmmaking. Susan Sontag unpacks the formal elements and themes of science fiction and disaster films in "The Imagination of Disaster." In the process, she shows how these movies meet certain cultural and psychological needs. In "Hollywood's Love Affair with Surveillance," Willie Osterweil makes the case that—in contrast to dystopian fiction like George Orwell's *1984*—contemporary American films reveal a "love of surveillance" that is "deeply entwined into our cultural products." David Denby ("Has Hollywood Murdered the Movies?") argues that commercial demands are forcing Hollywood to produce empty, oversized, and weightless blockbusters—and squeezing out the resources and audiences for higher quality films in the process. In "Seven Steps to the Perfect Story," the Content Marketing Association presents the essential elements of storytelling in a clever infographic, illustrating the formulaic quality of our movie dreams.

The paired readings explore the ways in which movies create myths in two different contexts. Linda Seger's classic "Creating the Myth" reveals the archetypal characters and mythical narratives that structure many popular films. In "The Asian Renovation of Biracial Buddy Action" Philippa Gates traces the racial, ethnic, and national myths encoded in action movies of the 1990s and early 2000s.

As you read, reflect on the way movies represent the collective imagination of our culture and society:

- How do popular Hollywood movies present and encourage particular ideologies or unconscious attitudes?
- How do films allegorically thematize contemporary issues, anxieties, or problems?
- What is the relationship between the artistic demands of filmmaking and the commercial demands of the film industry?

SUSAN SONTAG

The Imagination of Disaster

A prolific fiction writer, critic, and political activist, Susan Sontag (1933–2004) was a prominent, if often controversial, public intellectual—both in the United States and abroad—for nearly forty years. Her interests ranged widely, from art, philosophy, photography, literature, film, and drama to war, illness, morality, and aesthetics. She was also notable for her engagement with popular culture, evident in "The Imagination of Disaster," which appeared in her celebrated 1966 book Against Interpretation. *Her books include* Death Kit *(1967),* Styles of Radical Will *(1966),* On Photography *(1973), and* The Volcano Lover *(1992). She wrote for the* New York Times, *the* New Yorker, *the* Nation, Art in America, *and many other publications. In the following essay, Sontag unpacks the components of science fiction and disaster films, revealing the devices that give movies their shape, their meaning, and their cultural resonance. "The Imagination of Disaster" was first published in the mid-1960s.*

As you read, *note how many of the writer's claims and conclusions are still applicable now. What is the most fascinating motif—or theme—in science fiction films, according to Sontag? How does she break down these films into their component parts to make her argument? What does Sontag mean when she claims that such movies offer the satisfaction of "moral simplification"?*

Ours is indeed an age of extremity. For we live under continual threat of two equally fearful, but seemingly opposed, destinies: unremitting banality and inconceivable terror. It is fantasy, served out in large rations by the popular arts, which allows most people to cope with these twin specters. For one job that fantasy can do is to lift us out of the unbearably humdrum and to distract us from terrors, real or anticipated—by an escape into exotic dangerous situations which have last-minute happy endings. But another one of the things that fantasy can do is to normalize what is psychologically unbearable, thereby inuring us to it. In the one case, fantasy beautifies the world. In the other, it neutralizes it.

The fantasy to be discovered in science fiction films does both jobs. These films reflect worldwide anxieties, and they serve to allay them. They inculcate a strange apathy concerning the processes of radiation, contamination, and destruction that I for one find haunting and depressing. The naïve level of the films neatly tempers the sense of otherness, of alien-ness, with the grossly familiar. In particular, the dialogue of most science fiction films, which is generally of a monumental but often touching banality, makes them wonderfully, unintentionally funny. Lines like: "Come quickly, there's a monster in my bathtub"; "We must do something about this"; "Wait, Professor. There's someone on the telephone"; "But that's incredible"; and the old American standby (accompanied by brow-wiping), "I hope it works!"—are hilarious in the context of picturesque and deafening holocaust. Yet the films also contain something which is painful and in deadly earnest.

Science fiction films are one of the most accomplished of the popular art forms, and can give a great deal of pleasure to sophisticated film addicts. Part of the pleasure, indeed, comes from the sense in which these movies are in complicity with the abhorrent. It is no more, perhaps, than the way all art draws its audience into a circle of complicity with the thing represented. But in science fiction films we have to do things which are (quite literally) unthinkable. Here, "thinking about the unthinkable"—not in the way of Herman Kahn,[1] as a subject for calculation, but as a subject for fantasy—becomes, however inadvertently, itself a somewhat questionable act from a moral point of view. The films perpetuate clichés about identity, volition, power, knowledge, happiness, social consensus, guilt, responsibility which are, to say the least, not serviceable in our present extremity. But collective nightmares cannot be banished by demonstrating that they are, intellectually and morally, fallacious. This nightmare—the one reflected in various registers in the science fiction films—is too close to our reality.

---

[1]*Herman Kahn* (1922–1983): military strategist and systems theorist known for studying the possible effects of nuclear war and recommending ways of surviving such a disaster. [Editor's note.]

A typical science fiction film has a form as predictable as a Western, and is made up of elements which are as classic as the saloon brawl, the blonde schoolteacher from the East, and the gun duel on the deserted main street.

One model scenario proceeds through five phases: 5

1. The arrival of the thing. (Emergence of the monsters, landing of the alien spaceship, etc.) This is usually witnessed, or suspected, by just one person, who is a young scientist on a field trip. Nobody, neither his neighbors nor his colleagues, will believe him for some time. The hero is not married, but has a sympathetic though also incredulous girlfriend.

2. Confirmation of the hero's report by a host of witnesses to a great act of destruction. (If the invaders are beings from another planet, a fruitless attempt to parley with them and get them to leave peacefully.) The local police are summoned to deal with the situation and massacred.

3. In the capital of the country, conferences between scientists and the military take place, with the hero lecturing before a chart, map, or blackboard. A national emergency is declared. Reports of further atrocities. Authorities from other countries arrive in black limousines. All international tensions are suspended in view of the planetary emergency. This stage often includes a rapid montage of news broadcasts in various languages, a meeting at the UN, and more conferences between the military and the scientists. Plans are made for destroying the enemy.

4. Further atrocities. At some point the hero's girlfriend is in grave danger. Massive counterattacks by international forces, with brilliant displays of rocketry, rays, and other advanced weapons, are all unsuccessful. Enormous military casualties, usually by incineration. Cities are destroyed and/or evacuated. There is an obligatory scene here of panicked crowds stampeding along a highway or a big bridge, being waved on by numerous policemen who, if the film is Japanese, are immaculately white-gloved, preternaturally calm, and call out in dubbed English, "Keep moving. There is no need to be alarmed."

5. More conferences, whose motif is: "They must be vulnerable to   10 something." Throughout, the hero has been experimenting in his lab on this. The final strategy, upon which all hopes depend, is drawn up; the ultimate weapon—often a super-powerful, as yet untested, nuclear device—is mounted. Countdown. Final repulse of the monster or invaders. Mutual congratulations, while the hero and girlfriend embrace cheek to cheek and scan the skies sturdily. "But have we seen the last of them?"

The film I have just described should be in Technicolor and on a wide screen. Another typical scenario is simpler and suited to black-and-white films with a lower budget. It has four phases:

1. The hero (usually, but not always, a scientist) and his girlfriend, or his wife and children, are disporting themselves in some innocent ultra-normal middle-class house in a small town, or on vacation (camping, boating). Suddenly, someone starts behaving strangely or some innocent form of vegetation becomes monstrously enlarged and ambulatory. If a character is pictured driving an automobile, something gruesome looms up in the middle of the road. If it is night, strange lights hurtle across the sky.

2. After following the thing's tracks, or determining that It is radioactive, or poking around a huge crater—in short, conducting some sort of crude investigation—the hero tries to warn the local authorities, without effect; nobody believes anything is amiss. The hero knows better. If the thing is tangible, the house is elaborately barricaded. If the invading alien is an invisible parasite, a doctor or friend is called in, who is himself rather quickly killed or "taken possession of" by the thing.

3. The advice of anyone else who is consulted proves useless. Meanwhile, It continues to claim other victims in the town, which remains implausibly isolated from the rest of the world. General helplessness.

4. One of two possibilities. Either the hero prepares to do battle $\quad$ 15 alone, accidentally discovers the thing's one vulnerable point, and destroys it. Or, he somehow manages to get out of town and succeeds in laying his case before competent authorities. They, along the lines of the first script but abridged, deploy a complex technology which (after initial setbacks) finally prevails against the invaders.

Another version of the second script opens with the scientist-hero in his laboratory, which is located in the basement or on the grounds of his tasteful, prosperous house. Through his experiments, he unwittingly causes a frightful metamorphosis in some class of plants or animals, which turn carnivorous and go on a rampage. Or else, his experiments have caused him to be injured (sometimes irrevocably) or "invaded" himself. Perhaps he has been experimenting with radiation, or has built a machine to communicate with beings from other planets or to transport him to other places or times.

Another version of the first script involves the discovery of some fundamental alteration in the conditions of existence of our planet, brought about by nuclear testing, which will lead to the extinction in a few months of all human life. For example: the temperature of the earth is becoming too high or too low to support life, or the earth is cracking in two, or it is gradually being blanketed by lethal fallout.

A third script, somewhat but not altogether different from the first two, concerns a journey through space—to the moon, or some other planet. What the space-voyagers commonly discover is that the alien terrain is in a state of dire emergency, itself threatened by extra-planetary invaders or nearing extinction through the practice of nuclear warfare. The terminal dramas of the first and second scripts are played out there, to which is added a final problem of getting away from the doomed and/or hostile planet and back to Earth.

I am aware, of course, that there are thousands of science fiction novels (their heyday was the late 1940s), not to mention the transcriptions of science fiction themes which, more and more, provide the principal subject matter of comic books. But I propose to discuss science fiction films (the present period began in 1950 and continues, considerably abated, to this day) as an independent subgenre, without reference to the novels from which, in many cases, they were adapted. For while novel and film may share the same plot, the fundamental difference between the resources of the novel and the film makes them quite dissimilar. Anyway, the best science fiction movies are on a far higher level, as examples of the art of the film, than the science fiction books are, as examples of the art of the novel or romance. That the films might be better than the books is an old story. Good novels rarely make good films, but excellent films are often made from poor or trivial novels.

Certainly, compared with the science fiction novels, their film counterparts have unique strengths, one of which is the immediate representation of the extraordinary: physical deformity and mutation, missile and rocket combat, toppling skyscrapers. The movies are, naturally, weak just where the science fiction novels (some of them) are strong—on science. But in place of an intellectual workout, they can supply something the novels can never provide—sensuous elaboration. In the films it is by means of images and sounds, not words that have to be translated by the imagination, that one can participate in the fantasy of living

"[T]he science fiction film . . . is concerned with the aesthetics of destruction, with the peculiar beauties to be found in wreaking havoc . . ." How does this image from *War of the Worlds* (2006) evoke the beauty of destruction?

through one's own death and more, the death of cities, the destruction of humanity itself.

Science fiction films are not about science. They are about disaster, which is one of the oldest subjects of art. In science fiction films, disaster is rarely viewed intensively; it is always extensive. It is a matter of quantity and ingenuity. If you will, it is a question of scale. But the scale, particularly in the wide-screen Technicolor films (of which the ones by the Japanese director, Inoshiro Honda and the American director George Pal are technically the most brilliant and convincing, and visually the most exciting), does raise the matter to another level.

Thus, the science fiction film (like a very different contemporary genre, the Happening) is concerned with the aesthetics of destruction, with the peculiar beauties to be found in wreaking havoc, making a mess. And it is in the imagery of destruction that the core of a good science fiction film lies. This is the disadvantage of the cheap film—in which the monster appears or the rocket lands in a small dull-looking town. (Hollywood budget needs usually dictate that the town be in the Arizona or California desert. In *The Thing from Another World* [1951], the rather sleazy and confined set is supposed to be an encampment near the North Pole.) Still, good black-and-white science fiction films have been made. But a bigger budget, which usually means Technicolor, allows a much greater play back and forth among several model environments. There is the populous city. There is the lavish but ascetic interior of the space ship—either the invaders' or ours— replete with streamlined chromium fixtures and dials, and machines whose complexity is indicated by the number of colored lights they flash and strange noises they emit. There is the laboratory crowded with formidable machines and scientific apparatus. There is a comparatively old-fashioned-looking conference room, where the scientist brings charts to explain the desperate state of things to the military. And each of these standard locales or backgrounds is subject to two modalities—intact and destroyed. We may, if we are lucky, be treated to a panorama of melting tanks, flying bodies, crashing walls, awesome craters and fissures in the earth, plummeting spacecraft, colorful deadly rays; and to a symphony of screams, weird electronic signals, the noisiest military hardware going, and the leaden tones of the laconic denizens of alien planets and their subjugated earthlings.

Certain of the primitive gratifications of science fiction films— for instance, the depiction of urban disaster on a colossally magnified scale—are shared with other types of films. Visually there is little difference between mass havoc as represented in the old horror and monster films and what we find in science fiction films, except (again) scale. In the old monster films, the monster always headed for the great city where he had to do a fair bit of rampaging, hurling buses off bridges, crumpling trains in his bare hands, toppling buildings, and so forth. The archetype is King Kong, in Schoedsack's great film of 1933, running amok, first in the African village (trampling babies, a bit of footage excised from most prints), then in New York. This is really not any different from Inoshiro Honda's *Rodan* (1957), where two giant reptiles—with a wingspan of five-hundred feet and supersonic speeds—by flapping their wings whip up a cyclone that blows most of Tokyo to smithereens. Or, the tremendous scenes of rampage by the giant robot who destroys half of Japan with the great incinerating ray which shoots forth from his eyes, at the beginning of Honda's *The Mysterians* (1959). Or, the destruction, by the rays from a fleet of flying saucers of New York, Paris, and Tokyo, in *Battle in Outer Space* (1960). Or, the inundation of New

York in *When Worlds Collide* (1951). Or, the end of London in 1968 depicted in George Pal's *The Time Machine* (1960). Neither do these sequences differ in aesthetic intention from the destruction scenes in the big sword, sandal, and orgy color spectaculars set in biblical and Roman times—the end of Sodom in Aldrich's *Sodom and Gomorrah,* of Gaza in de Mille's *Samson and Delilah,* of Rhodes in *The Colossus of Rhodes,* and of Rome in a dozen Nero movies. D. W. Griffith began it with the Babylon sequence in *Intolerance,* and to this day there is nothing like the thrill of watching all those expensive sets come tumbling down.

In other respects as well, the science fiction films of the 1950s take up familiar themes. The famous movie serials and comics of the 1930s of the adventures of Flash Gordon and Buck Rogers, as well as the more recent spate of comic book super-heroes with extraterrestrial origins (the most famous is Superman, a foundling from the planet Krypton, currently described as having been exploded by a nuclear blast) share motifs with more recent science fiction movies. But there is an important difference. The old science fiction films, and most of the comics, still have an essentially innocent relation to disaster. Mainly they offer new versions of the oldest romance of all—of the strong invulnerable hero with the mysterious lineage come to do battle on behalf of good and against evil. Recent science fiction films have a decided grimness, bolstered by their much greater degree of visual credibility, which contrasts strongly with the older films. Modern historical reality has greatly enlarged the imagination of disaster, and the protagonists—perhaps by the very nature of what is visited upon them—no longer seem wholly innocent.

The lure of such generalized disaster as a fantasy is that it releases   25
one from normal obligations. The trump card of the end-of-the-world movies—like *The Day the Earth Caught Fire* (1962)—is that great scene with New York or London or Tokyo discovered empty, its entire population annihilated. Or, as in *The World, the Flesh, and the Devil* (1959), the whole movie can be devoted to the fantasy of occupying the deserted city and starting all over again—Robinson Crusoe on a worldwide scale.

   Another kind of satisfaction these films supply is extreme moral simplification—that is to say, a morally acceptable fantasy where one can give outlet to cruel or at least amoral feelings. In this respect, science fiction films partly overlap with horror films. This is the undeniable pleasure we derive from looking at freaks, at beings excluded from the category of the human. The sense of superiority over the freak conjoined in varying proportions with the titillation of fear and aversion makes it possible for moral scruples to be lifted, for cruelty to be enjoyed. The same thing happens in science fiction films. In the figure of the monster from outer space, the freakish, the ugly, and the predatory all converge—and provide a fantasy target for righteous bellicosity to discharge itself, and for the aesthetic enjoyment of suffering and disaster. Science fiction films are one of the purest forms of spectacle; that is, we are rarely inside anyone's feelings. (An exception to this is Jack Arnold's *The Incredible Shrinking Man* [1957].) We are merely spectators; we watch.

But in science fiction films, unlike horror films, there is not much horror. Suspense, shocks, surprises are mostly abjured in favor of a steady inexorable plot. Science fiction films invite a dispassionate, aesthetic view of destruction and violence—a *technological* view. Things, objects, machinery play a major role in these films. A greater range of ethical values is embodied in the décor of these films than in the people. Things, rather than the helpless humans, are the locus of values because we experience them, rather than people, as the sources of power. According to science fiction films, man is naked without his artifacts. *They* stand for different values, they are potent, they are what gets destroyed, and they are the indispensable tools for the repulse of the alien invaders or the repair of the damaged environment.

The science fiction films are strongly moralistic. The standard message is the one about the proper, or humane, uses of science, versus the mad, obsessional use of science. This message the science fiction films share in common with the classic horror films of the 1930s, like *Frankenstein, The Mummy, The Island of Doctor Moreau, Dr. Jekyll and Mr. Hyde*. (Georges Franju's brilliant *Les Yeux Sans Visage* [1959], called here *The Horror Chamber of Doctor Faustus,* is a more recent example.) In the horror films, we have the mad or obsessed or misguided scientist who pursues his experiments against good advice to the contrary, creates a monster or monsters, and is himself destroyed—often recognizing his folly himself, and dying in the successful effort to destroy his own creation. One science fiction equivalent of this is the scientist, usually a member of a team, who defects to the planetary invaders because "their" science is more advanced than "ours."

This is the case in *The Mysterians,* and, true to form, the renegade sees his error in the end, and from within the Mysterian space ship destroys it and himself. In *This Island Earth* (1955), the inhabitants of the beleaguered planet Metaluna propose to conquer Earth, but their project is foiled by a Metalunan scientist named Exeter who, having lived on Earth a while and learned to love Mozart, cannot abide such viciousness. Exeter plunges his space ship into the ocean after returning a glamorous pair (male and female) of American physicists to Earth. Metaluna dies. In *The Fly* (1958), the hero, engrossed in his basement-laboratory experiments on a matter-transmitting machine, uses himself as a subject, accidentally exchanges head and one arm with a housefly which had gotten into the machine, becomes a monster, and with his last shred of human will destroys his laboratory and orders his wife to kill him. His discovery, for the good of mankind, is lost.

Being a clearly labeled species of intellectual, the scientists in science fiction films are always liable to crack up or go off the deep end. In *Conquest of Space* (1955), the scientist-commander of an international expedition to Mars suddenly acquires scruples about the blasphemy involved in the undertaking, and begins reading the Bible mid-journey instead of attending to his duties. The commander's son, who is his junior officer and always addresses his father as "General," is forced to kill the old man when he tries to prevent the ship from landing on Mars. In this film, both sides of the ambivalence toward scientists are given voice. Generally, for a scientific enterprise to be treated entirely sympathetically in these films, it needs the certificate of utility. Science, viewed without ambivalence, means an efficacious response to danger. Disinterested intellectual curiosity rarely appears in any form other than caricature, as a maniacal dementia that cuts one off from normal human relations. But this suspicion is usually directed at the scientist rather than his work. The creative scientist may become a martyr to his own discovery, through an accident or by pushing things too far. The implication remains that other men, less imaginative—in short, technicians—would administer the same scientific discovery better and more safely. The most ingrained contemporary mistrust of the intellect is visited, in these movies, upon the scientist-as-intellectual.

The message that the scientist is one who releases forces which, if not controlled for good, could destroy man himself seems innocuous enough. One of the oldest images of the scientist is Shakespeare's Prospero,[2] the over-detached scholar forcibly retired from society to a desert island, only partly in control of the magic forces in which he dabbles. Equally classic is the figure of the scientist as satanist (*Dr. Faustus*, stories of Poe and Hawthorne). Science is magic, and man has always known that there is black magic as well as white. But it is not enough to remark that contemporary attitudes—as reflected in science fiction films—remain ambivalent, that the scientist is treated both as satanist and savior. The proportions have changed, because of the new context in which the old admiration and fear of the scientist is located. For his sphere of influence is no longer local, himself or his immediate community. It is planetary, cosmic.

One gets the feeling, particularly in the Japanese films, but not only there, that mass trauma exists over the use of nuclear weapons and the possibility of future nuclear wars. Most of the science fiction films bear witness to this trauma, and in a way, attempt to exorcise it.

The accidental awakening of the super-destructive monster who has slept in the earth since pre-history is, often, an obvious metaphor for the Bomb. But there are many explicit references as well. In *The Mysterians,* a probe ship from the planet Mysteroid has landed on earth, near Tokyo. Nuclear warfare having been practiced on Mysteroid for centuries (their civilization is "more advanced than ours"), 90 percent of those now born on the planet have to be destroyed at birth, because of defects caused by the huge amounts of Strontium 90 in their diet. The Mysterians have come to earth to marry earth women and possibly to take over our relatively uncontaminated planet. . . . In *The Incredible Shrinking Man,* the John Doe hero is the victim of a gust of radiation which blows over the water, while he is out boating with his wife; the radiation causes him to grow smaller and smaller, until at the end of the movie he steps through the fine mesh of a window screen to become "the infinitely small. . . ." In *Rodan,* a horde

---

[2]*Prospero:* character in Shakespeare's *The Tempest.* [Editor's note.]

of monstrous carnivorous prehistoric insects, and finally a pair of giant flying reptiles (the prehistoric Archeopteryx), are hatched from dormant eggs in the depths of a mine shaft by the impact of nuclear test explosions, and go on to destroy a good part of the world before they are felled by the molten lava of a volcanic eruption. . . . In the English film, *The Day the Earth Caught Fire*, two simultaneous hydrogen bomb tests by the U.S. and Russia change by eleven degrees the tilt of the earth on its axis and alter the earth's orbit so that it begins to approach the sun.

Radiation casualties—ultimately, the conception of the whole world as a casualty of nuclear testing and nuclear warfare—is the most ominous of all the notions with which science fiction films deal. Universes become expendable. Worlds become contaminated, burnt out, exhausted, obsolete. In *Rocketship X-M* (1950), explorers from Earth land on Mars, where they learn that atomic warfare has destroyed Martian civilization. In George Pal's *The War of the Worlds* (1953), reddish spindly alligator-skinned creatures from Mars invade Earth because their planet is becoming too cold to be habitable. In *This Island Earth*, also American, the planet Metaluna, whose population has long ago been driven underground by warfare, is dying under the missile attacks of an enemy planet. Stocks of uranium, which power the force-shield shielding Metaluna, have been used up; and an unsuccessful expedition is sent to Earth to enlist earth scientists to devise new sources of power.

There is a vast amount of wishful thinking in science fiction films, 35 some of it touching, some of it depressing. Again and again, one detects the hunger for a "good war," which poses no moral problems, admits of no moral qualifications. The imagery of science fiction films will satisfy the most bellicose addict of war films, for a lot of the satisfactions of war films pass, untransformed, into science fiction films. Examples: the dogfights between earth "fighter rockets" and alien spacecraft in the *Battle of Outer Space* (1959); the escalating firepower in the successive assaults upon the invaders in *The Mysterians*, which Dan Talbot correctly described as a nonstop holocaust; the spectacular bombardment of the underground fortress in *This Island Earth*.

Yet at the same time the bellicosity of science fiction films is neatly channeled into the yearning for peace, or for at least peaceful coexistence. Some scientist generally takes sententious note of the fact that it took the planetary invasion or cosmic disaster to make the warring nations of the earth come to their senses, and suspend their own conflicts. One of the main themes of many science fiction films—the color ones usually, because they have the budget and resources to develop the military spectacle—is this UN fantasy, a fantasy of united warfare. (The same wishful UN theme cropped up in a recent spectacular which is not science fiction, *Fifty-Five Days at Peking* [1963]. There, topically enough, the Chinese, the Boxers, play the role of Martian invaders who united the earthmen, in this case the United States, Russia, England, France, Germany, Italy, and Japan.) A great enough disaster cancels all enmities, and calls upon the utmost concentration of the earth's resources.

Science—technology—is conceived of as the great unifier. Thus the science fiction films also project a utopian fantasy. In the classic models of utopian thinking—Plato's Republic, Campanella's City of the Sun, More's Utopia, Swift's land of the Houyhnhnms, Voltaire's Eldorado—society had worked out a perfect consensus. In these societies reasonableness had achieved an unbreakable supremacy over the emotions. Since no disagreement or social conflict was intellectually plausible, none was possible. As in Melville's *Typee*, "they all think the same." The universal rule of reason meant universal agreement. It is interesting, too, that societies in which reason was pictured as totally ascendant were also traditionally pictured as having an ascetic and/or materially frugal and economically simple mode of life. But in the utopian world community projected by science fiction films, totally pacified and ruled by scientific consensus, the demand for simplicity of material existence would be absurd.

But alongside the hopeful fantasy of moral simplification and international unity embodied in the science fiction films, lurk the deepest anxieties about contemporary existence. I don't mean only the very real trauma of the Bomb—that it has been used, that there are enough now to kill everyone on earth many times over, that those new bombs may very well be used. Besides these new anxieties about physical disaster, the prospect of universal mutilation and even annihilation, the science fiction films reflect powerful anxieties about the condition of the individual psyche.

For science fiction films may also be described as a popular mythology for the contemporary *negative* imagination about the impersonal. The other-world creatures which seek to take "us" over, are an "it," not a "they." The planetary invaders are usually zombie-like. Their movements are either cool, mechanical, or lumbering, blobby. But it amounts to the same thing. If they are nonhuman in form, they proceed with an absolutely regular, unalterable movement (unalterable save by destruction). If they are human in form—dressed in space suits, etc.—then they obey the most rigid military discipline, and display no personal characteristics whatsoever. And it is this regime of emotionlessness, of impersonality, of regimentation, which they will impose on the earth if they are successful. "No more love, no more beauty, no more pain," boasts a converted earthling in *The Invasion of the Body Snatchers* (1956). The half earthling–half alien children in *The Children of the Damned* (1960) are absolutely emotionless, move as a group and understand each other's thoughts, and are all prodigious intellects. They are the wave of the future, man in his next stage of development.

These alien invaders practice a crime which is worse than mur- 40
der. They do not simply kill the person. They obliterate him. In *The War of the Worlds*, the ray which issues from the rocket ship disintegrates all persons and objects in its path, leaving no trace of them but a light ash. In Honda's *The H-Men* (1959), the creeping blob melts all flesh with which it comes in contact. If the blob, which looks like a huge hunk of red Jell-O, and can crawl across floors and up and down walls, so much as touches your bare boot, all that is left of you is a heap of clothes on the floor. (A more articulated, size-multiplying blob is the villain in the English film *The Creeping Unknown* [1956].) In another version of this fantasy, the body is preserved but the person is entirely reconstituted as the automatized servant or agent of the alien powers. This is, of course, the vampire fantasy in new dress. The person is really dead, but he doesn't know it. He's "undead," he has become an "unperson." It happens to a whole California town in *The Invasion of the Body Snatchers*, to several earth scientists in *This Island Earth*, and to assorted innocents in *It Came from Outer Space*, *Attack of the Puppet People* (1961), and *The Brain Eaters* (1961). As the victim always backs away from the vampire's horrifying embrace, so in science fiction films the person always fights being "taken over"; he wants to retain his humanity. But once the deed has been done, the victim is eminently satisfied with his condition. He has not been converted from human amiability to

monstrous "animal" bloodlust (a metaphoric exaggeration of sexual desire), as in the old vampire fantasy. No, he has simply become far more efficient—the very model of technocratic man, purged of emotions, volitionless, tranquil, obedient to all orders. The dark secret behind human nature used to be the upsurge of the animal—as in *King Kong*. The threat to man, his availability to dehumanization, lay in his own animality. Now the danger is understood as residing in man's ability to be turned into a machine.

The rule, of course, is that this horrible and irremediable form of murder can strike anyone in the film except the hero. The hero and his family, while grossly menaced, always escape this fact and by the end of the film the invaders have been repulsed or destroyed. I know of only one exception, *The Day That Mars Invaded Earth* (1963), in which, after all the standard struggles, the scientist-hero, his wife, and their two children are "taken over" by the alien invaders—and that's that. (The last minutes of the film show them being incinerated by the Martians' rays and their ash silhouettes flushed down their empty swimming pool, while their simulacra drive off in the family car.) Another variant but upbeat switch on the rule occurs in *The Creation of the Humanoids* (1964), where the hero discovers at the end of the film that he, too, has been turned into a metal robot, complete with highly efficient and virtually indestructible mechanical insides, although he didn't know it and detected no difference in himself. He learns, however, that he will shortly be upgraded into a "humanoid" having all the properties of a real man.

Of all the standard motifs of science fiction films, this theme of dehumanization is perhaps the most fascinating. For, as I have indicated, it is scarcely a black-and-white situation, as in the vampire films. The attitude of the science fiction films toward depersonalization is mixed. On the one hand, they deplore it as the ultimate horror. On the other hand, certain characteristics of the dehumanized invaders, modulated and disguised—such as the ascendancy of reason over feelings, the idealization of teamwork and the consensus-creating activities of science, a marked degree of moral simplification—are precisely traits of the savior-scientists. For it is interesting that when the scientist in these films is treated negatively, it is usually done through the portrayal of an individual scientist who holes up in his laboratory and neglects his fiancée or his loving wife and children, obsessed by his daring and dangerous experiments. The scientist as a loyal member of a team, and therefore considerably less individualized, is treated quite respectfully.

There is absolutely no social criticism, of even the most implicit kind, in science fiction films. No criticism, for example, of the conditions of our society which create the impersonality and dehumanization which science fiction fantasies displace onto the influence of an alien It. Also, the notion of science as a social activity, interlocking with social and political interests, is unacknowledged. Science is simply either adventure (for good or evil) or a technical response to danger. And, typically, when the fear of science is paramount—when science is conceived of as black magic rather than white—the evil has no attribution beyond that of the perverse will of an individual scientist. In science fiction films the antithesis of black magic and white is drawn as a split between technology, which is beneficent, and the errant individual will of a lone intellectual.

Thus, science fiction films can be looked at as thematically central allegory, replete with standard modern attitudes. The theme of depersonalization (being "taken over") which I have been talking about is a new allegory reflecting the age-old awareness of man that, sane, he is always perilously close to insanity and unreason. But there is something more there than just a recent, popular image which expresses man's perennial, but largely unconscious, anxiety about his sanity. The image derives most of its power from a supplementary and historical anxiety, also not experienced *consciously* by most people, about the depersonalizing conditions of modern urban society. Similarly, it is not enough to note that science fiction allegories are one of the new myths about—that is, ways of accommodating to and negating—the perennial human anxiety about death. (Myths of heaven and hell, and of ghosts, had the same function.) Again, there is a historically specifiable twist which intensifies the anxiety, or better, the trauma suffered by everyone in the middle of the twentieth century when it became clear that from now on to the end of human history, every person would spend his individual life not only under the threat of individual death, which is certain, but of something almost unsupportable psychologically—collective incineration and extinction which could come any time, virtually without warning.

From a psychological point of view, the imagination of disaster 45 does not greatly differ from one period in history to another. But from a political and moral point of view, it does. The expectation of the apocalypse may be the occasion for a radical disaffiliation from society, as when thousands of Eastern European Jews in the seventeenth century gave up their homes and businesses and began to trek to Palestine upon hearing that Shabbethai Zevi had been proclaimed Messiah and that the end of the world was imminent. But peoples learn the news of their own end in diverse ways. It is reported that in 1945 the populace of Berlin received without great agitation the news that Hitler had decided to kill them all, before the Allies arrived, because they had not been worthy enough to win the war. We are, alas, more in the position of the Berliners than of the Jews of seventeenth-century Eastern Europe; and our response is closer to theirs, too. What I am suggesting is that the imagery of disaster in science fiction films is above all the emblem of an *inadequate response*. I do not mean to bear down on the films for this. They themselves are only a sampling, stripped of sophistication, of the inadequacy of most people's response to the unassimilable terrors that infect their consciousness. The interest of the films, aside from their considerable amount of cinematic charm, consists in this intersection between a naïvely and largely debased commercial art product and the most profound dilemmas of the contemporary situation.

For Discussion and Writing

1. *Comprehension*   Sontag writes, "Science fiction films are not about science" (par. 21). What are they about, according to her? Why is this important to her argument?

2. *Critical Reading*   Sontag is well known for her writing about "high" art and culture. What is her attitude toward popular science fiction? How does this attitude come across in her **style**? Do the **structure** and tone of the essay suggest her relationship with her subject?

3. *Analysis*   Writing in the mid-1960s, Sontag asserts, "There is absolutely no social criticism, of even the most implicit kind, in science fiction films. No criticism, for example, of the conditions of our society which create the impersonality and dehumanization which

science fiction fantasies displace onto the influence of an alien It"
(par. 43). Is this assertion still accurate, when measured against the
science fiction films of the last decade or two? If you are familiar
with any science fiction films of the 1950s and 1960s, do you agree
with Sontag's claim that they contain "absolutely no social criticism"?

4. ***Connections***   Sontag writes that "it is not enough to note that
science fiction allegories are one of the new myths about—that is,
ways of accommodating to and negating—the perennial human
anxiety about death" (par. 44). Is Sontag using the term "myth" in
the same way that Linda Seger does in "Creating the Myth" (p. 367)?
Does the word have a different meaning in Sontag's essay than it
does in Seger's? Explain your answer.

5. ***Writing***   Although Sontag provides close readings of specific films
in her essay, she also proposes more general, theoretical strategies
for interpreting science fiction, disaster, and horror films: their
common themes, structural elements, moral values, and other
patterns. Choose a contemporary science fiction, disaster, or horror
film, and, in an essay, PowerPoint, or Prezi presentation, analyze it
using Sontag's critical approach. You may also want to show how
your choice subverts or challenges Sontag's argument.

WILLIE OSTERWEIL

Hollywood's Love Affair with Surveillance

A 2009 graduate of Cornell University, Willie Osterweil is an activist, writer, and editor at the New Inquiry. *His work has appeared in the* Paris Review, Al Jazeera America, *and other publications. Over the past several years, Americans have wrestled with questions about privacy and surveillance—from online sharing and government transparency to warrantless wiretapping and spying by the National Security Administration. In this essay, which appeared in the* Baffler, *Osterweil argues that the film industry is complicit in the American security state's culture of surveillance.*

As you read, note the writer's use of the word "ideological." What does the term mean in the context of his argument? Do you think movies, television shows, and other popular culture artifacts have an "ideology"? Why or why not?

One of the valences of the NSA[1] leaks has been opinionators wringing their hands over the lack of anger and shock. Where's the anger? The protests? Why are the people so complacent in the face of these revelations? Well, one reason might be that they're not all that revelatory.

Only liberals require repeated instances of one-hundred-percent verified documentary evidence to begin to entertain the idea that there might be something bad about the way the state is treating its subjects—at least when a Democrat is in the White House. Muslims, communities of color, immigrants, political activists, the incarcerated or formerly incarcerated, and anyone else who

---

[1]*National Security Agency* (NSA): the United States government defense agency that provides foreign and domestic intelligence through monitoring, decoding, translation, etc. [Editor's note.]

lives under police surveillance (not to mention the more than one million people who actually work in the intelligence industry and their families) know the surveillance-state first hand.

But knowledge of surveillance techniques—hacking into e-mail accounts, eavesdropping on phone calls, coordinating security cameras, or tracking people by GPS—has already been spread far and wide through movies and television, long before Edward Snowden's revelations. The *Bourne* films, the new *Iron Man* movies, *The Hunger Games,* and dozens more besides have featured state actors capable of knowing anything and everything at any time.

While the fantasy of a panoptical state in fiction goes back to George Orwell's *Nineteen Eighty-Four*,[2] and portrayals of police snooping, wiretapping, and trailing are as old as the cop-film genre, the image of total surveillance as something other than a dystopian nightmare has become an increasingly frequent cinematic and televisual motif in the last fifteen years.

Indeed, cinema has moved well beyond the fact that everything   5
might be heard and watched by state spooks into exploring the ramifications and possibilities presented by that fait accompli. Three recent examples, *Captain America: The Winter Soldier* (2014), *Robocop* (2014), and *Her* (2013), present three different ways of accommodating us to total surveillance, which viewed together can helpfully describe the ideological contours of the surveillance state.

As with all Marvel Studios films, part of the way *Captain America: The Winter Soldier* shows the audience that they're watching hundreds of millions of dollars being spent is to throw about thirty plots at them. But the main "Captain America versus the super-villains" plot could be summarized, only slightly sardonically, as, "What if Edward Snowden were a genetically-modified-super-soldier, and the NSA were a conspiracy hatched by a Nazi scientist who downloaded his consciousness onto a computer?" The answer to that intriguing what-if is that the massive surveillance would be used in the production of genocidal mega-drones who would preemptively eliminate millions of future dissidents in order to instantiate a fascist state. When Captain America

[2]*Nineteen Eighty-Four* (1949): dystopian novel by George Orwell that depicts a reality in which people are monitored by the totalitarian government. [Editor's note.]

Osterweil writes that *Captain America: The Winter Soldier* provides one way of "accommodating" Americans to "total surveillance." Do you think popular films perform such ideological functions?

reveals the internal fascist conspiracy to employees of SHIELD (Marvel's superhero-training military-industrial complex), he instructs them to rise up against their bosses.

Of course, the film has to walk back this radical analysis—namely, that mass surveillance can only be used towards forms of totalitarian state control, up to and including genocide. In one of the film's approximately nineteen different endings (love you, Marvel!), Black Widow explicitly states that, while SHIELD surveillance may produce certain vulnerabilities—like, say, funding and enabling a massive conspiracy of ultra-powerful neo-Nazis—it also produces the only available counter-power to such a conspiracy.

If *Captain America* takes the potential structural abuses of state power as its subject, *Robocop* and *Her* pretend to talk about robots and artificial intelligence (AI) while actually asking that all-important ideological question: what does it take to make ostensibly free subjects accept total surveillance?

The *Robocop* reboot answers that question sloppily: it takes *results*. The remake mimics a critique of the police and the security apparatus, like that of its visionary predecessor, but is ultimately a commercial for state omniscience. The film's meta-conflict is whether Congress, in 2028, will allow the use of surveillance robots (which we see them already using globally) to police the United States. Omnicorp, the makers of the drones, builds and mobilizes Robocop to sway public opinion. Robocop single-handedly and immediately drops the crime rate in Detroit by 90 percent. And if the American people love Robocop, well, Congress will have to act!

The conflict driving the film's plot is a totally false dilemma, because the use of unmanned drones by the state is already approved on U.S. soil now, in 2014, and also because public opinion hasn't mattered to whatever gets through Congress in maybe four decades. Furthermore, even if we're meant to recognize robot policing would be "bad," most of the film's meager pleasures come from action sequences we spend inside Robocop's robotic-visor, which is like Google Glass[3] on cop-steroids. With

10

[3]*Google Glass:* wearable technology developed by Google that allows users to view a small, hands-free display mounted in front of their eyes. [Editor's note.]

this system, Robocop has the ability to locate anyone (and ascertain their emotional and medical status) anywhere in the city through the instantaneous deployment of cameras, retinal scans, and biometric readings. The upshot of the film is that corrupt corporations might abuse surveillance, but that a "good cop" would use total omniscience to end crime.

Her has, by its critical and popular acclaim, found a much more convincing answer to the question of what it takes for us to submit to total surveillance: patriarchy. The fundamental question of *Her* actually has nothing to do with AI and everything to do with how much misogyny is required to convincingly tell a story about a man falling in love with his personal surveillance device—er, operating system. (Spoiler alert: a lot.)

From his first sexual encounter in the film, in which a stranger on a phone-sex hotline tells him to describe choking her with a dead cat, then cries into the phone after orgasm, the women Theodore encounters are all beings of inchoate and terrifying desire. It is only after a blind date with a gorgeous woman played by Olivia Wilde—who thrusts her hands down Theodore's pants before asking, terrified, "You're not just gonna sleep with me and not call me like all the other guys?"—that Theodore falls into the digital arms of Samantha.

Even the film's most interesting conceit, in which a woman shows up to be a body-surrogate stand-in for Samantha, allowing Samantha and Theodore to (sort of) have sex, ends the moment their interaction is marred by a tiny glimmer of insecurity or instability. The surrogate, again a beautiful woman who has put herself forward sexually, flees crying and screaming from the scene at the first sign of trouble, hiding in a closet and taking the blame for a fight between Samantha and Theodore. "I'm sorry my lip quivered," she says. "The way you guys love each other without any judgment, I wanted to be part of that."

But what does Samantha do, throughout the film, to make Theodore love her? She reads all of his e-mails. She watches him constantly: while he's sleeping, while he's working. She tells him whom to date, and what to do on those dates. She becomes his eyes. In a "romantic" scene at a carnival, he puts the video device through which she sees in his pocket and lets her lead him around with his eyes closed. *Her* shows that you just have to really hate (real-life) women in order to love the NSA.

Here, then, we see three strategies for accommodating people 15 to surveillance society. One, the most obvious and prevalent, the lie already getting a bit threadbare, is *Robocop*'s insistence that surveillance will actually stop crime and terrorism. If that doesn't work, you can always combine patriarchy with total alienation from our desire and our bodies, as in *Her*. And if none of that convinces you, there's always the liberal shrug embodied in *Captain America*: the military-industrial complex may constitute an existential threat, but it's so powerful that it's also the only thing capable of keeping us safe from itself.

For Discussion and Writing

1. **Comprehension**   According to Osterweil, what "all-important ideological question" (par. 8) do the films *Robocop* and *Her* ask their viewers?

2. **Critical Reading**   Who is the intended **audience** for this essay and what is the writer's attitude toward it? Does he think his readers overlap with the audiences for the movies he analyzes?

3. **Analysis**   What two oppositions does Osterweil use in paragraphs 3 and 4? Why are they important to his argument?

4. **Connections**   Osterweil suggests that Hollywood movies condition viewers to accept and perhaps even embrace the panoptical surveillance state. How does this process parallel the ideological conditioning of children that Roland Barthes describes in "Toys" (p. 36)? In what ways do toys accommodate children to society? How are Osterweil's and Barthes's analytical approaches similar? How are they different?

5. **Writing**   Osterweil reads three films, claiming that each suggests a different thesis about the surveillance state. According to the writer, regardless of their differences, all three movies work to "accommodat[e] us to total surveillance" (par. 5). Do you agree with his overall argument? Are his examples sufficient to make the case? Choose another contemporary film that includes surveillance in its story line or themes. Then, use this example either to extend Osterweil's argument, or to provide a counterexample that complicates or refutes his thesis.

DAVID DENBY

Has Hollywood Murdered the Movies?

David Denby (b. 1943) writes about film for the New Yorker. *Previously, he was the film critic for* New York *magazine. His work has appeared in the* Atlantic, *the* New Republic, *and other publications. Denby is also the author of* Great Books *(1996),* American Sucker *(2004), and* Snark: It's Mean, It's Personal, and It's Ruining Our Conversation *(2009). In this essay from the* New Yorker, *Denby laments the current state of American film and its "wearying, numbing, infuriating sameness." In the process, he balances the analytical detachment of a sophisticated critic evaluating movies with the passion of a fan ranting at an "enraging" trend that threatens the very existence of quality cinema.*

As you read, *pay attention to the cause-and-effect relationships Denby tries to establish in making his argument. What has changed in American filmmaking—and viewing—over the last three decades? What is Denby's thesis? Do you agree with his assessment of the contemporary film culture and the film industry?*

1.

Six hundred or so movies open in the United States every year, including films from every country, documentaries, first features spilling out of festivals, experiments, oddities, zero-budget movies made in someone's apartment. Even in the digit-dazed summer season, small movies never stop opening—there is always something to see, something to write about. Just recently I have been excited by two independent films—the visionary Louisiana bayou mini-epic, *Beasts of the Southern Wild,* and a terse, morally alert fable of authority and obedience called *Compliance.* Yet despite such pleasures, movies—mainstream American movies—

are in serious trouble. And this is hardly a problem that worries movie critics more than anyone else: many moviegoers feel the same puzzlement and dismay.

When I speak of moviegoers, I mean people who get out of the house and into a theater as often as they can; or people with kids, who back up rare trips to the movies with lots of recent DVDs and films ordered on demand. I do not mean the cinephiles, the solitary and obsessed, who have given up on movie houses and on movies as our national theater (as Pauline Kael called it) and plant themselves at home in front of flat screens and computers, where they look at old films or small new films from the four corners of the globe, blogging and exchanging disks with their friends. They are extraordinary, some of them, and their blogs and Web sites generate an exfoliating mass of knowledge and opinion, a thickening density of inquiries and claims, outraged and dulcet tweets. Yet it is unlikely that they can do much to build a theatrical audience for the movies they love. And directors still need a sizable audience if they are to make their next picture about something more than a few people talking on the street.

I have in mind the great national audience for movies, or what's left of it. In the 1930s, roughly eighty million people went to the movies every week, with weekly attendance peaking at ninety million in 1930 and again in the mid-1940s. Now about thirty million people go, in a population two and a half times the size of the population of the 1930s. By degrees, as everyone knows, television, the Internet, and computer games dethroned the movies as regular entertainment. By the 1980s, the economics of the business became largely event-driven, with a never-ending production of spectacle and animation that draws young audiences away from their home screens on opening weekend. For years, the tastes of young audiences have wielded an influence on what gets made way out of proportion to their numbers in the population. We now have a movie culture so bizarrely pulled out of shape that it makes one wonder what kind of future movies will have.

Nostalgia is history altered through sentiment. What's necessary for survival is not nostalgia, but defiance. I'm made crazy by the way the business structure of movies is now constricting the art of movies. I don't understand why more people are not made crazy by the same thing. Perhaps their best hopes have been defeated; perhaps, if they are journalists, they do not want to argue themselves out of a job; perhaps they are too frightened of sounding like cranks to point out what is obvious and have merely, with a suppressed sigh, accommodated themselves to the strange thing that American movies have become. A successful market-place has a vast bullying force to enforce acquiescence.

The Avengers (2013), which pulled together into one movie all   5
the familiar Marvel Comics characters from earlier pictures—Captain America, Thor, Iron Man, and so on—achieved a world-wide box-office gross within a couple of months of about $1.5 billion. That extraordinary figure represented a triumph of craft and cynical marketing: the movie, which cost $220 million to make, was mildly entertaining for a while (self-mockery was built into it), but then it degenerated into a digital slam, an endless battle of exacerbated pixels, most of the fighting set in the airless digital spaces of a digital city. Only a few critics saw anything bizarre or inane about so vast a display of technology devoted to so little. American commercial movies are now dominated by the instantaneous monumental, the senseless repetition of movies washing in on a mighty roar of publicity and washing out in a waste of semi-indifference a few weeks later. *The Green Hornet? The Green Lantern?* Did I actually see both of them? *The Avengers* will quickly be effaced by an even bigger movie of the same type.

This franchise-capping *Avengers* was a carefully built phenom-enon. Let's go back a couple of years and pick up a single strand that led to it. Consider one of its predecessors, *Iron Man 2*, which began its run in the United States, on May 7, 2010, at 4,380 the-aters. That's only the number of theaters: multiplexes often put new movies on two or three, or even five or six, screens within the complex, so the actual number of screens was much higher—well over 6,000. The gross receipts for the opening weekend were $128 million. Yet those were not the movie's first revenues. As a way of discouraging piracy and cheap street sale of the movie overseas, the movie's distributor, Paramount Pictures, had opened *Iron Man 2* a week earlier in many countries around the world. By May 9, at the end of the weekend in which the picture opened in America, cumulative worldwide theatrical gross was $324 mil-lion. By the end of its run, the cumulative total had advanced to $622 million. Let's face it: big numbers are impressive, no matter what produced them.

The worldwide theatrical gross of *Iron Man 2* served as a branding operation for what followed—sale of the movie to broadcast and cable TV, and licensing to retail outlets for DVD rentals and purchase. *Iron Man 2* was itself part of a well-developed franchise (the first *Iron Man* came out in 2008). The hero, Tony Stark, a billionaire industrialist-playboy, first appeared in a Marvel comic book in 1963 and still appears in new Marvel comics. By 2010, rattling around stores and malls all over the world, there were also *Iron Man* video games, soundtrack albums, toys, bobblehead dolls, construction sets, dishware, pillows, pajamas, helmets, T-shirts, and lounge pants. There was a hamburger available at Burger King named after Mickey Rourke, a supporting player in *Iron Man 2*. Companies such as Audi, LG Mobile, 7-Eleven, Dr Pepper, Oracle, Royal Purple motor oil, and Symantec's Norton software signed on as "promotional partners," issuing products with the *Iron Man* logo imprinted somewhere on the product or in its advertising. In effect, all of American commerce was selling the franchise. All of American commerce sells every franchise.

Iron Man movies have a lighter touch than many comparable blockbusters—for instance, the clangorous *Transformer* movies, which are themselves based on plastic toys, in which dark whirling digital masses barge into each other or thresh their way through buildings, cities, and people, and at which the moviegoer, sitting in the theater, feels as if his head were repeatedly being smashed against a wall. The *Iron Man* movies have been shaped around the temperament of their self-deprecating star, Robert Downey Jr., an actor who manages to convey, in the midst of a $200-million super-production, a private sense of amusement. By slightly distancing himself from the material, this charming rake offers the grown-up audience a sense of complicity, which saves it from self-contempt. Like so many big digital movies, the *Iron Man* films engage in a daringly flirtatious give-and-take with their own inconsequence: the disproportion between the size of the productions, with their huge sets and digital battles, and the puniness of any meaning that can possibly be extracted from them, may, for the audience, be part of the frivolous pleasure of seeing them.

Many big films (not just the ones based on Marvel Comics) are now soaked in what can only be called corporate irony, a mad discrepancy between size and significance—for instance, Christopher Nolan's widely admired *Inception,* which generates an extraordinarily complicated structure devoted to little but its own workings. Despite its dream layers, the movie is not really about dreams—the action you see on screen feels nothing like dreams. An industrialist hires experts to invade the dreaming mind of another industrialist in order to plant emotions that would cause the second man to change corporate plans. Or something like that; the plot is a little vague. Anyway, why should we care? What is at stake?

You could say, I suppose, that the movie is about different levels of representation, and then refine that observation and observe that the differences between fiction and reality, between subjective and objective, no longer exist—that what Nolan created is somehow analogous to our life in a postmodernist society in which the image and the real, the simulacrum and the original, have assumed, for many people, equal weight. (The literary and media theorist Fredric Jameson has made such a case for the movie.) You can say all of that, but you still haven't established why such an academic-spectacular exercise is worth looking at as a work of narrative art, or why any of it matters emotionally.

Nolan's movie was a whimsical, overarticulate nullity—a huge fancy clock that displays wheels and gears but somehow fails to tell the time. Yet *Inception* is nothing more than the logical product of a recent trend in which big movies have been progressively drained of sense. As much as two-thirds of the box office for these big films now comes from overseas, and the studios appear to have concluded that if a movie were actually *about* something, it might risk offending some part of the worldwide audience. Aimed at Bangkok and Bangalore as much as at Bangor, our big movies have been defoliated of character, wit, psychology, local color.

I do not hate all overscaled digital work. "God works too slowly," said Ian McKellen in *X-Men,* playing Magneto, who can produce mutations on the spot. So can digital filmmakers, who play God at will. Digital moviemaking is the art of transformation, and in the hands of a few imaginative people it has produced sequences of great loveliness and shivery terror—the literally mercurial reconstituted beings in *Terminator 2,* the floating high-chic battles in *The Matrix.* I loved the luscious purple beauty of *Avatar,* but

Avatar is off the scale in visual allure, and so is Alfonso Cuarón's *Harry Potter and the Prisoner of Azkaban,* the best of the Potter series.

Apart from these movies and a few others, however, many of us have logged deadly hours watching superheroes bashing people off walls, cars leapfrogging one another in tunnels, giant toys and mock-dragons smashing through Chicago, and charming teens whooshing around castles. What we see in bad digital action movies has the anti-Newtonian physics of a cartoon, but drawn with real figures. Rushed, jammed, broken, and overloaded, action now produces temporary sensation rather than emotion and engagement. Afterward these sequences fade into blurs, the different blurs themselves melding into one another—a vague memory of having been briefly excited rather than the enduring contentment of scenes playing again and again in one's head.

The oversized weightlessness leaves one numbed, defeated. Surely rage would seem an excessive response to movies so enormously trivial. Yet the overall trend is enraging. Fantasy is moving into all kinds of adventure and romantic movies; time travel has become a commonplace. At this point the fantastic is chasing human temperament and destiny—what we used to call drama—from the movies. The merely human has been transcended. And if the illusion of physical reality is unstable, the emotional framework of movies has changed, too, and for the worse. In time—a very short time—the fantastic, not the illusion of reality, may become the default mode of cinema.

Yes, of course, the studios, with greater or lesser degrees of 15 enthusiasm, make other things besides spectacles—thrillers and horror movies; chick flicks and teen romances; comedies with Adam Sandler, Will Ferrell, Jennifer Aniston, Katherine Heigl, and Cameron Diaz; burlesque-hangover debauches and their female equivalents; animated pictures for families. All these movies have an assured audience (or one at least mostly assured), and a few of them, especially the Pixar animated movies, may be very good. The studios will also distribute an interesting movie if their financing partners pay for most of it. And at the end of the year, as the Oscars loom, they distribute unadventurous but shrewdly written and played movies, such as *The Fighter,* which are made entirely by someone else. Again and again these *serioso* films win honors, but for the most part, the studios, except as distributors, don't want to get involved in them. Why not? Because they are "execution dependent"—that is, in order to succeed, they have to be good. It has come to this: a movie studio can no longer risk making good movies. Their business model depends on the assured audience and the blockbuster. It has done so for years and will continue to do so for years more. Nothing is going to stop the success of *The Avengers* from laying waste to the movies as an art form. The big revenues from such pictures rarely get siphoned into more adventurous projects; they get poured into the next sequel or a new franchise. Pretending otherwise is sheer denial.

2.

I can hear the retorts. If such inexpensive movies as *Please Give* (or *Winter's Bone,* an even better movie, which also came out in 2010, or *Beasts of the Southern Wild*) still get made, and they have an appreciative audience, however small; if directors such as Martin Scorsese and Steven Soderbergh and David O. Russell and Kathryn Bigelow and Noah Baumbach and David Fincher and Wes Anderson are doing interesting things within the system; if Terrence Malick can make a lyrical masterpiece such as *The Tree of Life*; if the edges of the industry are soulfully alive even as the center is mostly an algorithm for making money—if all of this is so, then why get steamed over the *Iron Man* or *Transformers* franchises?

The reason is this: not everything a film artist wants to say can be said with $3 million. Artists who want to work with, say, $30 million (still a moderate amount of money by Hollywood standards) often have an impossible time getting their movies made. At this writing, Paul Thomas Anderson (*There Will Be Blood*), one of the most talented men in Hollywood, has finished his Scientology movie, *The Master,* but it took years of pleading to get the money to do it. (An heiress came to his rescue.) After making *Capote,* Bennett Miller was idle for six years before making *Moneyball.* Alexander Payne had to wait seven years (after *Sideways*) before making *The Descendants.* Alfonso Cuarón hasn't brought out a movie since the brilliant *Children of Men* in 2006. Guillermo del Toro, the gifted man who made *Pan's Labyrinth,* is also having trouble getting money for his projects. By studio standards, there isn't a big enough audience for their movies: they can work if they want to, but only on very small budgets. You cannot mourn an unmade project, but you can feel its absence through the long stretches of an inane season.

And why isn't there a big enough audience for art? Consider that in recent years the major studios have literally gamed the system. American children—boys, at least—play video games, and read comic books and graphic novels. Latching onto those tastes, Disney purchased Marvel Comics for $4 billion, which gives it the right to make Marvel's superhero comic book characters into movies. Paramount has its own deal with Marvel for the Captain America character and others. Time Warner now owns DC Comics, and Warner Bros. will make an endless stream of movies based on DC Comics characters (the Superman, Batman, and Green Lantern pictures are just the beginning). For years, all the studios have tried to adapt video games into movies, often with disastrous results. So Warner Bros. went the logical next step: it bought a video game company, which is developing new games that the studio will later make into films.

"Give me the children until they are seven, and anyone may have them afterwards," Francis Xavier, one of the early Jesuits, is supposed to have said. The studios grab boys when they are seven, eight, or nine, command a corner of their hearts, and hold them with franchise sequels and product tie-ins for fifteen years. The *Twilight* series of teen vampire movies, which deliciously sell sex without sex—romantic danger without fornication—caught girls in the same way at a slightly older age. *The Hunger Games* franchise will be with us for years. In brief, the studios are not merely servicing the tastes of the young audience; they are also continuously creating the audience to whom they want to sell. (They have tied their fortunes to the birth rate.) Which raises an inevitable question: will these constantly created new audiences, arising from infancy with all their faculties intact but their expectations already defined—these potential *moviegoers*—will they ever develop a taste for narrative, for character, for suspense, for acting, for irony, for wit, for drama? Isn't it possible that they will be so hooked on sensation that anything without extreme action and fantasy will just seem lifeless and dead to them?

Apart from that dolorous autumn-leaves season (the Holocaust, 20 troubled marriages, raging families, self-annihilating artists), American movies during the rest of the year largely abandon older audiences, leaving them to wander about like downsized workers. Many gratefully retreat into television, where producer-writers such as David Chase, Aaron Sorkin, David Simon, and David Milch now enjoy the same freedom and status, at HBO, as the Coppola-Scorsese generation of movie directors forty years ago. Cable television has certainly opened a space for somber realism, such as *The Wire*, and satirical realism, such as *Mad Men* and Lena Dunham's mock-depressive, urban-dejection series *Girls*. But television cannot be the answer to what ails movies. I have been ravished in recent years by things possible only in movies—by Paul Thomas Anderson's *There Will Be Blood*, Julian Schnabel's *The Diving Bell and the Butterfly*, and Malick's *The Tree of Life*, which refurbished the tattered language of film. Such films as *Sideways*, *The Squid and the Whale*, and *Capote* have a fineness, a nuanced subtlety, that would come off awkwardly on television. Would that there were more of them.

The intentional shift in large-scale movie production away from adults is a sad betrayal and a minor catastrophe. Among other things, it has killed a lot of the culture of the movies. By culture, I do not mean film festivals, film magazines, and cinephile Internet sites and bloggers, all of which are flourishing. I mean that blessedly saturated mental state of moviegoing, both solitary and social, half dreamy, half critical, maybe amused, but also sometimes awed, that fuels a living art form. Moviegoing is both a private and a sociable affair—a strangers-at-barbecues, cocktail-party affair, the common coin of everyday discourse. In the fall season there may be a number of good things to see, and so, for adult audiences, the habit may flicker to life again. If you have seen one of the five interesting movies currently playing, then you need to see the other four so you can join the dinner-party conversation. If there is only one, as there is most of the year, you may skip it without feeling you are missing much.

These observations annoy many people, including some of the smartest people I know, particularly men in their late forties and younger, who have grown up with pop culture dominated by the conglomerates and don't know anything else. They don't disagree, exactly, but they find all of this tiresome and beside the point. They accept the movies as a kind of environment, a constant stream. There are just movies, you see, movies always and forever, and of course many of them will be uninspiring, and always have been. Critics, chalking the score on the blackboard, think of large-scale American moviemaking as a system in which a few talented people, in order to make something good, struggle against discouragement or seduction; but for my young media-hip friends, this view is pure melodrama. They see the movies not as a moral and aesthetic battleground, but as a media game that can be played either shrewdly or stupidly. There is no serious difference for them between making a piece of clanging, over-wrought, mock-nihilistic digital roughhouse for $200 million and a personal independent film for $2 million. They are not looking for art, and they do not want to be associated with commercial failure; it irritates them in some way; it makes them feel like losers. If I say that the huge budgets and profits are mucking up movie aesthetics, changing the audience, burning away other movies, they look at me with a slight smile and say something like this: "There's a market for this stuff. People are going. Their needs are being satisfied. If they didn't like these movies, they wouldn't go."

But who knows if needs are being satisfied? The audience goes because the movies are there, not because anyone necessarily loves them. My friends' attitudes are defined so completely by the current movie market that they do not wish to hear that movies, for the first eighty years of their existence, were essentially made for adults. Sure, there were always films for families and children, but, for the most part, ten-year-olds and teens were dragged by their parents to what the parents wanted to see, and this was true well after television reduced the size of the adult audience. The kids saw, and half understood, a satire such as *Dr. Strangelove,* an earnest social drama such as *To Kill a Mockingbird,* a cheesy disaster movie such as *Airport,* and that process of half understanding, half not, may have been part of growing up; it also laid the soil for their own enjoyment of grown-up movies years later. They were not expected to remain in a state of goofy euphoria until they were thirty-five. My friends think that our current situation is normal. They believe that critics are naïve blowhards, but it is they who are naïve.

3.

To understand what is so strange about big movies now, you have to remember a little of what movies once were and what audiences once wanted from them—how stories were told in different periods, how movies were put together. We are now trapped by an exasperating irony: employing all the devastating means at their command, movies have in some ways gone back to their crudest beginnings and are determined, perhaps, to stay there forever, or at least as long as the box-office and ancillary-market mother lode holds out.

A long time ago, at a university far away, I taught film, and I did what many teachers have no doubt done before and since: I tried to develop film aesthetics for the students as a historical progression toward narrative. After all, many of the first movies in the 1890s were not stories at all, but just views of things—a train coming into a station, a wave breaking toward the camera. These visual astonishments caused the audience to stare open-mouthed or duck under the seats for cover (or so the legend says, preserved recently in Scorsese's *Hugo*). I wanted my students to be astonished, too—to enjoy the development of film technique as a triumph of artistic and technical consciousness. I worked in straight chronological order, moving from those early "views" through Edwin S. Porter's 1903 experiments in linear sequencing in films such as *Life of an American Fireman* and *The Great Train Robbery* and then on through D. W. Griffith's consolidation a few years later of an actual syntax—long and medium shots, close-ups, flashbacks, parallel editing, and the like.

But I now think there was something merely convenient in teaching that way. The implication of my lesson plan was that the medium had by degrees come to a realization of itself, discovering in those early years—say, 1895 to 1915—its own true nature embedded within its technology: the leafy oak of narrative lodged within the acorn of celluloid. It is a teleological view, and it is probably false. In truth, there is nothing inherent in the process of exposing strips of film to light sixteen or eighteen times a second (later twenty-four times) that demanded the telling of a story.

At the beginning, after the views of trains and oceans, movies offered burlesque skits or excerpts from theatrical events, but still no stories. A completed movie was often just a single, fixed, long-lasting shot. It is likely, as David Bordwell, Janet Staiger, and Kristin Thompson explained in *The Classical Hollywood Cinema*, that narrative emerged less from the inherent nature of film than from the influence of older forms—novels and short stories and plays. And also from pressure to create work of greater power to attract more and more customers.

If creating fictions is not encoded in the DNA of film, then what is happening now has a kind of grisly logic to it. As the narrative and dramatic powers of movies fall into abeyance, and many big movies turn into sheer spectacle, with only a notional pass at plot or characterization, we are returning with much greater power to capers and larks that were originally performed in innocence. The kind of primitive chase, for instance, that in 1905 depended on some sort of accident or mischief rather than on character or plot has been succeeded by the endless up-in-the-air digital fight. The 1905 scene has a harum-scarum looseness and wit; the destructive action scenes in movies now are brought off with a kind of grim, faceless glee, an exultation in power and mass: We can do it, therefore we will do it, and our ability to do it is the meaning of it, and even if you're not impressed, it is still going to roll over you.

Sparked, perhaps, by the absence of sound, filmmakers developed the visual possibilities of film very quickly, and by the end of World War I the vocabulary of editing and the overall strategy of Hollywood moviemaking was set. Celluloid may not have carried storytelling in its genes, but, as David Bordwell puts it, "telling a story is the basic formal concern which makes the film studio resemble the monastery's scriptorium, the site of the transcription and transmission of countless narratives." In the scriptorium, an unspoken vow was repeated daily: audiences need to get emotionally involved in a story in order to enjoy themselves. The idea is so obvious that it seems absurd to spell it out. Yet in recent years this assumption, and everything that follows from it, have begun to weaken and even to disappear.

It is shocking to be reminded of some of the things that are now slipping away: that whatever is introduced in a tale has to mean something, and that one thing should inevitably lead to another; that events are foreshadowed and then echoed, and that tension rises steadily through a series of minor climaxes to a final, grand climax; that music should be created not just as an enforcer of mood but as the outward sign of an emotional or narrative logic; that characterization should be consistent; that a character's destiny is supposed to have some moral and spiritual meaning—the wicked punished, the virtuous rewarded or at least sanctified. It was a fictional world of total accountability.

The structure of the movie business—the shaping of production decisions by marketing—has kicked bloody hell out of the language of film. But the business framework is not operating alone. Film, a photographic and digital medium, is perhaps more vulnerable than any of the other arts to the postmodernist habits of recycling and quotation. Imitation, pastiche, and collage have become dominant strategies, and there is an excruciating paradox in this development: two of the sprightly media forms derived from movies—commercials and music videos—began to dominate movies. The art experienced a case of blowback.

As everyone knows, we can read an image much more quickly than anyone thought possible forty years ago, and in recent years many commercials have been cut faster and faster. The filmmakers know that we are not so much receiving information as getting a visual impression, a mood, a desire. A truly hip commercial has no obvious connection to the product being sold, though selling is still its job. What, then, is being sold at a big movie that is cut the same way? The experience of going to the movie itself, the sensation of being rushed, dizzied, overwhelmed by the images. Michael Bay wasn't interested in what happened at Pearl Harbor. He was interested in his whizzing fantasia of the event. Nothing important happens in *The Avengers*. As in half of these big movies, the world is about to end because of some invading force; but the world is always about to end in digital spectacles, and when everything is at stake, nothing is at stake. The larger the movie, the more "content" becomes incidental, even disposable.

In recent years, some of the young movie directors have come out of commercials and MTV. If a director is just starting out in feature films, he doesn't have to be paid much, and the studios can throw a script at him with the assumption that the movie, if nothing else, will have a great "look." He has already produced that look in his commercials or videos, which he shoots on film and then finishes digitally—adding or subtracting color, changing the sky, putting in flame or mist, retarding or speeding up movement. In a commercial for a new car, the blue-tinted streets rumble and crack, trees give up their roots, and the silver SUV, cool as a titanium cucumber, rides over the steaming fissures. Wow! What a filmmaker! Studio executives or production executives who get financing from studios do not have to instruct such a young director to cut a feature very fast and put in a lot of thrills, because for their big movies they hire only the kind of people who will cut it fast and put in thrills. That the young director has never worked with a serious dramatic structure, or even with actors, may not be considered a liability.

The results are there to see. At the risk of obviousness: techniques that hold your eye in a commercial or video are not suited to telling stories or building dramatic tension. In a full-length movie, images conceived that way begin to cancel each other out or just slip off the screen; the characters are just types or blurred spots of movement. The links with fiction and theater and classical film technique have been broken. The center no longer holds; mere anarchy is loosed upon the screen; the movie winds up a mess.

So are American movies finished, a cultural irrelevance? Despite almost everything, I don't think the game is up, not by any means. There are talented directors who manage to keep working either within the system or just on the edges of it. Some of the independent films that have succeeded, against the odds, in gaining funding and at least minimal traction in the theaters, are obvious signs of hope. Terence Malick is alive and working hard. Digital is still in its infancy, and if it moves into the hands of people who have a more imaginative and delicate sense of spectacle, it could bloom in any one of a dozen ways. The micro-budget movies now made on the streets or in living rooms might also take off if they give up on sub-Cassavetes ideas of improvisation, and accept the necessity of a script. There is enough talent sloshing around in the troubled vessel of American movies to keep the art form alive. But the trouble is real, and it has been growing for more than twenty-five years. By now there is a wearying, numbing, infuriating sameness to the cycle of American releases year after year. Much of the time, adults cannot find anything to see. And that reason alone is enough to make us realize that American movies are in a terrible crisis, which is not going to end soon.

For Discussion and Writing

1. **Comprehension**   How does Denby define the phrase "the culture of the movies" (par. 21)? Why is it important to his argument?

2. **Critical Reading**   How does the writer view his **audience**? How can you tell? Where in the essay does he address possible counter-arguments—and how effectively does he do so?

3. **Analysis**   According to Denby, "the fantastic is chasing human temperament and destiny—what we used to call drama—from the movies" (par. 14). What do you think he means by this assertion? Do you agree? How is the claim related to his larger point?

4. **Connections**   How are Denby's argument, tone, and writing situation similar to those of Saul Austerlitz in "The Pernicious Rise of Poptimism" (p. 240)? How are they different?

5. **Writing**   Denby writes, "In brief, the studios are not merely servicing the tastes of the young audience; they are also continuously creating the audience to whom they want to sell. . . . will [these audiences] ever develop a taste for narrative, for character, for suspense, for acting, for irony, for wit, for drama? Isn't it possible that they will be so hooked on sensation that anything without extreme action and fantasy will just seem lifeless and dead to them?" (par. 19). In a persuasive essay, address Denby's questions about the future of film.

CONTENT MARKETING ASSOCIATION

Seven Steps to the Perfect Story

The Content Marketing Association (CMA) is an organization that represents the publishing and content marketing agencies in the United Kingdom. The CMA provides research, education, training, and other services to its member companies. One such service addresses the popular trend of creating infographics, which often depict data visually to engage customers and spread the information or brand by going viral on social networks. This infographic, which originally appeared on the CMA's blog, breaks down plot, characters, and other elements of storytelling into specific categories.

As you read, *reflect on the reasons an organization focused on marketing and branding might be interested in the elements of powerful storytelling: What are the fundamental elements of plot? How does the infographic incorporate examples to support its claims? Do you think these visual representations are more effective than a straightforward explanation in prose? Why or why not?*

From structure and plot to heroes and characters, your story must have everything in place if it's to connect with the reader. Follow our guide to storytelling success.

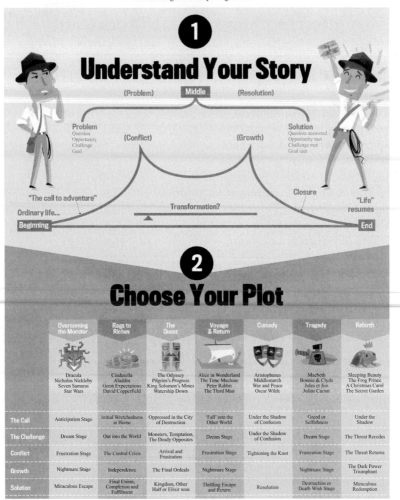

Understand Your Story

(Problem)   Middle   (Resolution)

Problem
Question
Opportunity
Challenge
Goal

(Conflict)

(Growth)

Solution
Question answered
Opportunity met
Challenge met
Goal met

"The call to adventure"
Ordinary life...
Beginning

Transformation?

Closure

"Life" resumes
End

Choose Your Plot

	Overcoming the Monster	Rags to Riches	The Quest	Voyage & Return	Comedy	Tragedy	Rebirth
	Dracula Nicholas Nickleby Seven Samurai Star Wars	Cinderella Aladdin Great Expectations David Copperfield	The Odyssey Pilgrim's Progress King Solomon's Mines Watership Down	Alice in Wonderland The Time Machine Peter Rabbit The Third Man	Aristophanes Middlemarch War and Peace Oscar Wilde	Macbeth Bonnie & Clyde Jules et Jim Julius Caesar	Sleeping Beauty The Frog Prince A Christmas Carol The Secret Garden
The Call	Anticipation Stage	Initial Wretchedness at Home	Oppressed in the City of Destruction	'Fall' into the Other World	Under the Shadow of Confusion	Greed or Selfishness	Under the Shadow
The Challenge	Dream Stage	Out into the World	Monsters, Temptation, The Deady Opposites	Dream Stage	Under the Shadow of Confusion	Dream Stage	The Threat Recedes
Conflict	Frustration Stage	The Central Crisis	Arrival and Frustration	Frustration Stage	Tightening the Knot	Frustration Stage	The Threat Returns
Growth	Nightmare Stage	Independence	The Final Ordeals	Nightmare Stage		Nightmare Stage	The Dark Power Triumphant
Solution	Miraculous Escape	Final Union, Completion and Fulfilment	Kingdom, Other Half or Elixir won	Thrilling Escape and Return	Resolution	Destruction or Death Wish Stage	Miraculous Redemption

continued

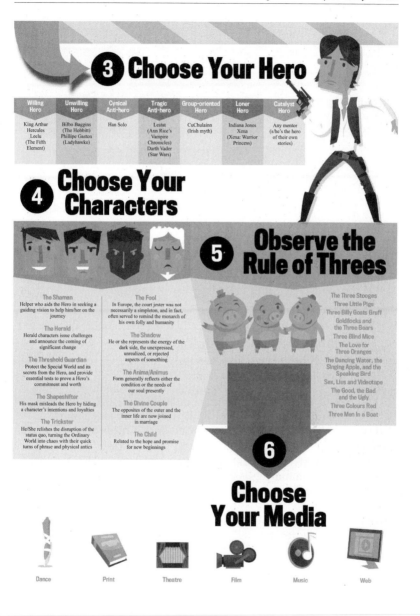

3 Choose Your Hero

Willing Hero	Unwilling Hero	Cynical Anti-hero	Tragic Anti-hero	Group-oriented Hero	Loner Hero	Catalyst Hero
King Arthur Hercules Leelu (The Fifth Element)	Bilbo Baggins (The Hobbitt) Phillipe Gaston (Ladyhawke)	Han Solo	Lestat (Ann Rice's Vampire Chronicles) Darth Vader (Star Wars)	CuChulainn (Irish myth)	Indiana Jones Xena (Xena: Warrior Princess)	Any mentor (s/he's the hero of their own stories)

4 Choose Your Characters

5 Observe the Rule of Threes

The Shaman
Helper who aids the Hero in seeking a guiding vision to help him/her on the journey

The Herald
Herald characters issue challenges and announce the coming of significant change

The Threshold Guardian
Protect the Special World and its secrets from the Hero, and provide essential tests to prove a Hero's commitment and worth

The Shapeshifter
His mask misleads the Hero by hiding a character's intentions and loyalties

The Trickster
He/She relishes the disruption of the status quo, turning the Ordinary World into chaos with their quick turns of phrase and physical antics

The Fool
In Europe, the court jester was not necessarily a simpleton, and in fact, often served to remind the monarch of his own folly and humanity

The Shadow
He or she represents the energy of the dark side, the unexpressed, unrealized, or rejected aspects of something

The Anima/Animus
Form generally reflects either the condition or the needs of our soul presently

The Divine Couple
The opposites of the outer and the inner life are now joined in marriage

The Child
Related to the hope and promise for new beginnings

The Three Stooges
Three Little Pigs
Three Billy Goats Gruff
Goldilocks and the Three Bears
Three Blind Mice
The Love for Three Oranges
The Dancing Water, the Singing Apple, and the Speaking Bird
Sex, Lies and Videotape
The Good, the Bad and the Ugly
Three Colours Red
Three Men In a Boat

6 Choose Your Media

Dance	Print	Theatre	Film	Music	Web

continued

Source: Visual Portrait of a Story, adapted by Ohler, J. (2001) from Dillingham, B. (2001).

For Discussion and Writing

1. **Comprehension** What plot genres does the infographic provide?

2. **Critical Reading** The infographic's **structure** is a sequence of seven steps. Do you think the order of the steps matters? Could the steps be arranged in a different order? Explain your answer.

3. **Analysis** According to the infographic, writers should follow the Golden Rule (step 7), which is a quotation from *WALL-E* director Andrew Stanton: "Don't give the audience 4, give them 2 plus 2." How do you interpret this advice? What does it mean? Do you agree?

4. **Connections** Like "Seven Steps to the Perfect Story," Linda Seger's "Creating the Myth" (p. 367) explores how archetypal characters and plots function in movies. Where do you see overlap between the two selections? In what ways does the infographic challenge, revise, or complicate Seger's explanations?

5. **Writing** The infographic provides specific examples to illustrate the elements of the "perfect" story. Choose your own example from film, fiction, or television, and then use the infographic's claims and categories to analyze it. Does it complicate the "steps" in any way, or fall outside the infographic's analysis? Explain your answer in an essay, blog post, or multimedia presentation.

LINDA SEGER

Creating the Myth

Dr. Linda Seger is a script consultant, author of twelve books—nine on screenwriting—and an international speaker on the subject of screenwriting. Her books include Creating Unforgettable Characters *(1990),* The Art of Adaptation: Turning Fact and Fiction into Film *(1992), and* When Women Call the Shots: The Developing Power and Influence of Women in Television and Film *(1996). In the following excerpt from* Making a Good Script Great *(1987), Seger reveals the archetypal characters and mythic narratives that underlie popular movies such as* Star Wars. *According to the writer, "Many of the most successful films are based on these universal stories."*

As you read, *think about the enduring appeal of these mythic characters and plots despite their familiarity: Why do we identify with mythic heroes? Does her analysis still apply to contemporary films? How does Seger organize and structure her essay?*

All of us have similar experiences. We share in the life journey of growth, development, and transformation. We live the same stories, whether they involve the search for a perfect mate, coming home, the search for fulfillment, going after an ideal, achieving the dream, or hunting for a precious treasure. Whatever our culture, there are universal stories that form the basis for all our particular stories. The trappings might be different, the twists and turns that create suspense might change from culture to culture, the particular characters may take different forms, but underneath it all, it's the same story, drawn from the same experiences.

Many of the most successful films are based on these universal stories. They deal with the basic journey we take in life. We identify with the heroes because we were once heroic (descriptive) or because we wish we could do what the hero does (prescriptive). When Joan Wilder finds the jewel and saves her sister, or James

Bond saves the world, or Shane saves the family from the evil ranchers, we identify with the character, and subconsciously recognize the story as having some connection with our own lives. It's the same story as the fairy tales about getting the three golden hairs from the devil, or finding the treasure and winning the princess. And it's not all that different a story from the caveman killing the woolly beast or the Roman slave gaining his freedom through skill and courage. These are our stories—personally and collectively—and the most successful films contain these universal experiences.

Some of these stories are "search" stories. They address our desire to find some kind of rare and wonderful treasure. This might include the search for outer values such as job, relationship, or success; or for inner values such as respect, security, self-expression, love, or home. But it's all a similar search.

Some of these stories are "hero" stories. They come from our own experiences of overcoming adversity, as well as our desire to do great and special acts. We root for the hero and celebrate when he or she achieves the goal because we know that the hero's journey is in many ways similar to our own.

We call these stories *myths*. Myths are the common stories at 5 the root of our universal existence. They're found in all cultures and in all literature, ranging from the Greek myths to fairy tales, legends, and stories drawn from all of the world's religions.

A myth is a story that is "more than true." Many stories are true because one person, somewhere, at some time, lived it. It is based on fact. But a myth is more than true because it is lived by all of us, at some level. It's a story that connects and speaks to us all.

Some myths are true stories that attain mythic significance because the people involved seem larger than life, and seem to live their lives more intensely than common folk. Martin Luther King Jr., Gandhi, Sir Edmund Hillary, and Lord Mountbatten personify the types of journeys we identify with, because we've taken similar journeys—even if only in a very small way.

Other myths revolve around make-believe characters who might capsulize for us the sum total of many of our journeys. Some of these make-believe characters might seem similar to the characters we meet in our dreams. Or they might be a composite of types of characters we've met.

In both cases, the myth is the "story beneath the story." It's the universal pattern that shows us that Gandhi's journey toward independence and Sir Edmund Hillary's journey to the top of Mount Everest contain many of the same dramatic beats. And these beats are the same beats that Rambo takes to set free the MIAs, that Indiana Jones takes to find the Lost Ark, and that Luke Skywalker takes to defeat the Evil Empire.

In *Hero with a Thousand Faces,* Joseph Campbell traces the elements that form the hero myth. In their own work with myth, writer Chris Vogler and seminar leader Thomas Schlesinger have applied this criteria to *Star Wars.* The myth within the story helps explain why millions went to see this film again and again."

The hero myth has specific story beats that occur in all hero stories. They show who the hero is, what the hero needs, and how the story and character interact in order to create a transformation. The journey toward heroism is a process. This universal process forms the spine of all the particular stories, such as the *Star Wars* trilogy.

THE HERO MYTH

1. In most hero stories, the hero is introduced in ordinary surroundings, in a mundane world, doing mundane things. Generally, the hero begins as a nonhero: innocent, young, simple, or humble. In *Star Wars,* the first time we see Luke Skywalker, he's unhappy about having to do his chores, which consist of picking out some new droids for work. He wants to go out and have fun. He wants to leave his planet and go to the Academy, but he's stuck. This is the setup of most myths. This is how we meet the hero before the call to adventure.

2. Then something new enters the hero's life. It's a catalyst that sets the story in motion. It might be a telephone call, as in *Romancing the Stone,* or the German attack in *The African Queen,* or the holograph of Princess Leia in *Star Wars.* Whatever form it takes, it's a new ingredient that pushes the hero into an extraordinary adventure. With this call, the stakes are established, and a problem is introduced that demands a solution.

© 20th Century Fox/Photofest

Seger writes, "A myth is a story that is 'more than true.'" What specific aspects of the "Hero Myth" do Obi-Wan Kenobi and Luke Skywalker illustrate?

3. Many times, however, the hero doesn't want to leave. He or she is a reluctant hero, afraid of the unknown, uncertain, perhaps, if he or she is up to the challenge. In *Star Wars,* Luke receives a double call to adventure. First, from Princess Leia in the holograph, and then through Obi-Wan Kenobi, who says he needs Luke's help. But Luke is not ready to go. He returns home, only to find that the Imperial Stormtroopers have burned his farmhouse and slaughtered his family. Now he is personally motivated, ready to enter into the adventure.

4. In any journey, the hero usually receives help, and the help often comes from unusual sources. In many fairy tales, an old woman, a dwarf, a witch, or a wizard helps the hero. The hero achieves the goal because of this help, and because the hero is receptive to what this person has to give.

   There are a number of fairy tales where the first and second son are sent to complete a task, but they ignore the helpers, often scorning them. Many times they are severely punished for their lack of humility and unwillingness to

15

accept help. Then the third son, the hero, comes along. He receives the help, accomplishes the task, and often wins the princess.

In *Star Wars,* Obi-Wan Kenobi is a perfect example of the "helper" character. He is a kind of mentor to Luke, one who teaches him the Way of the Force and whose teachings continue even after his death. This mentor character appears in most hero stories. He is the person who has special knowledge, special information, and special skills. This might be the prospector in *The Treasure of the Sierra Madre,* or the psychiatrist in *Ordinary People,* or Quint in *Jaws,* who knows all about sharks, or the Good Witch of the North who gives Dorothy the ruby slippers in *The Wizard of Oz.* In *Star Wars,* Obi-Wan gives Luke the light saber that was the special weapon of the Jedi Knight. With this, Luke is ready to move forward to do his training and meet adventure.

5. The hero is now ready to move into the special world where he or she will change from the ordinary into the extraordinary. This starts the hero's transformation, and sets up the obstacles that must be surmounted to reach the goal. Usually, this happens at the first Turning Point of the story, and leads into Act Two development. In *Star Wars,* Obi-Wan and Luke search for a pilot to take them to the planet of Alderaan, so that Obi-Wan can deliver the plans to Princess Leia's father. These plans are essential to the survival of the Rebel Forces. With this action, the adventure is ready to begin.

6. Now begin all the tests and obstacles necessary to overcome the enemy and accomplish the hero's goals. In fairy tales, this often means getting past witches, outwitting the devil, avoiding robbers, or confronting evil. In Homer's *Odyssey,* it means blinding the Cyclops, escaping from the island of the Lotus-Eaters, resisting the temptation of the singing Sirens, and surviving a shipwreck. In *Star Wars,* innumerable adventures confront Luke. He and his cohorts must run to the *Millennium Falcon,* narrowly escaping the Stormtroopers before jumping into hyperspace. They must make it through the meteor shower after Alderaan has been destroyed. They must evade capture on the Death Star, rescue the Princess, and even survive a garbage crusher.

7. At some point in the story, the hero often hits rock bottom. 20
He often has a "death experience," leading to a type of
rebirth. In *Star Wars*, Luke seems to have died when the
serpent in the garbage-masher pulls him under, but he's
saved just in time to ask R2D2 to stop the masher before
they're crushed. This is often the "black moment" at the
second turning point, the point when the worst is con-
fronted, and the action now moves toward the exciting
conclusion.

8. Now, the hero seizes the sword and takes possession of the
treasure. He is now in charge, but he still has not completed
the journey. Here Luke has the Princess and the plans, but
the final confrontation is yet to begin. This starts the third-
act escape scene, leading to the final climax.

9. The road back is often the chase scene. In many fairy tales,
this is the point where the devil chases the hero and the
hero has the last obstacles to overcome before really being
free and safe. His challenge is to take what he has learned
and integrate it into his daily life. He *must* return to renew
the mundane world. In *Star Wars*, Darth Vader is in hot
pursuit, planning to blow up the Rebel Planet.

10. Since every hero story is essentially a transformation story,
we need to see the hero changed at the end, resurrected into
a new type of life. He must face the final ordeal before being
"reborn" as the hero, proving his courage and becoming
transformed. This is the point, in many fairy tales, where
the Miller's Son becomes the Prince or the King and marries
the Princess. In *Star Wars*, Luke has survived, becoming
quite a different person from the innocent young man he
was in Act One.

   At this point, the hero returns and is reintegrated into his
society. In *Star Wars*, Luke has destroyed the Death Star, and
he receives his great reward.

This is the classic "Hero Story." We might call this example a *mis-* 25
sion or *task myth*, where the person has to complete a task, but
the task itself is not the real treasure. The real reward for Luke is
the love of the Princess and the safe, new world he had helped
create.

A myth can have many variations. We see variations on this myth in James Bond films (although they lack much of the depth because the hero is not transformed), and in *The African Queen,* where Rose and Allnutt must blow up the *Louisa,* or in *Places in the Heart,* where Edna overcomes obstacles to achieve family stability.

The *treasure myth* is another variation on this theme, as seen in *Romancing the Stone.* In this story, Joan receives a map and a phone call which forces her into the adventure. She is helped by an American birdcatcher and a Mexican pickup truck driver. She overcomes the obstacles of snakes, the jungle, waterfalls, shootouts, and finally receives the treasure, along with the "prince."

Whether the hero's journey is for a treasure or to complete a task, the elements remain the same. The humble, reluctant hero is called to an adventure. The hero is helped by a variety of unique characters. S/he must overcome a series of obstacles that transform him or her in the process, and then faces the final challenge that draws on inner and outer resources.

THE HEALING MYTH

Although the hero myth is the most popular story, many myths involve healing. In these stories, some character is "broken" and must leave home to become whole again.

The universal experience behind these healing stories is our 30 psychological need for rejuvenation, for balance. The journey of the hero into exile is not all that different from the weekend in Palm Springs, or the trip to Hawaii to get away from it all, or lying still in a hospital bed for some weeks to heal. In all cases, something is out of balance and the mythic journey moves toward wholeness.

Being broken can take several forms. It can be physical, emotional, or psychological. Usually, it's all three. In the process of being exiled or hiding out in the forest, the desert, or even the Amish farm in *Witness,* the person becomes whole, balanced, and receptive to love. Love in these stories is both a healing force and a reward.

Think of John Book in *Witness.* In Act One, we see a frenetic, insensitive man, afraid of commitment, critical and unreceptive to the feminine influences in his life. John is suffering from an "inner wound" which he doesn't know about. When he receives an "outer wound" from a gunshot, it forces him into exile, which begins his process of transformation.

At the beginning of Act Two, we see John delirious and close to death. This is a movement into the unconscious, a movement from the rational, active police life of Act One into a mysterious, feminine, more intuitive world. Since John's "inner problem" is the lack of balance with his feminine side, this delirium begins the process of transformation.

Later in Act Two, we see John beginning to change. He moves from his highly independent life-style toward the collective, communal life of his Amish hosts. John now gets up early to milk the cows and to assist with the chores. He uses his carpentry skills to help with the barn building and to complete the birdhouse. Gradually, he begins to develop relationships with Rachel and her son, Samuel. John's life slows down and he becomes more receptive, learning important lessons about love. In Act Three, John finally sees that the feminine is worth saving, and throws down his gun to save Rachel's life. A few beats later, when he has the opportunity to kill Paul, he chooses a nonviolent response instead. Although John doesn't "win" the Princess, he has nevertheless "won" love and wholeness. By the end of the film, we can see that the John Book of Act Three is a different kind of person from the John Book of Act One. He has a different kind of comradeship with his fellow police officers, he's more relaxed, and we can sense that somehow, this experience has formed a more integrated John Book.

COMBINATION MYTHS

Many stories are combinations of several different myths. Think of *Ghostbusters*, a simple and rather outrageous comedy about three men saving the city of New York from ghosts. Now think of the story of "Pandora's Box." It's about the woman who let loose all manner of evil upon the earth by opening a box she was told not to touch. In *Ghostbusters*, the EPA man is a Pandora figure. By shutting off the power to the containment center, he inadvertently unleashes all the ghosts upon New York City. Combine the story of "Pandora's Box" with a hero story, and notice that we have our three heroes battling the Marshmallow Man. One of them also "gets the Princess" when Dr. Peter Venkman finally receives the affections of Dana Barrett. By looking at these combinations, it is apparent that even *Ghostbusters* is more than "just a comedy."

Tootsie is a type of reworking of many Shakespearean stories where a woman has to dress as a man in order to accomplish a certain task. These Shakespearean stories are reminiscent of many fairy tales where the hero becomes invisible or takes on another persona, or wears a specific disguise to hide his or her real qualities. In the stories of "The Twelve Dancing Princesses" or "The Man in the Bearskin," disguise is necessary to achieve a goal. Combine these elements with the transformation themes of the hero myth where a hero (such as Michael) must overcome many obstacles to his success as an actor and a human being. It's not difficult to understand why the *Tootsie* story hooks us.

ARCHETYPES

A myth includes certain characters that we see in many stories. These characters are called *archetypes*. They can be thought of as the original "pattern" or "character type" that will be found on the hero's journey. Archetypes take many forms, but they tend to fall within specific categories.

Earlier, we discussed some of the helpers who give advice to help the hero — such as the *wise old man* who possesses special knowledge and often serves as a mentor for the hero.

The female counterpart of the wise old man is the *good mother*. Whereas the wise old man has superior knowledge, the good mother is known for her nurturing qualities, and for her intuition. This figure often gives the hero particular objects to help on the journey. It might be a protective amulet, or the ruby slippers that Dorothy receives in *The Wizard of Oz* from the Good Witch of the North. Sometimes in fairy tales it's a cloak to make the person invisible, or ordinary objects that become extraordinary, as in "The Girl of Courage," an Afghan fairy tale about a maiden who receives a comb, a whetstone, and a mirror to help defeat the devil.

Many myths contain a *shadow figure*. This is a character who is   40
the opposite of the hero. Sometimes this figure helps the hero on
the journey; other times this figure opposes the hero. The shadow
figure can be the negative side of the hero which could be the
dark and hostile brother in "Cain and Abel," the stepsisters in
"Cinderella," or the Robber Girl in "The Snow Queen." The
shadow figure can also help the hero, as the whore with the heart
of gold who saves the hero's life, or provides balance to his idealization of woman.

Many myths contain *animal archetypes* that can be positive or
negative figures. In "St. George and the Dragon," the dragon is
the negative force which is a violent and ravaging animal, not
unlike the shark in *Jaws*. But in many stories, animals help the
hero. Sometimes there are talking donkeys, or a dolphin which
saves the hero, or magical horses or dogs.

The *trickster* is a mischievous archetypical figure who is always
causing chaos, disturbing the peace, and generally being an anar-
chist. The trickster uses wit and cunning to achieve his or her
ends. Sometimes the trickster is a harmless prankster or a "bad
boy" who is funny and enjoyable. More often, the trickster is a con
man, as in *The Sting,* or the devil, as in *The Exorcist,* who demanded
all the skills of the priest to outwit him. The "Till Eulenspigel"
stories revolve around the trickster, as do the Spanish picaresque
novels. Even the tales of Tom Sawyer have a trickster motif. In all
countries, there are stories that revolve around this figure, whose
job it is to outwit.

"MYTHIC" PROBLEMS AND SOLUTIONS

We all grew up with myths. Most of us heard or read fairy tales
when we were young. Some of us may have read Bible stories, or
stories from other religions or other cultures. These stories are
part of us. And the best way to work with them is to let them come
out naturally as you write the script.

Of course, some filmmakers are better at this than others.
George Lucas and Steven Spielberg have a strong sense of myth
and incorporate it into their films. They both have spoken about
their love of the stories from childhood, and of their desire to
bring these types of stories to audiences. Their stories create

some of the same sense of wonder and excitement as myths. Many of the necessary psychological beats are part of their stories, deepening the story beyond the ordinary action-adventure.

Myths bring depth to a hero story. If a filmmaker is thinking 45 only about the action and excitement of a story, audiences might fail to connect with the hero's journey. But if the basic beats of the hero's journey are evident, a film will often inexplicably draw audiences, in spite of critics' responses to the film.

Take *Rambo*, for instance. Why was this violent, simple story so popular with audiences? I don't think it was because everyone agreed with its politics. I do think Sylvester Stallone is a master at incorporating the American myth into his filmmaking. That doesn't mean it's done consciously. Somehow he is naturally in sync with the myth, and the myth becomes integrated into his stories.

Clint Eastwood also does hero stories, and gives us the adventure of the myth and the transformation of the myth. . . . Eastwood's films have given more attention to the transformation of the hero, and have been receiving more serious critical attention as a result.

All of these filmmakers—Lucas, Spielberg, Stallone, and Eastwood—dramatize the hero myth in their own particular ways. And all of them prove that myths are marketable.

APPLICATION

It is an important part of the writer's or producer's work to continually find opportunities for deepening the themes within a script. Finding the myth beneath the modern story is part of that process.

To find these myths, it's not a bad idea to reread some of 50 Grimm's fairy tales or fairy tales from around the world to begin to get acquainted with various myths. You'll start to see patterns and elements that connect with our own human experience.

Also, read Joseph Campbell and Greek mythology. If you're interested in Jungian psychology, you'll find many rich resources within a number of books on the subject. Since Jungian psychology deals with archetypes, you'll find many new characters to draw on for your own work.

With all of these resources to incorporate, it's important to remember that the myth is not a story to force upon a script. It's more a pattern which you can bring out in your stories when they seem to be heading in the direction of a myth.

As you work ask yourself:

> Do I have a myth working in my script? If so, what beats am I using of the hero's journey? Which ones seem to be missing?
>
> Am I missing characters? Do I need a mentor type? A wise old man? A wizard? Would one of these characters help dimensionalize the hero's journey?
>
> Could I create new emotional dimensions to the myth by starting my character as reluctant, naïve, simple, or decidedly "unheroic"?
>
> Does my character get transformed in the process of the journey?
>
> Have I used a strong three-act structure to support the myth, using the first turning point to move into the adventure and the second turning point to create a dark moment, or a reversal, or even a "near-death" experience?

Don't be afraid to create variations on the myth, but don't start with the myth itself. Let the myth grow naturally from your story. Developing myths are part of the rewriting process. If you begin with the myth, you'll find your writing becomes rigid, uncreative, and predictable. Working with the myth in the rewriting process will deepen your script, giving it new life as you find the story within the story.

For Discussion and Writing

1. **Comprehension** Seger writes that both Luke Skywalker and James Bond are examples of the hero myth. What is the significant difference between the two characters, according to the writer?

2. **Critical Reading** What is Seger's **purpose** and who is her intended **audience**, and how do you know?

3. **Analysis** Seger claims: "A myth is a story that is 'more than true.' Many stories are true because one person, somewhere, at some time, lived it. It is based on fact. But a myth is more than true because it is lived by all of us, at some level. It's a story that connects and speaks to us all" (par. 6). For the writer, these myths are useful. What is the relationship between "myth" and "fact"? How might "more than true" myths become problematic or have negative consequences outside the realm of screenwriting?

4. ***Connections***   In "The Asian Renovation of Biracial Buddy Action" (p. 380), Philippa Gates writes about the "mainstream myths" of action movies, focusing on racial and ethnic stereotypes in the context of clichéd "Hollywood formulas." Does Gates's analysis fit into Seger's taxonomy of myths? Do you think Seger's essay encourages formulaic writing and the use of stereotypes or "stock" characters? Does Seger provide advice for avoiding these problems?

5. ***Writing***   View a contemporary film and analyze the myths behind the story line and characters. You may also choose to write more generally about a group of films, and how they use myths—or even work against the conventional archetypes and plots Seger describes.

PHILIPPA GATES

The Asian Renovation of Biracial Buddy Action

Philippa Gates is an associate professor of film studies at Wilfrid Laurier University in Canada. She earned her undergraduate degree from the University of Toronto, and her M.A. and Ph.D. from the University of Exeter. She has written numerous scholarly articles on film and film history. Her books include Detecting Men: Masculinity and the Hollywood Detective Film *(2006) and* Detecting Women: Gender and the Hollywood Detective Film *(2011). With Lisa Funnell, she also coedited* Transnational Asian Identities in Pan-Pacific Cinemas: The Reel Asian Exchange *(2011). In this article, which was published in the* Journal of Popular Film and Television, *Gates writes about race and Asian identity in "buddy cop" action movies. She argues that these films thematize "transnational mediation between China and the Western world," proving that pop culture can be not only a reflection but an agent of globalization.*

***As you read,** consider the following questions: How has the biracial buddy cop film changed over the last three decades? Where—and how—does Gates incorporate the work of other film critics into her own article? In what ways do these action movies comment on America's international relations?*

The buddy cop film became a popular staple of Hollywood action film in the 1980s, highlighting the relationship between two heroes of contrasting backgrounds who—initially at odds—learn to respect one another and work together to defeat a common enemy. In the 1980s, the contrast was most often based on racial and class differences as in *48 Hrs.* (1982), *Beverly Hills Cop* (1984), and *Lethal Weapon* (1987) and their sequels. The biracial buddy formula allowed Hollywood to capitalize on a broader audience base—black and white—but it also reflected Hollywood's reluctance to place a black star in a film without a white co-star and a black character without a white context to allow a point of identification for the white spectator. While these films offered a representation of African American experience, they simultaneously negated any perceived threat to white masculinity that the black buddy might pose (in terms of civil rights' gains) by placing him in a subordinate role to the more central white hero.

With the increasing popularity and visibility of African Americans in film by the mid-1990s, black stars were relocated from being the sidekick of a white star to being the central hero himself with a sidekick of his own—most often white and female as in *Kiss the Girls* (1997), *The Bone Collector* (1999), and *Along Came a Spider* (2001). By 2002, it was the white female star who moved from sidekick to central hero with a white, male buddy of her own in films such as *Murder by Numbers* (2002), *Twisted* (2004), and *Taking Lives* (2004). These films, however, did not necessarily represent as great a departure from their 1980s predecessors as their foregrounding of race and gender might suggest. As Barry Keith Grant argues, "Often these films merely plug in, or substitute, blacks, women, or gay characters for white male heroes but do little or nothing to challenge the sexist or racist assumptions that inform the myths by which they operate" (196). Rather than engage with racial or sexual politics, these films capitalized on race and gender as means by which to renovate the detective genre. The films, however, represented three important shifts in the detective genre: (1) the criminal was no longer an international terrorist or head of a vice racket but a serial killer; (2) there was rarely a clash and certainly no comedy derived from any differences between the two detectives; and (3) forensics and profiling replaced firepower and physical action as the means by which to catch the criminal. In other words, the films were not cop action films, and black and female bodies were denied the opportunity literally to fight crime through action. In fact, the buddy cop film had become all but extinct by the mid-1990s.[1]

---

[1]The few examples include *Rising Sun* (1993), the *Lethal Weapon* sequels (1992 and 1998), and *Bad Boys* (1995 and 2003)—although I would argue the *Bad Boys* series revival was due to the success of the *Rush Hour* films.

With the Hong Kong handover to China looming and its film industry in crisis, some Hong Kong action stars, directors, and choreographers migrated successfully to Hollywood in the mid-1990s, and in 1998, a new kind of buddy cop film appeared, bringing exciting action back to the fore and featuring buddies not only of different classes and races, but also of different nations. Hong Kong action stars were paired with American sidekicks—black and white, male and female: Chow Yun-Fat with Mira Sorvino in *The Replacement Killers* (1998) and Mark Wahlberg in *The Corruptor* (1999); Jet Li with Aaliyah in *Romeo Must Die* (2000), Bridget Fonda in *Kiss of the Dragon* (2001), and DMX in *Cradle 2 the Grave* (2003); and Jackie Chan with Lee Evans in *The Medallion* (2003) and, perhaps most famously, with Chris Tucker in the *Rush Hour* series (1998, 2001, and 2007). Chan has also teamed up with Owen Wilson for the buddy films *Shanghai Noon* (2000) and *Shanghai Knights* (2003); however, because these films are not cop action films and not set in the present, they are excluded from this discussion. In the post–civil rights era, the 1980s biracial buddy cop film assured audiences that the United States could rely on all Americans (black and white) to defeat any threats to its security—and that threat was often Asian in origin. As Brian Locke states, Asians, when present (e.g., in *Rising Sun*, 1993), were the common enemy that united the American buddies and embodied the displacement of white America's history of racism against African Americans onto Asians (11–12). In the globalized twenty-first century, however, the new millennial buddy cop film suggests that the United States can also rely on her international allies to join in the battle against their common foreign enemies. Other scholars have discussed *Rush Hour* as a commentary on domestic American "multicultural" relations with its teaming up of an African American with an Asian (although *not* Asian American) buddy (see Banerjee; Jayamanne; Wald). In contrast, this article discusses *Rush Hour* within the broader trend of millennial buddy cop films and their commentary on American international relations. This article explores how issues of racial otherness are negotiated in the millennial buddy cop film and how Hollywood's adoption of Hong Kong action stars and action cinema conventions have renovated the American genre of the cop action film for the new millennium, including with myths of transnational cooperation.

"OTHER" BODIES

Buddy cop films are known by—and sold to—audiences on the basis of their spectacular action sequences whether gunplay with Chow or martial arts with Chan and Li. As Julian Stringer demonstrates, action film fans do not necessarily consider stars like Chow to be Chinese but Asian American (229–30). This is because the presence of Chow (and similarly Li and Chan) at the center of a Hollywood film and battling America's enemies align him with Hollywood conventions of American heroism—namely through violent physical action. These Chinese stars, however, are differentiated from their American contemporaries through their specific kind of physical action, and the films highlight the "Asian" male body as spectacular and "other."[2] Chan's fame stems partly from the fact that he does all his own stunts, and his films often conclude with outtakes of stunts gone wrong as the credits roll: in other words, he is presented as a very human hero. Although the 1980s saw the height of the muscular action hero with Sylvester Stallone's Rambo and Arnold Schwarzenegger's Conan the Barbarian, the equating of "musculinity" with heroism continued, and many of American action stars at the turn of the millennium were still expected to bulk up and show off their bodies—including Brendan Fraser (*The Mummy*, 1999), Vin Diesel (*The Fast and the Furious*, 2001), and Matt Damon (*The Bourne Identity*, 2002). The body of the Asian hero is smaller and slimmer than that of the traditionally muscular American action hero and placed very much on display in choreographed balletic fight sequences (i.e., more feminine) rather than traditional fisticuffs (i.e., more masculine). Indeed, in *Romeo Must Die* and *Cradle 2 the Grave*, Li's short stature (5'6" according to IMDb) is a discussion point among characters. The Asian hero, thus, simultaneously embodies a complex system of masculine and feminine signifiers for North American audiences that can be relegated and contained by his being other and allow a variety of readings: He is non-American, and this facilitates the presentation of a more feminized body as smaller, graceful, and spectacular—one placed on unmediated display without the associated implications on his manliness that such a

---

[2]The term *Asian* is used in this article rather than *Chinese* (despite the ethnicity of the stars being discussed) because of Hollywood's tendency to ignore the specificity of different Asian cultures, instead, offering a generic image of "Asianness."

body and performance in an American film might otherwise invoke.

Rather than suggesting that Asian action heroes are somehow ⁵ inferior to American heroes, Yuan Shu argues that the "other" kind of action they embody is the reason for their wide appeal: "As a result of his move toward comedy, Chan unwittingly deconstructs the hard bodies of masculinity projected by both the Kung Fu tragedy and the American action cinema, and he demonstrates the vulnerability of the male body in a way that would appeal to the female viewership as well as the male viewer" (51).

Bruce Lee offered a very strongly coded Asian body (rather than an integrated Asian American hero) as an underclass hero who fought "dirty," in an attempt to redress the stereotype of Asian masculinity as asexual and emasculated (Shu 51). In contrast, Chan's heroes (as well as Chan himself) are fallible and often injured. His millennial heroes move toward an integration of sorts with American culture, embodying a desire to explore and forge a kind of Asian American identity. The question is, however, do audiences recognize Chan's deconstruction of American heroic masculinity, or is kung fu expertise regarded as merely other? Certainly, as Hollywood products themselves, the films do not appear to challenge the American action film but, instead, capitalize on the international appeal of the stars within that American genre. In reference to the biracial buddy cops of the 1980s, Ed Guerrero argues that mainstream cinema suppressed any threat that black masculinity might seem to imply by a variety of, using Fredric Jameson's term, "strategies of containment" — one of which is the denial of black romance and sexuality (237–38). While the millennial Asian stars are allowed to perform heroic action, notably however, they are also denied the opportunity to be sexually potent. James Kim argues that, despite his female costar, Aaliyah, in *Romeo Must Die* (also Bridget Fonda in *Kiss of the Dragon*), Li is presented as "neutered" (155). Even Chow who, as Floyd Cheung reminds us, is "[f]requently compared to Cary Grant and Clint Eastwood" and "has been dubbed 'Sexiest Action Star' by the U.S. publication *People Weekly*," does not "get the girl" (played by Sorvino) in *The Replacement Killers* (1) — as no doubt a white, American counterpart would have. These heroes are allowed to fight for America; however, their ability to embody American heroism is qualified. This is likely the reason that, just as the1980s black male was paired with a white hero, the millennial Asian star—despite his international fame— is always paired with an American buddy.

ASIAN HERO, WHITE BUDDY

The core convention of the buddy cop film, which demands resolution by the end of the film, is difference: the two buddies are contrasting types in terms of personality and background, but they must learn to respect one another's difference and work together to defeat their common enemy. In the 1980s, that difference was based on race and class; since the late 1990s, it has been based on race and nationality. There are two types of narrative in the millennial buddy cop film: (1) Some films are concerned with the infiltration of Asian crime into the United States, including Chow's *The Replacement Killers* and *The Corruptor;* Li's *Romeo Must Die* and *Cradle 2 the Grave,* and Chan's first *Rush Hour* film; (2) The other films take place in nations foreign to both buddies (i.e., both are fish out of water), including Chan's *The Medallion* (which takes place in Dublin, Ireland), Li's *Kiss of the Dragon,* and Chan's third *Rush Hour* (which both take place in Paris, France). Importantly, the heroes in all of the films come from Asia (whether Hong Kong, mainland China, or Taiwan); only Chow's cop hero in *The Corruptor* lives and works in America. The Asian hero is never fully integrated into American culture, and the films always flag up the cultural differences—from music to language, from food to fighting skills—between the Asian hero and his American partner. The differences also incite comic moments in the films (although far more so in Chan's films, which have a sustained comic tone).

These millennial buddy cop films echo the "cooperation model" of World War II films such as *The Great Escape* (1963)— thematizing that the heroes must put aside their personal differences to work together to defeat a common enemy. These Asian law enforcers want to be lone heroes—in effect, isolationists— and it is their American buddies who must teach them the value of being a team player.

ASIAN HERO, BLACK BUDDY

What made *Rush Hour* so groundbreaking, as actor Tzi Ma suggests, is that "to the best of my knowledge, this is the first Hollywood film with two heroes of color. . . . This movie is really a melting pot" (qtd. in Alliance 7). And, as director Brett Ratner explained in an interview for *Rush Hour 2*, "You could never have had a budget like this with a black and an Asian star—never. Not before *Rush Hour*" (qtd. in Kirkland 17). The first film was the seventh top grossing film of 1998, and the sequel, the fifth highest grossing film of 2001.[3] The series begins on the eve of the British handover of Hong Kong to China in 1997 as British Commander Griffin (Tom Wilkinson) hosts a dinner party to congratulate Consul Han (Tzi Ma) on his new appointment to the Chinese consulate in Los Angeles. Detective Inspector Lee (Chan) interrupts the celebration to report to Han that Chinese antiquities have been successfully recovered from a Hong Kong criminal ring run by the mysterious villain known only as Juntao. Two months later in Los Angeles, his daughter is kidnapped and Han requests Lee's assistance; however, the FBI agents in charge of the case consider Lee as unwanted (read: foreign) interference and assign Los Angeles Police Department (LAPD) Detective James Carter (Tucker) to "babysit" him. Carter is considered equally undesirable within his unit as he was in charge of an undercover operation that went wrong: his white superior volunteers Carter for the "bullshit assignment" (i.e., Lee) that he initially refuses to give to any of his other (read: white) detectives. Carter also has a reputation for not working well with others. As his colleague Detective Johnson (Elizabeth Peña) explains, "This is why nobody will work with you, man. But you're the only cop in the department without a partner." Carter wants to investigate the kidnapping alone and finds Lee a hindrance; similarly, Lee wants to see Consul Han so that he can begin working on the case.

From their first meeting, Lee and Carter are at odds as signaled 10
by their inability to communicate effectively. When Carter picks
Lee up at the airport, he says slowly and loudly in a patronizing
tone, "I'm Detective Carter. Do you speaka any English?" Lee
plays into Carter's assumptions and responds only with a polite

---

[3]*Rush Hour 3* did not fare quite so well as the sixteenth highest grossing film of 2007, but it still made its money back in worldwide box office.

"American and Asian must work together to protect their mutual global interests." Do Jackie Chan and Chris Tucker in *Rush Hour 3* (or other examples) "thematize" larger issues, problems, or questions?

smile. Incensed, Carter exclaims, "I cannot believe this shit! First, I get a bullshit assignment, now Mr. Rice-a-Roni don't even speak American." Later, Lee confesses to Carter, "I didn't say I didn't; you assumed so [. . .] I'm not responsible for your assumptions." The two cops, initially in opposition with one another, bond halfway through the film over the Edwin Starr song "War": Lee begins by singing the song focusing on the melody while Carter corrects him by singing the song with more power; similarly, Carter demonstrates some American dance moves, and Lee shares some of his Asian martial arts moves. Here is the moment of transnational cultural exchange and, with it, understanding and acceptance. With its declaration that war is good for "absolutely nothing," the song becomes a metaphor for transnational cooperation. When Carter and Lee are pulled off the case by the Feds and Lee is sent packing back to Hong Kong, Carter realizes that he can no longer be a lone hero and calls Johnson for assistance. He tells her, "You was right. Yeah, I was egotistic; I was inconsiderate; I was self-centered. I ain't used to working with partners but, look, it ain't

about me now—it's about the little girl." Although Lee is willing
to work with a partner, he feels that he has "disgraced" himself by
failing to return his friend's daughter and doesn't think that Carter
can understand how he feels. Carter, however, reveals that his
father—although a great police officer—died on the job in a random act of violence when his partner failed to have his back. This
is the reason that Carter cannot trust a partner, and he asks Lee
to prove to him that there is honor in dying to serve and protect
others and that he can trust in a buddy. The two, working together,
and with the assistance of Johnson as a bomb specialist, are able
to save Han's daughter and to bring Juntao to justice. There is a
twist here when it is revealed that the assumed-to-be Asian criminal mastermind is none other than Britain's Commander Griffin.

Rush Hour 2 begins where *Rush Hour* leaves off, with Carter
accompanying Lee to Hong Kong for a vacation: Whereas, in the
first film, Lee was the fish out of water, now it is Carter's turn. The
vacation is interrupted by an explosion at the American Embassy,
and the death of two Secret Service agents working undercover in
a smuggling ring see Lee put on the case. Again, the second film
thematizes the buddy relationship: not only is the ring leader,
Ricky Tan (John Lone), a former detective and the partner who
betrayed Lee's father five years earlier, but also Carter accuses Lee
of being a bad partner by not confiding in him about the embassy
attack and his history with Tan. When Lee requests his assistance,
Carter retorts, "There's two billion Chinese people here. Let one
of them be your partner." Carter and Lee, however, do end up
working together, pursuing leads to Los Angeles and later Las
Vegas where they bring Tan to justice. As Robert Koehler suggests
in his *Variety* review of the film, "This superior sequel . . . is the
very model of the limber, transnational Hollywood action comedy"(17).

In *Rush Hour 3*, the buddy relationship is elevated to the status
of family. The film begins in Los Angeles at the World Criminal
Court where Ambassador Han (Tzi Ma reprising his role from the
first film) gives a speech about the pervasive problem of the Triad
criminal organization. An assassination attempt is made on Han,
and Lee gives chase, discovering that the assassin is none other
than Kenji (Hiroyuki Sanada)—a Japanese orphan who became
Lee's "brother" at the orphanage in China where they spent time

as boys. Lee carries the weight of guilt from their youth—that he was adopted while Kenji ended up on the streets—and cannot bring himself to shoot Kenji. Kenji wants the "Shy Shen," the rumored list of Triad leader names, and Carter and Lee pursue him to Paris. Initially, Lee insists that the bond with his brother outweighs that with his partner, causing a rift between the cop buddies. Carter exclaims, "Fine. I'm not your brother," and storms out of their Paris hotel room. A sequence follows in which each man regrets his words to his buddy and seeks food that reminds him of the other: Carter orders Chinese moo shu and Lee, southern fried chicken with sweet potato pie—again suggesting an internalization of transnational cultural exchange. While Carter eats his take-out at a street café, a busker plays the Beach Boys's song "California Girls"—a song that the two buddies had listened to in the first film and that is Carter's ringtone on Lee's phone in this one. In the final showdown at the Eiffel Tower, Kenji insists that Lee will not kill him since he is the only family Lee has in the world; however, Lee disagrees and claims Carter as "his brother from another mother"—as Carter puts it. Importantly, these buddy relationships, although personal, enact an important function at a the level of national identity: American and Asian must work together to protect their mutual global interests.

Works Cited

Alliance Atlantis Pressbook for *Rush Hour* (1998). Toronto: Alliance Atlantis. Print.

Banerjee, Mita. "The *Rush Hour* of Black/Asian Coalitions? Jackie Chan and Black-face Minstrelsy." *AfroAsian Encounters: Culture, History, Politics*. Ed. Heike Raphael-Hernandez and Shannon Steen. New York: New York UP, 2006. 204–22. Print.

Cheung, Floyd. "Negative Attraction: The Politics of Interracial Romance in *The Replacement Killers*." *Americana: The Journal of American Popular Culture (1990–Present)* 1.2 (2002), Web. 1 May 2011. <www.americanpopularculture.com/journal/articles/fall_2002/cheung.htm>

The Corruptor. Dir. James Foley. Perf. Chow Yun-Fat and Mark Wahlberg. New Line Cinema and Illusion Entertainment Group, 1999. Film. USA.

Cradle 2 the Grave. Dir. Andrzej Bartkowiak. Perf. Jet Li and DMX. Silver Pictures, 2003. Film. USA.

Grant, Barry Keith. "Strange Days: Gender and Ideology in New Genre Films." *Ladies and Gentlemen, Boys and Girls: Gender in Film at the End of the Twentieth Century*. Ed. Murray Pomerance. Albany, NY: State U of New York P, 2001. 185–99. Print.

Guerrero, Ed. "The Black Image in Protective Custody: Hollywood's Biracial Buddy Films of the Eighties." *Black American Cinema*. Ed. Manthia Diawara. New York: Routledge, 1993. 237–46. Print.

Jameson, Fredric. *The Political Unconscious*. New York: Comell UP, 1981. Print.

Jayamanne, Laleen. "Let's Miscegenate: Jackie Chan and His African-American Connection." *Hong Kong Connections: Transnational Imagination in Action Cinema*. Ed. Meaghan Morris, Siu Leung Li, and Stephen Chan Ching-kiu. Durham, NC: Duke UP, 2005. 151–62. Print.

Kim, James. "The Legend of the White-and-Yellow Black Man: Global Containment and Triangulated Racial Desire in *Romeo Must Die*." *Camera Obscura* 19.1 (2004): 150–79. Print.

Kirkland, Bruce. "Chan's Finest Hour." Rev. of *Rush Hour 2*. *The Sunday Sun* (29 July 2001): Showcase 17. Print.

Kiss of the Dragon. Dir. Chris Nahon. Perf. Jet Li and Bridget Fonda. Twentieth Century-Fox Film Corporation, 2001. Film. France/USA.

Koehler, Robert. "Auds Get a Rush from '2.'" Rev. of *Rush Hour 2*. *Variety* (30 July–5 Aug. 2001): 17, 22. Print.

Locke, Brian. *Racial Stigma on the Hollywood Screen from World War II to the Present: The Orientalist Buddy Film*. New York: Palgrave Macmillan, 2009. Print.

The Medallion. Dir. Gordon Chan. Perf. Jackie Chan, Lee Evans, and Claire Forlani. Screen Gems, 2003. Film. Hong Kong/USA.

The Replacement Killers. Dir. Antoine Fuqua. Perf. Chow Yun-Fat and Mira Sorvino. Columbia Pictures, 1998. Film.

Romeo Must Die. Dir. Andrzej Bartkowiak. Perf. Jet Li and Aaliyah. Silver Pictures and Warner Bros. Pictures, 2000. Film. USA.

Rush Hour. Dir. Brett Ratner. Perf. Jackie Chan and Chris Tucker. New Line Cinema and Roger Bimbaum Productions, 1998. Film. USA.

Rush Hour 2. Dir. Brett Ratner. Perf. Jackie Chan and Chris Tucker. New Line Cinema and Roger Bimbaum Productions, 2001. Film. USA.

Rush Hour 3. Dir. Brett Ratner. Perf. Jackie Chan and Chris Tucker. New Line Cinema, 2007. Film. USA.

Shanghai Knights. Dir. David Dobkin. Perf. Jackie Chan and Owen Wilson. Spyglass Entertainment, 2003. Film. USA.

Shanghai Noon. Dir. David Dobkin. Perf. Jackie Chan and Owen Wilson. Spyglass Entertainment, 2000. Film. Hong Kong/USA.

Shu, Yuan. "Reading the Kung Fu Film in an American Context: From Bruce Lee to Jackie Chan." *Journal of Popular Film and Television* 31.2 (2003): 50–59. Print.

Stringer, Julian. "Scrambling Hollywood: Asian Stars/Asian American Star Cultures." *Contemporary Hollywood Stardom*. Ed. Thomas Austin and Martin Barker. London: Arnold, 2003. 229–42. Print.

Wald, Gayle. "Same Difference: Racial Masculinity in Hong Kong and Cop-Buddy Hybrids." *Chinese Connections: Critical Perspectives on Film, Identity, and Diaspora*. Ed. See-kam Tan, Peter X. Feng, and Gina Marchetti. Philadelphia: Temple UP, 2009, 68–81. Print.

For Discussion and Writing

1. **Comprehension**   According to Gates's article, why was the film *Rush Hour* so "groundbreaking" (par. 9)?

2. **Critical Reading**   Where in the essay does Gates use compare and contrast to support her **main points**? Find a specific example and explain how it furthers her argument.

3. **Analysis**   Gates refers to the critic Frederic Jameson's term "strategies of containment" (par. 6). How do such "strategies" operate with regard to black and Asian characters in movies? According to the theory, what supposedly needs to be contained and why?

4. **Connections**   In "Creating the Myth" (p. 367), Linda Seger claims that "every hero story is essentially a transformation story," in which the hero is changed and "reintegrated into his [or her] society" (pars. 23–24). Do the buddy action movies in Gates's article seem to fit this pattern? What transformations do these films illustrate? What is the larger significance of these changes?

5. **Writing**   According to Gates, films cam "thematize" topics and problems like interracial cooperation or international relations

between America and China. That is, such movies investigate, illustrate, explore, comment on, and attempt to resolve larger questions and issues through plot and characters. Choose a film that includes a relationship between two people of different races, ethnicities, or nationalities. Then, in an essay, blog post, or multimedia presentation, explain how the film uses that relationship to thematize a larger issue—and evaluate whether it does so successfully.

CHAPTER 7

Immersive Media

Can we get lost—and can we be found— in media?

From the earliest spoken tales and poems to the most recent blockbuster movie, we have always craved fictions and vicarious experiences. And for almost as long, we have tried to explain that hunger. The Greek philosopher Aristotle argued that tragedies allow spectators to purge themselves of excessive pity and fear through the vicarious experience of watching a play. For writers in the Romantic tradition, imaginative works reveal glimpses of transcendent truth and beauty: a glimmer of hope that the "world imagined is the ultimate good," in the words of poet Wallace Stevens. For thinkers like Sigmund Freud, fictional works function like dreams, allowing space for unconscious fears and wish fulfillment. These works perform more mundane tasks, too. They allow us to escape from the ordinariness of our daily lives and selves—or even from sorrow, pain, and unpleasant realities. In this context, our love of vicarious distraction contradicts the value we ascribe to "authenticity" and "truth." But as Jack Nicholson's character Colonel Jessup yells in *A Few Good Men*: "You can't handle the truth!"

If our love of imaginative escape has aroused the curiosity of philosophers and critics, it has also aroused their fear and loathing. A strong distrust of imaginative fictions and entertainments runs through the history of Western literature and culture. In *The Republic*, Plato famously banishes poets from his ideal society because fiction-makers mislead and debase people with their falsehoods. After the 1642 Puritan Revolution in England, all English theaters were closed to stop the corrupting influence of

393

theatrical performances. "To indulge the power of fiction and send imagination out upon the wing is often the sport of those who delight too much in silent speculation," says a character in Samuel Johnson's 1759 work *The History of Rasselas, Prince of Abissinia* (itself, a work of fiction). In these centuries-old concerns about the dangers of imaginative and vicarious experiences, we can see early versions of contemporary debates about whether the graphic imagery of video games desensitizes children or causes violent behavior.

All the selections in this section address the value of vicarious experience and take the measure of imaginative flights in popular culture. In "On Novel Reading," the eighteenth-century English moralist, educator, and critic Vicessimus Knox writes at a time when novels were a sensational pop culture phenomenon, as well as a potential danger to young, impressionable minds; for Knox, popular fictions "often pollute the heart . . . inflame the passions . . . and teach all the malignity of vice in solitude." Approaching fiction writing from a contemporary perspective, Robin Brenner ("Teen Literature and Fan Culture") considers the power and popularity of fan fiction: works in which fans of a particular book, movie, or television show will use its characters and story lines to write their own original works. For Brenner, these loving, speculative homages affirm a "creativity, talent, and sheer joy in stories." In "The Art of Immersion: Fear of Fiction," Frank Rose profiles two video-game developers and explores the ways in which people have feared the immersive power of fiction as every new technological medium "has increased the transporting power of narrative." Chuck Klosterman's "My Zombie, Myself: Why Modern Life Feels Rather Undead" reveals how monsters can reflect—and embody—both our fears and our felt experience of day-to-day life. Jacob Burak ("Escape from the Matrix") also writes about the implications of our new digital lives on real-world relationships as he analyzes the collective social and cultural disorder "FoMO," or "Fear of Missing Out." In "Why Videogames Should Be Played with Friends, Not Online with Strangers," Bo Moore investigates a gaming trend in which players actively pursue non-immersion and seek a "pre-Internet ideal of local play and social camaraderie."

In the paired readings, Gerard Jones ("Violent Media Is Good for Kids") and Michael Chabon ("Secret Skin: An Essay in Unitard Theory") affirm the importance and power of comic book superheroes—to help young readers understand identity, to help them manage personal transformation, and (in Chabon's words) to invite them "into the world of story."

As you read, reflect on your own experiences with immersive media and vicarious fictions:

- Why do we crave the virtual worlds and alternative realities provided by stories, games, media, and technology?
- How has technology changed our relationship with immersive fictions?
- Does immersive media provide merely escapist fantasy, or can it lead us to a deeper engagement with the "real"?

VICESSIMUS KNOX

On Novel Reading

Vicessimus Knox (1752–1821) was an English minister, educator, essayist, and author. He attended Oxford University and served as headmaster of Tonbridge School in Kent, England. As a writer and editor, Knox was preoccupied with the morality of literature and the effects of fiction on younger readers. He published the anthologies Elegant Extracts: or, Useful and Entertaining Passages in Poetry *(1784) and* Elegant Extracts: or, Useful and Entertaining Passages in Prose *(1785). These became well-known works—Jane Austen, for example, was a fan. Knox wrote about education in* Essays, Moral and Literary *(1778), from which this selection comes, and* Liberal Education *(1781). In this essay, Knox considers the dangers and pleasures of reading. In the process, he prescribes the qualities that define good and bad books for the young. Knox refers to several popular seventeenth- and eighteenth-century English novelists, including Samuel Richardson, Henry Fielding, Tobias Smollett, Laurence Sterne, and Daniel Defoe. Even if you are unfamiliar with their works, you should be able to understand Knox's evaluation of their suitability for younger readers.*

As you read, consider Knox's assumptions about young readers and their needs. What kind of books are "safe," according to Knox? Who do you think is the audience for this essay? Do you think that morally improving works and works that excite young readers are mutually exclusive categories?

If it be true, that the present age is more corrupt than the preceding, the great multiplication of novels has probably contributed to its degeneracy. Fifty years ago there was scarcely a novel in the kingdom. Romances, indeed, abounded; but they, it is supposed, were rather favorable to virtue. Their pictures of human nature were not exact, but they were flattering resemblances. By exhibiting patterns of perfection, they stimulated emulation to aim at it. They led the fancy through a beautiful wilderness of delights; and they filled the heart with pure, manly, bold, and liberal sentiments.

Those books also, which were written with a view to ridicule the more absurd romantic writers, are themselves most pleasing romances, and may be read without injury to the morals. Such is the immortal work of Cervantes.[1] Perhaps the safest books of entertainment for young people are those of decent humor, which excite a laugh, and leave the heart little affected.

Books are more read in youth than in the advanced periods of life; but there are few perfectly well adapted to the young mind. They should be entertaining, or they will not be attended to. They should not be profound, or they will not be understood. Entertaining books there are in great numbers; but they were not written solely for young people, and are therefore too unguarded in many of their representations. They do not pay that reverence which Juvenal[2] asserts to be due to the puerile age.

That Richardson's novels are written with the purest intentions of promoting virtue, none can deny. But in the accomplishment of this purpose scenes are laid open, which it would be safer to conceal, and sentiments excited, which it would be more advantageous to early virtue not to admit. Dangers and temptations are pointed out; but many of them are dangers which seldom occur, and temptations by which few in comparison are assaulted. It is to be feared, the moral view is rarely regarded by youthful and inexperienced readers, who naturally pay the chief attention to the lively description of love, and its effects; and who, while they read, eagerly wish to be actors in the scenes which they admire.

The writings of such men do, however, display the beauties of that genius, which allures and rewards the attention of the discreet reader. But the memoirs, private histories, and curious anecdotes, imported from our neighboring land of libertinism, have seldom any thing to recommend them to perusal but their profligacy. Yet even these, adorned with specious titles, and a pert vivacity of language, have found their way to the circulating libraries, and are often obtruded on the attention at an early age.

5

---

[1]*Miguel de Cervantes* (1547–1616): Spanish author best known for *Don Quixote* (1605). [Editor's note.]

[2]*Juvenal:* Roman poet of the late first and early second century A.D., known for a collection of satirical poems titled *Satires*. [Editor's note.]

The English press has teemed with similar original productions. That coarse taste, which was introduced in the reign of Charles the Second,[3] was greedily adopted by the juvenile reader. At an inflammatory age, the fuel of licentious ideas will always find a ready reception. The sentimental manner seems of late to have supplanted it. But it is matter of doubt, whether even this manner is not equally dangerous. It has given an amiable name to vice, and has obliquely excused the extravagance of the passions, by representing them as the effect of lovely sensibility. The least refined affections of humanity have lost their indelicate nature, in the ideas of many, when dignified by the epithet of sentimental; and transgressions forbidden by the laws of God and man have been absurdly palliated, as proceeding from an excess of those finer feelings, which vanity has arrogated to itself as elegant and amiable distinctions. A softened appellation has given a degree of gracefulness to moral deformity.

The languishing and affectedly sentimental compositions formed on the pattern of Sterne,[4] or of other less original novelists, not only tend to give the mind a degree of weakness, which renders it unable to resist the slightest impulse of libidinous passion, but also indirectly insinuate, that the attempt is unnatural. What then remains to support the feeble efforts of remaining virtue, but the absence of temptation?

Such books, however pernicious in their tendency, are the most easily attained. The prudence of their publishers suggests the expediency of making them conveniently portable. Every corner of the kingdom is abundantly supplied with them. In vain is youth secluded from the corruptions of the living world. Books are commonly allowed them with little restriction, as innocent amusements; yet these often pollute the heart in the recesses of the closet, inflame the passions at a distance from temptation, and teach all the malignity of vice in solitude.

There is another evil arising from a too early attention to novels. They fix attention so deeply, and afford so lively a pleasure,

[3]*King Charles II of England* (1630–1685): Known as the "Merry Monarch," his reign marked the end of England's Puritan rule that restricted "immoral" arts and entertainment. [Editor's note.]
[4]*Laurence Sterne* (1713–1768): British novelist and clergyman best remembered for his novels *The Life and Opinions of Tristram Shandy* (1759–1767) and *A Sentimental Journey* (1768). [Editor's note.]

that the mind, once accustomed to them, cannot submit to the painful task of serious study. Authentic history becomes insipid. The reserved graces of the chaste matron Truth pass unobserved amidst the gaudy and painted decorations of fiction. The boy who can procure a variety of books like *Gil Blas,* and *The Devil upon Two Sticks,* will no longer think his Livy, his Sallust, his Homer, or his Virgil pleasing. He will not study old Lilly, while he can read *Pamela* and *Tom Jones,* and a thousand inferior and more dangerous novels.

When the judgment is ripened by reflection, and the morals 10 out of danger, every well-written book will claim attention. The man of application may always find agreeable refreshment, after severer study, in the amusing pages of a Fielding;[5] but the fungous productions of the common novel-wright will be too insignificant to attract his notice.

The extreme insipidity of some of our later novels, it might have been supposed, would have prevented their reception. But insipid minds find in them entertainment congenial to their nature. And, indeed, the futility of the modern novel almost precludes its power of causing any other mischief, than the consumption of time that might be more usefully employed.

For Discussion and Writing

1. **Comprehension** Knox praises the virtuous intentions and moral messages of Samuel Richardson, whose most famous novel, *Clarissa* (1748), tells the story of a young woman's struggle to protect her virtue and chastity against a villainous suitor. But Knox ultimately finds Richardson's work unsuitable for young readers. Why?

2. **Critical Reading** In his **introduction**, Knox proposes a cause-and-effect relationship. What is it? How does it help establish the larger significance of his argument?

3. **Analysis** Are Knox's characterizations of young people still relevant today? He writes that "licentious [immoral, corrupt] ideas will always find a ready reception" among "juvenile" readers (par. 6). Do you agree that the minds of children and teenagers are easily corrupted and need to be protected from "libidinous passion" (par. 7)? Why or why not?

---

[5]*Henry Fielding* (1707–1754): English novelist best remembered for his comic novel *Tom Jones* (1749). [Editor's note.]

4. ***Connections*** Compare and contrast Knox's view of children and their emotional and intellectual needs with the view presented by Gerard Jones in "Violent Media Is Good for Kids" (p. 442). For example, Jones would likely agree with Knox that "while they read, [young readers] eagerly wish to be actors in the scenes which they admire" (par. 4). What is the power and influence of such vicarious experiences, according to Knox and Jones, respectively? How free should children be to choose their own vicarious pleasures? How do the two essays represent different conceptions of childhood?

5. ***Writing*** For Knox, the quality of a book is inseparable from the virtue of its moral message. Do you think art and entertainment should be "moral" and promote virtuous ideas and behavior? When you evaluate the quality of a book, movie, television show, or video game, do you include its morality in your judgment? Why or why not? What, if anything, makes a piece of popular culture "moral" or "immoral"? Write an essay that explains your answer.

ROBIN BRENNER

Teen Literature and Fan Culture

Robin Brenner is the teen librarian at the Brookline Public Library in Brookline, Massachusetts. She earned her undergraduate degree in creative writing from Bryn Mawr College and a graduate degree in library sciences from the University of Illinois. Brenner has written for Library Journal, VOYA, Knowledge Quest, *and other publications. She is also the editor-in-chief of* No Flying No Tights, *a Web site that reviews graphic novels. In this article, which appeared in the* Young Adult Library Services *journal, she considers the meaning and popularity of fan art— and fan fiction, in particular. Writers of fan fiction take the characters, plots, themes, and other aspects of their favorite books, television shows, or movies, and then create their own stories. As Brenner writes, these "devotees take the leap from speculation to creation" and "use their talents to fill in the gaps, to create alternative timelines, and mix universes."*

As you read, *reflect on a time when you have read a book or seen a movie, and then wondered "what happens next, what happened before, and what happened in scenes not shown." How has the meaning of "fan" changed, according to Brenner? What is her attitude toward fan fiction, and how does it come across in her tone? Would you ever consider writing fan fiction of your own?*

"Fan fiction is what literature might look like if it were reinvented from scratch after a nuclear apocalypse by a band of brilliant pop-culture junkies trapped in a sealed bunker. They don't do it for money. That's not what it's about. The writers write it and put it up online just for the satisfaction. They're fans, but they're not silent, couchbound consumers of media. The culture talks to them, and they talk back to the culture in its own language."[1]

Everyone has read a book and speculated about what might have been. When a work inspires, an engaged reader wonders

[1]Lev Grossman, qtd. in Robin Brenner, "Fanworks and Libraries Survey." *No Flying No Tights.* June 2012. Web. 23 Apr. 2013.

what happens next, what happened before, and what happened in scenes not shown. Many fans are content with contemplating the "what if" questions in their own imaginations, but with fan fiction, fan videos, and fan art, devotees take the leap from speculation to creation. They use their talents to fill in the gaps, to create alternative timelines, and mix universes. And that's just the beginning.

Once fans are satisfied with their effort, they share that work and vibrant communities build up rapidly. One power of the Internet is that if you really love a particular work, you can very easily find more people who love that work just as much as you do. Fans join forums and electronic discussion groups, and follow fan creators via social networking sites. Many create, but just as many participate by reading, commenting, editing, critiquing, and debating everything from character development and plot points to media tropes and minority representation. Everyone is involved in the creation, and everyone is involved in the conversation. All you need to join in is enthusiasm.

In my work as a teen librarian, I have noticed in the past ten years intersections between teen reading, literacy, creativity and the collaborative, creative world of fannish activity surrounding popular literature, television, and films. The engagement with creative works, from Harry Potter to *Twilight* to Star Trek to Sherlock, has led to adding voices, characters, points of view, and critique to any created universe. As author Lev Grossman notes in the quote above, being a fan today is about participation, community, and creative expression in a way that has never been quite so visible. In the past ten years, I've realized that not only are the teens I serve well aware of fan cultures, but many are active creators and participants.

The runaway success of works like E. L. James's *Fifty Shades of Grey*, which was originally written as fan fiction, to Stephenie Meyer's Twilight series, has brought fan creation front and center for people working in publishing and who may view fan culture as a rich creative training ground for new talent. In teen literature, published authors including Cassandra Clare, Marissa Meyer, Naomi Novik, Saundra Mitchell, and Claudia Gray[2] all started out writing in fan communities. 5

---

[2]Authors of *The Mortal Instruments*, *The Lunar Chronicles*, *Temeraire*, *Shadowed Summer*, and *Evernight*, respectively. [Editor's note.]

Being a fan is not new, of course, but today being a fan has become an increasingly public, shared act. The term originally applied to sports fans in the nineteenth century, and since science fiction enthusiasts adopted the label in the 1920s, the term has stuck for any enthusiast. A community of fans allied by their love for a particular source can be about anything from cats to a celebrity to a TV ad. When discussing fan culture in this article, the term identifies a community of fans that discuss, critique, and create around a particular source work, be it a film, a series of books, a television show, or a comic book. Fan works, which include creative writing (fan fiction), art (fan art), music (filk), video (fan vids), comics, costumes, and crafts, are as diverse as the people who create them.

A sticky question in this outpouring of creativity: just how legal is creating works so clearly inspired by and connected to copyrighted content? As panelists at the YALSA Young Adult Literature Symposium in St. Louis in November 2012 noted, the legal debate centers around whether fan works are considered derivative or transformative. If a work is considered derivative, adding nothing of value to the original work, then it is not allowed. If the work, however, is considered transformative, or building on what the original work created, then it is allowed. However, keep in mind, a lawsuit has yet to make its way through the courts and, without precedent, it is difficult to predict an outcome. Outside of the legal question, individual creators, including writers and artists, are increasingly moving toward a policy of permission and acceptance, especially as they recognize the harm in potentially alienating their fans if they pursue legal action. Recently, source material producers have shifted toward embracing fan culture by endorsing and hosting contests in creating fan works.

In order to help introduce fan creation and communities to library staff and others, I took part in a panel at the 2012 YALSA Young Adult Literature Symposium. (Other panelists included librarian and *School Library Journal* blogger Liz Burns, Aja Romano, fandom reporter for the *Daily Dot*; and Leslee Friedman, a representative from the Organization of Transformative Works and an ACLU Legal Fellow.)

Our symposium audience was full of librarians, authors, editors, and professionals interested in teen literature, and while some audience members were well versed in online fandom, many were hearing about these creations and communities for the first time. Given the continuing discussion about authorship, publishing, and fan communities around the world, it was definitely the right time to discuss what being a fan means, the influence fan culture has on what and how we read, and to consider where the creativity of the fan community will lead us.

In order to be sure attendees saw the many formats fan works take, we included in our presentation a gallery of fan art, showing the extraordinary talent, sense of humor, and communication that happens through visual media. Everything from Harry Potter single-panel cartoons to elaborate portraits of the Avengers' Steve Rogers (a.k.a. Captain America) in the style of renowned illustrator J. C. Leyendecker[3] showed a brief glimpse of what fans create and share.

In the months before the panel, I conducted a survey to gather a snapshot of the fan community. I sent out word of the survey online through librarian electronic discussion groups, social networks, and with the help of the Organization of Transformative Works, I gathered over 500 responses from self-identified fans.

Looking over our survey data, the majority of our respondents were over 18, although we did have over 40 teens respond. The ages of respondents ranged from 13 to over 65, with most in their 20s or 30s. Over 93 percent of the respondents identified as female, with 5 percent identifying as male and 3 percent as other, including transgender, genderqueer, and androgynous. This percentage supports the impression from fan communities that the majority of participants are female. In terms of sexuality, 62 percent declared their sexuality is straight or mostly straight, while 35 percent identified as bisexual, gay, or lesbian, or questioning, and 3 percent identified as asexual. This shows a significant participation by GBLTQ people, and goes toward debunking the perception that fan creators are almost entirely straight women.

From the teens who responded, 97 percent read, watched, or viewed fan fiction, fan vids, or fan art, 85 percent have written fan fiction, and 55 percent have created fan art. Of the adults who responded, 97 percent read, watched, or viewed fan fiction, fan

10

[3]*Joseph Christian Leyendecker* (1874–1951): popular twentieth-century American illustrator best remembered for his illustrated advertisements and covers for the *Saturday Evening Post*. [Editor's note.]

vids, or fan art, 71 percent have written fan fiction, and 33 percent have created fan art. Of both teens and adults, 79 percent actively participate in fan communities, and 70 percent of adults and teens have written or blogged about fan culture. Forty-nine percent of teens and 65 percent of adults have been what's known as a beta—worked with another creator as an editor, copy editor, and cheerleader in the creation of work. While smaller percentages (5 to 25 percent) participate in creating or listening to podfic (audio recordings of fan fiction), filk (fan music), or fan mixes (music playlists tailored to a source or fan work), the fact that these options exist show the many ways fans can and do participate.

So why are all these people drawn to fan culture? There are many reasons, but the stated reasons from our survey include a love of compelling stories, finding community, gaining courage to create as well as becoming a better creator, finding a safe space for expression, and becoming more critical consumers.

Given the urges that prompt creating fan works, it's unsur- 15 prising that output can be both incredibly creative and critical. Remixing, retelling, and reinventing characters, worlds, plot points, and stories are the norm. Alternate universes (AU), or works that explore what makes characters true to their nature if they're placed in an entirely different place, situation, or time, are a popular way to riff on the original. Crossover works, which connect one or more fan sources and intermingle characters and ideas, are a key example of remixing. A recent example has been dubbed Superwholock and features the main characters of the television shows *Supernatural, Doctor Who,* and the BBC's *Sherlock* solving crimes together. In today's world of strict media copyright, this kind of cross-pollination is virtually impossible through traditional channels.

The act of ripping apart source material and putting it together in new ways also allows fan creators to add in content they want to see but are not getting from professional published media. To put it simply, fan works are more inclusive than mainstream media. Fan works explore sexuality, gender identity, race, and class in an avenue of production that exists outside mainstream production gatekeepers. There is no budget bottom line or question of market appeal. By adding or giving more substantial voices to already existing characters of color, for example, fans can explore and comment on the diversity or lack thereof in a favorite world. Alternate sexuality is frequently a part of fan works, showing a strong interest in highlighting and creating LGBTQ characters. Expanding and subverting established worlds show what fans feel are missing; survey respondents cited this inclusion over and over again as a major reason for seeking out fan work.

For many fans, finding a fan community online increases their confidence in social interactions, connects them with people through common interests, and helps them feel less isolated. As fan culture is also a forum for exploring sexuality and gender, many respondents reported that discovering these issues in fan circles helped them articulate and feel comfortable in their own identities. Despite the fact that much of fan culture's interaction takes place online through social media, many respondents also reported that online connections and community have led to invaluable in-person friendships.

As fan culture is based around creativity, respondents also noted the encouragement, consultation, collaboration, and feedback that thrive in creating and sharing fan works that have led many to try their hand at creation, to improve dramatically, and to feel more confident in their work, and successfully seek professional publication. As one teen notes, "Before fandoms, I thought you needed a fancy degree or a medal from the queen to write actual stories. But when I figured out there was more to life than Internet Explorer and Neopets, I realized that kids were writing. Everyone was writing. And everyone could do it. Then I started to do it . . . I honestly think I started out writing stories because I started writing fanfiction. And now I want to minor in creative writing."

Fans also learn to view what they love critically as they examine the source material, criticizing plot, characters, and storytelling decisions—and all of this is far outside the traditional rigor of a classroom. Critiquing an original work is part of participating in a fandom, from writing an essay examining character motivation to unpacking what a film's costumes say about the characters' class. Similarly, participating in fan culture has provoked many fans to consider questions of authorship, storytelling, and copyright. Many cite fan culture as forming their thoughts about how created worlds are shared, understanding (and potentially dismissing) authorial intent, and looking at the collaborative agreement between author and consumer that creates each reading. Fans in our survey noted over and over again that they became more critical consumers of media through participating in fan debates and reading or writing critical essays.

Fans encourage and hope that fan creators may move on to 20 create original work, as many have. The success of titles like *Fifty Shades of Grey* has opened the door publicly to how fan works can become traditionally published works. Making significant money off of fan work, which is ostensibly available for free to celebrate the original source, is considered gauche and potentially dangerous if it draws the legal attention of media producers. Respondents reported varying levels of comfort with crossing the line from fan work to professional work, especially given how uncertain and new this practice is for creators and publishers alike. Creating prints of fan art for sale or running conventions and fan events are considered allowable, but taking a fan fiction story, changing all the names, and publishing it as original is much more problematic. However, many creators are not simply changing the names and places of their fan work in order to publish, as James reputedly did. Instead, many are using what they have learned in the trenches of fan creation to create original work. Those who come from fandom, such as Naomi Novik and Marissa Meyer, are accepted in both worlds, but writing professionally and writing fan fiction are considered separate endeavors for different goals both creatively and economically. As more creators move from one world to the other, and the lines between them begin to blur, attitudes will continue to change.

Fan culture has become a vibrant and creative part of being a fan, and participating is part of many teens' daily lives. As fan culture, publishing, and teen literature continue to evolve, all of these creative outlets will become more intertwined, and no one can guarantee smooth sailing. As attitudes seem to be shifting toward embracing the creativity, talent, and sheer joy in stories that define fan works, fan creators are visible, vocal, talented, creative, collaborative, and, undoubtedly, here to stay.

For Discussion and Writing

1. **Comprehension** According to Brenner's survey, what are the main reasons people are drawn to fan culture?

2. **Critical Reading** How does the writer use rhetorical questions to **structure** her article? How are these questions related to her assumptions about her **audience**?

3. **Analysis**   Brenner writes, "Being a fan is not new, of course, but today being a fan has become an increasingly public, shared act" (par. 6). What does she mean by this? Does it seem like a positive development? Can you think of examples that support her claim?

4. **Connections**   In "The Art of Immersion: Fear of Fiction" (p. 409), Frank Rose writes about game developers Jordan Weisman and Elan Lee, who supervised an elaborate online project (called *The Beast*) to engage fans of the 2001 film *A.I.* Look at the story behind—and the fan reaction to—this game. How is a fan-culture phenomenon like *The Beast* similar to the fan fiction or fan art described by Brenner? In what significant ways is it different?

5. **Writing**   Find a fan-work Web site devoted to a book, film, television show, or other popular culture phenomenon that interests you. Then write your own piece of fan fiction based on your chosen source material. Alternately, you may also find a fan-work Web site and then write a critique of the writing you find there. As Brenner points out, critical discussion—of plot, theme, character, source material—is part of the fan community phenomenon. Do you find the work engaging, intelligent, original, and transformative? Does it deepen your engagement with the source material? Why or why not? Describe your experience reading and writing fan fiction in a short reflection piece.

FRANK ROSE

The Art of Immersion: Fear of Fiction

Frank Rose began his journalism career at the Village Voice, *writing about the bourgeoning 1970s punk rock scene in New York City. Since then he has been a contributing editor at* Travel + Leisure *and* Esquire *magazines, as well as a contributing writer at* Premiere *and a contributing editor at* Wired *magazine. Rose's work has also appeared in the* New York Times Magazine, Vanity Fair, Rolling Stone, *and other publications. His most recent book is* The Art of Immersion: How the Digital Generation Is Remaking Hollywood, Madison Avenue, and the Way We Tell Stories *(2011). In this excerpt from* The Art of Immersion, *Rose tells the story of video game developers Jordan Weisman and Elan Lee. But he also explores the history of immersive media and cultural responses to evolving technologies of narrative.*

As you read, *think about your own experiences with—and reactions to—the "transporting power of narrative." What immersive, story-based game first inspired Jordan Weisman? What is Rose's attitude toward his subjects, and how does it come across in his tone and style? Why do you think vicarious experiences are so appealing to us?*

Jordan Weisman, a 14-year-old from the Chicago suburbs who would grow up to more or less invent the concept of alternate reality games, was back for his sixth summer—this time as a junior counselor. Camp Shewahmegon fronted on a remote and pristine lake, its thousand-foot shoreline dotted with sugar maples, yellow birches, white pines, and balsam firs. But for Jordan the fun started after dark, when the little kids were asleep and the older ones had the evening to themselves. That's when the camp's senior counselor brought out a new game he'd just discovered in college. The game was *Dungeons & Dragons*. The year was 1974.

When he was in second grade, Jordan had been diagnosed as severely dyslexic. In a way, he was lucky. Dyslexia had been identified by European physicians in the late nineteenth century, but American schoolteachers had only recently been introduced to the idea that otherwise normal kids might be unable to read because their brains couldn't process words and letters properly. Jordan's teacher had just attended a seminar on the disorder, and a nearby teachers' college was one of the few places in the country that tested for it. Since then, years of daily tutoring had given Jordan a way to cope, but reading was still difficult—so difficult he found it almost physically painful.

Dungeons & Dragons gave him a different kind of story—one he could act out instead of having to read. The first commercial example of what would become a long line of fantasy role-playing games, *D&D* provided an elaborate set of rules that guided players through an imaginary adventure as they sat around a table together. Each player got to pick a character with certain characteristics (human or elf, fighter or wizard) and abilities. The game started with the lead player, the "Dungeon Master," describing the setting and the plot to all the others. As the game progressed, the Dungeon Master determined the outcome of the players' actions, often with a roll of the dice. For those few hours, they weren't a bunch of knock-kneed mall rats in a cabin in the woods; they were axe-wielding warriors fighting goblins and orcs. The images that played out in Jordan's head during these sessions were so vivid, and the socialization with the other boys so intense, that decades later he remembered thinking, Wow—my life is going to be changed.

"Here was entertainment that involved problem solving and was story based and social," he recalled. "It totally put my brain on fire." Ultimately, it led him to fashion a career in game design and social interaction—two fields he sees as intimately connected. "Games are about engaging with the most entertaining thing on the planet," he added, "which is other people."

On his way home from Camp Shewahmegon that summer, Jordan convinced his parents to stop at Lake Geneva, Wisconsin, a small resort town near the Illinois border. He wanted to buy his own copy of *Dungeons & Dragons,* and the only way you could do that was to see Gary Gygax, the local insurance underwriter who had invented it with a friend. Gygax had a passion for games, but no publisher was interested in taking this one on, so he had published it himself and was selling it out of his house.

Jordan started a *Dungeons & Dragons* club when he went back to school that fall—the beginning of what would become a lifelong pattern of entrepreneurship. After graduation he attended the Merchant Marine Academy and then the University of Illinois, but before long he dropped out and started a company he called FASA Corporation—short for Freedonian Aeronautics and Space Administration, after the fictional nation in the Marx Brothers' film *Duck Soup*.

In 1999, Microsoft acquired a spin-off company called FASA Interactive and moved it from Chicago to the woodsy Seattle suburb of Redmond, not far from corporate headquarters. Weisman became creative director of Microsoft's new entertainment division, which was about to launch the Xbox—the console that would pit the company against Sony and its best-selling Play Station in the video game business.

Weisman's new role gave him creative oversight of everyone developing video games for the Xbox. One such group was Bungie Studios, another Chicago-based game developer that Microsoft had bought and moved to Seattle. Bungie's big project was *Halo,* a shooter that had generated rave reports after being demonstrated at game shows in prototype form. In 2000 and 2001, as the Bungie team was retooling *Halo* to be a game that could be played exclusively on the Xbox, Weisman helped the Bungie crew create a backstory for the game.

"You need characters," he explained. "You need plotlines that can be extended and moved to other media to create a more robust world." Weisman's team put together a *Halo* "bible," a compendium of information about the characters in the game and the universe in which it takes place. They made a deal with Del Rey Books to publish a series of novels that would flesh out the *Halo* story. But while Weisman was spending most of his days thinking about *Halo* and other new Xbox titles, on his own time he was thinking about an entirely different kind of game.

In truth, Weisman didn't really care that much about video games. He liked storytelling, and game developers at the time were far too busy trying to deliver gee-whiz computer graphics to pay much attention to story. Ever since his days at camp, he'd loved telling stories through interaction with other people. Now he was starting to think about how interactive stories could be told in a way that was organic to the Internet.

"What do we do on the Net?" he asked. "Mainly we search through a ton of crap looking for information we care about, like an archaeologist sifting through dirt." Gradually, after months of midafternoon rambles through Microsoft parking lots and 3:00 A.M. phone calls with a young protégé named Elan Lee, this line of thought evolved into the notion of a deconstructed narrative. They could write a story, fabricate the evidence that would have existed had it been real, and then throw the story out and get an online audience to reconstruct it. That was the theory anyway— that we humans would forage for information the same way other species forage for food, and use it to tell ourselves a story. Now all he needed was some way to try it out.

One of the video games Weisman was supervising at Microsoft was based on the upcoming Steven Spielberg movie *Artificial Intelligence: AI*. Originally developed by Stanley Kubrick in the 1970s, then taken over by Spielberg after Kubrick's death, the film was meant to be a futuristic retelling of the Pinocchio legend, with an android in place of the wooden puppet that dreamed of becoming an actual boy. Personally, Weisman had his doubts about the appeal of a video game centered on a boy who longed for his mother's love, even if the boy in question was a robot. But he also figured that the kind of deconstructed narrative he wanted to create could be used to establish a context for the game, and for the movie as well.

While overseeing development of the video game, Weisman worked closely with Spielberg and his producer, Kathleen Kennedy. One day he sat in Spielberg's headquarters at Universal Studios, a grandly appointed "bungalow" just down the hill from *Jurassic Park—The Ride*, and told them he wanted to explore a new way of telling stories.

Much as the theme park ride was designed to give the sensation of being hurled headlong into *Jurassic Park*, Weisman wanted to create an experience of being plunged into the world of *A.I.* But there the similarities stopped. The *Jurassic Park* ride was Hollywood's idea of participatory entertainment: a five-and-a-half minute boat trip past some robotic dinosaurs, with a scream-inducing eighty-five-foot drop at the end. It was an expensively produced theme park attraction that sought to match the public's desire for more *Jurassic Park* entertainment with Universal's desire for more *Jurassic Park* profits. Weisman's idea was to use the Internet to go beyond the very personal narrative of Spielberg's new film to tell the story of the world the movie was set in.

Weisman is a persuasive guy. At the end of the meeting, Kennedy 15 called the head of marketing at Warner Bros., which was making the picture. As Weisman recalls it, she made an announcement: "I'm sending Jordan over. I want you to write him a very big check. And don't ask what it's for."

"It's good to be king," Weisman remarked when the call was over.

"Yes," she said, "it is."

The experiment began in April 2001, twelve weeks before the release of the movie, when a credit for something called a "sentient machine therapist" appeared among the myriad other credits listed in trailers and posters for the film. The clue was so tiny you could easily miss it, but that was the point. Marketers were already encountering a growing problem: how to reach people so media saturated that they block any attempt to get through. "Your brain filters it out, because otherwise you'd go crazy," Weisman told me. So he opted for the subdural approach: instead of shouting the message, hide it. "I figured that if the audience discovered something, they would share it, because we all need something to talk about."

He was right. Within 24 hours, someone posted the discovery on the movie fan site Ain't It Cool News. Googling the therapist's name, people found a maze of bizarre Web sites about robot rights and a phone number that, when called, played a message from the therapist saying her friend's husband had just died in a suspicious boating accident. Within days, a 24-year-old computer programmer in Oregon had organized an online discussion forum to investigate. More than 150 people joined the forum in its first 48 hours. By the time the movie came out in June, some 3 million people around the planet were involved at one level or another.

Whatever they were experiencing seemed to know no boundar- 20 ies. Clues were liable to appear anywhere—on Web sites, on TV, in fake newspaper ads. Phone calls, faxes, and emails could come at any time, day or night. Almost the weirdest part was that no one announced or even acknowledged that anything unusual was going on.

One day a Warner Bros. marketing executive asked Elan Lee, who was essentially running the *AI* game, for a single line of text to go at the end of an *AI* movie trailer being made for TV. He needed it in 20 minutes. Lee was desperate. He wanted to make people feel good, or at least not silly, about responding to emails from a fictional character. So he came up with the line "This Is Not a Game." It was flashed for a few seconds on TV. This cryptic missive quickly became a mantra among the players, a neat summation of the mystique generated by a game that refused to acknowledge its own existence. It was the closest Lee or Weisman or any of them ever came to speaking publicly about the experience as it was happening.

They made mistakes, of course. When he and Lee were planning the game, Weisman had argued that no puzzle would be too hard, no clue too obscure, because with so many people collaborating online, the players would have access to any conceivable skill that would be needed to solve it. Where he erred was in not following that argument to its logical conclusion.

"Not only do they have every skill set on the planet," he told me, "but they have unlimited resources, unlimited time, and unlimited money. Not only can they solve anything—they can solve anything instantly." He had dubbed his game *The Beast* because originally it had 666 items of content—Web pages to pore over, obscure puzzles to decipher. These were supposed to keep the players busy for three months; instead, the players burned through them in a single day. With people clamoring for more, the name took on a different connotation: Weisman had created a monster.

It's little wonder that the game's success took Weisman by surprise. Its mix of real-world and online interaction violated every notion of what futuristic digital entertainment was expected to be. For years, science-fiction novels like Neal Stephenson's *Snow Crash* had conditioned readers to think the future would bring some swirling electronic phantasm so vivid that the real world could never compete. But Weisman didn't do virtual reality; he trafficked in alternate reality. *The Beast* wasn't about retreating into some digitally synthesized head space. It was about interacting with other humans in response to an alternate sequence of events.

The world in the spring of 2001 might have been trying to cope with the sudden deflation of the Internet bubble, but people caught up in the *A.I.* game had to deal not only with that issue but with the furor over civil rights for sentient machines in the year 2142. This was, if anything, more radical, and perhaps ultimately more in sync with the current direction of technology, than the gloves and goggles that kept popping up in the media's breathless reports about virtual reality. "What we're doing is a giant extrapolation of sitting in the kitchen playing *Dungeons & Dragons* with our friends," Weisman told me as we sat at the table in his guesthouse, gazing out across the placid surface of the lake. "It's just that now, our kitchen table holds three million people." [. . .]

Several years after he and Jordan Weisman staged *The Beast,* Elan Lee went to visit his parents at the antique shop they own in Los Angeles. The shop, which goes by the name Aunt Teek's, occupies a modest storefront on Ventura Boulevard, a commercial strip that lies like a fault line between the winding lanes and bougainvillea-clad homes of the Hollywood Hills and the sun-baked sprawl of the San Fernando Valley. When Lee walked in, his father pulled out a rare treasure: a first edition of *Robinson Crusoe,* published by Daniel Defoe in 1719 and generally regarded as the earliest novel in the English language. The author's name was nowhere on the book; the title page identified it as *The Life and Strange Surprizing Adventures of Robinson Crusoe, of York, Mariner: Written by Himself.* As Lee carefully examined the volume, which was falling apart yet strangely beautiful, he was struck by the disclaimer he read in its preface:

> If ever the Story of any private Man's Adventures in the World were worth making Pvblick, and were acceptable when Publish'd, the Editor of this Account thinks this will be so. . . . The Editor believes the thing to be a just History of Fact; neither is there any Appearance of Fiction in it . . . ; and as such he thinks, without farther Compliment to the World, he does them a great Service in the Publication.

This might seem a rather elaborately defensive justification for a work that today, nearly three centuries later, is considered a major landmark in English literature. With hindsight, we can see that *Robinson Crusoe* and the novels that followed it—Henry Fielding's *Tom Jones,* Samuel Richardson's *Pamela,* Laurence Sterne's *Tristram Shandy*—led to a fundamental shift in our view of the world. Where earlier forms of literature had been expected to hew to history, myth, or legend, novels were judged by their "truth to individual experience," as the critic Ian Watt put it. They gave readers for the first time a window onto other people's lives. Yet in the early 1700s, nearly three centuries after the invention of movable type in Europe, prose fiction remained highly suspect: it was categorized with history but had the flaw of not being true.

Defoe himself was equally suspect. Nearly 60 at the time of the book's publication, he was a failed businessman, chronic debtor, political pamphleteer, and occasional spy. Even his name was false; he'd been born Daniel Foe, the son of a tradesman, but had changed his name in an attempt to pass as an aristocrat. In 1703, despite years of propagandizing for king and government, he'd been jailed and pilloried for sedition. In 1704, after his release, he had started one of England's first periodicals, a proto-newspaper on political and economic affairs that he continued to write and publish for the next nine years. And then after that, he somehow used his imaginative powers to channel the tale of a shipwrecked sailor forced to live by his wits for 28 years on a remote Caribbean island.

Robinson Crusoe was an instant success. After its publication Defoe went on to write other novels—*Moll Flanders, The Journal of the Plague Year*—that vividly dramatized the lives of very different people: a prostitute and thief, a witness to the epidemic that killed 20 percent of London's population in 1665 and 1666. By this time, a modest rise in literacy and leisure was starting to create what seemed by contemporary standards to be an explosion of reading, and of writing as well. As Samuel Johnson wrote, "There never was a time in which men of all degrees of ability of every kind of education, of every profession and employment were posting with ardour so general to the press."

Yet decades would pass before the novel became a generally accepted literary form in England. And even after it did, literary figures would argue about its function. Is fiction merely a personal "impression of life," as Henry James maintained in "The Art of Fiction," an 1884 essay in *Longman's Magazine,* the London literary journal? Or is it something more fundamental—an abstraction of life, a simulation we use to help us understand our existence? "Life is monstrous, infinite, illogical, abrupt and poignant; a work of art in comparison is neat, finite, self-contained, rational, flowing, and emasculate," Robert Louis Stevenson wrote a few months later in response. Life is true; art is a construct. But Defoe was writing long before this particular type of construct became accepted as art. So never mind that every story is by definition a fiction of some sort—what Defoe was saying in his preface was, This is not a novel.

It was certainly a statement that resonated with Lee. In March 2002, nearly a year after he and Weisman had staged *The Beast*, Lee had given a talk about the experience at the Game Developers Conference, an annual expo that was held that year in San Jose, in the heart of Silicon Valley. He called his talk "This Is Not a Game"—the same enigmatic statement that had been flashed at the end of the TV trailer for *A.I.*—and in it he set out to explain their goal. They wanted to tell a story that would blend into your life—a story that would send you e-mail, page you when you were in business meetings, transmit secret messages through ringtones. They weren't building a game; they were building an experience that was capable of, as he put it, "transforming your life into an entertainment venue."

But of course it was a game, just as *Robinson Crusoe* was a novel. And as he sat in his parents' shop reading that preface from 300 years before, Lee had a sudden jolt of insight. By denying that they had created a game, he realized, he had fallen into a pattern that had been repeated many times before, whenever people were trying to figure out a way of telling stories that was new and unformed and not yet accepted. He was trying to make it seem okay.

"What Defoe was saying was, 'Take this seriously,'" Lee said as we sipped espresso at a café in a century-old commercial building in downtown Seattle, around the corner from the bustling, tourist-friendly waterfront. "Novels didn't exist yet, and he needed to justify this experience"—and what better way to justify a new medium than by pretending it's not new at all? Early moviemakers, Lee figured, were making the same plea with the proscenium arch shot—filming the story as if it were a play, with a single, stationary camera from the perspective of a spectator in the center row. "That's them screaming, 'This is not a game.' It wasn't until later that they took the camera and started doing zooms and pans."

That sort of thing began around 1903, a decade after films were first shown publicly. In *The Great Train Robbery*, generally considered to be the first Western, Edwin S. Porter, a director at the Edison Manufacturing Company, used crosscutting to link parallel events. It took years for such practices to become commonplace. But by the time D. W. Griffith made *The Birth of a Nation* in 1915, directors had developed a grammar of film, abandoning stage conventions in favor of dramatic close-ups and sophisticated editing techniques—flashbacks, crosscuts, point-of-view shots—that took full advantage of the new medium's possibilities. Even before sound and color, film conveyed a degree of realism viewers had never encountered before.

Television, too, began by mimicking familiar forms. America's   35
first big hits—Milton Berle's *Texaco Star Theater* and Ed Sullivan's *Toast of the Town*—were pure vaudeville, the variety format that a half century before had lured people to theaters to see a bill of singers and dancers and novelty acts. Popular dramatic series— *Man Against Crime, Philco Television Playhouse, Kraft Television Theatre*—were broadcast live from New York, just as radio dramas had been. So were comedy series like *The George Burns and Gracie Allen Show*. Not until the 1951 debut of *I Love Lucy*—shot on film in the now-classic, then-revolutionary sitcom format— did television begin to find success on its own terms.

The demise of live drama and comedy brought with it the end of the so-called Golden Age of Television, the brief period when broadcasters were as likely to challenge the audience as to pander. But by inviting viewers into Lucy and Desi's living room, producers found a far more dependable and cost-effective way to get audiences to turn on the tube. Inadvertently, as Clay Shirky has pointed out, they also found a way of soaking up all the free time created by vacuum cleaners, automatic dishwashers, and post– World War II prosperity. Now, two decades into the development of the Web, the sitcom in its classic form—three cameras and a laugh track—has given way to more psychologically involving comedies like *The Office* and *Curb Your Enthusiasm*, even as the concept of leisure time has all but evaporated in a constant bombardment of information.

But no new medium's attempt to cloak itself in familiar garb has succeeded in rendering it immune from attack. Janet Murray made this point in her 1997 book *Hamlet on the Holodeck,* a prescient look at narrative in cyberspace: Every new medium that has been invented, from print to film to television, has increased the transporting power of narrative. And every new medium has aroused fear and hostility as a result.

Ray Bradbury's *Fahrenheit 451,* written in the early fifties—the dawn of the television era—concerns a man named Montag whose job is burning books. Montag's wife, like her friends, is enthralled by the weirdly nonlinear yet mesmerizing video transmissions on the giant "televisors" on her living room walls. Lulled by their narcotic effect, Mildred and most of the rest of the population are too distracted to register the coming nuclear holocaust. "My wife says books aren't 'real,'" the book burner tells Faber, the former English professor who gradually transforms him into a preserver of books. Faber replies,

> "Thank God for that. You can shut them and say, 'Hold on a moment!' But who has ever torn himself from the claw that encloses you when you drop a seed in a TV parlor? . . . It is an environment as real as the world. It becomes and is the truth. Books can be beaten down with reason. But with all my knowledge and skepticism, I have never been able to argue with . . . those incredible parlors."

A claw that encloses you. An environment as real as the world. That was Bradbury's beef with television—it was just too immersive. Logical, linear thought was no match for its seductively phosphorescent glow. It became and was the truth.

Before television came along, the same danger could be found in the movies. In Aldous Huxley's *Brave New World*—published in 1932, five years after talkies finally gave motion picture actors a voice—young John the Savage is taken to the "feelies." There, viewing an "All-Super-Singing, Synthetic-Talking, Coloured, Stereoscopic Feely," he is revolted by the sensation of phantom lips grazing his own as the actors kiss. "Suddenly, dazzling and incomparably more solid-looking than they would have seemed in actual flesh and blood, far more real than reality, there stood the stereoscopic images, locked in one another's arms, of a gigantic negro and a golden-haired young brachycephalic Beta-Plus female. The Savage started. That sensation on his lips!"

Too real. Dangerously, immersively, more-real-than-reality real, Huxley would say. Better to curl up with a good book.

But once upon a time, books, too, had seemed more real than reality. They offered a passport to imaginary worlds. They triggered delusions. They were new, and not to be trusted. More than a century before *Robinson Crusoe*, Don Quixote went tilting at windmills because he'd lost his mind from reading:

> [He] so buried himself in his books that he read all night from sundown to dawn, and all day from sunup to dusk, until with virtually no sleep and so much reading he dried out his brain and lost his sanity. He filled his imagination full to bursting with everything he read in his books, from witchcraft to duels, battles, challenges, wounds, flirtations, love affairs, anguish, and impossible foolishness, packing it all so firmly into his head that these sensational schemes and dreams became the literal truth. . . . Indeed, his mind was so tattered and torn that, finally . . . he decided to turn himself into a knight errant, traveling all over the world with his horse and his weapons, seeking adventures and doing everything that, according to his books, earlier knights had done.

So Don Quixote was a book geek, and an embarrassing one at that. It's little wonder Defoe felt need of a disclaimer.

For Discussion and Writing

1. *Comprehension*   Besides video games, list other narrative technologies and examples of immersive media in this excerpt. What point does Rose make by using them?

2. *Critical Reading*   How does Rose shift from his narrative account of Jordan Weisman and Elan Lee to a literary–historical discussion of *Robinson Crusoe* and the history of the English novel? Find the passage where Rose manages this **transition**. What makes this **structure** technique effective?

3. *Analysis*   According to Rose, game designer Jordan Weisman "didn't do virtual reality; he trafficked in alternate reality" (par. 24). What does Rose mean by this distinction? Why is the difference significant?

4. *Connections*   How can we understand "The Art of Immersion" by using Clay Shirky's analysis and approach in "Gin, Television, and Social Surplus" (p. 167) or Neil Postman's argument in "The Judg-

ment of Thamus" (p. 151)? For example, how might Shirky explain *The Beast*—and the public response to it? What does the game reveal about the nature of (in Rose's words) "participatory entertainment" (par. 14)? Or do Postman and Shirky have similar attitudes toward and conclusions about their subjects?

5. **Writing** According to Rose, every new narrative medium "has aroused fear and hostility" (par. 37) toward the dangers of its immersive power. Do you think contemporary immersive media— from the Internet to violent video games—are uniquely harmful or dangerous to their users? Or are contemporary anxieties about their immersive power unfounded and overstated, as in the past when critics feared the dangerous effects of novels (see Knox, p. 396)? Explain your answer in a persuasive essay that draws on your own media habits and experiences.

CHUCK KLOSTERMAN

My Zombie, Myself:
Why Modern Life Feels
Rather Undead

A prolific author, essayist, and pop culture critic, Chuck Klosterman (b. 1972) has written for Esquire, *the* New York Times Magazine, Spin, *the* Washington Post, *and many other publications. His books include* Fargo Rock City: A Heavy Metal Odyssey in Rural North Dakota *(2001),* Sex, Drugs, and Cocoa Puffs: A Low Culture Manifesto *(2003), and* I Wear the Black Hat: Grappling with Villains (Real and Imagined) *(2013). In this* New York Times *column, Klosterman argues that zombies are the representative monsters of our age: "Zombies are like the Internet and the media and every conversation we don't want to have." For the writer, zombies are less important for the unconscious fears they represent than for the way they capture the experience of living in the contemporary world.*

As you read, *consider the metaphorical and allegorical significance of monsters. Why does Klosterman think zombies are "becoming more intriguing to us"? How does he support his thesis? Do you fear being "consumed"?*

Zombies are a value stock. They are wordless and oozing and brain-dead, but they're an ever-expanding market with no glass ceiling. Zombies are a target-rich environment, literally and figuratively. The more you fill them with bullets, the more interesting they become. Roughly 5.3 million people watched the first episode of *The Walking Dead* on AMC, a stunning 83 percent more than the 2.9 million who watched the Season 4 premiere of *Mad Men*. This means there are at least 2.4 million cable-ready Americans who might prefer watching Christina Hendricks if she were an animated corpse.

Statistically and aesthetically that dissonance seems perverse. But it probably shouldn't. Mainstream interest in zombies has steadily risen over the past 40 years. Zombies are a commodity that has advanced slowly and without major evolution, much like the staggering creatures George Romero popularized in the 1968 film *Night of the Living Dead*. What makes that measured amplification curious is the inherent limitations of the zombie itself: You can't add much depth to a creature who can't talk, doesn't think and whose only motive is the consumption of flesh. You can't humanize a zombie, unless you make it less zombie-esque. There are slow zombies, and there are fast zombies—that's pretty much the spectrum of zombie diversity. It's not that zombies are changing to fit the world's condition; it's that the condition of the world seems more like a zombie offensive. Something about zombies is becoming more intriguing to us. And I think I know what that something is.

Zombies are just so easy to kill.

When we think critically about monsters, we tend to classify them as personifications of what we fear. Frankenstein's monster illustrated our trepidation about untethered science; Godzilla was spawned from the fear of the atomic age; werewolves feed into an instinctual panic over predation and man's detachment from nature. Vampires and zombies share an imbedded anxiety about disease. It's easy to project a symbolic relationship between vampirism and AIDS (or vampirism and the loss of purity). From a creative standpoint these fear projections are narrative linchpins; they turn creatures into ideas, and that's the point.

But what if the audience infers an entirely different metaphor?   5

What if contemporary people are less interested in seeing depictions of their unconscious fears and more attracted to allegories of how their day-to-day existence feels? That would explain why so many people watched the first episode of *The Walking Dead:* They knew they would be able to relate to it.

A lot of modern life is exactly like slaughtering zombies.

If there's one thing we all understand about zombie killing, it's that the act is uncomplicated: you blast one in the brain from point-blank range (preferably with a shotgun). That's Step 1. Step 2 is doing the same thing to the next zombie that takes its place. Step 3 is identical to Step 2, and Step 4 isn't any different from Step 3. Repeat this process until (a) you perish, or (b) you run out of zombies. That's really the only viable strategy.

Andrew Lincoln as Rick Grimes in *The Walking Dead*. Are those slow-moving figures in the background zombies, or are they really "the Internet and the media and every conversation we don't want to have"?

Every zombie war is a war of attrition. It's always a numbers game. And it's more repetitive than complex. In other words, zombie killing is philosophically similar to reading and deleting 400 work e-mails on a Monday morning or filling out paperwork that only generates more paperwork, or following Twitter gossip out of obligation, or performing tedious tasks in which the only true risk is being consumed by avalanche. The principal downside to any zombie attack is that the zombies will never stop coming; the principal downside to life is that you will never be finished with whatever it is you do.

The Internet reminds us of this every day.   10

Here's a passage from a youngish writer named Alice Gregory, taken from a recent essay on Gary Shteyngart's dystopic novel *Super Sad True Love Story* in the literary journal *n+1*: "It's hard not to think 'death drive' every time I go on the Internet," she writes. "Opening Safari is an actively destructive decision. I am asking that consciousness be taken away from me."

Ms. Gregory's self-directed fear is thematically similar to how the zombie brain is described by Max Brooks, author of the fictional oral history *World War Z* and its accompanying self-help manual, *The Zombie Survival Guide*: "Imagine a computer programmed to execute one function. This function cannot be paused, modified, or erased. No new data can be stored. No new commands can be installed. This computer will perform that one function, over and over, until its power source eventually shuts down."

This is our collective fear projection: that we will be consumed. Zombies are like the Internet and the media and every conversation we don't want to have. All of it comes at us endlessly (and thoughtlessly), and—if we surrender—we will be overtaken and absorbed. Yet this war is manageable, if not necessarily winnable. As long we keep deleting whatever's directly in front of us, we survive. We live to eliminate the zombies of tomorrow. We are able to remain human, at least for the time being. Our enemy is relentless and colossal, but also uncreative and stupid.

Battling zombies is like battling anything . . . or everything.

Because of the *Twilight* series it's easy to manufacture an argument in which zombies are merely replacing vampires as the monster of the moment, a designation that is supposed to matter for metaphorical, nonmonstrous reasons. But that kind of thinking is deceptive. The recent five-year spike in vampire interest is only about the multiplatform success of *Twilight,* a brand that isn't about vampirism anyway. It's mostly about nostalgia for teenage chastity, the attractiveness of its film cast and the fact that contemporary fiction consumers tend to prefer long serialized novels that can be read rapidly. But this has still created a domino effect. The 2008 Swedish vampire film *Let the Right One In* was fantastic, but it probably wouldn't have been remade in the United States if *Twilight* had never existed. *The Gates* was an overt attempt by ABC to tap into the housebound, preteen *Twilight* audience; HBO's *True Blood* is a camp reaction to Robert Pattinson's flat earnestness. 15

The difference with zombies, of course, is that it's possible to like a specific vampire temporarily, which isn't really an option with the undead. Characters like Mr. Pattison's Edward Cullen in *Twilight* and Anne Rice's Lestat de Lioncourt, and even boring old Count Dracula can be multidimensional and erotic; it's possible to learn why they are and who they once were. Vampire love can be singular. Zombie love, however, is always communal. If you dig zombies, you dig the entire zombie concept. It's never personal. You're interested in what zombies signify, you like the way they move, and you understand what's required to stop them. And this is a reassuring attraction, because those aspects don't really shift. They've become shared archetypal knowledge.

A few days before Halloween I was in upstate New York with three other people, and we somehow ended up at the Barn of Terror, outside a town call Lake Katrine. Entering the barn was mildly disturbing, although probably not as scary as going into an actual abandoned barn that didn't charge $20 and doesn't own its own domain name. Regardless, the best part was when we exited the terror barn and were promptly herded onto a school bus, which took us to a cornfield about a quarter of a mile away. The field was filled with amateur actors, some playing military personnel and others what they called the infected. We were told to run through the moonlit corn maze if we wanted to live; as we ran, armed soldiers yelled contradictory instructions while hissing zombies emerged from the corny darkness. It was designed to be fun, and it was. But just before we immersed ourselves in the corn, one of my companions sardonically critiqued the reality of our predicament.

"I know this is supposed to be scary," he said. "But I'm pretty confident about my ability to deal with a zombie apocalypse. I feel strangely informed about what to do in this kind of scenario."

I could not disagree. At this point who isn't? We all know how this goes: If you awake from a coma, and you don't immediately see a member of the hospital staff, assume a zombie takeover has transpired during your incapacitation. Don't travel at night and keep your drapes closed. Don't let zombies spit on you. If you knock a zombie down, direct a second bullet into its brain stem. But above all, do not assume that the war is over, because it never is. The zombies you kill today will merely be replaced by the zombies of tomorrow. But you can do this, my friend. It's disenchanting, but it's not difficult. Keep your finger on the trigger. Continue the termination. Don't stop believing. Don't stop deleting. Return your voice mails and nod your agreements. This is the zombies' world, and we just live in it. But we can live better.

For Discussion and Writing

1. **Comprehension**   How are zombies different from vampires, according to Klosterman? Why are these distinctions important to his argument?

2. **Critical Reading**   Where does the writer use classification and division to **structure** his essay? Locate an example and explain how it furthers his **main point**.

3. **Analysis**   Klosterman writes about monsters as illustrative metaphors—and the ways these metaphors "turn creatures into ideas" (par. 4). What ideas do zombies represent for Klosterman? Does it make sense to read monsters metaphorically? Explain your answer.

4. **Connections**   In "Escape from the Matrix" (p. 428), Jacob Burak writes about the "Fear of Missing Out," which is a "cultural disorder that is insidiously undermining our peace of mind" (par. 5). Does this "disorder" seem related to the "undead" texture of modern life as described by Klosterman? Are the coping and management strategies suggested by both writers compatible? Why or why not?

5. **Writing**   According to Klosterman, "When we think critically about monsters, we tend to classify them as personifications of what we fear" (par. 4). But he also claims that people may be drawn to monsters as "allegories of how their day-to-day existence feels" (par. 6). Choose a monster from legend, film, fiction, or television, and then analyze it in either of the two ways Klosterman suggests here. For example, what is the "symbolic relationship" (par. 4) between your chosen monster and a particular social or cultural anxiety?

JACOB BURAK

Escape from the Matrix

Jacob Burak is an Israeli author and activist. In 1987, he founded the venture capital firm Evergreen, which focused on investments in technology. In 2005, he left Evergreen to write about popular science, psychology, economics, technology, and culture. Burak's books include Do Chimpanzees Dream of Retirement: An Encounter between Psychology, Evolution and Business *(2007) and* Why Kamikaze Pilots Wear Helmets *(2009). He is also the founder of* Alaxon, *a digital magazine devoted to culture, art, and popular sciences. In this essay, which appeared in* Aeon, *Burak investigates "FoMO" or the "Fear of Missing Out": a "cultural disorder that is insidiously undermining our peace of mind." As Burak notes, this phenomenon is not new, but our hyperconnected and networked culture may be making it more acute than ever.*

As you read, *consider: Given its long history, how has the Fear of Missing Out changed over time? What is Burak's strategy in his introduction, and how effective is it? How does Burak's article connect with your own experiences of FoMO?*

Here's a test you might enjoy: rate these scenarios on a number scale, ranging from 1 for mild discomfort to 7 for outrageous distress.

Scenario 1: you're flicking through news websites, as you do every morning. Today, however, you're behind schedule and have only 15 minutes to read articles, instead of your usual 30. You have to skip some of your favorite columns and sections. How would you rate your level of discomfort? (Most of us would probably choose a low level, say 2.)

Scenario 2: you're visiting New York City and realize there's no way you'll be able to get to all the exhibits, see all the recommended plays, or take in even a fraction of the "musts" your local friends have raved about. How do you feel now? Something like 5?

Scenario 3: you're at dinner with friends, and you've all agreed to make it a strictly phone-free evening. But your smartphone won't stop beeping Twitter and text alerts. Something is obviously up in your social network, but you can't check. Even 7 wouldn't match the stress you're feeling now.

Welcome to FoMO (Fear of Missing Out), the latest cultural disorder that is insidiously undermining our peace of mind. FoMO, a spawn of technological advancement and proliferating social information, is the feeling that we're missing out on something more exciting, more important, or more interesting going on somewhere else. It is the unease of feeling that others are having a more rewarding experience and we are not a part of it. According to a recent study, 56 percent of those who use social networks suffer this modern plague.

Of course, that sense of missing out is nothing new. An entire body of literature describes the heart-wrenching conflict between romantic aspirations and social conservatism. Edith Wharton, Charlotte Brontë, and Stendhal,[1] to name but a few, described the angst of missing out long before we could look up high-school friends on Facebook.

But while 19th-century protagonists spent a lifetime grappling with a single missed opportunity, today's incessant flow of information is a disturbing reminder of the world rushing by. As you read this, you might be missing a party that some friends are throwing or the meal that other friends are eating without you. Perhaps you're willing to cut one phone call short—in mid-sentence—to take another call, without even knowing who might be on the other end. At night, when you've solemnly sworn yet again to put the phone aside or turn off the computer, you grab one last peek at the screen on your way to bed—lest you miss some tidbit supplied by mere acquaintances or even strangers requesting your "friendship" or announcing news.

We all know the studies showing that end-of-life regrets center on what we didn't do, rather than on what we did. If so, constantly watching others doing things that we are not is fertile ground for a future of looking back in sorrow. A lively conversation at the

---

[1]*Edith Wharton* (1862–1937), *Charlotte Brontë* (1816–1855), and *Stendahl* (b. Marie-Henri Beyle, 1783–1842): American, English, and French authors, respectively, known for the realism and social commentary of their fiction. [Editor's note.]

other end of the table can give us the FoMO itch, just as can the dizzying array of shows, parties, books, or the latest in consumer trends pumped at us by social media.

Our attractive online personas—so alluring from afar—make FoMO more virulent still. The Massachusetts Institute of Technology social psychologist Sherry Turkle, author of *Alone Together: Why We Expect More from Technology and Less from Each Other* (2011), says that technology has become the major construct through which we define intimacy. We confuse our hundreds, or even thousands, of "friends" on social networks with the handful of intimate friends we have in reality. Drawing on hundreds of interviews, Turkle claims that the price we are paying for technological prosperity is the gradual decline of important relationships—with our parents, children, or partners—and the birth of a new type of loneliness. "Insecure in our relationships, and anxious about intimacy," she writes, "we look to technology for ways to be in relationships, and protect ourselves from them at the same time." If you have ever looked on in wonder as someone taps out an endless text message instead of actually talking to the person they're with, you will find comfort in Turkle's assessment that our relationship with technology is still maturing. Being connected to everyone, all the time, is a new human experience; we're just not equipped to cope with it yet.

Turkle says our dependence on technology can be mitigated if 10 we manage to detach ourselves, even for short periods of time, from our gadgets. Will we one day buy devices from FA (FoMO Anonymous) to help us recover from our technology addiction? I envision devices that relay information at random, unanticipated intervals—with neither sender nor receiver cognizant of the delay in advance—that would force owners to miss out on some communiqués and discover, to their surprise, that they can still function without them.

Even with such interventions, the problem might be resolved only when we grasp that our brains and our humanity—not our technologies—enable this addiction, in the end. We cannot seek solutions without honestly asking ourselves why we are so afraid of missing out.

The University of Oxford social scientist Andrew Przybylski recently conducted the first empirical study on the exploding disorder, with the results published in *Computers in Human Behavior* in 2013. Among his conclusions, there and elsewhere, is that

FoMO is a driving force behind social media use. FoMO levels are highest in young people, in particular young men. It is high in distracted drivers, who engage in other activities while behind the wheel. And perhaps most revealing, FoMO occurs mostly in people with unfulfilled psychological needs in realms such as love, respect, autonomy, and security. All in all, we are afraid of missing out on love and on feeling that we belong; those of us heavily invested in work also fear missing an opportunity for professional advancement or a profitable deal.

The University of Oxford evolutionary psychologist Robin Dunbar, author of *How Many Friends Does a Person Need?* (2010), says that the problem might be mitigated if only we understood ourselves more. Dunbar claims that we lack the emotional and intellectual capacity to distinguish between more than about 150 members of a group—the average size of a Neolithic farming village. But just tell that to the average U.S. teen, who sends 3,000 text messages a month (according to a 2010 report by Nielsen, the marketing-survey giant) and who fears that she will be ostracized if she doesn't respond immediately, sometimes dealing with a cast of thousands online.

Freedom from other people's opinions and release from social comparison is a triumph reserved for very few. The self-discipline strong enough to withstand the power of FoMO is no less rare. In 2012, the University of Chicago social psychologist Wilhelm Hofmann studied the use of willpower to resist daily temptation: his participants found it far easier to abstain from food and sex through willpower alone than to stay away from online networks, where the failure rate was 42 percent.

What, then, can we do about something so detrimental to our quality of life? Psychotherapy for the underlying emotional causes of FoMO is far too costly and invasive, and simply vowing to disconnect from our gadgets fails to work. Instead, the best way to cope with FoMO might be to recognize that, at our frenetic pace of life, we are sometimes bound to miss out. And that, when we do, we might actually improve the outcomes of the options we have chosen. 15

This simple approach was first introduced in 1956 by Herbert Simon, an American multidisciplinary researcher and Nobel Prize Laureate in Economics. He used the term "satisfice"—a portmanteau of "satisfy" and "suffice"—to suggest that instead of trying to maximize our benefits, we seek a merely "good enough" result. Simon's strategy relies on the assumption that we simply do not have the cognitive capacity to optimize complex decision making. We cannot process the mass of information entailed in weighing all available options and probable outcomes—both on the social networks and off. Thus, the best move is "satisficing"—choosing the first available option that meets our predetermined criteria, which is good enough.

In 1996, Simon published an autobiography describing his life as a series of discrete decisions in which he chose the "good enough" option over a possible best one. Simon claims that most people who favor optimization are unaware of the heavy toll that gathering information takes on their overall benefit. In routine decisions, the price we pay is in well-being: anyone with a friend who will not agree to eat anywhere but the most fashionable restaurant or who insists on shopping until the perfect outfit is found can appreciate the relief of a "good enough" strategy.

Studies of Simon's method have shown that people who insist on optimizing decisions are ultimately less satisfied with their choices than those who made do with "good enough." Other studies clarify why: the achievements of the former are actually lower than those of the latter, especially when the decision involved weighing possible outcomes. In a series of experiments led by the Swarthmore College social psychologist Barry Schwartz, participants filled out a self-assessment questionnaire determining their tendency to optimize decisions (based on their agreement with statements such as "I never settle for second best" or "I often find it difficult to shop for gift for a friend"). Another questionnaire measured subjects' propensity to feel regret; participants were then classified according to their answers on both questionnaires. The researchers found a negative correlation between the tendency to optimize and happiness, self-esteem, and satisfaction, and a positive correlation between the same tendency and depression, perfectionism, and regret. Another study in the series found that people who optimize also engage in more social comparison, and are adversely affected when they come up short.

Wait a minute—isn't FoMO of the social networks based exactly on this type of comparison? If so, could "satisficing" bring relief? Analyzing FoMO through Simon's parameters reveals an uncanny similarity to the decision-making processes he studied, marked by cognitive overload and a heavy toll on well-being.

Today's wealth of information, especially online, is costing us   20
another valuable resource: our attention, which is limited enough
to begin with. The difficulty of spreading our already taxed attention over unprecedented amounts of information derives not just
from our cognitive problem with prioritizing, but also from our
inability to consume and process it all. FoMO-related distress is
our soul crying out for help, imploring us to limit our superficial
connectivity and our frantic hopping from site to site before our
quality of life and our ability to express intimacy and individualism erode.

Taking the "good-enough" approach to this crushing problem
is not merely a tactic for improving our decision making. It is first
and foremost a worldview, a way of life; some researchers even
believe it is a hereditary personality trait.

Testimony to the method's effectiveness abounds. In business,
sacrificing maximization in favor of a predefined "good enough"
is known to be the best strategy in the long run. As the saying
goes, "Bulls make money, bears make money, pigs get slaughtered": greediness that looks to maximize doesn't pay. Business
people also know to "leave something on the table," especially
in deals leading to long-term partnerships. Experienced capital
market investors understand that aiming to "sell at the peak" will
ultimately be less profitable than selling once a satisfactory profit
is gained. Corporate graveyards are full of companies that did not
stop at a "good enough," profitable product that they could easily
market, surrendering instead to ambitious engineers with sophisticated specifications and unrealistic plans.

In his outstanding book *Why the Allies Won* (1995), the British
historian Richard Overy analyzes the outcomes of the Second
World War, which were not, he claims, a given. One explanation
he offers is the German army's attempt to optimize use of its military munitions at the expense of tactical combat efficiency. At
one point in the war, the Germans had no fewer than 425 different kinds of aircraft, 151 kinds of trucks, and 150 kinds of
motorcycles. The price they paid for the technical superiority of
German-made munitions was difficulty in mass-production, which
was ultimately more important from a strategic point of view.
In the decisive battles fought in Russia, one German force had
to carry approximately one million spare parts for hundreds of
types of armed carriers, trucks, and motorcycles. The Russians,

in contrast, used only two types of tanks, making for much simpler munitions maintenance during war. It was "good enough" for them.

Perfectionism is the personality trait most associated with aspiring towards maximizing the outcome of decisions. However, those of us who know perfectionists, know that for them life is one never-ending score sheet that throws them into a self-assessment tizzy of frustration, anxiety, and sometimes even depression. Perfectionists tend to confuse error with failure, and their attempt to hide their errors, even the inevitable ones, prevents them from accepting the critical feedback so necessary for personal growth. They would probably give a great deal for the relief of being able to "satisfice."

Even when it comes to emotional intimacy and love, "good 25 enough" works best. It was the British psychologist Donald Winnicott who gave us the concept of the "good-enough mother" — a mother sufficiently attentive and adequately responsive to her baby's basic needs. As the baby develops, the mother occasionally "fails" to answer his needs, preparing him for a reality in which he will not always get exactly what he wants, whenever he wants it. The child learns to delay gratification, a key to any form of adult success. As we mature, we make do with "good enough" partners almost by definition. Yes, out there is someone probably more suited to our needs—but we might not live long enough to find him or her.

Even if feeling that we are missing out is testament to our spirited drive for life, the way in which social networks now enhance our optimization fallacy beyond all proportion is taking a serious toll on our quality of life. If you still doubt that "good enough" is the best antidote to FoMO, the words of the American essayist and poet Ralph Waldo Emerson might strike the right chord: "For everything you have missed, you have gained something else, and for everything you gain, you lose something else."

For Discussion and Writing

1. **Comprehension**   What demographic has the highest levels of FoMO, according to Burak?
2. **Critical Reading**   How does Burak end his article in the concluding paragraph? Do you find his choice effective? What other strategies could he have used in his **conclusion**? Provide a specific alternative.

3. *Analysis* Burak acknowledges that technology and connectivity contribute to the prevalence and urgency of FoMO. At the same time, he argues that technology is not the real problem. How does he reconcile this apparent tension? What misperception is he trying to correct?

4. *Connections* In "Why Video Games Should Be Played with Friends, Not Online with Strangers" (p. 436), Bo Moore reports on a trend in which gamers are gathering at local events, in real time, with real people, rather than merely connecting online. Does this trend appear to be a strategy for managing or fighting the Fear of Missing Out? Or does it seem like a development likely to aggravate FoMO?

5. *Writing* Burak explains the distinction between "optimizing" and "satisficing" (par. 16). Ultimately, the writer argues that "satisficing" is the more effective approach. Spend a day, a few days, or a week testing Burak's claim. Then, write about your experience in an essay or blog post. Did focusing on making "good enough" decisions (rather than "perfect" ones) lead to more peace of mind, happiness, or success? What were the consequences? Did trying this approach mean changing your attitude and behavior, or were you already in the habit of "satisficing"? Explain.

BO MOORE

Why Videogames Should Be Played with Friends, Not Online with Strangers

Bo Moore is a San Francisco-based culture and entertainment writer. His work has appeared in Paste, Kill Screen, Game Life, *and other publications. In this article from* Wired, *Moore reports on a trend in which individuals seek real connections with others at a local space, a "wave of games meant to be played together—truly together." At public events like Wild Rumpus parties, or in private homes where offline games like* Johann Sebastian Joust *are played, gamers may be recapturing the social spirit and camaraderie of the arcade.*

As you read, *think about the social pleasures people derive from games. What originally "killed" the social aspect of video games, according to Moore? Does he include enough evidence to support the claim that these current games represent a "wave" or a real trend? Do you think that games serve an important social function and, therefore, should be "played with friends, not online with strangers"?*

In the beginning, there were the arcades. We crowded around massive cabinets, seven-foot-tall monoliths containing a single videogame, arrayed like columns in movie theaters and bowling alleys. We would jostle for position, laying down our quarters to reserve a turn. Games were filled with smack talk, and a well-placed fireball could draw cheers.

Gaming was in many ways a social endeavor, something that continued as we bought consoles like the Atari 2600 and Nintendo NES. There were two controllers, which let us play with a friend. Then came the Nintendo 64 in 1996, giving us four standard controller ports. It ushered in a new era of offline social gaming; most designers included four-player modes in their N64 games. *GoldenEye 007* became a new religion, and its devotees moved on to the Xbox and *Halo*, which let us link four consoles for epic 16-player matches. But just as soon as these social gatherings were becoming the next big thing, game consoles adopted an innovation that would all but kill them: Internet play. Suddenly we were playing together alone. "It was just easier to monetize online games," said game designer Douglas Wilson. "You could be alone—you didn't have to bring a bunch of people over to enjoy it. Companies were getting bigger, and they had to be more conservative."

As netplay increased in popularity, IRL[1] gamer nights died. Wilson wants to bring them back. He's the cofounder of Die Gute Fabrik, an indie game studio in Copenhagen that recently released the Kickstarter-funded game *Sportsfriends*. It's a collection of offline multiplayer games for PlayStation 3, PlayStation 4, Windows, Mac, and Linux. "A lot of my best gaming memories are all on the couch with friends, or playing in front of a big crowd at a party, and cheering and all that stuff," said Wilson. "It's about the whole social context around the occasion—the ritual of play."

The collection's flagship title is *Johann Sebastian Joust*, developed by Wilson. Its design gets players to interact with each other, not the screen. It pits as many as seven players in a dance-like competition of balance, movement, and reflexes. Each player holds a PlayStation motion controller with extreme delicacy, like an egg balanced on a spoon. The objective: Jostle your opponents' controllers while keeping yours steady. Last one standing wins. The kicker is the classical music in the background. The slightest burst of movement can knock you out of the game, but the music periodically speeds up, signaling a brief period in which the controllers are less sensitive. A direct jostle still knocks someone out, but players have greater freedom to move quickly or reach out with a quick jab. "Inevitably, if you play *Joust* long enough, someone breaks the rules," says Max Temkin, creator of the smash hit card game *Cards Against Humanity*. Things happen in real life that can't be replicated in code. "Like, someone throws a chair at someone else. And they're rewarded, because they win. There's a lot to learn about life from that kind of game," he says.

---

[1]*IRL:* short for "in real life," a slang phrase that distinguishes actual, off-line events from digital, virtual, or fictional events. [Editor's note.]

Wild Rumpus parties spotlight the "social and physical aspects of local multiplayer games by throwing huge parties around them." How is the experience depicted here different from conventional video gaming?

The games in *Sportsfriends* promote this pre-Internet ideal of local play and social camaraderie, but they're not the only ones doing so. We've seen a wave of games meant to be played together—truly together. These games wouldn't work online, even if you wanted them to. They appeal to players and spectators alike. And it's just the beginning. 5

Walking into a Wild Rumpus party is like stepping into a dance club in an arcade. Neon lights flash and spin, a DJ pumps out electronic music at eardrum-busting volume, and everyone's got a drink. The difference is the indie videogames throughout the room, projected on walls, each with a cluster of revelers.

Wild Rumpus, based in London, spotlights the social and physical aspects of local multiplayer games by throwing huge parties around them. Since 2011, they've hosted events in London, Toronto, and one in San Francisco, one night in March after the Game Developers Conference. To the side of the dance floor, a crowd watched as two people squared off in *Nidhogg*, a blend of fencing and tug-of-war with an Atari aesthetic. Behind them, partygoers used fur-covered controllers to portray body-building felines in *MuscleCat Showdown*. Upstairs, they slid into sleeping bags and writhed on the floor to control their apple-chomping avatars in a game of *Roflpillar*.

"Events like Wild Rumpus are bringing back the feel of the arcade," says event cofounder Marie Foulston. They're "creating spaces for people to come into games, people that haven't come into physical spaces and engaged with games before. For me, it was about finding the right sort of games that work in that space, games that worked together instead of playing in isolation. When we started out, we wondered if we could sustain running more events, since we didn't want to drop the quality of the games we curate. But it feels almost like a self-fulfilling prophecy. Since there's been . . . so many other events that are showcasing games in physical spaces, there's many more spaces for people to create these games for. I think that in turn has encouraged people to create more of these games."

Foulston says many people tell her that they had a great time. But when she asks them what game they liked most, many give a surprising answer. They hadn't played any. They were happy enough spectating. "It's about creating a sporting environment," Foulston said. "You need games that an audience can get into."

There's also an effort to level the playing field. New four-player, 10 local fighting games like *Towerfall* and *Samurai Gunn* are much simpler, in a good way, than genre mainstays like *Street Fighter*. You can learn the games' mechanics in seconds; from there, it's just strategy. "They all have one-hit kills," says *TowerFall* creator Matt Thorson: Get hit one time and you're dead. "It distills it down to the most tense moments of the match." One-hit kills, in which the outcome rests on a split-second twitch, is another reason these games are suited for local play. The best Internet connections have a ping of around 10 or 20 milliseconds. It might not seem like much, but it's everything in a game of one-hit kills. Games designed to be played online compensate for latency or bad ping, calculating after the fact whether or not a shot hit its target—but it means subjecting the game's entire design to those concessions.

It's tough telling players used to Xbox Live that they can't play your game online. The inability to play online was the most common feedback the creators of *TowerFall* and *Samurai Gunn* received.

Thorson deliberated for months on whether to include online play in *TowerFall*, ultimately deciding against it when he imagined someone's experience the first time they played the game. "I think most people would play it online first, since it's harder to get people [to visit]," Thorson said. "So they're playing online against complete strangers who are probably way better than them, and who either don't care about them at all, or actively hate them. Imagining that being someone's first *TowerFall* experience just makes me cringe, and I really couldn't get past that."

One of the biggest challenges facing developers of local multiplayer games is hardware. Most people playing single-player or online multiplayer games can get by with the controller included with the console. They might have a second one. But who has four? Especially when an Atari 2600 joystick costs $9.95 and a Dual Shock 4 for PS4 costs $60. For this reason, Wilson doesn't see *TowerFall*, *Samurai Gunn*, or *Nidhogg* as competition to *Johann Sebastian Joust*. He sees them as allies. They're all fighting the same hardware battle, and if someone buys controllers for one game, they have the controllers needed to play another. "It's not a zero-sum game," Wilson said. "The battle is 'do people have enough hardware to enjoy these games?' And, like board games, are people in the habit of inviting people over on Friday nights to play?"

Max Temkin thinks that's an apt comparison. "People are constantly connected to everyone in their life, but they're also constantly lonely," he says. Through his company Maxistentialism, Temkin has invested some of his *Cards Against Humanity* earnings into publishing local multiplayer games, starting with *Samurai Gunn*. "There's something super addictive and super satisfying about just sitting down with your friends and having that real-world experience," he says. "I think a lot of the times people play *Cards*, they have this great time and they often attribute it to the game, but it's really just that the game was the pretext for them to sit down and have this real-world interaction."

Wilson hopes *Sportsfriends* will similarly act as a "Trojan horse" that gets gamers back into the living room, socializing in person, recapturing the magic of the off-line games he played in his youth. "We see these games," he says, "as almost an intervention."

For Discussion and Writing

1. **Comprehension** According to Moore, game designer Douglas Wilson hopes his games function as a "Trojan horse" (par. 14). What does this mean, both generally and in the context of Moore's article?

2. **Critical Reading** This article appeared in *Wired* magazine, which covers the intersection of technology with culture, economics, and politics. What does Moore assume about this **audience**? Does the article seem written for general readers or readers with specialized knowledge of video games and gaming culture? Are there places where Moore could have provided more explanation or background information?

3. **Analysis** Moore makes a hard distinction between the "pre-Internet ideal of local play and social camaraderie" (par. 5) and "Internet play," which moved away from social gatherings in favor of gamers playing "together alone" (par. 2). Do you accept this dichotomy? Or do you believe that Internet play is a valid and worthy form of socialization?

4. **Connections** As Moore does in this article, Frank Rose profiles game developers and their games in "The Art of Immersion" (p. 409). In both articles, the developers have particular tastes, preferences, and aspirations for their products. Are the visions of gaming in the articles compatible? For example, do Jordan Weisman and Elan Lee share the same ideals and goals as Douglas Wilson or Max Temkin?

5. **Writing** According to Max Temkin, "There's something super addictive and super satisfying about just sitting down with your friends and having that real-world experience" (par. 13). Do you play games—card games, board games, or video games? Do you agree with Temkin that the satisfactions of playing derive from the in-person interactions rather than the game itself? Or are there other sources of value, such as the pleasure in being skilled at a particular game? Write an essay that explains the significance of games and gaming from your perspective. You may choose to structure it as a response or rejoinder to Moore's article.

GERARD JONES

Violent Media Is Good for Kids

An author, critic, and comic book writer, Gerard Jones (b. 1957) spent fourteen years writing for Marvel Comics, DC Comics, and other publishers. His books include Killing Monsters: Why Children Need Fantasy, Super Heroes, and Make-Believe Violence *(2002), and* Men of Tomorrow: Geeks, Gangsters, and the Birth of the Comic Book *(2004). In this provocative essay from* Mother Jones *magazine, Jones argues that "every aspect of even the trashiest pop-culture story can have its own developmental function." Jones thus enters the ongoing conversation about kids and their exposure to violence in television, movies, video games, and books with a surprising move: He argues that pop-culture violence can be more beneficial than people realize— especially for children.*

As you read, consider your own views of "violent media." What circumstances led Jones to research the effects of "junk culture" on children? How does the writer connect his personal experiences and observations with a larger, more general argument? Do you agree with Jones that we are conditioned to fear strong emotions like rage—even (or especially) our own?

At 13 I was alone and afraid. Taught by my well-meaning, progressive, English-teacher parents that violence was wrong, that rage was something to be overcome, and cooperation was always better than conflict, I suffocated my deepest fears and desires under a nice-boy persona. Placed in a small, experimental school that was wrong for me, afraid to join my peers in their bumptious rush into adolescent boyhood, I withdrew into passivity and loneliness. My parents, not trusting the violent world of the late 1960s, built a wall between me and the crudest elements of American pop culture.

Then the Incredible Hulk smashed through it.

442

One of my mother's students convinced her that Marvel Comics, despite their apparent juvenility and violence, were in fact devoted to lofty messages of pacifism and tolerance. My mother borrowed some, thinking they'd be good for me. And so they were. But not because they preached lofty messages of benevolence. They were good for me because they were juvenile. And violent.

The character who caught me, and freed me, was the Hulk: overgendered and undersocialized, half-naked and half-witted, raging against a frightened world that misunderstood and persecuted him. Suddenly I had a fantasy self to carry my stifled rage and buried desire for power. I had a fantasy self who was a self: unafraid of his desires and the world's disapproval, unhesitating and effective in action. "Puny boy follow Hulk!" roared my fantasy self, and I followed.

I followed him to new friends—other sensitive geeks chasing their own inner brutes—and I followed him to the arrogant, self-exposing, self-assertive, superheroic decision to become a writer. Eventually, I left him behind, followed more sophisticated heroes, and finally my own lead along a twisting path to a career and an identity. In my 30s, I found myself writing action movies and comic books. I wrote some Hulk stories, and met the geek-geniuses who created him. I saw my own creations turned into action figures, cartoons, and computer games. I talked to the kids who read my stories. Across generations, genders, and ethnicities I kept seeing the same story: people pulling themselves out of emotional traps by immersing themselves in violent stories. People integrating the scariest, most fervently denied fragments of their psyches into fuller senses of selfhood through fantasies of superhuman combat and destruction.

I have watched my son living the same story—transforming himself into a bloodthirsty dinosaur to embolden himself for the plunge into preschool, a Power Ranger to muscle through a social competition in kindergarten. In the first grade, his friends started climbing a tree at school. But he was afraid: of falling, of the centipedes crawling on the trunk, of sharp branches, of his friends' derision. I took my cue from his own fantasies and read him old Tarzan comics, rich in combat and bright with flashing knives. For two weeks he lived in them. Then he put them aside. And he climbed the tree.

But all the while, especially in the wake of the recent burst of school shootings, I heard pop psychologists insisting that violent stories are harmful to kids, heard teachers begging parents to keep their kids away from "junk culture," heard a guilt-stricken friend with a son who loved Pokémon lament, "I've turned into the bad mom who lets her kid eat sugary cereal and watch cartoons!"

That's when I started the research.

"Fear, greed, power-hunger, rage: these are aspects of ourselves that we try not to experience in our lives but often want, even need, to experience vicariously through stories of others," writes Melanie Moore, Ph.D., a psychologist who works with urban teens. "Children need violent entertainment in order to explore the inescapable feelings that they've been taught to deny, and to reintegrate those feelings into a more whole, more complex, more resilient selfhood."

Moore consults to public schools and local governments, and 10 is also raising a daughter. For the past three years she and I have been studying the ways in which children use violent stories to meet their emotional and developmental needs—and the ways in which adults can help them use those stories healthily. With her help I developed Power Play, a program for helping young people improve their self-knowledge and sense of potency through heroic, combative storytelling.

We've found that every aspect of even the trashiest pop-culture story can have its own developmental function. Pretending to have superhuman powers helps children conquer the feelings of powerlessness that inevitably come with being so young and small. The dual-identity concept at the heart of many superhero stories helps kids negotiate the conflicts between the inner self and the public self as they work through the early stages of socialization. Identification with a rebellious, even destructive, hero helps children learn to push back against a modern culture that cultivates fear and teaches dependency.

At its most fundamental level, what we call "creative violence"—head-bonking cartoons, bloody videogames, playground karate, toy guns—gives children a tool to master their rage. Children will feel rage. Even the sweetest and most civilized of them, even those whose parents read the better class of literary magazines, will feel rage. The world is uncontrollable and incomprehensible; mastering it is a terrifying, enraging task. Rage can be an energizing emotion, a shot of courage to push us to resist greater threats, take more control, than we ever thought we could. But rage is also the emotion our culture distrusts the most. Most of us are taught early on to fear our own. Through immersion in imaginary combat and identification with a violent protagonist, children engage the rage they've stifled, come to fear it less, and become more capable of utilizing it against life's challenges.

I knew one little girl who went around exploding with fantasies so violent that other moms would draw her mother aside to whisper, "I think you should know something about Emily. . . . " Her parents were separating, and she was small, an only child, a tomboy at an age when her classmates were dividing sharply along gender lines. On the playground she acted out *Sailor Moon* fights, and in the classroom she wrote stories about people being stabbed with knives. The more adults tried to control her stories, the more she acted out the roles of her angry heroes: breaking rules, testing limits, roaring threats.

Then her mother and I started helping her tell her stories. She wrote them, performed them, drew them like comics: sometimes bloody, sometimes tender, always blending the images of pop culture with her own most private fantasies. She came out of it just as fiery and strong, but more self-controlled and socially competent: a leader among her peers, the one student in her class who could truly pull boys and girls together.

I worked with an older girl, a middle-class "nice girl," who held   15
herself together through a chaotic family situation and a tumultuous adolescence with gangsta rap. In the mythologized street violence of Ice T, the rage and strutting of his music and lyrics, she found a theater of the mind in which she could be powerful, ruthless, invulnerable. She avoided the heavy drug use that sank many of her peers, and flowered in college as a writer and political activist.

I'm not going to argue that violent entertainment is harmless. I think it has helped inspire some people to real-life violence. I am going to argue that it's helped hundreds of people for every one it's hurt, and that it can help far more if we learn to use it well. I am going to argue that our fear of "youth violence" isn't well-founded on reality, and that the fear can do more harm than the reality. We act as though our highest priority is to prevent our

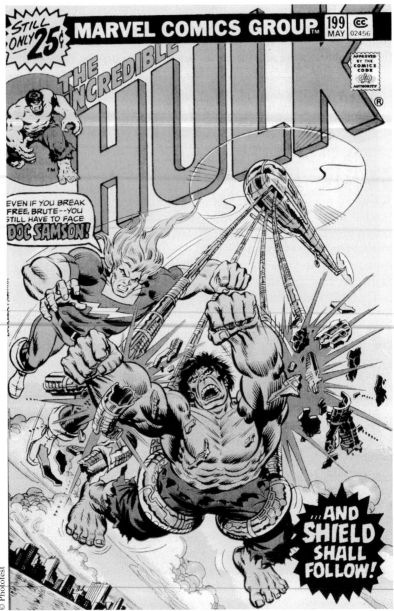

The Incredible Hulk: "overgendered and undersocialized, half-naked and half-witted, raging against a frightened world. . . ." How do fictional characters help real children learn to manage their anger?

children from growing up into murderous thugs—but modern kids are far more likely to grow up too passive, too distrustful of themselves, too easily manipulated.

We send the message to our children in a hundred ways that their craving for imaginary gun battles and symbolic killings is wrong, or at least dangerous. Even when we don't call for censorship or forbid *Mortal Kombat,* we moan to other parents within our kids' earshot about the "awful violence" in the entertainment they love. We tell our kids that it isn't nice to playfight, or we steer them from some monstrous action figure to a *pro-social doll.* Even in the most progressive households, where we make such a point of letting children feel what they feel, we rush to substitute an enlightened discussion for the raw material of rageful fantasy. In the process, we risk confusing them about their natural aggression in the same way the Victorians confused their children about their sexuality. When we try to protect our children from their own feelings and fantasies, we shelter them not against violence but against power and selfhood.

For Discussion and Writing

1. **Comprehension**   How, specifically, did Jones help his son overcome his fears? What point does this anecdote illustrate?

2. **Critical Reading**   What is Jones's **writing situation** in this essay? How does Jones include and address **counterarguments**? Point out specific moments where he engages an opposing point of view. Is his response effective?

3. **Analysis**   Jones asserts, "We act as though our highest priority is to prevent our children from growing up into murderous thugs—but modern kids are far more likely to grow up too passive, too distrustful of themselves, too easily manipulated" (par. 16). Jones makes two claims in this sentence. Do you agree with them?

4. **Connections**   In "Secret Skin: An Essay in Unitard Theory" (p. 449), Michael Chabon writes about the significance and power of comic book superheroes. Chabon argues that, for children, the appeal of such stories and characters is not about escapism but transformation. Would Jones agree with this claim? Is it compatible with his argument in "Violent Media Is Good for Kids"? Why or why not?

5. **Writing**   Jones writes about the need—especially in childhood—for a "fantasy self" (par. 4): "The dual-identity concept at the heart of many superhero stories helps kids negotiate the conflicts between the inner self and the public self as they work through the early

stages of socialization. Identification with a rebellious, even destructive, hero helps children learn to push back against a modern culture that cultivates fear and teaches dependency" (par. 11). How do you respond to this claim? Do you agree? What experiences do you have with vicarious "identification," whether from comic books or other sources? Explain your answer in a personal essay that includes both narrative and analysis.

MICHAEL CHABON

Secret Skin: An Essay in Unitard Theory

A prolific fiction writer and essayist, Michael Chabon (b. 1963) earned his B.A. from the University of Pittsburgh and an M.F.A. in creative writing from the University of California, Irvine. He is best known as the author of the novels The Mysteries of Pittsburgh *(1988),* The Amazing Adventures of Kavalier & Clay *(2000), and* Telegraph Avenue *(2012). Additionally, Chabon has written a young adult novel,* Summerland *(2002), and a children's book,* The Astonishing Secret of Awesome Man *(2011), along with books of short stories and essays. He is the winner of the Pulitzer Prize for Fiction (2001) as well other literary honors and awards. In this essay, which appeared in the* New Yorker, *Chabon writes about one of his persistent preoccupations: comic book superheroes. Chabon focuses his analysis on the rich and paradoxical meaning of their costumes, arguing that "like the being who wears it, the superhero costume is, by definition, an impossible object."*

As you read, reflect on your own childhood superhero fantasies. Why does Chabon's Jewish ethics teacher dislike comic books? How does Chabon use his memory of Mr. Spector's criticism of comics as a pretext and a prompt for his own discussion of superheroes? What themes does Chabon explore in this essay?

When I was a boy, I had a religious-school teacher named Mr. Spector, whose job was to confront us with the peril we presented to ourselves. Jewish Ethics was the name of the class. We must have been eight or nine.

Mr. Spector used a workbook to guide the discussion; every Sunday, we began by reading a kind of modern parable or cautionary tale, and then contended with a series of imponderable questions. One day, for example, we discussed the temptations of shoplifting; another class was devoted to all the harm to oneself

449

and to others that could be caused by the telling of lies. Mr. Spector was a gently acerbic young man with a black beard and black Roentgen-ray[1] eyes. He seemed to take our moral failings for granted and, perhaps as a result, favored lively argument over reproach or condemnation. I enjoyed our discussions, while remaining perfectly aloof at my core from the issues they raised. I was, at the time, an awful liar, and quite a few times had stolen chewing gum and baseball cards from the neighborhood Wawa. None of that seemed to have anything to do with Mr. Spector or the cases we studied in Jewish Ethics. All nine-year-olds are sophists and hypocrites; I found it no more difficult than any other kid to withhold my own conduct from consideration in passing measured judgment on the human race.

The one time I felt my soul to be in danger was the Sunday Mr. Spector raised the ethical problem of escapism, particularly as it was experienced in the form of comic books. That day, we started off with a fine story about a boy who loved Superman so much that he tied a red towel around his neck, climbed up to the roof of his house, and, with a cry of "Up, up, and away," leaped to his death. There was known to have been such a boy, Mr. Spector informed us—at least one verifiable boy, so enraptured and so betrayed by the false dream of Superman that it killed him.

The explicit lesson of the story was that what was found between the covers of a comic book was fantasy, and "fantasy" meant pretty lies, the consumption of which failed to prepare you for what lay outside those covers. Fantasy rendered you unfit to face "reality" and its hard pavement. Fantasy betrayed you, and thus, by implication, your wishes, your dreams and longings, everything you carried around inside your head that only you and Superman and Elliot S! Maggin (exclamation point and all, the principal Superman writer circa 1971) could understand—all these would betray you, too. There were ancillary arguments to be made as well, about the culpability of those who produced such fare, sold it to minors, or permitted their children to bring it into the house.

These arguments were mostly lost on me, a boy who consumed   5 a dozen comic books a week, all of them cheerfully provided to him by his (apparently iniquitous) father. Sure, I might not be

---

[1]*Roentgen:* a unit of measurement for X-rays and gamma rays. [Editor's note.]

prepared for reality—point granted—but, on the other hand, if I ever found myself in the Bottle City of Kandor, under the bell jar in the Fortress of Solitude, I would know not to confuse Superman's Kryptonian double (Van-Zee) with Clark Kent's (Vol-Don). Rather, what struck me, with the force of a blow, was recognition, a profound moral recognition of the implicit, indeed the secret, premise of the behavior of the boy on the roof. For that fool of a boy had not been doomed by the deceitful power of comic books, which after all were only bundles of paper, staples, and ink, and couldn't hurt anybody. That boy had been killed by the irresistible syllogism of Superman's cape.

One knew, of course, that it was not the red cape any more than it was the boots, the tights, the trunks, or the trademark "S" that gave Superman the ability to fly. That ability derived from the effects of the rays of our yellow sun on Superman's alien anatomy, which had evolved under the red sun of Krypton. And yet you had only to tie a towel around your shoulders to feel the strange vibratory pulse of flight stirring in the red sun of your heart.

I, too, had climbed to a dangerous height, with my face to the breeze, and felt magically alone of my kind. I had imagined the streak of my passage like a red-and-blue smear on the window-pane of vision. I had been Batman, too, and the Mighty Thor. I had stood cloaked in the existential agonies of the Vision, son of a robot and grandson of a lord of the ants. A few years after that Sunday in Mr. Spector's class, at the pinnacle of my career as a hero of the imagination, I briefly transformed myself (more about this later) into a superpowered warrior–knight known as Aztec. And all that I needed to effect the change was to fasten a terry-cloth beach towel around my neck.

It was not about escape, I wanted to tell Mr. Spector, thus unwittingly plagiarizing in advance the well-known formula of a (fictitious) pioneer and theorist of superhero comics, Sam Clay. It was about *transformation*.

The American comic book preexisted the superhero, but just barely, and with so little distinction that in the cultural mind the medium has always seemed indistinguishable from its first stroke of brilliance. There were costumed crime-fighters before

Superman (the Phantom, Zorro), but only as there were pop quartets before the Beatles. Superman invented and exhausted his genre in a single bound. All the tropes, all the clichés and conventions, all the possibilities, all the longings and wishes and neuroses that have driven and fed and burdened the superhero comic during the past seventy years were implied by and contained within that little red rocket ship hurtling toward Earth. That moment — Krypton exploding, *Action Comics No. 1* — is generally seen to be Minute Zero of the superhero idea.

About the reasons for the arrival of Superman at that zero 10 moment there is less agreement. In the theories of origin put forward by fans, critics, and other origin-obsessives, the *idea* of Superman has been accounted the offspring or recapitulation, in no particular order, of Friedrich Nietzshe; of Philip Wylie (in his novel *Gladiator*); of the strengths, frailties, and neuroses of his creators, Jerry Siegel and Joe Shuster, of Cleveland, Ohio; of the aching wishfulness of the Great Depression; of the (Jewish) immigrant experience; of the mastermind stratagems of popular texts in their sinister quest for reader domination; of repressed Oedipal[2] fantasies and homoerotic wishes; of facism; of capitalism; of the production modes of mass culture (and not in a good way); of celebrated strongmen and proponents of physical culture like Eugen Sandow; and of a host of literary not-quite-Superman precursors, chief among them Doc Savage.

Most of these rationales of origin depend, to some extent, on history; they index the advent of Superman, in mid-1938, to various intellectual, social, and economic trends of the Depression years, to the influence or aura of contemporary celebrities and authors, to the structure and demands of magazine publishing and distribution, et cetera. To suit my purpose here, I might construct a similar etiology of the superhero costume, making due reference, say, to professional-wrestling and circus attire of the early twentieth century, to the boots-cloak-and-tights ensembles worn by swashbucklers and cavaliers in stage plays and Hollywood films, to contemporary men's athletic wear, with its unitard construction and belted trunks, to the designs of Alex Raymond

---

[2]*Oedipal:* relating to the Oedipus complex, which develops from a boy's sexual desire toward his mother and jealous feelings toward his father. [Editor's note.]

For Chabon, "the superhero costume is, by definition, an impossible object. It cannot exist." Nevertheless, hope springs eternal every Halloween. This map shows the most popular superhero costumes by state in 2013.

and Hal Foster and the amazing pulp-magazine cover artist Frank R. Paul. I could cite the influence of Art Deco and Streamline Moderne aesthetics, with their roots in fantasies of power, speed, and flight, or posit the costume as a kind of fashion alter ego of the heavy, boxy profile of men's clothing at the time. When in fact the point of origin is not a date or a theory or a conjunction of cultural trends but a story, the intersection of a wish and the tip of a pencil.

Now the time has come to propose, or confront, a fundamental truth: like the being who wears it, the superhero costume is, by definition, an impossible object. It cannot exist.

One may easily find suggestive evidence for this assertion at any large comic-book convention by studying the spectacle of the brave and bold convention attendees, those members of the general comics-fan public who show up in costume and go shpatziring around the ballrooms and exhibition halls dressed as

Wolverine, say, or the Joker's main squeeze, Harley Quinn. Without exception, even the most splendid of these getups is at best a disappointment. Every seam, every cobweb strand of duct-tape gum, every laddered fish-net stocking or visible ridge of underpants elastic—every stray mark, pulled thread, speck of dust—acts to spoil what is instantly revealed to have been, all along, an illusion.

The appearance of realism in a superhero costume made from real materials is generally recognized to be difficult to pull off, and many such costumes do not even bother to simulate the presumable effect on the eye and the spirit of the beholder were Black Bolt to stride, trailing a positronic lace of Kirby crackle, into a ballroom of the Overland Park Marriott. This disappointing air of saggy trouser seats, bunchy underarms, and wobbly shoulder vanes may be the result of imaginative indolence, the sort that would permit a grown man to tell himself he will find gratification in walking the exhibition floor wearing a pair of Dockers, a Jägermeister hoodie, and a rubber Venom mask complete with punched-out eyeholes and flopping rubber bockwurst of a tongue.

But realism is not, in fact, merely *difficult*; it is hopeless. A 15 plausibly heroic physique is of no avail in this regard, nor is even the most fervent willingness to believe in oneself as the man or woman in the cape. Even those costumed conventioneers who go all out, working year-round to amass, scrounge, or counterfeit cleverly the materials required to put together, with glue gun, soldering iron, makeup, and needle and thread, a faithful and accurate Black Canary or Ant-Man costume, find themselves prey to forces, implacable as gravity, of tawdriness, gimcrackery, and unwitting self-ridicule. And in the end they look no more like Black Canary or Ant-Man than does the poor zhlub in the Venom mask with a three-day pass hanging around his neck on a lanyard.

This sad outcome even in the wake of thousands of dollars spent and months of hard work given to sewing and to packing foam rubber into helmets has an obvious, an unavoidable, explanation: a superhero's costume is constructed not of fabric, foam rubber, or adamantium but of halftone dots, Pantone color values, inked containment lines, and all the cartoonist's sleight of hand. The superhero costume *as drawn* disdains the customary relationship in the fashion world between sketch and garment. It makes no suggestions. It has no agenda. Above all, it is not waiting to find fulfillment as cloth draped on a body. A constructed superhero costume is a replica with no original, a model built on a scale of $x:1$. However accurate and detailed, such a work has the tidy airlessness of a model-train layout but none of the gravitas that such little railyards and townscapes derive from making faithful reference to homely things. The graphic purity of the superhero costume means that the more effort and money you lavish on fine textiles, metal grommets, and leather trim the deeper your costume will be sucked into the silliness singularity that swallowed, for example, Joel Schumacher's Batman and Robin and their four nipples.

In fact, the most reliable proof of the preposterousness of superhero attire whenever it is translated, as if by a Kugelmass device,[3] from the pages of comics to the so-called real world can be found in film and television adaptations of superhero characters. George Reeves's stogy pajamas-like affair in the old *Superman* TV series and Adam West's mod doll clothes in *Batman* have lately given way to purportedly more "realistic" versions, in rubber, leather, and plastic, pseudo-utilitarian coveralls that draw inspiration in equal measure from spacesuits, catsuits, and scuba suits, and from (one presumes) regard for the dignity of actors who have seen the old George Reeves and Adam West shows, and would not be caught dead in those glorified Underoos. In its attempts to slip the confines of the paneled page, the superhero costume betrays its nonexistence, like one of those deep-sea creatures which evolved to thrive in the crushing darkness of the seabed, so that when you haul them up to the dazzling surface they burst.

One might go farther and argue not only that the superhero costume has (and needs) no referent in the world of textiles and latex but also that, even within its own proper comic-book context, it can be said not to exist, not to *want* to exist—can be said to advertise, even to revel in, its own notional status. This illusionary quality of the drawn costume can readily be seen if we

---

[3]*Kugelmass device:* reference to Woody Allen's short story "The Kugelmass Episode" (1977), in which a magician's device projects real human beings into works of fiction and fictional characters into the real world. [Editor's note.]

attempt to delimit the elements of the superhero wardrobe, to inventory its minimum or requisite components.

We can start by throwing away our masks. Superman, arguably the first and the greatest of all costumed heroes, has never bothered with one, nor have Captain Marvel, Luke Cage, Wonder Woman, Valkyrie, and Supergirl. All those individuals, like many of their peers (Hawkman, Giant-Man), also go around barehanded, which suggests that we can safely dispense with our gauntlets (whether finned, rolled, or worn with a jaunty slash at the cuff). Capes have been an object of scorn among discerning superheroes at least since 1974, when Captain America, having abandoned his old career in protest over Watergate, briefly took on the nom de guerre Nomad, dressed himself in a piratical ensemble of midnight blue and gold, and brought his first exploit as a stateless hero to an inglorious end by tripping over his own flowing cloak.

So let's lose the cape. As for the boots—we are not married to 20 the boots. After all, Iron Fist sports a pair of kung-fu slippers, the Spirit wears brown brogues, Zatanna works her magic in stiletto heels, and Beast, Ka-Zar, and Mantis wear no shoes at all. Perhaps, though, we had better hold on to our unitards, crafted of some nameless but readily available fabric that, like a thin matte layer, at once coats and divulges the splendor of our musculature. Assemble the collective, all-time memberships of the Justice League of America, the Justice Society of America, the Avengers, the Defenders, the Invaders, the X-Men, and the Legion of Super-Heroes (and let us not forget the Legion of Substitute Heroes), and you will probably find that almost all of them, from Nighthawk to the Chlorophyll Kid, arrive wearing some version of the classic leotard-tights ensemble. And yet—not everyone. Not Wonder Woman, in her star-spangled hot pants and eagle bustier; not the Incredible Hulk or Martian Manhunter or the Sub-Mariner.

Consideration of the last named leads us to cast a critical eye, finally, on our little swim trunks, typically worn with a belt, pioneered by Kit Walker (for the Ghost Who Walks), the Phantom of the old newspaper strip, and popularized by the super-trendsetter of Metropolis. The Sub-Mariner wears nothing *but* a Eurotrashy green Speedo, suggesting that, at least by the decency standards of the old Comics Code, this minimal garment marks the zero degree of superheroic attire. And yet, of course, the Flash, Green Lantern, and many others make do without trunks over their tights; the forgoing of trunks in favor of a continuous flow of fabric from legs to torso is frequently employed to lend a suggestion of speed, sleekness, a kind of uncluttered modernism. And the Hulk never goes around in anything but those tattered purple trousers.

So we are left with, literally, nothing at all: the human form, unadorned, smooth, muscled, and ready, let's say, to sail the starry ocean of the cosmos on the deck of a gleaming surfboard. A naked spacefarer, sheathed in a silvery pseudoskin that affords all the protection one needs from radiation and cosmic dust while meeting Code standards by neatly neutering one, the shining voice between the legs serving to signify that one is not (as one often appears to be when seen from behind) naked as an interstellar jaybird.

Here is a central paradox of superhero attire: from panther black to lantern green, from the faintly Hapsburg pomp of the fifties-era Legion of Super-Heroes costumes to the *Mad Max* space grunge of Lobo, from sexy fishnet to vibranium — for all the mad recombinant play of color, style, and materials that the superhero costume makes with its limited number of standard components, it ultimately takes its deepest meaning and serves its primary function in the depiction of the naked human form, unfettered, perfect, and free. The superheroic wardrobe resembles a wildly permutated alphabet of ideograms conceived only to express the eloquent power of silence.

A public amnesia, an avowed lack of history, is the standard pretense of the costumed superhero. From the point of view of the man or woman or child in the street, gaping up at the sky and skyscrapers, the appearance of a new hero over Metropolis or New York or Astro City is always a matter of perfect astonishment. There have been no portents or warnings, and afterward one never learns anything new or gains any explanations.

The story of a superhero's origin must be kept secret, occulted 25 as rigorously from public knowledge as the alter ego, as if it were a source of shame. Superman conceals, archived in the Fortress of Solitude and accessible only to him, not only his own history — the facts and tokens of his birth and arrival on Earth, of his Smallville childhood, of his exploits and adventures — but the history of his Kryptonian family and, indeed, of his entire race. Batman similarly hides his story and its proofs in the trophy chambers of the Batcave.

In theory, the costume forms part of the strategy of concealment. But in fact the superhero's costume often functions as a kind of magic screen onto which the repressed narrative may be projected. No matter how well he or she hides its traces, the secret narrative of transformation, of rebirth, is given up by the costume. Sometimes this secret is betrayed through the allusion of style or form: Robin's gaudy uniform hints at the murder of his circus-acrobat parents, Iron Man's at the flawed heart that requires a life-support device, which is the primary function of his armor.

More often, the secret narrative is hinted at with a kind of enigmatic, dreamlike obviousness right on the hero's chest or belt buckle, in the form of the requisite insignia. Superman's "S," we have been told, only coincidentally stands for Superman: in fact, the emblem is the coat of arms of the ancient Kryptonian House of El, from which he descends. A stylized bat alludes to the animal whose chance flight through a window sealed Bruce Wayne's fate; a lightning bolt encapsulates the secret history of Captain Marvel; an eight-legged glyph immortalizes the bug whose bite doomed Peter Parker to his glorious and woebegone career.

We say "secret identity," and adopt a series of cloaking strategies to preserve it, but what we are actually trying to conceal is a narrative: not who we are but the story of how we got that way — and, by implication, of all that we lacked, and all that we were not, before the spider bit us. Yet our costume conceals nothing, reveals everything: it is our secret skin, exposed and exposing us for all the world to see. Superheroism is a kind of transvestism; our superdrag serves at once to obscure the exterior self that no longer defines us while betraying, with half-unconscious panache, the truth of the story we carry in our hearts, the story of our transformation, of our story's recommencement, of our rebirth into the world of adventure, of story itself.

I became Aztec in the summer of 1973, in Columbia, Maryland, a planned suburban utopia halfway between Smallville and Metropolis. It happened one summer day as I was walking to the swimming pool with a friend. He wore a pair of midnight-blue bathing trunks; my trunks were loud, with patches of pink, orange, gold, and brown overprinted with abstract patterns that we took for Aztec (though they were probably Polynesian). In those days, a pair of bathing trunks did not in the least resemble the baggy board shorts that boys and men wear swimming today. Ours were made of stretchy polyester doubleknit that came down the thigh just past the level of the crotch, and fashion fitted them with a sewn-on, false belt of elastic webbing that buckled at the front with a metal clasp. They looked, in other words, just like the trunks favored by costumed heroes ever since the last son of Krypton came voguing down the super-catwalk, back in 1938. Around our throats we knotted our beach towels (his was blue, mine a fine 1973 shade of burnt orange), those enchanted cloaks whose power Mr. Spector had failed to understand or to recall from his own childhood. They fluttered out behind us, catching the breeze from our imaginations, as Darklord and Aztec walked along.

Darklord carried a sword, and wore a Barbuta helmet, with a 30 flowing crusader cloak and invulnerable chain mail of "lunar steel." Aztec wore tights and a feathered cloak and wielded a magic staff tipped with obsidian. We had begun the journey that day, through the street-melting, shimmering green Maryland summer morning, as a pair of lonely boys with nothing in common but that loneliness, which we shared with Superman and Batman, who shared it with each other—a fundamental loneliness and a wild aptitude for transformation. But with every step we became Darklord and Aztec a little more surely, a little more irrevocably, transformed by the green-lantern rays of fancy, by the spider bite of inspiration, by the story we were telling each other and ourselves about two costumed superheroes, about the new selves that had been revealed by our secret skin.

Talking, retying the knots of our capes, flip-flops slapping against the soles of our feet, we transformed not only ourselves. In the space of that walk to the pool we also transformed the world, shaping it into a place in which such things were possible: the reincarnation of an Arthurian knight could find solace and partnership in the company of a latter-day Mesoamerican wizard. An entire world of superheroic adventure could be dreamed up by a couple of boys from Columbia, or Cleveland. And the self you knew you contained, the story you knew you had inside you, might find its way like an emblem onto the spot right over your heart. All we needed to do was accept the standing invitation that superhero comics extended to us by means of a towel. It was an invitation to enter into the world of story, to join in the ongoing business of comic books, and, with the knotting of a magical beach towel, to begin to wear what we knew to be hidden inside us.

For Discussion and Writing

1. **Comprehension** What is the "central paradox of superhero attire" (par. 23)? What "secret narrative" (par. 28) is often represented on such costumes?

2. **Critical Reading** How would you describe Chabon's prose **style**? What are its identifying characteristics (e.g., in terms of diction, sentence length, syntax, use of figurative language, tone)? Do you find it accessible? Engaging? Difficult? Appealing? Explain your answer by pointing to specific examples from the text.

3. **Analysis** Retrospectively responding to his Jewish ethics teacher, Chabon writes that the appeal of comic books "was not about escape. . . . It was about transformation" (par. 8). How do you see this distinction, both as Chabon discusses it and as you understand it? For example, are "transformation" and "escape" mutually exclusive? Why or why not?

4. **Connections** For Chabon's ethics teacher, comic books and vicarious fantasies "failed to prepare you for what lay outside those covers" and "rendered you unfit to face 'reality' and its hard pavement" (par. 4). Is Mr. Spector's criticism similar to the criticism of violent media that Gerard Jones responds to in "Violent Media Is Good for Kids" (p. 442)? Is the criticism now different? Was Mr. Spector worried about "ethical problems" similar to the ones that preoccupy protective and "progressive" parents today?

5. **Writing** In the essay, Chabon performs skillful and illuminating close readings—careful, detailed interpretations and explanations—of superhero costumes worn by figures like Superman, Batman, and Spiderman. Choose another superhero, comic book villain, or other, similar character and perform your own close reading of his or her costume. What do the specific details reveal about the character's origin, identity, or story? Do the character's specific powers reflect any larger thematic or allegorical meanings? You may present your analysis in essay form, or as a presentation with visual images or video.

Acknowledgments

Lessley Anderson. "Seduced by 'Perfect' Pitch: How Auto-Tune Conquered Pop Music." From *The Verge*, February 27, 2013. Copyright © 2013 by Vox Media, Inc. Reprinted by permission of Vox Media, Inc.

Liz Armstrong. "An Argument for Being a Poser." Originally published as "Identity Kit: An Argument for Being a Poser" online by *Rookie* magazine, June 14, 2012. Copyright © 2012 by Liz Armstrong. Reprinted by permission of author.

Chiara Atik. "Public Displays of Transaction." Originally published by *Matter.com*, July 20, 2014. Copyright © 2014 by Matter.com. Reprinted by permission of Matter/Medium.

David Auerbach. Excerpts from "You Are What You Click" by David Auerbach from the *Nation*, March 4, 2013. Reprinted with permission from the March 4, 2013, issue of the *Nation*. For subscription information, call 1-800-333-8536. Portions of each week's *Nation* magazine can be accessed at http://www.thenation.com.

Ken Auletta. Excerpts from "Netflix and the Future of Television" by Ken Auletta from the *New Yorker*, February 3, 2014. Copyright © 2014 by Ken Auletta. Used by permission. All rights reserved.

Saul Austerlitz. "The Pernicious Rise of Poptimism." From the *New York Times*, April 6, 2014, The *New York Times*. All rights reserved. Used by permission and protected by the Copyright Laws of the United States. The printing, copying, redistribution, or retransmission of this Content without express written permission is prohibited.

Benjamin Barber. "Overselling Capitalism with Consumerism." Published originally in the *Los Angeles Times*, April 4, 2007. Copyright © 2007 by Benjamin Barber. Reprinted with the permission of the author.

Roland Barthes. "Toys." From *Mythologies* by Roland Barthes, translated by Annette Lavers. Translation copyright © 1972 by Jonathan Cape Ltd. Reprinted by permission of Hill and Wang, a division of Farrar, Straus and Giroux, LLC. Canada: published by Vintage. Reprinted by permission of the Random House Group Limited.

Judy Berman. "Concerning the Spiritual in Indie Rock." From the *Believer*, August 2009. Copyright © 2009 by Judy Berman. Reprinted by permission of the author.

Jennifer Bleyer. "Love the One You're Near." From *Psychology Today*, July 1, 2014. Copyright © 2014 by Sussex Publishers, LLC. Reprinted with permission from *Psychology Today* magazine.

Robin Brenner. "Teen Literature and Fan Culture." From *Young Adult Library Services*, Summer 2013 (pp. 33–36). Copyright © 2013 by American Library Association. Reprinted by permission of American Library Association.

Bill Bryson. "The Hard Sell: Advertising in America." Chapter 14 (pp. 235–47) from *Made in America* by Bill Bryson. Copyright © 1994 by Bill Bryson. Reprinted by permission of HarperCollins Publishers.

Jacob Burak. "Escape from the Matrix." From *Aeon* magazine, May 28, 2014. Copyright © 2014 by *Aeon* magazine. Reprinted by permission of *Aeon* magazine.

Paul A. Cantor. "The Apocalyptic Strain in Popular Culture: The American Nightmare Becomes the American Dream." From the *Hedgehog Review*: Vol. 15, No. 2 (Summer 2013). Copyright © 2013. Reprinted by permission of the *Hedgehog Review*, University of Virginia/IASC.

Index of Authors and Titles

465

Preface

Because the questions provided after each selection in *Reading Pop Culture: A Portable Anthology* are meant to stimulate dialogue and debate—to provoke discussion and writing—they rarely lend themselves to a single appropriate response. While this manual tries to clarify the intention of a few of the more challenging questions, it doesn't offer a list of "right" answers.

The notes on individual selections underscore the purpose behind the piece; they anticipate students' reactions and suggest productive pedagogical approaches and strategies for reading and interpretation. Key concepts for particularly challenging selections are discussed; thumbnail answers are offered for some of the more difficult questions. The discussions, however, are meant to help you understand our reading of the selection in question, not to supply you with definitive or complete answers. This manual also highlights especially fruitful connections between specific readings, as well as between particular chapters. You can use these suggestions to construct a syllabus around a theme traced throughout the text.

Jeff Ousborne

Contents

3. Technology: How do new devices and apps transform experience?   13

4. Music: How does popular music reflect and express our identities?   18

5. Television: Are we living in a Golden Age of television?   24

Sample Syllabi

Thematic Syllabus (14 weeks)

Eng 100
Composition/Expository Writing

COURSE OBJECTIVES

- To develop your ability to think critically and with a questioning attitude
- To develop your ability to identify and cut through faulty logic
- To help you gain confidence in using correctly the mechanics of language (grammar, usage, punctuation)
- To give you useful practice in writing a variety of types of essays
- To improve your writing skills, including organization, development, support, and logical flow
- To help you develop a more effective writing style
- To develop skills in revising and editing

REQUIRED TEXTS

Ousborne, *Reading Pop Culture*, Second Edition (RPC)
Hacker, *A Writer's Reference*, Eighth Edition (handbook)

STUDENT REQUIREMENTS

- Read and respond to texts as assigned
- Compose essays as assigned
- Complete exploration, focus, and editing exercises
- Complete quizzes and exams
- Participate in classroom discussions

POLICIES

Participation is essential. Your attendance, your contributions to discussions, and your performance on occasional reading quizzes are part of your grade. Please come to class on time and prepared, with your cell phone turned off. Frequent unexcused absences will significantly lower your grade. Assignments are due on assigned dates.

PLAGIARISM

Plagiarism is a serious violation of class—and university—policy, and will be treated as such. Please see the *Student Policies and Procedures* handbook regarding the penalties for academic dishonesty. If you have any questions about using the work of others in your own essays, please check with me first.

SCHEDULE

Week 1
Introduction: Analyzing Popular Culture
   Diagnostic essay
   Subject-verb agreement (handbook)
   Assign essay on consumption and advertising (Essay 1)

Week 2
Consumption and Advertising
   Using active verbs (handbook)
   Benjamin Barber, "Overselling Capitalism with Consumerism,"
      pp. 22–25 (RPC)
   Virginia Postrel, "In Praise of Chain Stores," pp. 47–52 (RPC)
   William Lutz, "With These Words I Can Sell You Anything,"
      pp. 26–35 (RPC)

Week 3
Consumption and Advertising (cont.)
  Avoiding sentence fragments (handbook)
  Bill Bryson, "The Hard Sell: Advertising in America," pp. 53–69
    (RPC)
  Ellen Huet, "Snaps to Riches: The Rise of Snapchat Celebrities,"
    pp. 70–77 (RPC)
  Chiara Atik, "Public Displays of Transaction," pp. 78–81 (RPC)

Week 4
Identity
  Essay 1 due
  Finding print and online sources (handbook)
  Liz Armstrong, "An Argument for Being a Poser," pp. 85–89 (RPC)
  danah boyd, "Impression Management in a Networked Setting,"
    pp. 122–127 (RPC)
  Assign essay on identity (Essay 2)

Week 5
Identity (cont.)
  Misplaced modifiers (handbook)
  Malcolm Gladwell, "The Sports Taboo," pp. 109–121 (RPC)
  Ariel Levy, "Women and the Rise of Raunch Culture," pp. 128–132
    (RPC)
  Sonali Kohli, "Pop Culture's Transgender Moment," pp. 133–136
    (RPC)

Week 6
Technology
  Essay 2 due
  Run-on sentences (handbook)
  Neil Postman, "The Judgment of Thamus," pp. 151–166 (RPC)
  Clay Shirky, "Gin, Television, and Social Surplus," pp. 167–173
    (RPC)
  Assign essay on technology (Essay 3)

Week 7
Technology (cont.)
  Pronouns (handbook)
  Commas (handbook)

Week 13

Immersive Media (cont.)

Writing workshop

Chuck Klosterman, "My Zombie, Myself: Why Modern Life Feels Rather Undead," pp. 422–427 (RPC)

Jacob Burak, "Escape from the Matrix," pp. 428–435 (RPC)

Week 14

Immersive Media (cont.)

Writing Workshop

Gerard Jones, "Violent Media Is Good for Kids," pp. 442–448 (RPC)

Michael Chabon, "Secret Skin: An Essay in Unitard Theory," pp. 449–468 (RPC)

Essay 5 due

Rhetorical Syllabus (14 weeks)

Eng 100
Composition/Expository Writing

COURSE OBJECTIVES

- To develop your ability to think critically and with a questioning attitude
- To develop your ability to identify and cut through faulty logic
- To help you gain confidence in using correctly the mechanics of language (grammar, usage, punctuation)
- To give you useful practice in writing a variety of types of essays
- To improve your writing skills, including organization, development, support, and logical flow
- To help you develop a more effective writing style
- To develop skills in revising and editing

REQUIRED TEXTS

Ousborne, *Reading Pop Culture*, Second Edition (RPC)
Writer's Help 2.0 (handbook)

STUDENT REQUIREMENTS

- Read and respond to texts as assigned
- Compose essays as assigned
- Complete exploration, focus, and editing exercises
- Complete quizzes and exams
- Participate in classroom discussions

POLICIES

Participation is essential. Your attendance, your contributions to discussions, and your performance on occasional reading quizzes are part of your grade. Please come to class on time and prepared, with your cell phone turned off. Frequent unexcused absences will significantly lower your grade. Assignments are due on assigned dates.

PLAGIARISM

Plagiarism is a serious violation of class—and university—policy, and will be treated as such. Please see the *Student Policies and Procedures* handbook regarding the penalties for academic dishonesty. If you have any questions about using the work of others in your own essays, please check with me first.

SCHEDULE

Week 1
Introduction: Analyzing Popular Culture
    Diagnostic essay
    Bill Bryson, "The Hard Sell: Advertising in America," pp. 53–69
        (RPC)
    Assign Writing Assignment 1: Exemplification essay on advertising,
        film, or music

Week 2
Exemplification: Illustrating points and ideas by using effective examples

Paul A. Cantor, "The Apocalyptic Strain in Popular Culture: The American Nightmare Becomes the American Dream," pp. 279–293 (RPC)

Willie Osterweil, "Hollywood's Love Affair with Surveillance," pp. 342–347 (RPC)

Week 3
Exemplification (cont.)

Writing Assignment 1 due

Avoiding sentence fragments (handbook)

Judy Berman, "Concerning the Spiritual in Indie Rock," pp. 247–255 (RPC)

Tina Vasquez, "Riffs of Passage," pp. 232–239 (RPC)

Assign Writing Assignment 2: Cause and effect essay on media consumption or multiculturalism

Week 4
Cause and Effect: Explaining why and how things happen

Finding print and online sources (handbook)

Gerard Jones, "Violent Media Is Good for Kids," pp. 442–448 (RPC)

Vicessimus Knox, "On Novel Reading," pp. 396–400 (RPC)

Week 5
Cause and Effect (cont.)

Writing Assignment 2 due

Misplaced modifiers (handbook)

Hua Hsu, "The End of White America?" pp. 96–108 (RPC)

David Denby, "Has Hollywood Murdered the Movies?" pp. 348–362 (RPC)

Assign Writing Assignment 3: Comparison and contrast essay on sports, technology, or video games

Week 6
Comparison and Contrast: Understanding similarities, making distinctions

Run-on sentences (handbook)

Malcolm Gladwell, "The Sports Taboo," pp. 109–121 (RPC)

Nikil Saval, "Wall of Sound: The iPod Has Changed the Way We Listen to Music," pp. 139–150 (RPC)

Week 7
Comparison and Contrast (cont.)

Writing Assignment 3 due

Pronouns (handbook)

Commas (handbook)

Bo Moore, "Why Videogames Should Be Played with Friends, Not Online with Strangers," pp. 436–441 (RPC)

Nathan Jurgenson, "The IRL Fetish," pp. 191–197 (RPC)

Assign Writing Assignment 4: Classification and division essay on language, myth, or genre

Week 8
Classification and Division: Sorting, categorizing, breaking down, and analyzing

Colons and semicolons (handbook)

William Lutz, "With These Words I Can Sell You Anything," pp. 26–35 (RPC)

Linda Seger, "Creating the Myth," pp. 367–379 (RPC)

Week 9
Classification and Division (cont.)

Writing Assignment 4 due

Parallel structure (handbook)

Susan Sontag, "The Imagination of Disaster," pp. 324–341 (RPC)

Content Marketing Association, "Seven Steps to the Perfect Story," pp. 363–366 (RPC)

Assign Writing Assignment 5: Definition essay on a new or controversial term

Week 10
Definition: Identifying, explaining, distinguishing

Cohesion and coherence (handbook)

Clay Shirky, "Gin, Television, and Social Surplus," pp. 167–173 (RPC)

Jacob Burak, "Escape from the Matrix," pp. 428–435 (RPC)

Week 11

Definition (cont.)

> **Writing Assignment 5 due**
>
> Concision (handbook)
>
> Raquel Cepeda, "The N-Word Is Flourishing among Generation Hip-Hop Latinos: Why Should We Care Now?" pp. 90–95 (RPC)
>
> Ariel Levy, "Women and the Rise of Raunch Culture," pp. 128–132 (RPC)
>
> Assign Writing Assignment 6: Argumentation essay on television or gender

Week 12

Argumentation: Making your case and persuading

> Strategies for revision (handbook)
>
> Neil Postman, "The Judgment of Thamus," pp. 151–166 (RPC)
>
> Chuck Klosterman, "My Zombie, Myself: Why Modern Life Feels Rather Undead," pp. 422–427 (RPC)

Week 13

Argumentation (cont.)

> Jake Flanagin, "Stay Unlikable—for the Good of TV," pp. 315–321 (RPC)
>
> Roxane Gay, "Girls, Girls, Girls," pp. 270–278 (RPC)

Week 14

Argumentation (cont.)

> **Writing Assignment 6 due**
>
> Writing/editing workshop
>
> Research and sourcing (handbook)
>
> Revision (handbook)

1. Consumption and Advertising
How can we become more critical consumers?

Benjamin Barber

Overselling Capitalism with Consumerism

Barber's challenging essay is not so much an attack on consumer capitalism as it is an argument about how capitalism should function within a democratic society. For Barber, the crisis facing contemporary capitalism is that the "'Protestant ethos' of hard work and deferred gratification has been replaced by an infantilist ethos of easy credit and impulsive consumption" (par. 1). You might note the long tradition of criticism directed at societies that are—or are perceived to be—decadent and self-indulgent. Is that charge especially true now? In the past, did people work harder and defer gratification more persistently? How would we know? You might also ask students if they agree with Barber's claim that, ideally, capitalism "marries altruism and self-interest" (par. 2). For Barber, private economic decisions have public consequences and entail public responsibility: Individual consumer choice and economic liberty should be restrained by the "public logic fashioned by democracy" (par. 6). Do students think of their consumer choices in this way?

William Lutz

With These Words I Can Sell You Anything

You might want to begin discussing Lutz's essay by using his "Quick Quiz" on advertising doublespeak (p. 30). The exercise can focus students on the specifics of Lutz's argument rather than, say, generalities

1

about advertising being "bad." Most of us probably pay little attention to the language of packaging and advertisements in our day-to-day lives. But Lutz proposes that we approach these texts in almost the same way that we analyze poetry: "Every word in an ad is there for a reason; no word is wasted. Your job is to figure out exactly what each word is doing in an ad—what each word really means, not what the advertiser wants you to think it means" (par. 19). The third person creates a conversational intimacy with the reader, but it also reinforces the idea that Lutz's essay can function as a how-to guide for resisting the misleading or empty claims about consumer products. "With These Words I Can Sell You Anything" was written in the 1980s. You might discuss whether the rhetoric of packaging and advertising has changed since then, especially as many of the products and brands Lutz cites (Domino's Pizza, Advil, Miller Lite Beer) are still popular. Moreover, students can reflect on how new media forms such as the Internet or mobile apps influence or change the language—or strategies—of advertisers. Obviously, this text connects well with Bill Bryson's "The Hard Sell: Advertising in America" (p. 53), which provides history and context for the development of the techniques Lutz describes. One particularly apt pop-culture pairing for this selection is *Mad Men* (2007–2015); you might choose to show students an episode in which the characters make a particular pitch, then have students identify and analyze examples of doublespeak by using Lutz's framework. Be sure to use the advertisements on pages 32–33 as well, and ask students to analyze the design and use of words (or lack thereof) on these print ads.

ROLAND BARTHES

Toys

You might introduce "Toys" by explaining it as part of Barthes's larger project in *Mythologies* (1957). He outlined his motivation as follows: "I resented seeing Nature and History confused at every turn, and I wanted to track down, in the decorative display of *what-goes-without-saying*, the ideological abuse which, in my view, is hidden there." He did that by focusing on everyday objects, foods, events, and spectacles, from the enigmatic face of movie star Greta Garbo to the meaning of professional wrestling. For Barthes, toys prepare children to accept the constructed and historically specific "adult" world as a "natural," "universal" given: "Toys here reveal the list of all the things the adult does not find unusual:

war, bureaucracy, ugliness, Martians, etc. (par. 3). Barthes's most obvious example may be the dolls that socialize girls "for the causality of
house-keeping, to 'condition' her to her future role as mother" (par. 3).
This example stands out particularly well when put in context with the
recent awareness and discussions of feminism (e.g., Sheryl Sandberg,
#yesallwomen, etc.). Students can push back against Barthes's readings,
which suggest that there's little joy, wonder, or healthy pleasure in modern playthings. Is there another way to "read" toys? Consider putting
students in small groups to tease out the meanings of familiar objects
and products—from their own childhood toys to smartphones. Do our
consumer goods generally encourage us to be "users" or "creators"?
What's the difference?

SOLEIL HO

Craving the Other

Students may not have considered the ways in which food is part of
popular culture. What role does it play in the process of American
assimilation, for example? To what degree do representations of food
in commercials/infomercials or in meals portrayed on television shows
condition our response to particular foods? Students may also be surprised by the indignant—and even stinging—tone of Ho's polemic,
which cuts against the grain of familiar platitudes about "tasting" other
cultures or understanding ethnic differences by consuming ethnic cuisine. She scorns American "foodies," who "flit from *bibimbap* to *roti
canai*, fetishizing each dish as some adventure-in-a-bowl and using it as
a springboard to make gross generalizations about a given culture's
'sense of family and community,' 'lack of pretense,' 'passion,' and 'spirituality'" (par. 6). Ask students if she achieves her provocative purpose
without simply sounding like (as she puts it) a "sourpuss." But as Ho was
the Americanized child of Vietnamese immigrants, "Craving the Other"
is also a personal essay about her own desire to assimilate to American
food culture. If authenticity-seeking dilettantes "crave the other," Ho did
as well: "I wanted the straightforward, prefabricated snacks that I saw on
television: Bagel Bites, Pop-Tarts, chicken nuggets" (par. 2). Her repeated
characterizations of racial and cultural "whiteness" intersect well with
Hua Hsu's "The End of White America?" (p. 96), and her claims of cultural appropriation reflect the focus on language in Raquel Cepeda's
"The N-Word Is Flourishing among Generation Hip-Hop Latinos: Why

Should We Care Now?" (p. 90). Hsu quotes a sociologist who claims that "to be white is to be culturally broke" (par. 31), regardless of any social or economic privilege bestowed by "whiteness." Might this help explain the behavior of the American foodies who irk Ho?

VIRGINIA POSTREL

In Praise of Chain Stores

Postrel's essay rebukes claims that chain stores and restaurants are eliminating local color and destroying the regional character of American towns and cities. Point out that the writer is careful to avoid making a straw-man argument: From the very beginning she uses specific examples from Thomas Friedman and Rachel Dresbeck to establish conventional wisdom that she can then refute. You might also note that while Postrel gently mocks the "well-traveled cosmopolite," that stereotypical figure is clearly based on real attitudes among the kind of people who read the *New York Times*, watch *The Charlie Rose Show*, or use *Insiders' Guides* when traveling. This essay should prompt students to consider their own sense of both geography and consumer behavior. Postrel states, "Stores don't give places their character. Terrain and weather and culture do" (par. 6). Do students agree? How are commercial establishments a part of regional culture? Are students conscious of the differences between, say, a local diner and a chain restaurant? Are "mom and pop" stores inherently superior to large retailers like Wal-Mart? Do these differences matter?

BILL BRYSON

The Hard Sell: Advertising in America

Bryson's style is a remarkable achievement: He strikes an appealing balance between the accessibility of his prose, on the one hand, and the sophistication of his arguments, on the other. His ears are tuned not only to the language of advertising but also to the sound of his own voice as a writer. He also reads advertisements with the rigor of a literary critic. You may want to focus on paragraph 20, for example, to show how close reading can illuminate ads as effectively as it can unravel the meaning of a poem. In a way, the "cruel paradox" (par. 22) of brands is a testament to the care advertisers and packagers bring to their craft: Brand names like Tabasco, Kleenex, Coca-Cola, and Thermos are "indistinguishable in the public mind from the product itself" (par. 22). You might point out that Bryson incorporates several different writing patterns into this essay, including compare and contrast (par. 22) and cause and effect (par. 37). Given its exploration of the ad industry, this essay pairs well with William Lutz's "With These Words I Can Sell You Anything" (p. 26), which also focuses on the language of advertising.

PAIRED READINGS: M(E)-COMMERCE

ELLEN HUET

Snaps to Riches: The Rise of Snapchat Celebrities

Many undergraduates are likely to be familiar with photo and video messaging applications like Snapchat, Instagram, and Vine. For those who are not, have students provide a brief explanation or even give a demonstration; this is also a great way for students to take ownership of their pop-culture expertise and ability to rhetorically analyze these applications. Huet's essay builds on students' familiarity by investigating how Snapchat works and why brands want to use it as a marketing tool. Point out her strategy of cutting back and forth between profiling Shaun McBride and reporting on the app itself and its implications for users and marketers. Students may want to use this approach—which allows a writer to balance a sharp focus with a wider perspective—in their own writing. You might ask them about Snapchat (or a similar app) as a branding tool: If they use the app, how aware are they of the broader context in which companies are paying "for advertising deals with McBride and other power users, hoping to reach Snapchat's demographic: the fickle and influential 13- to 25-year-old bracket" (par. 4)? Does this affect how they understand Snapchat and their own photo messaging habits? Do they agree with Huet's point about the "great irony" that "everything that's appealing to brands and creators about Snapchat today—its youth appeal, its novelty, its authenticity—will fade as more brands and creators flock to it" (par. 33)?

PAIRED READINGS: M(E)-COMMERCE

Chiara Atik

Public Displays of Transaction

Like Ellen Huet (p. 70), Chiara Atik writes about a specific app, Venmo. But her essay touches on a range of issues—and questions—about life online that transcend any social networking site or electronic financial transaction platform. In the company's own words, Venmo is a "free digital wallet that allows you to pay and request money from your friends." These transactions can be displayed for other users within a network to view, which means that the app serves as an opportunity for a kind of coy financial exhibitionism, even if users are not fully aware of what they are revealing. Atik makes two related points that you may want to highlight for discussion. First, she argues that our personal financial lives make juicier voyeuristic fodder than our romantic lives: "Don't get me wrong, Facebook, Twitter, and Instagram are great for glimpses at how couples *want* to be perceived: that carefully cropped and filtered picture, the self-consciously flirtatious tweet. But money is intimate, far more intimate, in fact, than sex" (par. 7). Second, Atik notes our purchases can be read as a kind of narrative and "on Venmo, for better or for worse, these interactions are public, open to speculation and interpretation from your second cousin, your ex-boyfriend, your mom's work colleague, and, uhm, me" (par. 11). You might ask students whether they agree with Atik that discussing sex openly is easier than discussing money or personal financial status. What do they make of her suggestion that online social networking is primarily a place for "stalkers, gossips, and know-it-alls" (par. 6)? This essay is paired with Huet's "Snaps to Riches: The Rise of Snapchat Celebrities" (p. 70), but you might also link it with Nathan Jurgenson's "The IRL Fetish" (p. 191) and Jacob Burak's "Escape from the Matrix" (p. 428), which both provide wider context and explore the implications of our lives online.

2. Identity
Where do we discover ourselves in pop culture?

Liz Armstrong

An Argument for Being a Poser

As its title indicates, Liz Armstrong makes a clear argument in this very accessible selection. But her essay is also exploratory and contemplative: She writes to work through issues of identity, authenticity, and adolescent role-playing. Armstrong even includes an older passage from her diary, which suggests the open-ended quality of personal writing: Writers can always revisit and reinterpret past experiences as their perspective changes. You might ask students about their own experiences seeking their "subgenre," community, or identity. Are they searching for the "thing that takes a seam-ripper to the sewed-up reality [they've] been living in" (par. 4)? Are they as conscious of this process as Armstrong? Ultimately, she argues that "posing" and trying on different identities — even if they are inauthentic — are good things, despite the negative connotations of the word "poser": "You get smart and possibly eccentric from experience; your fantasies become richer, your dreams engorged with possibility. Because that's what this is all about, right?" (par. 8). Do students agree with her endorsement of "dabbling"? In a way, she recommends immersive experience, which makes her essay pair well with others about seeking identity and community in subcultures and vicarious media forms, especially Robin Brenner's "Teen Literature and Fan Culture" (p. 401) and Gerard Jones's "Violent Media Is Good for Kids" (p. 442). Because of their intended teenage audiences and their recurring themes of self-discovery, several high school comedies (a film genre that reached its height of popularity — and saturation — in the 1980s and 1990s) would pair well with this reading, especially as an introduction to the theme of identity.

RAQUEL CEPEDA

The N-Word Is Flourishing among Generation Hip-Hop Latinos: Why Should We Care Now?

The "n-word" has a long, controversial, and painful history in the United States. You might begin a discussion by talking about its significance historically as well as its lingering legacy. For example, a 2011 edition of Mark Twain's *The Adventures of Huckleberry Finn* excised the word from the novel. Yet the n-word's meaning seems to depend on cultural, racial, ethnic, and personal contexts, particularly who's ascribing it to whom. While Cepeda highlights the word as it's now used in the Latino and Dominican community, her essay may evoke a more general discussion about identity and language, especially with regard to taboo terms. The example of Jennifer Lopez suggests that the hip-hop industry and culture applies two sets of rules: Men can "get away with murder" while "women are held to impossibly high standards" (par. 10). But the negative reaction to Lopez's use of the word also raises questions about her "authenticity." Cepeda associates authenticity with "authentic urban native Fat Joe" (par. 2) and Afro-Peruvian rapper Immortal Technique. For her, the word connotes in-group membership: "For us, the word usually surfaces in the same context that arises among young African-Americans: as a term of inclusion and solidarity" (par. 4). It also serves as a "reminder that [Afro-Latinos] too have been oppressed and are products of the transatlantic slave trade" (par. 6). Ask students to consider the notion of "authenticity" here: Is it a function of race, class, ethnicity, past oppression? Or you may ask them if they see parallels and contrasts between this reappropriation of the n-word and the reappropriation of female stereotypes embraced by women in Ariel Levy's "Women and the Rise of Raunch Culture" (p. 128).

HUA HSU

The End of White America?

You might start a discussion with your students by asking about Hsu's provocative title. Does it seem threatening? How does one define "white America"? For the writer, the country is in the process of transformation:

"Whether you describe it as the dawning of a post-racial age or just the end of white America, we're approaching a profound demographic tipping point" (par. 7). That "tipping point" means not only changes in the makeup of the US population, but also shifts in the meaning of race, ethnicity, culture, and American identity. Hsu places special emphasis on the significance of "whiteness." For earlier generations of immigrants, to be "recognized as a 'white American' . . . was to enter the mainstream of American life" and gain the social, cultural, and economic power that membership entailed (par. 8). Accordingly, to be outside this category of whiteness "was to be permanently excluded" from those benefits (par. 8). Immigrants thus strove to assimilate and "blend in" as an ideal. Now, as Lind's so-called beiging of America continues, people of various races and ethnicities who identify as white will do so "out of convenience and even indifference, rather than aspiration and necessity" (par. 8). While students have likely discussed race and ethnicity before, they probably have not considered the meaning of "whiteness" as Hsu examines it or done a close analysis of its meaning and representations in pop culture. Ask them if their own relationship to culture and socioeconomics matches sociologist Matt Wray's characterization that regardless of their race and ethnicity, "to be white is to be culturally broke" (par. 31). Hsu also points to hip-hop music and pop culture as a major factor in the transformation of America. You may want to link this idea to Will Wilkinson's "Country Music, Openness to Experience, and the Psychology of Culture War" (p. 214), which suggests that, in several ways, country music sets itself in opposition to the kind of social and cultural changes described by Hsu.

Malcolm Gladwell

The Sports Taboo

For Gladwell, the "sports taboo" is, in part, the general prohibition against openly discussing "what whites are supposed to be good at and what blacks are supposed to be good at" (par. 1) or, more generally, "talking openly about the racial dimension of sports" (par. 3). Ask students how they react to the "racial taxonomy" described in the first paragraph of his essay: Do they accept his premises and preliminary observations? In his youth, Gladwell kept an eye on fellow runner Arnold Stotz because the writer suspected that the white Stotz could "not keep winning," that his "whiteness" was like a "degenerative disease, which would eventually claim and cripple him" (par. 2). The anecdote supports Gladwell's main point about the connection between race and athletic talent: Stotz dropped from the rankings, reinforcing the young Gladwell's presumption that "we were better because we were black, because of something intrinsic to being black" (par. 3). Gladwell's analogy is provocative and forceful, but it also suggests a slippery slope: If predispositions toward athletic talent or diabetes can be linked to race, should we think the same way about intelligence or a propensity toward criminality? Ask students to consider the representations or assumptions about race in sports portrayed in pop culture, from film to sports commentary programs on networks such as ESPN. You might also note that our ideas of "race"—and racial categories themselves—are socially constructed in many ways. Gladwell's essay can pair well with "The End of White America?" (p. 96), as Hua Hsu writes about race largely as a cultural construct rather than as an innate biological phenomenon.

DANAH BOYD

Impression Management in a Networked Setting

Begin a discussion of this selection from boyd's *It's Complicated: The Social Lives of Networked Teens* by focusing on the first three paragraphs. boyd begins by summarizing the work of sociologist Erving Goffman in his 1959 book *The Presentation of Self in Everyday Life*. Note how boyd uses summary, paraphrase, and direct quotation to present Goffman's key ideas clearly and accessibly to a general audience—that is, readers who are likely unfamiliar with his text. Then, she draws on Goffman's work to create an intellectual framework for her own approach to analyzing teen behavior in the context of online social networking. Student writers can find all of these rhetorical and intellectual moves difficult; boyd provides an excellent model for communicating, adapting, and applying the ideas of other thinkers and writers to one's own work. Students are likely to be intimately familiar with the issues of social networking that boyd discusses, which should lead to lively, wide-ranging discussion about self-presentation, self-censorship, and rhetorical contexts of digital writing. But note that the writer's examples lead her to form conclusions in the final paragraph, including her assertion that the online experience forces teens to navigate questions of identity in "one heck of a cultural labyrinth" (par. 10). Like Willie Osterweil in "Hollywood's Love Affair with Surveillance" (p. 342), boyd is concerned with surveillance, but in a different context. You might discuss these essays together, focusing on the ubiquity of surveillance and, perhaps, our increasing acceptance of it as a fact of life.

PAIRED READINGS: IT'S COMPLICATED

ARIEL LEVY

Women and the Rise of Raunch Culture

Levy grounds her broader cultural diagnosis in personal observations. It's especially revealing that the first verb in the essay is *noticed*. Levy illustrates how to integrate personal writing and reflection with wider subjects and themes: The process begins with paying attention, being perceptive, and noticing things. She starts with pop-culture phenomena such as Britney Spears, the early 2000s *Charlie's Angels* films, and the emergence of the "Lad Mag," then sharpens the focus to her own experiences and relationships, calling attention to female friends who like going to strip clubs and watching pornography. Levy also notes that even she has started to use the word *chick* and has "taken to wearing thongs" (par. 4). She argues that a "tarty" and cartoonish version of female sexuality now crowds out all other kinds of sexual expression. For Levy, this is a problem: The idea of an autonomous and "liberated" woman is now bound up with women choosing to behave like the oversexed, objectified stereotypes men imagine them to be. Ask students whether they have noticed the "raunch culture" identified by the writer and whether they agree with her analysis. Do they view the elements of raunch culture as "empowering"? In the years since this essay was published, has raunch culture evolved, intensified, or receded? Is peer pressure still placed on women to be "one of the guys"? Ask students to consider these questions with specific examples from pop culture, or bring in some of your own for applied analysis. Responses may break down along gender lines, but be careful to avoid too many assumptions. Roland Barthes's "Toys" (p. 36) makes an interesting pairing and an opportunity to discuss social gendering and expectations.

PAIRED READINGS: IT'S COMPLICATED

Sonali Kohli

Pop Culture's Transgender Moment

In this essay, Kohli traces the emergence of transgender characters and themes in popular culture—especially in online television programming like *Orange Is the New Black* and *Transparent*. In the past, transgender characters were often "victims or villains" (par. 2). Now, representations of transgendered people are fuller and more multidimensional. Kohli implies that writers and producers of shows for Amazon or Netflix have more artistic freedom than they would on network or cable television; the youthful audience for streaming services is more open to, accepting of, and interested in such portrayals. For Kohli, artistic and social aims match commercial goals: "Amazon and Netflix are building a loyal audience of young, web-savvy people by investing in shows that address what they want to see in TV" (par. 6). You might ask students whether they watch any of these shows and how they respond to such portrayals. You might also place this question in the broader context suggested by Kohli, namely, that pop culture is having a "transgender moment." Do they agree? Or is Kohli overstating—or even just inventing—a trend that is much more limited? Do students agree that net-based companies like Netflix and Amazon produce noticeably different content than their cable and network counterparts? David Charpentier's "Story or Spectacle? Why Television Is Better Than the Movies" (p. 308) can provide a useful lens for Kohli's essay as you can discuss whether the emergence of richly drawn transgender characters is merely part of a more general trend toward complexity in television programing.

3. Technology
How do new devices and apps transform experience?

NIKIL SAVAL

Wall of Sound: The iPod Has Changed the Way We Listen to Music

Saval's subject is music, but he is primarily concerned with its social functions and with the ways technology shapes our musical consumption. While the writer draws on critics and theorists such as Theodor Adorno, Pierre Bourdieu, George Steiner, and Allan Bloom, students should not be put off by the name-dropping. Saval puts these figures to good use (note his quick, compare-and-contrast summary of Adorno and Bourdieu in paragraph 15, for example) and deploys them to provide a framework of ideas about music and society. Moreover, Saval's style and diction remain accessible throughout the essay, and he does not hesitate to highlight the "blind spots" of these theorists. Nevertheless, you might want to go through this essay slowly, making sure that students follow Saval's argument. They will likely grasp his early claims about popular music, even if they disagree. For example, Saval claims that the "big difference" between music in the 1960s and 1970s was that '60s music was an "incitement to social change," while '70s music "more or less forfeited its capacity to promote social movements" (pars. 5–6). Ask students if they agree with this claim. Do any of them still see music as a site of "radical hope" (par. 6)? Does popular music still promote social movements? Should it? Saval avoids writing about specific songs, artists, and musical styles; such distinctions are largely irrelevant to his argument. In fact, he claims the endless classification and division of genres and subgenres has reached a "climax of absurdity" (par. 16). While he thinks these labels and genres perform "a lot of handy social sorting," all of them reinforce the "omnipresence of music" in daily life (par. 16). Still, you might have students consider his riffs on class distinctions, musical preferences, and the "total pluralism of taste" (pars. 17–18). Saval's essay suggests some evocative parallels with Frank Rose's "The Art of Immersion: Fear of Fiction" (p. 409). While Rose suggests that people generally

13

want vicarious fantasies and immersive fictions rather than reality, Saval argues that silence—the refusal to be condemned to a "lifetime of listening" (par. 24)—might be the most radical option in a culture where music is everywhere, always.

NEIL POSTMAN

The Judgment of Thamus

While Postman writes sophisticated prose about complex subjects (Plato, Freud, epistemology, ideology, technological change), you should highlight his clarity and accessibility. Postman writes in the first person, frequently using "I." He draws on philosophy, psychology, history, and previous scholarship, but he is never pedantic, obscure, or condescending. For example, his reading of *Phaedrus* provides a marvelous and memorable explication of an ancient text for a general audience. While Postman appreciates Thamus's reservations, the writer concedes that Thamus is also a "one-eyed prophet" who errs in only seeing the downsides of a new technology. Postman's main point is that technology is always both a "burden and a blessing; not either-or, but this-and-that" (par. 2). Postman's argument should give students a powerful lens to evaluate the benefits and drawbacks of technology—especially as it might get them to think critically about metaphors such as technological "progress." This essay pairs well with Clay Shirky's more optimistic "Gin, Television, and Social Surplus" (p. 167), but you might also have students read "The Judgment of Thamus" alongside Nathan Jurgenson's "The IRL Fetish" (p. 191) or Jacob Burak's "Escape from the Matrix" (p. 428). Postman's essay comes from his 1993 book *Technopoly*, published before the proliferation of smartphones, the Internet, and other innovations. Encourage students to apply his intellectual framework and his view of technology to newer devices.

CLAY SHIRKY

Gin, Television, and Social Surplus

Is participation a value in and of itself? Does the quality of one's participation matter? The well-known intellectual Stanley Fish once said that a particular type of literary criticism "relieves me of the obligation to be right . . . and demands only that I be interesting." You might keep that principle in mind as you read and discuss Shirky's freewheeling essay (adapted from a talk), which examines the notion of "cognitive surplus" and the cultural transformation from gin-soaked, eighteenth-century London to situation comedies like *Gilligan's Island*. Shirky does not shy away from sweeping generalizations, broad assertions of cause and effect, and provocative analogies between gin, television, and the Internet. But according to the writer, the Internet is different from television in that it invites participation and production of cultural content: "Media [today] is actually a triathlon. . . . People like to consume, but they also like to produce, and they like to share" (par. 24). Shirky's ideas can illuminate other readings that focus on participatory forms of media and pop culture, such as Robin Brenner's "Teen Literature and Fan Culture" (p. 405) and Bo Moore's "Why Videogames Should Be Played with Friends, Not Online with Strangers" (p. 436). You might also discuss Shirky's essay in the context of Neil Postman's "The Judgment of Thamus" (p. 151), which suggests that "technology giveth and technology taketh away" (par. 3). What do we lose when we gain the cognitive surplus articulated by Shirky?

JENNIFER BLEYER

Love the One You're Near

Bleyer's article looks like a relatively lighthearted review of new mobile dating apps, but the writer raises important issues about the intersection of technology and romantic relationships. Charting an evolution from online dating sites like Match.com and OKCupid to mobile apps like Grindr and Tinder, she surveys a shifting "landscape of love-seeking" (par. 5). This shift has its downsides. Quoted in the article, author Ken Page refers to the "superficiality and coldness" (par. 6) encouraged by these apps, as well as technology-enabled "cultural of unkindness" that has "created a lot more micro-jerkiness in early-stage dating than there has ever been before" (par. 8). Moreover, a relationship that begins with flattering pictures and witty text messages may not survive the awkwardness and imperfections of a real-life meeting. But another expert suggests that these apps can "infuse the spontaneity of real-world dating into online dating" (par. 11). Ask students whether they agree with Page that meeting "through a vast and dehumanizing virtual marketplace . . . encourages people to see each other more as products and less as people, and to not afford each other common courtesy, let alone the focused attention it takes to forge a real, intimate connection" (par. 7). Are our technologies turning our quest for intimate relationships into another form of shallow, online consumerism? These apps are ostensibly designed to facilitate real-life relationships. How might Nathan Jurgenson ("The IRL Fetish," p. 191) view them? Do Bleyer and her sources seem to privilege the "offline" and turn it into a fetish?

PAIRED READINGS: CLICKBAIT

David Auerbach

You Are What You Click

"You Are What You Click" is sophisticated, dense, and closely argued. You can begin by pointing out the writer's opening strategy: While Auberbach is concerned about online privacy issues, he starts by discussing the misleading and context-free ways these problems are covered by the media—and, as a result, misunderstood by the public. According to Auerbach, periodic news stories and outrages about privacy violations, hacking, identity theft, and data sniffing are "red herrings" that "provide false assurances that . . . our privacy is not being invaded on the Internet, that our personal data is safe, and that we are anonymous in our online—and offline—activities" (par. 2). In contrast, he argues, the real problem lies in the way private companies ("Big Salesman") engage in "a slow, unstoppable process of profiling who we are and what we do, to be sold to advertisers and marketing companies" (par. 5). As students live much of their lives online, you should be able to generate a lively discussion from this essay. How conscious are they of these privacy issues? Are they aware that sites like Twitter and Amazon are "tracking and retaining everything you're doing on their sites and on any other sites that host their scripts and widgets" (par. 17)? How do they think about—and manage or protect—their anonymity, if at all? You might pair "You Are What You Click" with Willie Osterweil's "Hollywood's Love Affair with Surveillance" (p. 342). For Osterweil, certain blockbuster movies function ideologically to accustom viewers to the constant surveillance of an outsized national security state. Auerbach is writing about a more subtle loss of privacy in the context of private corporations and the accumulation of consumer data. Ask students which of these seems like a bigger problem.

PAIRED READINGS: CLICKBAIT

Nathan Jurgenson

The IRL Fetish

In this essay, Jurgenson argues against the conventional wisdom that people are spending too much time online at the expense of their real lives. It may be helpful to walk students through the way the writer accomplishes this—especially in the way he presents and addresses counterarguments. In particular, focus on paragraphs 3 to 6, where Jurgenson lays out common complaints that "people, especially young people, have logged on and checked out" (par. 3) and entreaties that we need to "go out into the 'real' world, lift our chins, and breathe deep the wonders of the offline" (par. 5). Students should be mindful that these are not the writer's views, but rather the views of those he disagrees with—as such, he is employing an argumentative strategy of engaging opposing points. For Jurgenson, such laments, along with books like Sherry Turkle's *Alone Together* and initiatives like the digital sabbath movement, are examples of a misguided and mistaken "digital dualism": "The common (mis)understanding is [that] experience is zero-sum: time spent online means less spent offline" (par. 12). For Jurgenson, online and off-line are not separate realms or spheres. Both are part of an "augmented reality that exists at the intersection of materiality and information, physicality and digitality, bodies and technology, atoms and bits, the off and the online" (par. 14). Therefore, people are wrong when they use the term "IRL" to "mean offline: *Facebook is real life*" (par. 14). You may want to connect Jurgenson's argument to Jacob Burak's "Escape from the Matrix" (p. 428), which argues that our online social lives are contributing to FoMO, the "fear of missing out," a "cultural disorder that is insidiously undermining our peace of mind" (par. 5). How might Jurgenson respond to Burak? Does Burak seem to engage in "digital dualism" in his essay?

4. Music

How does popular music reflect and express our identities?

PAMELA HOLLANDER

"Elevate My Mind": Identities for Women in Hip-Hop Love Songs

Writing in a scholarly context, Pamela Hollander is explicit about her approach and her rationale. She uses the analytical tools of Critical Discourse Analysis to explore female identity and gender relationships in the lyrics of hip-hop songs. Her essay is carefully structured: It begins with a brief explanation of Critical Discourse Analysis (pars. 2–6), a theory that helps explain how identities, social relationships, power relationships, values, and ideologies are not simply reflected or expressed by language but coded and constructed by it as well. As Critical Discourse Analysis refers to an entire field of interdisciplinary academic inquiry, you may want to encourage students to investigate it further—especially if they want to use it for their own research and writing projects. However, while Hollander's approach is sophisticated and "academic," point out that the article emerged from personal observation and interest: "Through my teaching of a class called The Culture and Language of Hip Hop, I began to notice some recent hip hop love songs which seemed to push against the accepted identities for women in hip hop and point toward love as involving 'nurturing' and 'spiritual growth.' This essay is an examination of those love songs" (par. 1). Consequently, the body of Hollander's article provides both close readings of hip-hop, neo-soul, and R&B lyrics along with classifications of different identities and relationships based on her lyrical analysis. Besides being a good model of classification and division, this scholarly article provides a good example of academic discourse. You might highlight its structure, formality, and style to contrast it with other selections from magazines, Web sites, or other less specialized writing contexts. You may also want to have students read the article with Will Wilkinson's "Country Music, Openness to Experience, and the Psychology of Culture War" (p. 214), which, in a sense, considers the country genre as a discourse with a particular ideology. You may also ask students to apply the methodology Hollander uses to current hip-hop, soul, and R&B songs, which would provide an opportunity for close analysis.

WILL WILKINSON

Country Music, Openness to Experience, and the Psychology of Culture War

Will Wilkinson identifies the cultural preoccupations and political contours of contemporary country music: "Country has an ideology. Not to say country has a position on abortion, exactly. But country music, taken as a whole, has a position on life, taken as a whole" (par. 1). He mixes several approaches—social and political psychology, the science of personality types, personal observation, close analysis of lyrical themes—to build an argument about the meaning and purpose of this genre: "My conjecture, then, is that country music functions in part to reinforce in low-openness individuals the idea that life's most powerful, meaningful emotional experiences are precisely those to which conservative personalities living conventional lives are most likely to have access. And it functions as a device to coordinate members of conservative-minded communities on the incomparable emotional weight of traditional milestone experiences" (par. 7). In a way, then, country music emerges as a form of resistance to change—"more bomb shelter than bomb," as Wilkinson describes it (par. 12). You might ask students what the writer means by "culture war" in the context of this essay. If this musical form represents a kind of "shelter" or a defensive action by those who "sense that their values are under attack" (par. 8), what specific changes do these people seek to resist? You might point out the ways Wilkinson self-consciously mixes diction and discourses in this essay—from slang terms ("Gettin' hitched") to academic terms ("low-openness individuals") and from chatty autobiographical asides ("Last night, on my way to fetch bok choy . . .") to quotations from scholarly journals. According to Wilkinson, country music presents for its fans ideals about what makes for a stable, orderly, and meaningful life in America. This essay could pair well with Paul A. Cantor's "The Apocalyptic Strain in Popular Culture: The American Nightmare Becomes the American Dream" (p. 279), which might suggest the precise opposite of country music's fantasy. For example, is country music a "shelter" from both the breakdown of social and familial institutions and the lost ideals of American individuality?

You could also have students consider Wilkinson's claims as they listen to a number of more recent country songs that recognize the conservatism in country music and challenge it.

LESSLEY ANDERSON

Seduced by "Perfect" Pitch: How Auto-Tune Conquered Pop Music

Lessley Anderson dives deeply into her topic: the seemingly ubiquitous pitch-correction device and vocal effect Auto-Tune. In the process, she gives a revealing take on its history and use, as well as its implications for our notions of authenticity and even morality. But Anderson ends the essay on a personal note. As an Auto-Tune skeptic and amateur musician, she finds herself impressed with it after hearing her own vocals treated with a "natural-sounding" version of the effect. Students who are music fans should be familiar with both the vocal effect and the debates around its use. Indeed, the controversy was even the subject of a 2009 song, "D.O.A. (Death of Auto-Tune)," by hip-hop superstar Jay-Z. You might note that Anderson runs into roadblocks as a writer and acknowledges them in the article, as when she tries to get artists to discuss Auto-Tune: "Big producers like Max Marlin and Dr. Luke, responsible for mega hits from artists like Ke$ha, Pink, and Kelly Clarkson, either turned me down or didn't respond to interview requests. And you can't really blame them" (par. 22). But she does include an interview with Auto-Tune's creator, Andy Hildebrand, who playfully disowns any abuse of his creation with a coy analogy: "I just make the car. I don't drive it down the wrong side of the road" (par. 31). Moreover, she makes effective use of secondary sources. The article should lead to a provocative discussion of aesthetics and authenticity. As Anderson points out, "recorded music is, by definition, artificial" (par. 32). How is Auto-Tune any less authentic than, say, amplified electric guitars or other recording studio practices such as overdubbing and multi-tracking? As suggested in the Connections question, Anderson's discussion pairs well with Saul Austerlitz's "The Pernicious Rise of Poptimism" (p. 240): a poptimist might like Auto-Tuned vocals *because* of the effect rather than despite it. But you might also consider Anderson's article in the context of selections such as Nathan Jurgenson's "The IRL Fetish" (p. 191) or Frank Rose's "The Art of Immersion: Fear of Fiction" (p. 409), both of which explore our complex relationship with ideas like "authenticity" and "reality."

Tina Vasquez

Riffs of Passage

"It's not 'political' when it's your life," says a member of the Los Angeles band La Santa Cecilia, whom Vasquez profiles in her essay. She is referring to her band's involvement in a campaign called Not One More Deportation, an action which—along with a music video—got the band labeled as "political." Her statement suggests one of Vasquez's key themes: the ways in which the personal, the musical, and the political overlap and reflect one another. Mixing personal narrative with a journalistic survey of Los Angeles's Latino music scene, Vasquez provides a lively and earthy musical account of this musical landscape that "reveal[s] a bigger narrative about the beauty and brutality of migration" (par. 6). You might want to highlight the ways in which the writer evokes the feel of a vital subculture's scene: a passionate community of bands and fans knitted together by both the love of a certain kind of music *and* a shared sense of identity, ethnicity, and even hardship. As a member of the band Las Cafeteras claims, "a lot of us are using music as a tool to share our stories and communicate our struggles and successes as a people" (par. 18). Vasquez captures this community by skillfully combining exemplification and narration. You can pair her essay with other selections that focus on connecting through shared pop culture, such as Judy Berman's "Concerning the Spiritual in Indie Rock" (p. 247) or Robin Brenner's "Teen Literature and Fan Culture" (p. 401) or Bo Moore's "Why Videogames Should Be Played with Friends, Not Online with Strangers" (p. 436).

PAIRED READINGS: POP OF AGES

Saul Austerlitz

The Pernicious Rise of Poptimism

At first glance, "The Pernicious Rise of Poptimism" has an insular, media-focused "inside baseball" quality, as movie and book critic Saul Austerlitz reflects on the "reigning style of music criticism" among music writers (par. 4). But Austerlitz's article should provoke students to evaluate not only their own tastes in music but also their attitudes toward authenticity and artificiality in pop culture as a whole. He argues that the current critical orthodoxy "privilege[s] the deliriously artificial over the artificially genuine" (par. 5). It is a "studied response" to the traditional preferences of "rockists" who (presumably) overvalue authenticity, musicianship, sincerity, and integrity. For such critics, who have what Austerlitz calls "Rolling Stone disease": Bob Dylan and Bruce Springsteen are "geniuses," while Marvin Gaye and Madonna are "mere pop singers" (par. 7). The "rockist" musical canon is overwhelmingly white and male. But while Austerlitz acknowledges poptimism's populist virtues, he finds it stifling and dogmatic: "a cudgel with which to selectively club music that aims for something other than the whoosh of an indelibly catchy riff" (par. 12). He also points out that the poptimist aesthetic, applied to other forms (film criticism, food criticism), would lead to shallow writing that merely "cheer[ed] on the winners" (par. 10). You might find it illuminating to pair this essay with Virginia Postrel's "In Praise of Chain Stores" (p. 47). While their topics and points of view are different, both Austerlitz and Postrel are writing about forms of pop-culture snobbishness, as well as about the tension between populism and accessibility on one hand and authenticity and quality on the other hand. Postrel's image of the "bored cosmopolite," for example, corresponds almost exactly to the negative stereotype of a "rockist" music critic.

PAIRED READINGS: POP OF AGES

JUDY BERMAN

Concerning the Spiritual in Indie Rock

Judy Berman's contemplative essay on indie rock and spirituality provides a virtuoso performance of thoughtful, reflective pop-culture writing. Even if students are unfamiliar with the bands she discusses, they can learn much about exploring a topic by following the example of her strategy and approach. Considering the lyrics, performances, and aesthetics of bands such as Neutral Milk Hotel and Animal Collective, Berman proposes that these artists offer their fans metaphysical and spiritual sustenance. For example, at live performances, bands and audience members "fuse into an army of true believers, baptized in sweat and whinnying in tongues" (par. 11). The Yeasayer's album *All Hour Cymbals* functions as a "nonbeliever's attempt to understand what devotion and awe might feel like" (par. 16), while for indie rock audiences, "Bible study is replaced by ritualistic listening and re-listening to tease out the meaning or simply bask in the bliss of favorite albums" (par. 17). You might spend time discussing Berman's opening strategy, in which she quotes abstract artist Wassily Kandinsky; the quotation functions as a keynote for her discussion, and she both explains it in the introduction and returns to it near the end of her essay. Student writers often try to use this strategy (beginning with a quotation), and Berman models how to do it effectively and thoughtfully, rather than shallowly. That is, the quasi-epigraph is not a placeholder or the opening gimmick of a writer who does not know how to begin. Rather, Kandinsky's statement suggests the theme and structure of the entire essay. Note that Berman writes about spirituality and religion, which can be sensitive topics for students. Try to be mindful of that, especially given the writer's generalizations about contemporary "mainstream religion" (par. 17). You might have students pair this selection with Will Wilkinson's "Country Music, Openness to Experience, and the Psychology of Culture War" (p. 214). In both essays, fans of a specific genre seek ritual, enchantment, and community from music. How are the values of these fan communities different? How are they similar? Wilkinson writes that country music "has an ideology" (par. 1). Does the indie rock described by Berman also have an ideology? Encourage students to broaden the discussion and consider other pop-culture areas or artifacts around which communities form and "worship."

5. Television
Are we living in a Golden Age of television?

ROBERT KUBEY AND MIHALY CSIKSZENTMIHALYI

Television Addiction Is No Mere Metaphor

Kubey and Csikszentmihalyi's data-driven argument might be timelier than ever, given new developments in instant viewing, online streaming, and "binge watching." But you might use this essay to discuss not only television but also smartphones, laptops, and other "addictive" technologies. The "Slave to the Computer Screen" section will be helpful in making this connection. The writers define the "orienting response" as "our instinctive visual or auditory reaction to any sudden or novel stimulus" (par. 13). Scientists understand it as "part of our evolutionary heritage, a built-in sensitivity to movement and potential predatory threats" (par. 13). Television triggers that reactiveness. Essentially, humans are hardwired to react to sudden noises, cuts, edits, and other "formal features" of television. Ask students about their own experiences with the "orienting response": Do they find lighted screens irresistible or "feel hypnotized" by them, as one research subject claims in the essay (par. 15)? Kubey and Csikszentmihalyi integrate a range of research and evidence into their writing. Point out how they move from general assertion to specific evidence and then back to generality. Even though the writers cite laboratory experiments and specialized studies, they define technical terms clearly, and their prose remains accessible. Consider asking students how they feel after watching television as opposed to other activities. According to the essay, they may feel "depleted" (par. 9) or have more difficulty concentrating when they turn the television off. The authors point out that studies show less stimulation in the brains of people watching TV than in those of people who are reading. Ask students to consider also the "hypnotizing" and depleting effects of binge watching on new streaming platforms like Netflix and Hulu, which are featured in Ken Auletta's "Netflix and the Future of Television" (p. 294).

ROXANE GAY

Girls, Girls, Girls

In this chapter, excerpted from her bestselling 2014 book *Bad Feminist*, Roxane Gay begins in a speculative autobiographical register: "A television show about my twenties would follow the life of a girl who is lost, literally and figuratively" (par. 1). As you follow her elaborate account of this hypothetical TV program, you might note the freedom of Gay's chosen form: the extended personal essay, which allows her the space and leisure to move from narrative to reflection to analysis. Point out how this contrasts with the limitations of, say, an online magazine column or even the formal demands of a scholarly article. Ultimately, Gay shifts to a more critical mode, noting: "We put a lot of responsibility on popular culture, particularly when some pop artifact somehow distinguishes itself as not terrible" (par. 8). Her example of "not terrible" pop culture is the HBO series *Girls*, created by and starring Lena Dunham. In this comprehensive evaluation of the controversial show, Gay embodies a model of critically engaged writing. She admires many aspects of *Girls*: its clever writing; its presentation of its female protagonist as a rich, round, and multifaceted character; its groundbreaking quality. At the same time, Gay identifies its weaknesses, from its "forced premise" to its nearly exclusive representation of affluent characters living a "privileged existence" (par. 18). Yet her analysis goes well beyond a formal evaluation of *Girls* to examine the "discourse surrounding" the show: the wider discussions of "nepotism, privilege, race" (par. 16). Highlight how Gay uses *Girls* to enter a broader conversation, as these are exactly the kinds of connections we hope students learn how to make as they engage with popular culture. *Girls* is known for its unflinching approach to sexuality, presenting (in Gay's words) "sex scenes so uncomfortable they defy imagination"; consequently, you might want to pair this essay with Ariel Levy's "Women and the Rise of Raunch Culture" (p. 128). Do Lena Dunham and *Girls* suggest a new iteration of "raunch culture"? Do they suggest a subversion or refutation of raunch culture, or a backlash against it?

PAUL A. CANTOR

The Apocalyptic Strain in Popular Culture: The American Nightmare Becomes the American Dream

Cantor writes about our current fascination with apocalyptic fantasies in the context of the American Dream. After briefly defining the American Dream, Cantor notes that this collective aspirational vision was traditionally "bound up with trust in American institutions" (par. 3): financial, scientific, medical, educational, corporate, and—most of all— governmental. Now, according to the writer, faith in such institutions has declined in the wake of political scandals, failing schools, and economic collapse: "At this point, it becomes tempting for Americans to wish away their banks, their hospitals, their schools, and their government. Perhaps life might be easier and more fulfilling without them" (par. 7). Cantor then reads shows like *Falling Skies* and *The Walking Dead* as libertarian allegories for the desire to return to America's founding ideals or myths, such as rugged individualism, self-reliance, and small government: "One might even describe these shows as 'federalist' in spirit. The aim seems to be to reduce the size of government radically and thereby to bring it closer to the people" (par. 9). His interpretations are deft and illuminating. Point out that Cantor cannot assume that his audience has seen these television shows. Therefore, he must give brief explanations and context, highlighting important themes, plot points, characterizations, and specific details without either confusing his readers with unfamiliar material or boring them with elaborate and unnecessary summary. Cantor's argument—especially his reading of zombies both as metaphors for globalization and as "a powerful image of what governments try to do to their citizens" (par. 15)—makes a provocative and illuminating counterpoint to Chuck Klosterman's "My Zombie, Myself: Why Modern Life Feels Rather Undead" (p. 422), which provides an alternative interpretation of zombies.

Ken Auletta

Netflix and the Future of Television

In this informative piece from the *New Yorker*, Ken Auletta provides a long, journalistic account of the online-streaming and video-rental service Netflix. But, as its title indicates, the article also explores the implications of newer technologies on television, television programming, and television-viewing habits. Auletta argues that traditional television faces "two major threats" (par. 25). The first threat is to its advertising model, as many viewers with DVR technologies can simply avoid watching commercials altogether. The second is "existential": as streaming video and devices like Google's Chromecast become more prevalent, people "are bound to ask why they bother subscribing to cable television" (par. 26). The writer also considers the ways in which television has become more immersive and character driven in this "golden age of scripted drama" (par. 32). Students are likely to be familiar with these technologies, as Awesomeness TV founder Brian Robbins claims: "The next generation, our audience and even younger, they don't even know what live TV is. They live in an on-demand world" (par. 39). Ask them how their own views of television—and their viewing habits—compare with the descriptions and predictions in Auletta's article. What are the upsides and downsides of living in an "on-demand world"? You might ask students to consider this argument in light of live events like awards shows and sporting events as well. Auletta suggests that, in a sense, new technology has enabled a "golden age of scripted television." You might therefore have students make connections between this article and David Charpentier's "Story or Spectacle? Why Television Is Better Than the Movies" (p. 308), which also argues that television has become the preeminent media for long, involved narrative and deep, complex characters.

PAIRED READINGS: CHARACTERS WANTED

David Charpentier

Story or Spectacle? Why Television Is Better Than the Movies

People frequently argue that contemporary television is in a "golden age" of scripted drama, with shows such as *House of Cards* and *The Walking Dead* that feature long, novelistic narratives and complex characters who evolve over time. But that was not always the case, as small-screen television (with its frivolous sitcoms and clunky dramas, interrupted by commercials) was generally seen as an inferior medium to its big-screen counterpart, film or "cinema" (with its auteurs and grand artistic ambitions). David Charpentier investigates this reversal of fortune and argues that "it all comes down to the characters" (par. 6). Longer-form cable and streaming-service shows have "the ability to let elements unfold slowly, like a well-structured novel" and to develop highly textured and layered characters (par. 13). In contrast, the standard two-hour length and formulaic, three-act structure of most movies is "far too limiting in its service to the mechanics of plot rather than character" (par. 11). Charpentier's essay should get students to reflect on their own viewing preferences and their own vicarious relationships with character and narrative. What does it mean to say that a character has "layers"? In what ways do current television series mimic the structures of written novels rather than the patterns of older television shows or films? Why would novelistic narratives be more immersive and appealing, as well as more addictive? According to Charpentier, morally ambiguous characters "embody certain elements that we both admire and despise" (par. 7). Ask students to consider whether this preoccupation with moral ambiguity suggests any larger impulse or tendency in American culture. The writer discusses the schematic structures of Hollywood movies, so you might consider how his accounts intersect with those of Linda Seger in "Creating the Myth" (p. 367). Is it possible that film remains a superior form for these "mythic" plots, while television is better at presenting "realistic" narratives? If so, you might introduce the *Star Wars* franchise into your classroom as a phenomenon that complicates these ideas, as it involves characters that unfold over decades—both in the narrative and in the films' production.

PAIRED READINGS: CHARACTERS WANTED

JAKE FLANAGIN

Stay Unlikable—for the Good of TV

Here, Jake Flanagin considers Mindy Kaling's comedy series, *The Mindy Project*, which presents the lead character—a Princeton-educated physician of South Asian descent played by Kaling—as "kind of a jerk" (par. 1). But the writer is troubled by the possibility that Kaling has considered reshaping the character to make her "less unlikable" to television audiences (par. 6). He argues that doing so would not only harm the show, which "intentionally subverts sugary rom-com tropes" (par. 7), but also undermine the importance of *The Mindy Project* in the broader context of television characterizations: "Mindy, who is neither definitively good nor bad, presents a new kind of female sitcom lead. . . . She's exasperating—empirically so—but also human, lovelorn, and self-deprecating" (par. 12). Flanagin notes the recent prevalence of popular antiheroic male characters on television and states that Kaling has the corresponding "opportunity to usher in a new era of sitcoms: the era of the complicated woman" (par. 18). Flanagin's essay explores some of the same character-driven themes as its paired reading, David Charpentier's "Story or Spectacle? Why Television Is Better Than the Movies" (p. 308). But you might also make connections with Roxane Gay's "Girls, Girls, Girls" (p. 270), given Gay's focus on representations of women, or even Vicessimus Knox's "On Novel Reading" (p. 396), given Knox's concerns with fictional models of virtue, vice, and "human nature." Questions of gender might be especially useful in generating class discussion: Why do antiheroic, nuanced, or three-dimensional male characters seem more acceptable than their female counterparts? Flanagin asserts that we need more obnoxious women on television to "rectify a double standard" (par. 8). Do students agree?

6. Movies
Does the big screen still shape our dreams?

SUSAN SONTAG

The Imagination of Disaster

Susan Sontag's essay is a tour de force of criticism, coolly illuminating the tropes, themes, structures, plots, and other patterns in science fiction and disaster films. Yet she also acknowledges the genuine pleasures of these movies, writing with a sense of admiration (even if Sontag sounds a little condescending to a reader several decades later): "Science fiction films are one of the most accomplished of the popular art forms, and can give a great deal of pleasure to sophisticated film addicts" (par. 3). Students often assume that there are, on the one hand, "serious" subjects that require critical thinking and "work," and, on the other, mindless entertainment that should be consumed passively, for pleasure or fun. "The Imagination of Disaster" shows that these two categories overlap and that the process of analysis can be revealing and even pleasurable in its own right. In arguing that science fiction films are about disaster, not science, Sontag shows the link between a popular genre and "one of the oldest subjects of art" (par. 12). She also excavates the subtexts and assumptions of these films, like their deep concern with the "aesthetics of destruction," rather than real-world scientific progress, for example (par. 13). Several of the essays in this book examine the importance of fiction, immersion, and vicarious experience in popular culture. Gerard Jones ("Violent Media Is Good for Kids," p. 442) would likely agree with Sontag about the allure and need for a "morally acceptable fantasy where one can give outlet to cruel or at least amoral feelings" (par. 17). At the same time, ask students if there are any possible dangers to such "extreme moral simplification" (par. 17) in film, fiction, or other vicarious experiences. You might even have them give examples of how movies make morality "simple."

WILLIE OSTERWEIL

Hollywood's Love Affair with Surveillance

In this essay from the *Baffler*, Osterweil argues that Hollywood movies engage in the process of "accommodating people to surveillance society" (par. 15). He uses three well-chosen films to illustrate three different strategies that "describe the ideological contours of the surveillance state" (par. 5). Indeed, Osterweil's essay demonstrates exemplification especially well. To emphasize writing strategies for student modeling, focus on how he highlights specifics within *Captain America: The Winter Soldier*, *Robocop*, and *Her* to support his main idea: selecting plot details, interpreting specific scenes, and noting how each of the movies suggests a different thesis about surveillance. Students may be somewhat familiar with the context of Osterweil's essay, but you might want to begin by briefly discussing privacy, hacking, the Edward Snowden case, and—especially—the pervasiveness of surveillance in both the private and public spheres. In many ways, we have become accustomed and inured to surveillance—and that is Osterweil's point. You probably want to note that he is not arguing that screenwriters deliberately and consciously strive to justify National Security Administration policies in their scripts. Roland Barthes's "Toys" (p. 36) might be helpful in clarifying this point. Osterweil analyzes the implicit ideology of these films, underlying principles akin to the assumptions that Barthes finds in "Toys" that is hidden in pop cultural artifacts.

DAVID DENBY

Has Hollywood Murdered the Movies?

In "Has Hollywood Murdered the Movies?" long-time film critic David Denby makes a point that is hardly new: The total commercialization of Hollywood and the film industry's single-minded focus on blockbusters crowds out higher-quality cinema. But his stylish, introspective, and closely argued polemic is a rant of the highest order, making this piece great fodder for discussions of tone and ethos. Denby recasts what could be a tedious exercise in snobbery as an informative, wide-ranging examination of movies and the movie business; in the process, he illuminates the relationships between the commercial, aesthetic, and technological pressures (among other demands) that shape contemporary filmmaking. Denby begins, in part, with his reactions to big-budget films like *The Avengers* and the *Iron Man* franchise, but also to supposedly more cerebral fare like Christopher Nolan's *Inception*. He sees in them frivolity, along with "what can only be called corporate irony, a mad discrepancy between size and significance" (par. 9). Discussing an endless lineup of action movies, he writes that they "produc[e] temporary sensation rather than emotion and engagement" and that their "oversized weightlessness leaves one numbed, defeated" (pars. 13, 14). Point out how Denby anticipates and responds to his critics in paragraphs 16 and 17, knocking down the counterargument that good movies "still get made, and they have an appreciative audience, however small" (par. 16). Ultimately, he traces a shift away from mature films for adult audiences and mourns the loss of the "culture of movies": "that blessedly saturated mental state of moviegoing, both solitary and social, half dreamy, half critical, maybe amused, but also sometimes awed, that fuels a living art form" (par. 21). The writer clearly loves movies, but the pleasure he takes as a fan is matched by his insight as a critical viewer and writer—as when he describes *Inception* as a "whimsical, over-articulate nullity—a huge fancy clock that displays wheels and gears but somehow fails to tell the time" (par. 11). You might want to pair Denby's essay about the decline of both movies and the "culture of movies" with David Charpentier's "Story or Spectacle? Why Television Is Better Than the Movies" (p. 308). Does the emergence of television as a superior medium for narrative and character exploration correspond to the decline described by Denby? As part of the discussion, ask students to consider current films and/or television series to support their points.

CONTENT MARKETING ASSOCIATION

Seven Steps to the Perfect Story

"Seven Steps to the Perfect Story" is a clever infographic that illuminates plot, character, theme, and other aspects of storytelling. Its inclusion here provides an opportunity to focus on visual rhetoric and discuss with your students how pop culture can be read—and argued—in a wide variety of media. How do design decisions support the ideas in the infographic? Are they effective in their cartoonishness, or should the presentation be different? The infographic highlights narrative elements (in any medium) that we often take for granted, as well as the recurring patterns and archetypes in the structures of common stories. For example, the writers suggest that stories work out problems—a point echoed in the concluding quotation from *WALL-E* director, Andrew Stanton: "Don't give the audience 4, give them 2 plus 2." You might want to discuss this idea of story-as-problem (or question), but try to get students to move beyond canned responses about how good writers leave much to the reader's imagination or other, similar clichés. Instead, have them think about movies or TV shows they are familiar within the context of questions and problems: What question (or questions) are at the heart of *The Walking Dead* or *Game of Thrones*? What problems or dilemmas do fictions such as *The Hunger Games* or movies like *Star Wars* explore? Is it possible to rate the quality of a story based on the significance of the questions it asks—and the complexity of the answers it provides? While this selection obviously pairs well with Linda Seger's "Creating the Myth" (p. 367), you might want to read it in connection with other readings that look at structure and stereotype, such as Susan Sontag's "The Imagination of Disaster" (p. 324) or Philippa Gates's "The Asian Renovation of Biracial Buddy Action" (p. 380). As the infographic focuses on the creation of stories, you can also pair it with Robin Brenner's "Teen Literature and Fan Culture" (p. 401), which discusses participatory "fan fiction."

PAIRED READINGS: THE IMITATION GAME

LINDA SEGER

Creating the Myth

Many students will associate the word *myth* primarily with classical Greek mythology. They may also understand myth as it refers to false belief (e.g., from urban legends or a television show like *MythBusters*). Use Seger's essay to introduce students to another evocative definition of the term: "A myth is a story that is 'more than true' . . . because it is lived by all of us, at some level" (par. 6). Of course that does not mean that we actually "live" as mythic characters in mythic stories. Rather, these figures personify certain ideals, aspirations, and fears. Their journeys serve as resonant allegories or fables for our own lives. Seger's essay was written in the 1980s, but students can update, illustrate, and test her analysis of movie myths with their own examples. According to the writer, James Bond is different from Luke Skywalker because Bond is not "transformed" by missions and experiences. The Bond character has gone through different movie iterations since this essay first appeared, so ask students if that distinction is still true; that is, in more recent Bond films, does the character change or grow? Of course, our love of mythic stories and heroes is obvious in many different forms of media and entertainment. You might connect this analysis of myth to the appeal of superheroes in selections such as Gerard Jones's "Violent Media Is Good for Kids" (p. 442) and Michael Chabon's "Secret Skin: An Essay in Unitard Theory" (p. 449), which explore our vicarious relationship to such characters as well as their role in the formation of our identities. You may even want to discuss the power of myth more generally. That myths seem "more than true" makes them powerful as well as problematic. For example, a racial, ethnic, national, or gender stereotype—onscreen or in real life—can feel "true" on a visceral level, even if the stereotype is not representative, accurate, or factually "true."

PAIRED READINGS: THE IMITATION GAME

Philippa Gates

The Asian Renovation of Biracial Buddy Action

Gates primarily uses exemplification here, but she also deploys comparison and contrast, classification and division, and argumentation in this deft reading of "buddy" action movies. She begins by noting the way Hollywood action films of the '80s highlighted "the relationship between two heroes of contrasting backgrounds who—initially at odds—learn to respect one another and work together to defeat a common enemy" (par. 1). Gates then traces the evolution of this formula over the next decades, as it moves through different racial and ethnic iterations. Like other writers in this anthology such as Paul A. Cantor and Susan Sontag, Gates models a perceptive, ingenious, and allegorical mode of interpretation that can be eye-opening for students. Among her other conclusions, Gates claims that "these buddy relationships, although personal, enact an important function at the level of national identity: American and Asian must work together to protect their mutual global interests" (par. 12). This idea—that individual characters working their way through a movie plot can thematize or explore or represent large themes, problems, or ideas—is one key to consuming popular culture in a thoughtful, engaged way. Students may be resistant to these kinds of allegorical readings (e.g., *"Movie producers are just trying to provide entertainment— stop overthinking it"*). But point to Gates's supple and persuasive close reading of *The Rush Hour* films; whatever the individual intentions of a writer or director, Gates shows how specific details from the movies (plot, dialogue, setting, etc.) lead her—and the reader—to persuasive arguments about what these films are really "about." The Content Marketing Association's "Seven Steps to the Perfect Story" (p. 363) implies that stories are, among their other functions, ways of working out problems or answering questions. You might point out that Gates's essay demonstrates this process at work; that is, she illustrates how these action movies attempt to answer questions such as "How might China and the West cooperate to protect their global interests?"

7. Immersive Media
Can we get lost—and can we be found—in media?

VICESSIMUS KNOX

On Novel Reading

Vicessimus Knox's essay on reading popular fiction—and the potential dangers of the activity—appeared in 1778. He begins with the premise that if the "present age is more corrupt than the preceding," then the popularity and proliferation of novels "has probably contributed to its degeneracy" (par. 1). He argues that certain kinds of "licentious" books should be avoided because they can corrupt young minds. At first glance, Knox's references and concerns may seem remote and confusing to students. But as they work through his assertions, they should begin to recognize a familiar argument about the potentially pernicious influence of "coarse" popular culture and the dangerous effects of immersive media: Novels that "fix attention so deeply, and afford so lively a pleasure, that the mind, once accustomed to them, cannot submit to the painful task of serious study" (par. 9). You might want to give a brief explanation of the eighteenth-century novelists such as Samuel Richardson and Henry Fielding—writers who were concerned with questions of morality and virtue, even if their books often included racy or sensational content. Ask students to consider "On Novel Reading" in the context of contemporary debates about the dangers of violent media, immersive first-person shooter video games, or even highly sexualized aspects of contemporary popular culture. As an activity, you might ask them to bring in a contemporary op-ed or even a comment stream that displays the same reactionary morality that Knox presents. How do Knox's concerns parallel those of his contemporary counterparts? How do they diverge or contrast? "On Novel Reading" provides a good keynote for several of the readings in this chapter, but you might want to pair it with Frank Rose's "The Art of Immersion: Fear of Fiction" (p. 409), which refers to perennial fears about the power of narrative, or Robin Brenner's "Teen Literature and Fan Culture" (p. 401), which explores the timeless appeal of fiction for younger readers.

Robin Brenner

Teen Literature and Fan Culture

Robin Brenner identifies the creative and participatory impulses at the heart of fan fiction: "Many fans are content with contemplating the 'what if' questions in their own imaginations, but with fan fiction, fan videos, and fan art, devotees take the leap from speculation to creation. They use their talents to fill in the gaps, to create alternative timelines, and mix universes. And that's just the beginning" (par. 2). Indeed, Brenner describes fan cultures that are not merely outlets for isolated individual creativity but also opportunities for community, conversation, and broader literary engagement. Fan art can lead to commercial success as well, as in the case of *Fifty Shades of Grey*, which began as fan fiction based on the *Twilight* series. Brenner highlights some of the thornier issues raised by such works, including legal and copyright questions. But she notes that "individual creators including writers and artists are increasingly moving toward a policy of permission and acceptance, especially as they recognize the harm in potentially alienating their fans if they pursue legal action" (par. 7). Ask students about the implications for the idea of originality, as well. Can such "derivative" creations be called "original" in any sense? Does shifting the media form complicate this question? For example, what if a person turns scenes from a Harry Potter novel into a comic strip or retells a story from a *Star Wars* comic book as a film using only finger puppets and household objects? You might note that, according to Brenner, participating in fan culture sharpens critical reading and thinking skills: "Fans in our survey noted over and over again that they became more critical consumers of media through participating in fan debates and reading or writing critical essays" (par. 19). Brenner stresses the social component of fan fiction and fan culture, as participants build confidence and create lasting friendships. You may want to discuss this aspect of popular culture in the context of Gerard Jones's "Violent Media Is Good for Kids" (p. 442) and Michael Chabon's "Secret Skin: An Essay in Unitard Theory" (p. 449), which show how pop culture can be a conduit for personal growth and social connection.

Frank Rose

The Art of Immersion: Fear of Fiction

In this excerpt from his book *The Art of Immersion*, Frank Rose provides a narrative account of the creative life of author, game designer, and entrepreneur Jordan Weisman, known for creating fictions and games across a range of platforms, such as the BattleTech franchise. Rose recalls Weisman's collaboration with game designer Elan Lee on a 2001 gaming project, *The Beast*, which was part of the marketing of Steven Spielberg's movie *A.I. Artificial Intelligence*. But the narrative is also a pretext for examining the lure and appeal of immersive, participatory, vicarious, and alternative realities. Students may be familiar with fears about violent movies or video games, but they may be surprised by the claim that "every new medium that has been invented, from print to film to television, has increased the transporting power of narrative" and aroused "fear and hostility" (par. 37). You might point out that fears about immersive fictions — and anxieties about the conflation of fiction and reality — is one of the enduring themes of literature, from Miguel de Cervantes's *Don Quixote*, Jane Austen's *Northanger Abbey*, and Gustave Flaubert's *Madame Bovary* to Woody Allen's short story "The Kugelmass Episode." Many films explore similar problems of "immersion," too, including Buster Keaton's silent *Sherlock, Jr.*, Allen's *The Purple Rose of Cairo*, David Fincher's *Fight Club*, James Cameron's *Avatar*, and the work of screenwriter Charlie Kaufman (*Adaptation*; *Synecdoche, New York*). You should encourage students to reflect on their own relationships with "immersive" technologies. Postman's essay ("The Judgment of Thamus," p. 151) may provide a useful lens. As Postman writes, technology "imperiously commandeers our most important terminology. It redefines 'freedom,' 'truth,' 'intelligence,' 'fact,' 'wisdom,' 'memory,' 'history' — all the words we live by" (par. 6). How do our high-tech forms of immersion change the meaning of "authenticity" and "reality" itself?

Chuck Klosterman

My Zombie, Myself: Why Modern Life Feels Rather Undead

Chuck Klosterman writes with a strong, knowing voice: He's fluent both in the particulars of monsters and the larger generalities of popular culture. You might point out that although he does not shy away from grand pronouncements and even overstatement — "Zombies are like the Internet and the media and every conversation we don't want to have" (par. 13) — his argument is hard to resist because he grounds it in concrete examples and because his exuberant style carries us along. You might discuss how Klosterman manages to be playful and serious at the same time, an admirable trick for a writer. This essay should also help introduce students to the idea that culture — as perceived through our books, movies, music, television, media, and so on — may suggest allegories and reflections of our collective anxieties and preoccupations: "Godzilla was spawned from the fear of the atomic age; werewolves feed into an instinctual panic over predation . . ." (par. 4). In that context, you may want to pair "My Zombie, Myself" with Paul A. Cantor's "The Apocalyptic Strain in Popular Culture: The American Nightmare Becomes the American Dream" (p. 279), which suggests an alternative interpretation of zombies. Likewise, you might encourage students to do their own readings of monsters — or other fear-inducing phenomena in popular culture, fictional or real — as manifestations of "our collective fear projection" (Klosterman, par. 13).

JACOB BURAK

Escape from the Matrix

In this essay, Jacob Burak investigates and diagnoses a "cultural disorder" afflicting many of us: "FoMO," or the "Fear of Missing Out." According to the writer, FoMO is the "spawn of technological advancement and proliferating social information, is the feeling that we're missing out on something more exciting, more important, or more interesting going on somewhere else. It is the unease of feeling that others are having a more rewarding experience and we are not a part of it" (par. 5). More specifically, it's the stress we feel when we cannot check the beeping messages on our smartphones or complete activities within a limited time frame. Point out how he integrates the work of MIT social psychologist Sherry Turkle, researchers at the University of Oxford (pars. 8–13), and other outside sources effectively: He depends on these sources to build his argument, but he also controls them. He uses various rhetorical patterns for his purposes as well. Along with definition and exemplification, he relies on compare and contrast when explaining the differences between "satisficers," who take a "good enough" approach to making decisions, and "perfectionists," who try to maximize the outcome of every decision. Ultimately, Burak argues that satisficing is a better strategy for managing the FoMO, given the welter of choices and information that we face in our technologically connected day-to-day lives: "Taking the 'good-enough' approach to this crushing problem is not merely a tactic for improving our decision making. It is first and foremost a worldview, a way of life" (par. 21). Students should identify with these problems and issues in their own lives. In addition to discussing this essay with Bo Moore's "Why Videogames Should Be Played with Friends, Not Online with Strangers" (p. 436) and Chuck Klosterman's "My Zombie, Myself: Why Modern Life Feels Rather Undead" (p. 422), you might also ask students to discuss their own experience with FoMO, as well as their strategies for alleviating it. For example, how does Burak's endorsement of "satisficing"—taking a "good enough" approach to decisions—square with other values and pressures, such as competition or the desire for perfection? Would the "good enough" approach work for career choices or romantic partners?

BO MOORE

Why Videogames Should Be Played with Friends, Not Online with Strangers

In this *Wired* magazine article, Bo Moore sees signs of a trend in gaming toward more direct, in-person social interaction. He begins with a brief history of video games, moving from arcades, with their enormous, monolithic *Asteroids* cabinets and their implicit notion of gaming as a "social endeavor," to sociable off-line gaming at home on Atari and Nintendo consoles in the 1980s and 1990s, and (finally) to highly monetized, but largely isolated Internet play: "Suddenly we were playing together alone" (pars. 1–3). Point out this capsule history to students, which both deftly condenses the transformation of video games *and* highlights the point Moore wants to make without getting bogged down in extraneous detail and unnecessary summary. Then Moore turns his attention to current games like the screenless, graphics-free *Johann Sebastian Joust*, which "pits as many as seven players in a dance-like competition of balance, movement, and reflexes" (par. 4). He also attends a Wild Rumpus party, which sets games in a quasi-disco or club setting and (according to its cofounder) "creat[es] spaces for people to come into games, people that haven't come into physical spaces and engaged with games before" (par. 8). You might ask students about their own gaming habits as well as their sense of games as either isolated experiences or activities embedded in a social context. You can also test designer Douglas Wilson's hope that these games might "[get] gamers back into the living room, socializing in person, recapturing the magic of the offline games he played in his youth" (par. 14). Consider reading Moore's article alongside Nathan Jurgenson's "The IRL Fetish" (p. 191). Jurgenson argues against "digital dualism": the contention that online and off-line experience is a zero-sum relationship or binary opposition. He frames the relationship as complementary; our online lives enable our offline lives, and vice versa. Ask students how Jurgenson might respond to Bo Moore's article. Does it support his thesis or work against it?

PAIRED READINGS: WE CAN BE HEROES

GERARD JONES

Violent Media Is Good for Kids

You might begin discussion of this reading by asking students about their own experiences with "violent media," as well as their views of its social consequences. Like several other writers in this collection, Jones stakes out a position diametrically opposed to conventional wisdom and common assumptions. No doubt students will be familiar with hand-wringing over violent media (from music and movies to video games) and its presumed negative influence on real-world behavior. Integrating personal experience with observations about culture and psychology, Jones argues that vicarious experiences, especially immersion in "violent stories," perform an important "developmental function" for children (par. 11). Do students find his examples representative and effective? Point out that Jones carefully qualifies his arguments and acknowledges the validity of other points of view in paragraph 16, yet this concession helps strengthen his case: He anticipates the objections of readers and addresses them persuasively. Jones's essay was originally published in 2000. In the years since, has the discourse and controversy over violent media changed, given the number of high-profile mass shootings and the accessibility of media on the Internet? This essay will work well with other selections that explore similar themes, like Sontag's "The Imagination of Disaster" (p. 324), Seger's "Creating the Myth" (p. 367), and Rose's "The Art of Immersion: Fear of Fiction" (p. 409). All of these essays investigate the meaning of vicarious experience and immersion in imaginary worlds.

PAIRED READINGS: WE CAN BE HEROES

Michael Chabon

Secret Skin: An Essay in Unitard Theory

"Secret Skin: An Essay in Unitard Theory" explores the allure and power of immersive fiction and vicarious experience. Chabon begins with a personal anecdote about a religious school teacher who warned about the "ethical problem of escapism" (par. 3) and the dangers of consuming fantasies—especially comic book fantasies—that "rendered you unfit to face 'reality' and its hard pavement" (par. 4). But Chabon moves outward to a broader meditation on the meaning of superheroes and the nature of personal identity. Like several of the writers in this collection, novelist Michael Chabon is a dazzling prose stylist. As you discuss this essay with students, you might want to direct them to the *how* as much as the *what* of the writing: Chabon's command of language; his sense of rhythm, sentence variety, and word choice; the way his prose unfurls like skeins of gold. Indeed, it is perhaps fitting that Chabon ultimately focuses on the form and style of superhero costumes, not merely as a superficial, incidental, or decorative garment but as screens that simultaneously reveal and conceal: "In theory, the costume forms part of the strategy of concealment. But in fact the superhero's costume often functions as a kind of magic screen onto which the repressed narrative may be projected" (par. 26). His attention to costuming illustrates to students how even one aspect of a pop-culture trend is ripe for analysis and discussion. Ultimately, Chabon is interested in revealing the connections between the immersive fantasy, superhero narratives, and personal transformation. His essay pairs especially well with Gerard Jones's similarly themed "Violent Media Is Good for Kids" (p. 442), but you might also read it alongside Vicessimus Knox's "On Novel Reading" (p. 396) or Frank Rose's "The Art of Immersion: Fear of Fiction" (p. 409), which raise similar issues. You can also draw parallels between Chabon's essay and selections in the Identity chapter of this collection, particularly Liz Armstrong's "An Argument for Being a Poser" (p. 85) and danah boyd's "Impression Management in a Networked Setting" (p. 122), which explore the stories we tell about—and *to*—ourselves about who we really are.